A SIMPLE METHOD OF READING THE ≡≡ I CHING ≡≡

To find your fortune and fate in the I CHING, you must find your hexagram. In ancient China, this was done by a complicated ritual involving Yarrow sticks. Centuries passed before the shorter method of using Chinese bronze coins was common. Today three pennies may be substituted for the Chinese coins.

The three pennies are thrown down together six times, and each throw determines one line of the hexagram. The six lines are drawn from the bottom up.

EXAMPLE HEXAGRAM

6th throw	— — line 6	3rd throw	—— line 3
5th throw	—— line 5	2nd throw	— — line 2
4th throw	— — line 4	1st throw	—— line 1

Heads has a value of 2; tails has a value of 3. By adding the values of the pennies, the character of the line is derived. 3 heads = 6. 3 tails = 9. 2 heads + 1 tail = 7. 2 tails + 1 head = 8.

EXAMPLE PENNIES

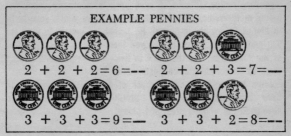

$2 + 2 + 2 = 6 = --$ $2 + 2 + 3 = 7 = ——$

$3 + 3 + 3 = 9 = ——$ $3 + 3 + 2 = 8 = --$

You then find your hexagram by matching the lines you have drawn with the hexagram that corresponds to plate 1.

In addition to the two basic texts, there are extensive appendixes with which you can probe deeply into the meaning of your reading.

FU HSI INVENTING THE EIGHT DIAGRAMS

Fu Hsi (2953–2838 B.C.), the first of the Five Emperors of the legendary period, is said to have been miraculously conceived by his mother who, after a gestation of twelve years, gave birth to him at Ch'eng-chi in Shensi. He taught his people to hunt, to fish and to keep flocks. He showed them how to split the wood of the t'ung tree, and then how to twist silk threads and stretch them to form rude musical instruments.

From the markings on the back of a tortoise, he is said to have constructed the EIGHT DIAGRAMS from which were developed the whole system of **I Ching**.

I CHING
BOOK OF CHANGES

Translated by JAMES LEGGE

Edited with Introduction and Study Guide
By CH'U CHAI with WINBERG CHAI

BANTAM BOOKS

TORONTO · NEW YORK · LONDON · SYDNEY · AUCKLAND

This low-priced Bantam Book
contains the complete text of
the original hard-cover edition.
NOT ONE WORD HAS BEEN OMITTED.

I CHING

A Bantam Book / published by arrangement with
University Books, Inc.

PRINTING HISTORY

University Books edition published September 1964

2nd printing . . . . January 1966	3rd printing . . . . . . March 1969
4th printing . . . July 1969	

Bantam edition / November 1969

2nd printing . . . . March 1970	9th printing . . . . . January 1976
3rd printing . . . . May 1970	10th printing . . . . . . April 1977
4th printing . . . . February 1971	11th printing . . . . . August 1978
5th printing . . . . July 1971	12th printing . . September 1979
6th printing . . . . July 1972	13th printing . . November 1980
7th printing . . . . . . August 1973	14th printing . . December 1982
8th printing . . . . June 1975	15th printing . . . . . March 1984
16th printing . . . February 1986	

Except for the new material added by the editors, the text of this edition
is that published in a second edition in 1899 as Volume XVI of The
Sacred Books of the East and also designed as Part II of The Texts of
Confucianism.

All rights reserved.
Copyright © 1964 by University Books, Inc.
This book may not be reproduced in whole or in part, by
mimeograph or any other means, without permission.
For information address: University Books, Inc.,
Div. of Lyle Stuart, Inc., 120 Enterprise Avenue, Secaucus, NJ 07094.

ISBN 0-553-26002-2

Published simultaneously in the United States and Canada

Bantam Books are published by Bantam Books, Inc. Its trademark, consisting of the words "Bantam Books" and the portrayal
of a rooster, is Registered in U.S. Patent and Trademark Office
and in other countries. Marca Registrada. Bantam Books, Inc.,
666 Fifth Avenue, New York, New York 10103.

PRINTED IN THE UNITED STATES OF AMERICA

O   25   24   23   22   21   20   19   18   17   16

PLATE I

THE HEXAGRAMS, in the order in which they appear in the Yî, and were arranged by king Wăn.

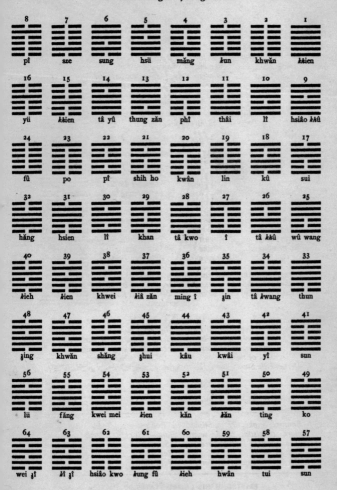

8	7	6	5	4	3	2	1
pî	sze	sung	hsü	măng	kun	khwăn	khien

16	15	14	13	12	11	10	9
yü	khien	tâ yû	thung zăn	phî	thâi	lî	hsiâo khû

24	23	22	21	20	19	18	17
fû	po	pî	shih ho	kwăn	lin	kû	sui

32	31	30	29	28	27	26	25
hăng	hsien	lî	khan	tâ kwo	î	tâ khû	wû wang

40	39	38	37	36	35	34	33
kieh	kien	khwei	kiâ zăn	ming î	zin	tâ kwang	thun

48	47	46	45	44	43	42	41
zing	khwăn	shăng	zhui	kâu	kwâi	yî	sun

56	55	54	53	52	51	50	49
lü	făng	kwei mei	kien	kăn	kăn	ting	ko

64	63	62	61	60	59	58	57
wei zî	kî zî	hsiâo kwo	kung fû	kieh	hwăn	tui	sun

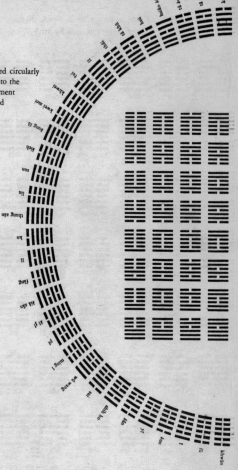

PLATE II

FIGURE 1

THE HEXAGRAMS, exhibited circularly
and in a square, according to the
natural process of development
from the whole and divided
lines, and the order of
arrangement ascribed
to Fû-hsî.

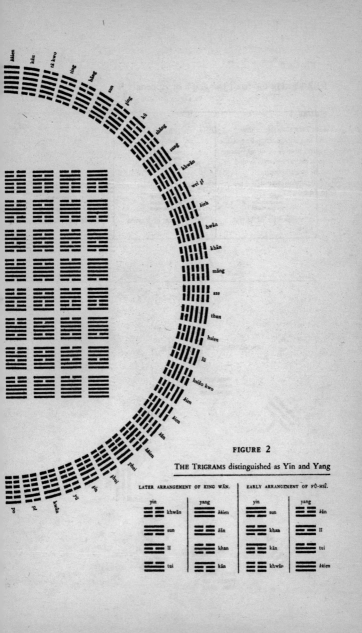

FIGURE 2

THE TRIGRAMS distinguished as Yin and Yang

LATER ARRANGEMENT OF KING WĂN.		EARLY ARRANGEMENT OF FŪ-HSĬ.	
yin	yang	yin	yang
khwăn	ķhien	sun	kăn
sun	ķăn	khan	li
li	khan	kăn	tui
tui	kăn	khwăn	ķhien

PLATE III

FIGURE 1

Illustrating the tenth paragraph of Appendix V

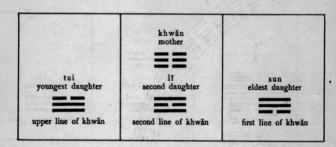

tui youngest daughter	khwăn mother	sun eldest daughter
upper line of khwăn	lî second daughter second line of khwăn	first line of khwăn

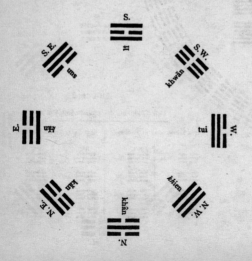

ACCORDING TO KING WĂN.

FIGURE 2   ORDER OF THE TRIGRAMS, with the cardinal and other

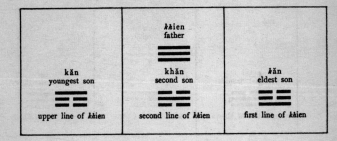

	*kh*ien father	
kăn youngest son	**khăn** second son	**kăn** eldest son
upper line of *kh*ien	second line of *kh*ien	first line of *kh*ien

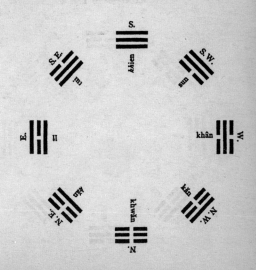

points to which they are severally referred.

CONTENTS

THE APPENDIXES

I TREATISE ON THE THWAN, THAT IS, ON KING WĂN'S
  EXPLANATIONS OF THE ENTIRE HEXAGRAMS

SECTION I

SECTION II

II TREATISE ON THE SYMBOLISM OF THE HEXAGRAMS,
   AND OF THE DUKE OF *K*ÂU'S EXPLANATIONS OF
   THE SEVERAL LINES

SECTION I

SECTION II

SUGGESTED STUDY GUIDE

At the beginning, it is advisable to read Dr Chu Chai's new introduction to James Legge's translation of the *Book of Changes*, so as to know the general structure of the great book and its fundamental concepts, as well as the basic rules and philosophical significance concerning the interpretations of the "Ten Wings." Then we should read the Discourses on the Trigrams (*Shuo Kuo;* i.e., Legge's Appendix V) before we read the text. The *Shuo Kuo* interprets the two primary trigrams making up each hexagram, and the symbolic significance involved in each trigram. In reading the text, it is best to follow the order given below. If we do so, we will generally start with the respective hexagrams and their separate lines. Then take up their pertinent Judgments (*T'uan*) and Commentaries (*Chuan*) presented in the Appendices.

In the breakdowns below, the following abbreviations are used:

TC	*T'uan Chuan*, the Treatise on the T'uan; i.e., Legge's Appendix I
HC	*Hsiang Chuan*, the Treatise on the Symbols; i.e., Legge's Appendix II
HTC	*Hsi Tz'u Chuan*, the Commentary on Appended Judgments; i.e., Legge's Appendix III
WY	*Wen Yen*, the Explanation of the Words and Sentences; i.e., Legge's Appendix IV
SK	*Shuo Kuo*, the Discourses on the Trigrams; i.e., Legge's Appendix V
HK	*Hsü Kuo*, the Treatise on the Sequence of the Hexagrams; i.e., Legge's Appendix VI
TK	*Tsa Kua*, the Miscellaneous Remarks on the Hexagrams; i.e., Legge's Appendix VII

TEXT.   SECTION I.

I.   The Ch'ien Hexagram

1. The hexagram and its lines.
2. TC   Section I, I, 1-5.
3. HC   Section I, I & 1-7.
4. WY   Section I, I, 1-3; II, 4-9; III, 10-16; IV, 17-23; V, 24-29; VI, 30-36.

II.   The K'un Hexagram

1. The hexagram and its lines.
2. TC   Section I, II, 1-5.
3. HC   Section I, II & 1-7.
4. WY   Section II, I, 1-4; II, 5-10.

III.   The Chun Hexagram

1. The hexagram and its lines.
2. TC   Section I, III, 1-3.
3. HC   Section I, III & 1-6.

IV.   The Mêng Hexagram

1. The hexagram and its lines.
2. TC   Section I, IV, 1-2.
3. HC   Section I, IV & 1-6.

V.   The Hsü Hexagram

1. The hexagram and its lines.
2. TC   Section I, V, 1-2.
3. HC   Section I, V & 1-6.

VI.   The Sung Hexagram

1. The hexagram and its lines.
2. TC   Section I, VI, 1-2.
3. HC   Section I, VI & 1-6.

VII.   The Shih Hexagram

1. The hexagram and its lines.
2. TC   Section I, VII, 1-2.
3. HC   Section I, VII & 1-6.

VIII.   The Pi Hexagram

1. The hexagram and its lines.
2. TC   Section I, VIII, 1-2.
3. HC   Section I, VIII & 1-6.

IX.   The Hsiao Ch'u Hexagram

1. The hexagram and its lines.
2. TC   Section I, IX, 1-3.
3. HC   Section I, IX & 1-6.

X.   The Lü Hexagram

1. The hexagram and its lines.
2. TC   Section I, X, 1-3.
3. HC   Section I, X & 1-6.

XI.   The T'ai Hexagram

1. The hexagram and its lines.
2. TC   Section I, XI, 1.
3. HC   Section I, XI & 1-6.

XII.   The P'i Hexagram

1. The hexagram and its lines.
2. TC   Section I, XII, 1.
3. HC   Section I, XII & 1-6.

XIII.   The T'ung Jen Hexagram

1. The hexagram and its lines.
2. TC   Section I, XIII, 1-3.
3. HC   Section I, XIII & 1-6.

XIV   The Ta Yu Hexagram

1. The hexagram and its lines.
2. TC   Section I, XIV, 1-2.
3. HC   Section I, XIV & 1-6.

XV.   The Ch'ien Hexagram

1. The hexagram and its lines.
2. TC   Section I, XV, 1-2.
3. HC   Section I, XV & 1-6.

XVI.   The Yü Hexagram

1. The hexagram and its lines.
2. TC   Section I, XVI, 1-3.
3. HC   Section I, XVI & 1-6.

XLIX. The Kó Hexagram

1. The hexagram and its lines.
2. TC Section II, XLIX, 1-3.
3. HC Section II, XLIX & 1-6.

L. The Ting Hexagram

1. The hexagram and its lines.
2. TC Section II, L, 1-2.
3. HC Section II, L & 1-6.

LI. The Chen Hexagram

1. The hexagram and its lines.
2. TC Section II, LI, 1-2.
3. HC Section II, LI & 1-6.

LII. The Kên Hexagram

1. The hexagram and its lines.
2. TC Section II, LII, 1-2.
3. HC Section II, LII & 1-6.

LIII. The Chien Hexagram

1. The hexagram and its lines.
2. TC Section II, LIII, 1-4.
3. HC Section II, LIII & 1-6.

LIV. The Kuei Mei Hexagram

1. The hexagram and its lines.
2. TC Section II, LIV, 1-3.
3. HC Section II, LIV & 1-6.

LV. The Fêng Hexagram

1. The hexagram and its lines.
2. TC Section II, LV, 1-3.
3. HC Section II, LV & 1-6.

LVI. The Lü Hexagram

1. The hexagram and its lines.
2. TC Section II, LVI, 1-2.
3. HC Section II, LVI & 1-6.

LVII. The Sun Hexagram

1. The hexagram and its lines.
2. TC Section II, LVII, 1-2.
3. HC Section II, LVII & 1-6.

LVIII. The Tui Hexagram

1. The hexagram and its lines.
2. TC Section II, LVIII, 1-2.
3. HC Section II, LVIIII & 1-6.

LIX. The Huan Hexagram

1. The hexagram and its lines.
2. TC Section II, LIX, 1-3.
3. HC Section II, LIX & 1-6.

LX. The Chieh Hexagram

1. The hexagram and its lines.
2. TC Section II, LX, 1-4.
3. HC Section II, LX & 1-6.

LXI. The Chung Fu Hexagram

1. The hexagram and its lines.
2. TC Section II, LXI, 1-3.
3. HC Section II, LXI & 1-6.

LXII. The Hsiao Kuo Hexagram

1. The hexagram and its lines.
2. TC Section I, LXII, 1-5.
3. HC Section II, LXII & 1-6.

LXIII. The Chi Chi Hexagram

1. The hexagram and its lines.
2. TC Section II, LXIII, 1-4.
3. HC Section II, LXIII & 1-6.

LXIV. The Wei Chi Hexagram

1. The hexagram and its lines.
2. TC Section II, LXIV, 1-2.
3. HC Section II, LXIV & 1-6.

After the text, we shall read the remaining portion of the Appendices, that is, the *Hsi Tz'u Chuan, Hsü Kua,* and *Tsa Kua.*

COMPARATIVE
TRANSCRIPTION TABLE

I. SIXTY-FOUR HEXAGRAMS

LEGGE	WADE-GILES SYSTEM		MEANINGS*
KHIEN	CH'IEN		Heaven, king, father, etc., the symbol of firmness.
KHWĂN	K'UN		Earth, people, mother, etc., the symbol of submission.
KUN	CHUN		Initial difficulties, the symbol of bursting.
MĂNG	MÊNG		Youthful inexperience, the symbol of obscurity.
HSÜ	HSÜ		Delaying, the symbol of waiting.
SUNG	SUNG		Conflict, the symbol of contention.
SZE	SHIH		Group action, the symbol of multitude.
PÎ	PI		Union, concord, the symbol of collaboration.
HSIAO KHU	HSIAO CH'U		Minor restraint, the symbol of taming force.
LÎ	LÜ		Treading carefully, the symbol of deliberate action.
THÂI	T'AI		Peace, progress, the symbol of success.
PHÎ	P'I		Retrogression, stagnation, the symbol of failure.
THUNG ZĂN	T'UNG JÊN		Companionship, the symbol of community.
TÂ YÛ	TA YU		Great possession, the symbol of abundance.

*These meanings are mostly derived from the text itself and from the commentaries.

KHIEN	CH'IEN		Modesty, the symbol of humility.
YÜ	YÜ		Harmonious joy, the symbol of enthusiasm.
SUI	SUI		Following, the symbol of succession.
KÛ	KU		Decaying, destroying, the symbol major power.
LIN	LIN		Approach, the symbol of advance.
KWÂN	KUAN		Observation, the symbol of contemplation.
SHIH HO	SHIH HO		Biting through, the symbol of criminal proceedings.
PÎ	PI		Ornamental, the symbol of model.
PO	PO		Collapse, splitting apart, the symbol of dispersion.
FÛ	FU		Returning, the symbol of reversal.
WÛ WANG	WU WANG		Freedom from error, the symbol of innocence.
TÂ KHÛ	TA CH'U		Major restraint, the symbol of great taming force.
Î	I		Nourishment, the symbol of sustenance.
TÂ KWO	TA KUO		Large excess, the symbol of major preponderance.
KHAN	K'AN		Abysmal, the symbol of sinking.

LÎ	LI		Clinging, brightness, the symbol of adherence, or of fire and light.
HSIEN	HSIEN		Influence, wooing, the symbol of mutual influence.
HĂNG	HÊNG'		Constancy, duration, the symbol of perseverance.
THUN	TUN		Retreat, the symbol of regression.
TÂ KWANG	TA CHUANG		Great strength, the symbol of major power.
3IN	CHIN		Advance, the symbol of progress.
MING Î	MING I		Darkening of the light, the symbol of lack of appreciation.
KIÂ ZĂN	CHIA JÊN		Members of a family, the symbol of the family.
KHWEI	K'UEI		Division and disunion, the symbol of opposition.
KIEN	CHIEN		Inhibition, obstruction, the symbol of difficulty.
KIEH	CHIEH		Loosening, the symbol of deliverance.
SUN	SUN		Decrease, lessening, the symbol of diminution.
YÎ	I		Increase, the symbol of addition.
KWÂI	KUAI		Break-through, the symbol of resoluteness.
KÂU	KOU		Meeting, intercourse, the symbol of coming to meet.

ȝHUI	TS'UI		Gathering together, the symbol of collection.
SHĂNG	SHÊNG		Rising and advancing, the symbol of pushing upward.
KHWĂN	K'UN		Oppression, the symbol of repression.
ȝING	CHING		Well, the symbol of source.
KO	KO		Revolution, the symbol of change.
TING	TING		Cauldron, the symbol of nourishment.
KĂN	CHEN		Shock, the symbol of exciting power.
KĂN	KÊN		Checking, keeping still, the symbol of stability.
KIEN	CHIEN		Progressive advance, the symbol of gradual progress.
KWEI MEI	KUEI MEI		Marrying maiden, the symbol of marriage.
FĂNG	FÊNG		Abundance, the symbol of prosperity.
LÜ	LÜ		Wanderer, the symbol of wandering.
SUN	SUN		Mildness, the symbol of penetration.
TUI	TUI		Joy, lake, the symbol of pleasure.
HWĂN	HUAN		Dissolution, the symbol of dispersion.
KIEH	CHIEH		Regulation, limitation, the symbol of regulated restriction.

LEGGE	WADE-GILES		MEANINGS
KUNG FÛ	CHUNG FU		Central sincerity, the symbol of truth.
HSIÂO KWO	HSIAO KUO		Small excess, the symbol of minor preponderance.
KÎ 3Î	CHI CHI		Completion, consummation, the symbol of accomplishment.
WEI 3Î	WEI CHI		Not quite up to accomplishment, the symbol of what is not yet accomplished.

II. APPENDICES AND OTHER RELATED PROPER NAMES

LEGGE	WADE-GILES SYSTEM	MEANINGS
THWAN KWAN	T'UAN CHUAN	The Treatise on the T'uan.
HSIANG KWAN	HSIANG CHUAN	The Treatise on the Symbols, or the Treatise on Symbolism.
TÂ KWAN	TA CHUAN or HSI TS'U CHUAN	The Commentary on the Appended Judgments, or the Great Appendix.
WĂN YEN	WÊN YEN	The Explanation of the Words and Sentences.
	SHUO KUA	The Discourses on the Trigrams.
	HSÜ KUA	The Treatise on the Orderly Sequence of Hexagrams.
A KWA	TSA KUA	The Miscellaneous Remarks on the Hexagrams.
LIEN-SHAN	LIEN SHAN	The Manifestation of Change in the Mountains.
KWEÎ-3HANG	KUEI TSANG	The Flow and Return to Womb and Tomb.
KÂU YÎ	CHOU I	Book of Changes of the Chou Dynasty.
YÎ KING	I CHING	The Book of Changes.
SHÛ KING	SHU CHING	The Book of History.
SHIH KING	SHIH CHING	The Book of Odes.
HSIÂO KING	HSIAO CHING	The Book of Filial Piety.
3O KWAN	TSO CHUAN	Tso Chiu-ming's Supplement to Spring and Autumn Annals.

INTRODUCTION

PART ONE

THE ORIGIN AND
STRUCTURE OF THE *I CHING*

I. The Canonical Text, or *Ching* Proper (*Pen Ching*)

THE MOST IMPORTANT LITERATURE of the five Confucian Classics[1] is the *I Ching*, usually called in translations the *Book of Changes*. The original corpus of the *I Ching* is made up of the famous *Pa Kua* (Eight Trigrams), consisting of various combinations of straight lines (*hsiao*) and arranged in a circle as follows:

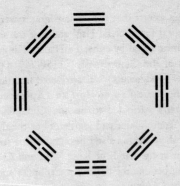

These lines consist of two primary forms: a continuous undivided line called *yang-hsiao* (———————), the symbol of the

---

[1] The five Confucian Classics consist of the *I Ching*, the *Shu Ching* or *Book of History*, the *Shih Ching* or *Book of Odes*, the *Li Chi* or *Book of Rituals*, and the *Ch'un-ch'iu* or *Spring and Autumn Annals*. These works have traditionally been accepted by the Chinese as a cultural heritage of the ancient times.

male or positive principle, and a divided line called *yin-hsiao* (———— ————), the symbol of the female or negative principle. These are the basic symbols used in the *I Ching,* representing the dualistic origin of their primary constitution. Various combinations were made by putting together the *yang-hsiao* and the *yin-hsiao* to form eight trigrams and by putting together any two of the trigrams to form sixty-four hexagrams, all known as *kua.* The *kua* are arranged in the *I Ching* in accordance with a definite order. Each *kua* is given a brief statement known as the *Kua-Tz'u* or *T'uan,* which has been translated "Judgment" or "Decision." Then there is a commentary on each of the six lines of a hexagram, known as the *Hsiao-Tz'u* or *Hsi-Tz'u,* which has been translated "Appended Judgments." The canonical text, or *Ching* proper *(Pen Ching),* consists of these symbols — *hsiao* (lines) and *kua* (trigrams and hexagrams) — with their statements and commentaries.

Tradition asserts that the eight trigrams were invented by the mythological Emperor Fu Hsi,[2] and that the sixty-four hexagrams were formulated by either Fu Hsi[3] or King Wen,[4] one of the founders of the Chou dynasty (1150-249 B.C.). The *Kua-Tz'u* or *T'uan* (Judgments) was attributed traditionally to King Wen,[5] and the *Hsiao-Tz'u* or *Hsi-Tz'u* (Appended Judgments) was traditionally attributed to his son Chou Kung (Duke of Chou),[6] the "consolidator and legislator" of the dynasty. This is to show that these trigrams and hexagrams first received systematic treatment at the hands of King Wen and Chou Kung and that they then became the basis of metaphysics and occultism as set forth in the *I Ching.*

Legge followed the traditional view, particularly in attribut-

[2]The legendary culture hero Fu Hsi, who is said to have invented writing, fishing, and trapping, represented a mixture of supernatural features and mock reality.
[3]This is maintained by Wang Pi (A.D. 226-249), the famous commentator on the *I Ching.*
[4]According to Ssu-ma Ch'ien (145c. 86 B.C.), noted for his *Shih Chi* or *Records of the Historian.*
[5]Also according to Ssu-ma Chi'en.
[6]This is maintained by Ma Yung (A.D. 79-166), the noted commentator on the Classics.

ing the composition of the text to King Wen and his son Chou
Kung (see his Introduction, page 10). However, although modern scholarship has advanced the theory that the trigrams and
hexagrams were invented early in the Chou dynasty in imitation
of ancient divination procedures by means of tortoise shells or
milfoil stalks, no recent scholar considers that either King Wen
or Chou Kung had anything to do with the *I Ching*.[7] So far as
we know, the *I Ching* was first of all a book of divination. To
divine is to resolve doubts of the mind or mysteries of the universe. Would a particular day be auspicious for hunting or an
expedition? Would rain come to relieve a long drought and the
threat of dearth and famine? And, even more important, would
Heaven or Shang Ti (Supreme Being) be gracious enough to
grant deliverance from the menacing calamities of the day such
as the eclipse of the sun, the falling of meteors, and the incursion
of barbaric tribes? Indeed, could its divine blessings be invoked
and relied upon on the eve of a great battle against an enemy
attack?

The proper course of action for such weighty affairs was
usually sought from the indications on the tortoise shell or the
way in which the milfoil stalks grouped themselves. The *I-wen
Chih,* the catalogue of the imperial library of the Han dynasty,
now found in the *Ch'ien Han Shu* (ch. 30), speaks of these two
methods of divination as follows:

The milfoil stalks and the tortoise shell are used by the Sages. The
Shu says: "When you have doubts about great matters, consult the tortoise shell and milfoil stalks." And the *I* says: "For making certain of

---

[7]There is another tradition which maintains that the present book might have
resulted from the revision of two earlier books. From the *Chou Li* (The Ritual of the
Chou Dynasty), we find that the Grand Augur (Ta Pu) was supposed to be in
charge of the three *I*: the *Lien Shan* (Mountains Standing Together), the *Kuei
Ts'ang* (Reverting to the Hidden), and *Chou I* (Book of Changes of the Chou
Dynasty). The *Yu Hai* quoted from the *San-hai Ching:* "Fu Hsi obtained the map
from the Ho, which the Hsia adopted as the *I*, called the *Lien Shan. Huang Ti*
[legendary culture hero] obtained the map from the Ho, which the Shang adopted
as the *I*, called the *Kuei Ts'ang.* Ni Shan obtained the map from the Ho, which
the Chou adopted as the *I*, called the *Chou I.*" Little is known, however, of the *Lien
Shan* and *Kuei Ts'ang,* for only the *Chou I* survived, as the *I Ching.* We agree
with Legge that "it would be a waste of time to try to discover the meaning of these
designations." (See Legge's Introduction, page 4 and note.)

good and bad fortune, and accomplishing things requiring strenuous effort, there is nothing better than the milfoil stalks and tortoise shell. Therefore the Superior Man, whenever he is about to do something or to carry out some action, asks [the *I*] and makes his inquiry in words. It receives his order, and the answer comes as the echo's response. Be the subject remote or near, mysterious or deep, he forthwith knows what will be the coming result. [If the *I*] were not the exquisite thing under Heaven, would it be concerned in such an operation as this?"[8] (p. 47)

Tortoise shell divination was practiced as early as the Shang dynasty. The belly surface of the tortoise shell having been incised with a red-hot stylus, it was then heated with fire by the diviner until cracks formed in it, from which the diviner read the oracles. But the cracks thus formed were intricate and difficult to interpret and, moreover, the prognostications based on the cracks were complicated and difficult to remember. Later, in Chou times, a new process of augury was devised with the use of a fixed number of milfoil stalks arranged in a definite order, the judgment for every possible combination and permutation of the stalks having been previously made and recorded in a work of divination known as the *I Ching*. The use of the milfoil stalks in conjunction with the *I Ching's* symbols was designed to simplify the divination procedures of the tortoise shell, as well as to provide for a standard prognostication in accordance with whichever *kua* and *hsiao* in the *kua* happened to be encountered. This was certainly a far easier method of divination than that of the tortoise shell. This is the reason why the *I Ching* is also called the

---

[8]Cf. Legge's translation, Appendix III, Sec. I, Ch. 10.

In the *Tso Chuan*, the divination by the tortoise shell and milfoil stalks is often mentioned. With the feudal lords, divination was a very important practice, from which they sought guidance in state affairs as well as in their life and activities. Hence attached to the feudal court was a group of hereditary diviners who, through the mysterious signs on the tortoise shell and by means of the milfoil stalks, spoke as the deputies of spirits and deities. A very interesting story about the relative merits of the two divination methods is told in the *Tso Chuan* under the 4th year of Duke Hsi of Lu (656 B.C.). When Duke Hsien of Tsin was about to make his favorite concubine, Lady Li of the barbaric Jung tribe, his wife, he referred the matter to divination. "The tortoise shell indicated that it would be unlucky, but the milfoil pronounced it lucky. The duke said: 'I will follow the milfoil.' The diviner by the tortoise shell said: 'The milfoil is reckoned inferior in its indications to the tortoise shell. You had better follow the latter.' But the duke did not listen to the advice, and in consequence, the state was thrown into great turmoil after his death." (Legge, *Chinese Classics*, V, 141.)

Chou I. "It was named Chou from the fact that it was composed by the people of the Chou dynasty, and *I* because its method of divination was an easy one." The word "I" means "easy" as well as "change".[9]

This, then, was the probable origin of the basic text of the *I Ching,* and explains its title in regard to the various combinations of lines. This book was originally a Chou manual on divination, "very valuable for its practical wisdom," but "we find nothing [in it] to justify"[10] its name as one of the Confucian Classics, until the commentaries and appendices known as the "Ten Wings" *(Shih I)* were added to it. The whole group of additional texts will be discussed in the following section.

II. The Ten Appendices, or Ten Wings (*Shih I*)

The basic text of the *I Ching* is ascribed, with a certain validity, to the early Chou period. Now let us turn to the supplementary commentaries and appendices, known as the Ten Wings *(Shih I),* which were later added to the *I Ching.* The first two of these constitute the Treatise on the T'uan *(T'uan Chuan),* which uses the structure of the individual hexagrams to interpret their Judgments *(T'uan).*[11] The third and fourth constitute the Treatise on the Symbols *(Hsiang Chuan),* which interprets the symbolism of the hexagrams, as well as that of the several lines.[12] The fifth and sixth constitute the Commentary on the Appended Judgments *(Hsi Tz'u Chuan),* also known as the Great Appendix *(Ta Chuan).*[13] This commentary deals with the fundamental ideas of the basic trigrams, as well as those of the hexagrams, some of which it interprets in terms of culture patterns and development.

[9]See Fung Yu-lan's *A History of Chinese Philosophy,* trans. by Derk Bodde (Princeton: Princeton University Press, 1952), I, 380.

[10]Legge, Introduction, p. 26.

[11]These form Appendix I in Legge's translation.

[12]Appendix II in Legge.

[13]Appendix III in Legge.

The seventh, known as the Explanation of the Words and Sentences (*Wen Yen*), deals with the first two hexagrams, Ch'ien and K'un, in connection with: "man's nature and doings."[14] The eighth appendix, the Discourses on the Trigrams (*Shuo Kua*), consists of eleven short chapters and deals with the symbolic correlations in regard to the system and content of the *I Ching* as a whole.[15] The last two constitute the Treatise on the Sequence of the Hexagrams (*Hsu Kua*), "intended to trace the connection of meaning between them in the order in which they follow one another in the Text,"[16] and the Miscellaneous Remarks on the Hexagrams (*Tsa Kua*), intended to define each of the sixty-four hexagrams.[17]

These appendices offer various interpretations of the *kua* as well as of their separate *hsiao*. In the old edition,[18] as given in Legge's edition, the Ten Appendices are a separate book from the text of the *I Ching*. In the modern edition[19] the *T'uan Chuan*, the *Hsiang Chuan*, and the *Wen Yen* are divided up and placed under the respective *kua* to which they correspond, but the Great Appendix, together with the last three appendices, is left at the end of the text. For the convenience of study, the pertinent portions of the appendices should be incorporated into the text of the *I Ching*, so that the respective *kua* and their separate *hsiao* could be studied together with their pertinent Judgments (*T'uan*) and Commentaries (*Chuan*).

There is a great controversy as to how much Confucius (551-479 B.C.) put into the *I Ching*. The traditional view maintains that the Sage arranged the book and wrote the appendices and commentaries together with the famous "Ten Wings." The heretics, on the other hand, deny his authorship altogether.

---

[14]Appendix IV in Legge.

[16]Appendix VI in Legge.

[15]Appendix V in Legge.

[17]Appendix VII in Legge.

[18]The old edition is authoritative for its formality, being put back into this form by Chu Hsi (1130-1200) and adopted in the imperial edition of the Ching dynasty (1644-1911).

[19]The modern edition is favored for its practicability, being modified by Fei Chih of the former Han dynasty or the two Ch'eng brothers (Ch'eng Hao, 1032-85, and Ch'eng Yi, 1033-1108).

considering all the extraneous material as forgeries by later writers. And finally, modern scholars particularly trained in textual criticism maintain that, even if in his later years Confucius was extremely fascinated by the *I Ching*,[20] these "Ten Wings" could never have been written by the Sage.[21]

Not one of these theories has been conclusively established, and this is not the place to undertake an extended analysis of the controversy. Probably the most plausible assumption is that these appendices must have been the product not of one but of many authors, who gave the *I* various interpretations and read into it their own ideas — some moral, some metaphysical, and some cosmological — but that they were not composed until the latter part of the Chou dynasty. This theory also explains why both Confucians and Taoists used the *I* to express their ideas, so that the *I* served as a bridge between the teachings of the opposing schools.

In this connection, the following passage from the chapter on the Ju School in the *Ch'ien Han Shu* is worth quoting:

> During the Ch'in interdiction of learning [i.e., the Burning of the Books in 213 B.C.], the *I*, being a book of divination, was the only work which had not been forbidden, and therefore its transmission was not interrupted. With the rise of the Han [in 206 B.C.], T'ien Ho, because he was of the royal family of T'ien of Ch'i, was moved to Tu-ling, and hence he was called Tu T'ien-sheng. Then he [T'ien Ho] gave [the *I*] to Wang T'ung and his son, Chung, of Tung-wu. Chou Wang-sun and Ting K'uan of Loyang, as well as Fu Sheng of Ch'i, all wrote commentaries [*chuan*] on the *I* in several chapters.

We do not know whether these "commentaries" are among the "Ten Wings" or not; however, the most pertinent thing that can be said in this connection is that, apart from considerations

---

[20] In the *Analects* (vii. 16) Confucius said: "If a few more years were added to my life, I would give fifty to the study of the *I;* only then I might be free from grave faults."

[21] A great debate on this subject, by a number of modern scholars, including Ku Chieh-kang, Ma Heng, Hu Shih, Chien Mu, Li Ching-chih, and others, will be found in *Ku Shih Pien*, vol. III. See also Fung Yu-lan's "Confucius' Position in Chinese History", in *Ku Shih Pien*, vol. II. James Legge seems to have ascribed all the appendices except the third and fourth—the fifth, sixth, and seventh "wings"—to Confucius.

of exact authorship, it is generally conceded that the "Ten Wings" "are in character similar to, and date from about the same period as, these commentaries."[22]

III. James Legge's Translation of the *I Ching*

James Legge, the English Sinologist, tells us that his original plan, formed in 1858, was to translate the *Four Books* and *Five Classics* in seven volumes:

Vol. I.   *Analects, Great Learning,* and *Doctrine of the Mean.*
Vol. II.   *Mencius.*
Vol. III. *Book of History (Shu Ching).*
Vol. IV. *Book of Odes (Shih Ching).*
Vol. V.   *Ch'un Ch'iu with the Tso Chuan.*
Vol. VI. *Book of Changes (I Ching).*
Vol. VII. *Book of Ritual (Li Chi).*

The first five volumes were published in Hong Kong in 1861, 1861, 1865, 1871, and 1872, with Chinese text and full commentary, while the last two volumes, without Chinese text or extensive commentary, were published in 1882 and 1885 in the Sacred Books of the East series edited by Friedrich Max Müller. Translations of the *Classic of Filial Piety (Hsiao Ching)* in 1879 and of the Taoist texts *Tao Te Ching* and *Chuang Tzu* in 1891 also appeared in the Sacred Books of the East.

There have been many translations of the *I Ching,* and Legge's work, in our opinion, is most popular and useful, as its frequent quotation in the study of Chinese philosophy proves. However, no matter how well a translation has been done, it is always capable of improvement, in order to reveal the richness of the *I Ching* in its original version.

Translation of technical philosophical terms is extremely difficult. For many of the Chinese terms only approximately equivalent terms can be found in English. Hence, translation must often be accompanied by interpretation, if the meaning is to be grasped by Western readers. It should be remembered that many of the most profound as well as the most difficult human

[22]Fung Yu-lan, *History of Chinese Philosophy*, I, 382.

conceptions are to be found in the *I Ching.* Moreover, a single Chinese character often carries the meaning of many English words. Then, too, such philosophical ideas are difficult in themselves, however lucidly translated and interpreted.

In this new publication of James Legge's *I Ching,* some changes have been introduced and useful additions have been made, so as to make the great Sinological work a closer translation from the original text. For instance, in the *I Ching,* throughout its *kua,* every *yang-hsiao* (i.e., undivided line——————) is called NINE, and every *yin-hsiao* (i.e., divided line—— ——) is called SIX, as can be seen in the hexagrams *Ch'ien* and *K'un:*

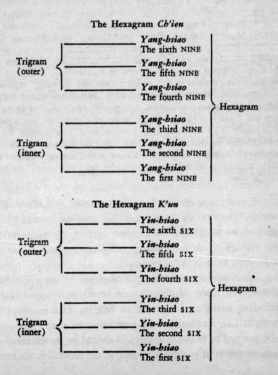

The Hexagram *Ch'ien*

Trigram (outer)
- Yang-hsiao — The sixth NINE
- Yang-hsiao — The fifth NINE
- Yang-hsiao — The fourth NINE

Trigram (inner)
- Yang-hsiao — The third NINE
- Yang-hsiao — The second NINE
- Yang-hsiao — The first NINE

} Hexagram

The Hexagram *K'un*

Trigram (outer)
- Yin-hsiao — The sixth SIX
- Yin-hsiao — The fifth SIX
- Yin-hsiao — The fourth SIX

Trigram (inner)
- Yin-hsiao — The third SIX
- Yin-hsiao — The second SIX
- Yin-hsiao — The first SIX

} Hexagram

Note: The lines are counted from the bottom up, i.e., the lowest is taken as the first.

In regard to the application of the numbers NINE and SIX, Legge offers two explanations in his notes to the *Ch'ien* hexagram as follows:

Each hexagram consists of two of the trigrams...the lower being called "the inner," and the one above "the outer." The lines, however, are numbered from one to six, commencing with the lowest.... As the lines must be either whole or divided, technically called strong and weak, yang and yin, this distinction is indicated by the application to them of the numbers NINE and SIX. All whole lines are NINE, all divided lines, SIX.

Two explanations have been proposed of this application of these numbers. The Khien trigram, it is said, contains 3 strokes (———————), and the Khwan 6 (——— ———). But the yang contains the yin in itself, and its representative number will be $3 + 6 = 9$, while the yin, not containing the yang, will only have its own number or 6. This explanation, entirely arbitrary, is now deservedly abandoned. The other is based on the use of the "four Hsiang," or emblematic figures (———————) the great or old yang, (——— ———) the young yang, (——— ———) the old yin, and (——— ———) the young yin. To these are assigned (by what process is unimportant for our present purpose) the numbers 9, 8, 7, 6. They were "the old yang," represented by 9, and "the old yin," represented by 6, that, in the manipulation of the stalks to form new diagrams, determined the changes of figure; and so 9 and 6 came to be used as the names of a yang line and a yin line respectively. This explanation is now universally acquiesced in. The nomenclature of first nine, nine two, &c., or first six, six two, &c., however, is merely a jargon; and I have preferred to use, instead of it, in the translation, in order to describe the lines, the names "undivided" and "divided." (pp. 58-59)

Hence Legge preferred to use the names of "undivided" and "divided" for all the *yang-hsiao* and *yin-hsiao*, instead of the numbers NINE and SIX. As a matter of fact, the numbers NINE and SIX are to be found in the Chinese original. They were originally used not as "mere jargon," but as important terms, to designate undivided and divided lines in the manipulation of stalks in the divination process. In the *Hsi Tz'u*, we find the following statement: "To Heaven belongs (the number) one; to Earth, two; to Heaven, three; to Earth, four; to Heaven, five; to Earth, six; to Heaven, seven; to Earth, eight; to Heaven, nine; to Earth, ten." (Sec. I, Ch. 9)

This gives the *Yang* (i.e., Heaven or the *Ch'ien* hexagram) a progression of odd numbers running from one to nine. In accordance with the *I-wei Ch'ien-tso-tu* (Apocryphal Treatise on the Changes: A Penetration of the Laws of Ch'ien),[23] one is the number with which the *Yang* first comes into being; three is its "correct position";[24] seven is the number of the unchanging line of *Ch'ien*, that is of the *Yang;* nine is the number of its changing line. This also gives the *Yin* (i.e., Earth or the *K'un* hexagram) a progression of even numbers: two is the number with which the *Yin* first comes into being; four is its "correct position";[25] eight is the number of the unchanging line of *K'un*, that is, of the *Yin;* six is the number of its changing line. As is said in the *I-wei Ch'ien-tso-tu:* "The *Yang* in movement advances forward; the *Yin* in movement draws back." This explains why the *Yang* advances from seven to nine, and the *Yin* withdraws from eight to six. This also explains why nine and six are key numbers, with the result that among the sixty-four hexagrams the number NINE is assigned to all the *yang-hsiao* (———————), whereas the number SIX is assigned to all the *yin-hsiao* (——— ———). Because of this, we have reinserted the two numbers NINE and SIX in their proper places throughout the text, as may be seen in the following quotations:

Concerning the number NINE, in the *Ch'ien* hexagram, the *Hsiao* read: "In the first NINE, (we see its subject as) the dragon lying hid (in the deep). It is not the time for active doing."

Concerning the number SIX, in the *K'un* hexagram, the *Hsiao* read: "In the first SIX, (we see its subject) treading on hoarfrost. The strong ice will come (by and by)."

For added clarity, a glossary (see Comparative Transcription Table) has been included in the present volume to suggest the

---

[23]One of the Han apocrypha on the *I Ching*.

[24]Cheng Hsüan (127-200) pointed out that the diameter of a circle (i.e., symbol of Heaven) is to its circumference as 1 to 3.

[25]Cheng Hsüan pointed out that the one side of a square (i.e., symbol of Earth) is to its four sides as 1 is to 4.

equivalence of important Chinese terms and their Western counterparts. This, in our opinion, will assist the reader to a better understanding of the text.

For those who are not familiar with the *I Ching* a few suggestions may be helpful. First, when one begins to read the *I Ching,* the first impression one gets is of the brevity of the statements. It is well to bear in mind that these brief statements are not simply conclusions from certain premises which have not been written in the text. They are in fact aphorisms full of suggestions and implications. The *I Ching* is like a good poem; the number of words is limited, but the ideas it suggests are limitless. Just as an intelligent reader of poetry reads what is beyond the poem, so a good reader of the *I Ching* reads "what is between the lines." This means that those latent ideas form an essential, often a principal, part of the *I Ching,* so that in an appreciative, generally reflective approach to its material the reader himself often supplies all the "links" that are necessary to turn these "aphorisms" into a form of reasoning and arguments.

In the second place, it is difficult for one to have a complete understanding and full appreciation of the *I Ching* if one cannot read it in the original. This is because of the language barrier. As we know, the Chinese language, in its written form, has become a secret code of subtle suggestions. There is nothing quite like this language elsewhere, nothing to match it in the simplicity and brevity of phrases conveying so many ideas. Moreover, a single character often includes the meaning of many words in English. Because of this suggestive quality of the Chinese language, it is well at the outset not to attempt to pin down fixed definitions of words such as *Yin* and *Yang, Ch'ien* and *K'un, Tao* and *Te.* Most often for these special terms we can find no precise English equivalents. We prefer to allow them to stand without rendering because their meanings are generally best sensed by observing their uses in various contexts. It is, however, advisable for the reader to consult the Glossary at the back of the book.

In the third place, the *I Ching,* being originally a book of divination, was later expanded and developed in a series of appendices or "wings" into a comprehensive system of philosophy. All the theories and principles advocated in the *I* Appendices are not entirely new creations. We find when we come to examine them that there are many respects in which the main thesis of the *I* Appendices corresponds with that of the *Chung Yung (Doctrine of the Mean).*[26] Moreover, the *I* Appendices borrow many ideas from the *Lao Tzu* (i.e., *Tao Te Ching*), so that they have a good deal in common with Taoism. Because of their close connection, the *Chung Yung* and the *Lao Tzu* may be read side by side with the *I Ching*, and may help the reader to understand the meaning of the latter and to grasp its richness.

PART TWO

THE FUNDAMENTAL CONCEPTS OF THE *I CHING*

THE WORD *I* (Change) has given its name to the book known as the *I Ching*. The system of the book has as its basis the eight trigrams, which symbolize the eight fundamental elements or factors of the universe and the different attributes that should be suggested by and associated with them. Then the eight trigrams were combined until there were sixty-four hexagrams — each symbolizing one or more phenomena of the universe, either natural or human. Together, all the hexagrams were supposed to represent symbolically all the possible situations or mutations of creation, a universe in miniature. The book is indeed a remarkable treatise in the history of philosophy. Its practical tendency and its simple symbols are important features of the artistic genius of the Chinese people; therefore, the *I Ching* is

---

[26]It was traditionally supposed to have been written by Confucius' grandson, Tzu Szu. The *Chung Yung*, like the *I* Appendices, was not the work of one man.

not simply a book of philosophy, but a work of art as well. Chinese philosophy, as well as Chinese art and literature, is predominantly practical, and yet at the same time it tends to be simple and penetrating. This is a significant characteristic of the Chinese character, as well as of the Chinese civilization — the art of using simple means to symbolize the complexity of nature. This explains why, with the symbols of the *I*, "the Sages were able to survey all the complex phenomena of the universe."[27] In understanding the significance of the *I Ching* as a book of philosophy, practical and simple, this remarkable characteristic must be taken into consideration.

Let us start with some of the fundamental concepts of the *I Ching* — *I* (Change), *Hsiang* (Symbols), and *Tz'u* (Judgment) — which have been important factors in the development of the *I*. The significance of the *I Ching* as a book of philosphy lies in its adaptability to varying circumstances and its magnetism, which attracts whatever is good and useful in Chinese philosophy, indeed, in Chinese culture.

I. The Concept of *I*

One of the fundamental concepts is the word *I*, which, it is said, has three meanings: "(1) ease and simplicity, (2) transformation and change, and (3) invariability."[28] These three meanings of the word *I* are in fact not clearly defined in the *I Ching*. However, we shall try to take these meanings as our guides to the study of the book.

The word *I* primarily means change. In the *I Ching*, the word *I* is used interchangeably with the word *Tao*, since *Tao* is

---

[27]*Hsi Tz'u*, Sec. I, Ch. 12.

[28]See the *I-wei Ch'ien-tso-tu*, which has a commentary by Cheng Hsüan (127-200), quoted by K'ung Ying-ta (547-648) in his commentary on Wang Pi's (226-49) *Commentary on the I.*

life, spontaneity, evolution, or, in one word, change itself. In the *Analects,* we read: "Standing by a stream, Confucius said 'Ah! that which is passing is just like this, never ceasing day or night.'" (IX, 16) What is "passing" is ever changeable and changing. All that happens in the universe ever flows and changes like the "flowing stream"; that is, to borrow an expression from Heraclitus of Ephesus (530-470 B.C.), *panta rhei* (everything flows). This expresses the real meaning of the word *I.*

All changes and transformations are the result of movements. For in the universe there are two primal forces: the virile called the *Yang* (the positive element, the male) and the docile called the *Yin* (the negative element, the female). Interaction of these two primal forces produces all kinds of movements and changes. In the *Hsi Tz'u,* we find the following statement: "The virile and the docile displace each other and produce the changes and transformation" (Sec. I, Ch. 2), and again:

> One *Yin* and one *Yang* constitute what is called *Tao.* That which is perpetuated by it is good. That which is completed by it is the natures (of men and things).[29]... How prolific is its *Te* (Power) and how great its achievement! The abundance of it is what is meant by "great achievement" and the daily renewal of it is what is meant by "prolific *Te*". (Sec. I, Ch. 5)

The *Tao* given here as the result of the unceasing movement of the *Yin* and the *Yang* corresponds to the *Tao* of Taoism. The *Tao* is the great spontaneous stream of life through which all things are produced. Everything produced by the *Tao* is a part of "the unceasing movement" and hence it is good. Everything transforms and completes its *Te* in the "unceasing movement." Because of this, the *Tao* achieves "the great achievement," being abundant and daily renewed. Indeed, its achievement is achieved

---

[29]About this passage, Chiao Hsün says: "That which is divided from *Tao* is called Fate. That which is manifested in the individual is called nature. The united *Tao* separates itself so as to give completeness to the natures of individual men. The natures of all things are united so as to give completeness to the whole of *Tao.* One *Yin* and one *Yang* are what make *Tao* never ending." See his *Lun-yü T'ung-shih Chung-shu.*

in daily renewal; that is, "the unceasing movement going on in the world." As the *Hsi Tz'u* says: "The great attribute *(Te)* of Heaven is to produce." (Sec. II, Ch. 1) "Production and reproduction are what the *I* represents." (Sec. I, Ch. 5) This of course does not mean that the *I* itself produces and reproduces, but that producing and reproducing go on in accordance with "the unceasing movement of the *Yin* and the *Yang*," that is, the *Tao*.

Moreover, the *I Ching* equates the *Yang* and the *Yin* with the *Ch'ien* and the *K'un*, the male and female principles, as physically represented by Heaven and Earth. As the *Hsi Tz'u* says:

> The *Ch'ien* and the *K'un* may be regarded as the gate of the *I*. The *Ch'ien* represents *Yang*-subjects; the *K'un* represents *Yin*-subjects. The *Yin* and the *Yang* are united in their *Te* and the virile and the docile receive form, thus giving manifestation to the phenomena of Heaven and Earth and comprehension to the *Te* of spiritual enlightenment. (Sec. II, Ch. 6)

Because of the union of *Ch'ien* and *K'un*, all things come into existence, and hence come all changes and transformations. As is said in the *Hsi Tz'u*: "There is an intermingling of the genial influences of Heaven and Earth, and transformation of all things proceeds abundantly. There is intercommunication of seed between male and female, and all creatures are born and transform." (Sec. II, Ch. 5)

Another important passage in the *Hsi Tz'u* is the following: "Thus, the shutting of a door is analogous to *K'un;* the opening of a door to *Ch'ien*. One shutting plus one opening is the meaning of transformation. The unceasing process, moving first one way and then the other, is known as effective evolving." (Sec. I, Ch. 11) The content of the course of transformation is the unceasing process of "the opening and shutting" symbolizing the primal forces — the *Ch'ien* and the *K'un*, the *Yang* and the *Yin*. Of these two primal forces, the one is virile, the other docile; the one gives forth, the other receives; to the one all things owe their beginning, and to the other they all owe their birth. Thus in the *Hsi Tz'u* we find the statement: "There is *Ch'ien:* When it is quiescent, it is self-absorbed; when it is active, it goes straight forward. Therefore it produces on the grand scale. There is *K'un:* When it is quiescent, it is shut in; when it is active, it opens out. Therefore it produces on a wide scale." (Sec. I, Ch. 6) Thus the *Ch'ien* and the *K'un* complement each other, and so the things in the universe ever change and transform. This is the first aspect of the *I*-concept.

The second aspect of the *I*-concept is the easy and the simple. The *I* in the midst of complexities reveals simplicity. In the *Hsi Tz'u*, there is the statement:

> Therefore, in (the system of) the *I*, there is the Supreme Ultimate *(T'ai Chi)*, which produced the Two Modes *(Yi)*. The Two Modes produced the Four *Hsiang* (Symbols), which in turn produced the Eight Trigrams *(Kua)*.[30]

> The Eight Trigrams determine good fortune and misfortune, from which comes great achievement. (Sec. I, Ch. 11)

The "great achievement," in relation to the Supreme Ultimate, consists in the symbols and formulae connected with all the *kua* and *hsiao*. These symbols and formulae represent the process of transforming what is simple and easy into what is complex and difficult. The Supreme Ultimate *(T'ai Chi)* given here is different from the *T'ai-chi Tu* (Diagram of the Supreme Ultimate), in which the Sung scholar Chou Tun-yi (1011-77) elucidated the origins of "Heavenly Principle" and probed into the beginning and end of all things. According to the *Shuo-wen Chieh-tzu* (Explanation of Script and Elucidation of Characters),[31] the word *chi* is the ridgepole — i.e., the horizontal beam along the ridge

---

[30]A similar passage is found in Ch. 42 of the *Lao Tzu.*

[31]A dictionary composed *ca.* A.D. 100 by Hsü Shen, in 15 sections, each divided into 2 parts.

of a roof — a simple line symbolizing the positing of oneness (———————). Out of the Supreme Ultimate, the Two Modes are produced and designated as the *Yang* (———————) and the *Yin* (———— ————). Through the Two Modes, there arise the Four *Hsiang:*

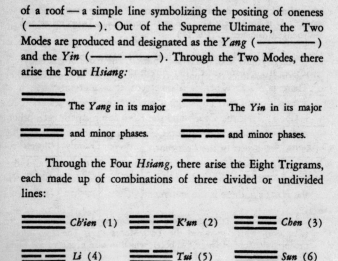

The *Yang* in its major

and minor phases.

The *Yin* in its major

and minor phases.

Through the Four *Hsiang*, there arise the Eight Trigrams, each made up of combinations of three divided or undivided lines:

Ch'ien (1) *K'un* (2) *Chen* (3)

Li (4) *Tui* (5) *Sun* (6)

K'an (7) *Ken* (8)

Originally these Eight Trigrams may not have had any specific meanings attached to them, but later on they were elaborated so that each came to be symbolically representative of certain things or ideas. The *Shuo Kua* says:

The *Ch'ien* (1) Trigram is Heaven, and hence is called father. *K'un* (2) is Earth, and hence is called mother. *Chen* (3) by its first (i.e., lowest) line is male (i.e., an undivided line), and so is called the eldest son. *Sun* (6) by its first line is female (i.e., a divided line), and so is called the eldest daughter. *K'an* (7) by its second (i.e., middle) line is male, and so is called the second son. *Li* (4) by its second line is female, and so is called the second daughter. *Ken* (8) by its third (i.e., upper) line is male, and so is called the youngest son. *Tui* (5) by its third line is female, and so is called the youngest daughter. (Ch. 10)

Ch'ien is Heaven, round, and is the ruler and the father....*K'un* is Earth and is the mother....*Chen* is thunder and the dragon....*Sun* is wood and wind, and the eldest daughter,...*K'an* is water... and the moon....*Li* is fire and the sun....*Ken* is mountain....*Tui* is marsh and the youngest daughter.... (Ch. 11)

The trigrams also symbolize animals, the parts of the body, and various qualities or situations, as may be seen in the following table:

Trigrams	Symbols	Attributes[1]	Symbolic Animals[2]	Parts of Body[3]	Family[4]	Natural Objects[5]
Ch'ien	☰	strength	horse	head	father	Heaven
K'un	☷	docility	ox	belly	mother	Earth
Chen	☳	movement	dragon	foot	eldest son	thunder
Sun	☴	penetration	fowl	thigh	eldest daughter	wood and wind
K'an	☵	danger	pig	ear	second son	water and moon
Li	☲	brightness	pheasant	eye	second daughter	fire and sun
Ken	☶	stand-still	dog	hand	youngest son	mountain
Tui	☱	pleasure	sheep	mouth	youngest daughter	marsh

[1]See the *Shuo Kua*, Ch. 7. [2]*Ibid.*, Ch. 8. [3]*Ibid.*, Ch. 9. [4]*Ibid.*, Ch. 10. [5]*Ibid.*, Ch. 11.

The objects or attributes thus symbolized by the Eight Trigrams are made the constituents of the universe, which form the basis of a cosmological system elaborated by the Han scholars in connection with the Theory of Five Elements. By combining any two of these trigrams to form a diagram of six lines, a total of sixty-four combinations is obtained, known as the Sixty-four Hexagrams. The Eight Trigrams, together with the Sixty-four Hexagrams formed by their combinations, therefore, represent all the possible situations and mutations of creation, a universe in miniature. This offers a good illustration of the transformation from simplicity to complexity.

The *I* makes *Ch'ien* and *K'un* represent what is easy and simple; for only from what is easy and simple can there be "complex phenomena" and "great movements." As the *Hsi Tz'u* puts it:

> The *Ch'ien* by its easiness is knowable, the *K'un* by its simplicity is do-able. What is easy, is easy to know; what is simple, is simple to follow.... With ease and simplicity, then all the principles in the world are successfully obtained. (Sec. I, Ch. 1)

> The *Ch'ien* represents the strongest of all things in the world. The expression of its *Te* is unvariably the easy, so as to know dangers. The *K'un* represents the most docile of all things in the world. The expression of its *Te* is invariably the simple, so as to know obstructions. (Sec. II, Ch. XII)

This idea of ease and simplicity attached to the *I* explains why the emphasis is often placed on ease and simplicity as the gateway to the true province of the *I*. Because of the good that lies in the easy and the simple, the *I* "can speak of the most complex phenomena in the world without arousing aversion, and speak of the subtlest movement without causing confusion." (*Hsi Tz'u*, Sec. I, Ch. 8)

Finally, we approach the third aspect associated with the concept of *I:* invariability. The *I* in the midst of variability also reveals an element of invariability. We see that things in the universe are ever in a state of flux and change. They are all part of "the unceasing movement going on in the universe." In the *T'uan*, we find the following statements: "When Heaven and Earth are released (from the grip of winter), we have thunder and rain. When these come, the buds of the plants and trees that produce the various fruits begin to burst."[32] "Heaven and Earth undergo their changes, and the four seasons complete their functions."[33]

---

[32]About *Hsieh*, the fortieth hexagram.   [33]About *Ko*, the forty-ninth hexagram.

Nevertheless, these phenomenal changes all follow a constant order. As is said in the *T'uan:*

Heaven and Earth move in concord, and hence the sun and moon do not err (in time), and the four seasons do not deviate (from their order).[34]

Heaven and Earth observe their regular terms, and we have the four seasons complete.[35]

The *Tao* of Heaven of Earth is constant and unceasing.

"When it is said, movement in any direction whatever will be advantageous," (this implies that) when there is an end, there is a beginning. The sun and moon, pertaining to Heaven, can shine forever. The four seasons, changing and transforming, can forever bring to completion. The sages remain forever in their *Tao,* and the world is transformed to completion. When we see how they are constant, the nature of Heaven, Earth, and all things can be seen.[36]

As a further expression of the *"Tao* of Heaven and Earth" which everything obeys, we present the following passage from the *Hsi Tz'u:*

Good fortune and misfortune are constantly overcoming one another (by an exact rule). The *Tao* of Heaven and Earth is constantly to manifest themselves. The *Tao* of the sun and moon is constantly to emit their light. All movements of the world are constantly subject to one and the same rule. (Sec. II, Ch. 1)

All the passages quoted above clearly indicate that all things in the universe follow a definite order — i.e., the *Tao* of Heaven and Earth — according to which they change and transform constantly. These passages also imply the ideas of invariability as a necessary attribute of the *I*-concept.

In conclusion, the concept of *I* has three important attributes: ease and simplicity, change and transformation, and invariability. These attributes should make clear two points,

---

[34]About *Yü,* the sixteenth hexagram.   [35]About *Chieh,* the sixtieth hexagram.

[36]About *Heng,* the thirty-second hexagram.

which we need mention only briefly. First, the process of transformation starts from the easy and the simple, and hence when we know the causes of the easy and the simple, we can predict the effects of the complex and the difficult. This is why the *I* in the midst of complexities reveals simplicity. Second, things in the universe are ever changing and changeable, but their underlying principles, for which the *Tao* can be employed, are constant and invariable. This is why the *I* also reveals an element of invariability in the midst of all phenomenal change. Because of this, although all the things in the universe are complex, forever changing, yet among the complexities simplicity can be found, among the changes something unchanging. Thus it is said: "The *I* dovetails with Heaven and Earth, with the result that it completely interweaves the *Tao* of Heaven and Earth."[37] This is the first fundamental concept of the *I Ching*.

II. The Concept of *Hsiang* (Symbol)

The whole *I* book is then a system of symbols (*hsiang*). As the *Hsi Tz'u* says, "Thus the *I* consists of symbols. By symbol is meant something resembling." (Sec. II, Ch. 3) Also it says: "The Eight Trigrams are arranged in their proper order; thus the symbols are contained in them. Thereupon they are doubled; thus the lines (*hsiao*) are contained in them. . . . By *hsiao* is meant something imitating this. By *hsiang* is meant something resembling this." (Sec. II, Ch. 1) According to the *Hsi Tz'u*, the sixty-four hexagrams and the three hundred and eighty-four *hsiao* (lines which comprise the hexagrams) are all symbols.

In fact, the word *hsiang* not only refers to the symbolic representation of an object, but includes the object itself as well.

[37] *Hsi Tz'u*, Sec. I, Ch. 4.

There comes to mind a passage in the *Lao Tzu:*

> *Tao* is a thing, elusive and evasive.
> Evasive and elusive,
> Yet there is a Symbol *{Hsiang}* in it.
> Elusive and evasive,
> Yet there is a Substance *{Wu}* in it. (Ch. 21)

By *wu* is meant something having shapes and features, and the *Lao Tzu* speaks of the *Tao* as transcending shapes and features, as when it says: "The *Tao* is invariable, unnamable — the Uncarved Block" (Ch. 32) and also: "When the Block diversifies, it becomes vessels" (Ch. 28). The *Tao* and the *Wu* (i.e., physical things) are opposites. The *Hsi Tz'u* also says, "That which is above shapes and features is called the *Tao;* that which is within shapes and features is called the vessel." (Sec. II, Ch. 12) The *Tao* and the *Wu* are opposites in the same way.

The basic idea in the passages quoted above is that first the *Tao* produces the *Hsiang,* and then out of the *Hsiang* the *Wu* comes into being. In other words, symbols serve as models or patterns, from which physical objects are evolved. The *Hsi Tz'u* says: "In the heavens there are the symbols *(hsiang)* there completed; on earth there are shapes and features *(hsing)* there formed. In this way changes and transformations are exhibited." (Sec. I, Ch. 1) This means that symbols come into existence in precedence of substances. The hexagrams and the *hsiao,* therefore, are symbols, which can be used as models for the making of physical objects. As the *Hsi Tz'u* expresses it:

> The sages were able to survey all the complex phenomena of the world. They then considered how to represent their physical forms and symbolize their character. Hence these (symbols) are designated the *hsiang.* (Sec. I, Ch. 8)
> The appearance of anything is called a symbol *(hsiang).* When it has received its physical form, it is called a vessel. When it is regulated

and used, this is called the *fa* (laws).[38] And when benefit arises from it
in external and internal matters, so that the people all use it, it is called
mysterious *(shen)*. (Sec. I, Ch. 11)

Thus from these symbols (i.e., hexagrams and *hsiao*) which the
Sage has drawn to represent the things of the universe, he makes
the vessels and laws for the use of the people and benefit of
the world. Therefore:

> The Sages, fully understanding the *Tao* of Heaven and knowing
> the needs of the people, thus made these mysterious things *(shen wu)*
> for the use of the people....The result is that Heaven produced the
> mysterious things and the Sages modeled themselves on them. Heaven
> and Earth have their changes and transformations, and the Sages imitated
> them. Heaven hangs out its symbols, from which are seen good fortune
> and misfortune, and the Sages made symbols *(hsiang)* of them. The Ho
> {i.e., Yellow River} brought forth the map and the Lo the writing, and
> the Sages took these as models. (Sec. I, Ch. 11)

According to the *Hsi Tz'u*, the *I* was composed so as to
represent, through these symbols, various objects of the universe,
as models for human conduct and institutions. As the *Hsi Tz'u*
says, "If we led on these (hexagrams) and expanded them, if
we prolonged each by the addition of the proper lines, then all
possible situations in the world might be represented." (Sec. I,
Ch. 9) One of the commentaries is the *Hsiang Chuan*, a text
that derives, from the symbols suggested by the primary trigrams,
a precept, corresponding to the situation represented by the
hexagram, which may serve as a model for human conduct:

> Heaven, in its motion, is vigorous. The Superior Man, in accordance
> with this, nerves himself to ceaseless activity (concerning the *Ch'ien*
> hexagram).
> The power of Earth is denoted by *K'un.* The Superior Man, in
> accordance with this, supports men and things with his sublime virtue
> *(te)* (concerning the *K'un* hexagram).

---

[38]The word *fa,* literally meaning law, is used here in the sense of a pattern or model.

As to society as whole, the *Hsi Tz'u* says:

> In the *I* there is a fourfold *Tao* of the Sages. Its judgment *(Tz'u)* serves as the model of our speech. Its changes serve as the models of our action. Its symbols *(Hsiang)* serve as the models for the making of vessels. Its prognostications serve as the model of the practice of divination. (Sec. I, Ch. 10)

Thus the *I,* originally a book of divination, can guide our speech by its words, and our conduct by its symbols. The *Hsi Tz'u* offers a good illustration of how the legendary sages instructed the people in the arts of civilization, and how their inventions or discoveries were inspired by the symbolic meanings of the hexagrams:

> In ancient times when Pao Hsi [i.e., Fu Hsi] ruled the world, he looked up to observe the symbols in the heavens, and gazed down to observe the patterns on earth. He observed the markings of birds and beasts and their adaptations to the regions. Some ideas he took from his own body and other ideas from other things. Thereupon he first devised the Eight Trigrams in order to comprehend the attributes *(te)* of the mysterious and represent the conditions of all things of creation. (Sec. II, Ch. 2)

This is to show that the Eight Trigrams devised by the Sage were supposed to be the symbolic representations of the basic constituents of the universe and the different attributes suggested by and associated with them. Following this passage, the *Hsi Tz'u* goes on to show how the important inventions of the sages all originated under the suggestion of the different symbols represented by the varied combinations of the trigrams, that is, the hexagrams. In the same chapter, we read: "He [Fu Hsi] knotted cords to make nets and baskets, for both hunting and fishing. The idea of this was taken, probably, from *Li.*"

Li

Li, the thirtieth hexagram — a symbol of empty space — is composed of trigrams (☲) and (☲) meaning "being attached to" or "being caught on something." Hence the *Li* hexagram inspired the Sage to invent nets and baskets for the use of the people. Then: "On the death of Pao Hsi, there arose Shen Nung.[39] He fashioned wood to form the share, and bent wood to make the plough-handle. The advantages of ploughing and weeding were then taught to the world. The idea of this was taken, probably, from *I*."

 I

I, the forty-second hexagram — a symbol of advantage — is composed of the trigrams *Sun* (☴) above, meaning wind, wood, and penetrating, and *Chen* (☳) below, meaning thunder, motion, and growth. Hence the *I* hexagram, representing the symbol of wood above and growth below, inspired the Sage to invent the art of agriculture. The same chapter continues:

After the death of Shen Nung, there were Huang Ti, Yao, and Shun.[40] They carried through the changes, so that the people did not grow weary. They exerted the mysterious transformation, so that the people were rightly ordered.... Then they hollowed out trees to make boats, and cut trees to make oars. Thus by the advantage of boats and oars they provided the means of communication with distant places for the profit of the world. The idea of this was taken, probably, from *Huan*.

[39]Shen Nung is said to have taught the people agriculture.

[40]They were all cultural heroes.

Huan

Huan, the fifty-ninth hexagram, is composed of the trigrams *Sun* ( ) above, meaning wind and wood, and *K'an* ( ) below, meaning water. Hence the *Huan* hexagram, composed of wood floating on water, suggested the idea of constructing boats and oars. And again: "They also tamed oxen and yoked horses so as to pull heavy loads and to go long distances, thus benefiting the world. The idea of this was taken, probably, from *Sui*."

Sui

Sui, the seventeenth hexagram, is composed of the trigrams *Tui* ( ) above, meaning marshes and contentment, and *Chen* ( ) below, meaning movement. Hence the *Sui* hexagram, composed of contentment above and movement below, suggested the idea of utilizing animals for transport. This was the origin of civilization. Such selections could be multiplied, but those quoted are sufficient to illustrate the point before us. The significance of these symbols provided models not only for the making of vessels and institutions, but also for the conduct of mankind. Civilization is after all not so much the conquest of Nature as a humble imitation of it. The *I*, in short, is a reflection of the universe in miniature. As the *Hsi Tz'u* says:

> In its breadth and greatness, the *I* corresponds to Heaven and Earth; in its ever-recurring changes, it corresponds to the four seasons; in its idea of the *Yin* and the *Yang*, it corresponds to the sun and moon; in the good seen in its ease and simplicity, it corresponds to the supreme power *(te)*. (Sec. I, Ch. 6)

There is another passage from the *Hsi Tz'u* worth inserting here for the sake of the clear conception of *Hsiang* which the *I* characterizes. It is as follows:

Thus, the shutting of a door is analogous to *K'un;* the opening of a door to *Ch'ien.* One shutting plus one opening is the meaning of transformation. The unceasing process, moving first one way and then the other, is known as effective evolving. The appearance of anything is called a symbol. When it has received its physical form, it is called a vessel. When it is regulated and used, this is called law. When benefit arises from it in external and internal matters, so that the people all use it, it is called mysterious.

"One shutting plus one opening" and "unceasing process of moving" may be regarded as the natural phenomena, from which, as conceived in the mind, is evolved the idea. When the idea has a physical form, it comes to be an object; when we regulate and use it, it becomes a "law," in order to be a model for our action. This explains why "the *I* consists of symbols; the sixty-four hexagrams and the three hundred and eighty-four *hsiao* are all symbols." Symbols are rather like what, in symbolic logic, are called variables, and a variable can represent a class or a number of classes of objects or ideas. In this connection, we present a few more illustrations:

The *Meng* hexagram (4)

above *Ken* (Mountain)

below, *K'an* (Water)

This is the symbol representing the idea "a spring rising at the foot of a mountain" — i.e., the fountainhead of a stream. Hence the idea of "child education" is evolved from this hexagram. This is why it is said in the *Hsiang:* "*Meng:* the Superior Man, in accordance with this, strives to be resolute in his conduct and nourishes his virtue *(te)*."

The Lü hexagram (10)

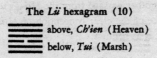

above, *Ch'ien* (Heaven)

below, *Tui* (Marsh)

This is the symbol representing the idea of "Heaven above, the marsh below" — i.e., the difference between high and low upon which proper social conduct depends. Hence it is said in the *Hsiang:* "The Superior Man, in accordance with this, discriminates between high and low, and thereby determines the aims of the people."

The T'ai hexagram (11)

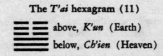

above, *K'un* (Earth)

below, *Ch'ien* (Heaven)

This is the symbol representing the idea of "the union of Heaven and Earth"; i.e., the interaction of Heaven and Earth, so that all things bloom and prosper. Hence it is said: *"T'ai:* The sovereign, in harmony with this, through his wealth completes the *Tao* of Heaven and Earth, and assists what is appropriate to Heaven and Earth, so as to benefit the people."

The Fu hexagram (24)

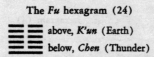

above, *K'un* (Earth)

below, *Chen* (Thunder)

This is the symbol representing the idea of "Thunder within the Earth" — i.e., the idea of rest, from which is evolved the idea of holidays. Hence it is said in the *Hsiang:* "*Fu:* The ancient kings, in accordance with this, closed the passes on the day of solstice, so that merchants and strangers could not pursue their journeys, nor could the princes go on with the inspection of their states."

The *Ta Ch'u* hexagram (26)

above, *Ken* (Mountain)

below, *Ch'ien* (Heaven)

This is the symbol representing the idea of "Heaven within the mountain," which points to limited knowledge. Hence it is said in the *Hsiang:* "*Ta Ch'u:* The Superior Man, in accordance with this, stores in his memory the words of antiquity and deeds of the past, in order to strengthen his virtue thereby."

It seems that every object or idea can be represented by a certain hexagram. As the *Hsi Tz'u* says:

> Thus good fortune and misfortune are symbols *(Hsiang)* and gain and loss; repentance and regret are symbols of sorrow and anxiety. Changes and transformations are symbols of advance and retrogression; the virile and the docile are symbols of day and night. The movements of the six lines *(hsiao)* show the *Tao* of the three primal powers.... Hence the Superior Man, when at rest, contemplates the symbols and studies the judgments *(Tz'u)*. When in activity, he contemplates their changes and studies their prognostications. Thus he "is blessed by Heaven, with good fortune and nothing that is not beneficial." (Sec. I, Ch. 2)

Herein the importance of *Hsiang* is made evident. This is the second fundamental concept of the *I Ching*.

III. The Concept of *Tz'u* (Judgment)

In the *I Ching*, there are sixty-four hexagrams and three hundred eighty-four *hsiao* (the single lines which comprise the hexagram). Each hexagram and each line has a symbol, representing a certain object or idea. However, symbols *(hsiang)* alone cannot bring out the meaning and significance of the *I*. As the *Hsi Tz'u* says:

In the *I*, there are four symbols,[41] so as to give information; there are judgments *(tz'u)* appended, so as to give interpretation; and a determination either fortunate or the reverse, so as to resolve the doubts. (Sec. I, Ch. 11)

The Sages set up the symbols in order to express fully their ideas; they devised hexagrams in order to show fully truth and falsehood; they appended judgments in order to give the full expression of their words. (Sec. I, Ch. 12)

The Sages devised hexagrams, so that symbols might be perceived therein; they appended judgments, so that good fortune and misfortune might be made clear. (Sec. I, Ch. 2)

From these passages it should be clear that *hsiang* (symbol) can be substituted for objects or ideas, but it is *tz'u* (judgment) attached to a hexagram or a *hsiao* that is a formula representing the *Tao* to determine good fortune and misfortune as "symbols of gain and loss." For instance:

The *Ch'ien* hexagram (15)

≡≡ above, *K'un* (Earth)
≡≡ below, *Ken* (Mountain)

This is a symbol of modesty or humility, about which the *hsiang* says: "Within the earth, there is a mountain," but it does not indicate whether there is good fortune or misfortune attached to the hexagram. Therefore the *Kua Tz'u* (Judgment on the Hexagram) says:

Ch'ien indicates progress and success.
The Superior Man will carry his work through.

This shows what modesty is and how it functions, as implied and suggested in the hexagram; thus the Superior Man can carry out his work to the end by being modest. And again, the first *hsiao* (counted from the bottom) of *Ch'ien* is *Yin-hsiao*

[41]The word "four" before "symbols," being superfluous, should be omitted.

(———— ————), that is, the lowest line, symbolizing "modesty to modesty," but not telling fortune, good or bad. Hence the *Tz'u* on the *hsiao* says:

> The first Six means:
> A Superior Man adds modesty to modesty;
> The great stream must be crossed with this,
> And there will be good fortune.

A dangerous enterprise, such as the crossing of a great stream, will be turned to "good fortune," if it is attended to modestly and humbly. This shows how modesty functions, as suggested in the lines *(hsiao)*.

The function of the *Tz'u* is to point out good fortune and misfortune attached to the *kua*-symbol or to the *hsiao*-symbol. As the *Hsi Tz'u* expresses it, "The Sages . . . appended judgments, so that good fortune and misfortune might be made clear" (Sec. I, Ch. 2), and "the discriminations of good fortune and misfortune are based upon the judgments" (Sec. I, Ch. 3). The word *tz'u*, in the *Shuo Wen Chieh-tzu*,[42] means "legal action" or "dispute." The original meaning of the word *tz'u* is in the sense of decisions or judgments of a legal action. In the *I Ching*, the *tz'u* is used in the sense of "decision" and "discrimination." Etymologically speaking, *hsiang* is a symbol in the sense of "a term" or "a concept," while *tz'u* is a statement in the sense of "a judgment" or "a decision." For instance, in the *Ch'ien* hexagram, we read: *"Ch'ien: progress and success."* Here *Ch'ien* is the symbol of modesty; "progress and success" is the statement. To interpret the symbol with the statement is called *Tz'u* or Judgment.

As to the definition of the word *Tz'u*, there is a passage in the *Hsi Tz'u:* "Thus of the *kua*, some are small and some are great, and of the *Tz'u*, some speak of danger and some speak of safety. The *Tz'u* in each case indicates the tendency (shown in the symbols)." (Sec. I, Ch. 3) Therefore the *Tz'u* attached to

---

[42] See above, note 31 on p. xliii.

a certain hexagram or a certain *hsiao* indicates the tendency as to what brings good fortune and what brings misfortune, so that we can take advantage of good fortune and avoid misfortune.

The *Tz'u* is better understood in the light of *Hsiang*. In the *Hsi Tz'u*, there are two sets of statements, one with regard to the *Hsiang*, the other with regard to the *Tz'u*. With regard to the *Hsiang*, there is the statement already quoted, "Thus to speak of *Hsiang:* the Sages were able to survey all the complex phenomena of the world. They then considered how to represent their physical forms and symbolize their character. Hence these *(Hsiang)* are designated the *Hsiang*." (Sec. I, Ch. 8) With regard to the *Tz'u,* there is the statement: "The Sages were able to survey all the movements of the world. They then contemplated the way in which these movements became interrelated, in order to put into effect right rituals. They appended *Tz'u,* in order to determine good fortune and misfortune. Hence these (judgments) are denominated *Tz'u*".[43] *(Ibid.)* Then the *Hsi Tz'u* concludes: "Then the most thorough mastery of all the complex phenomena of the world is obtained from the *kua* (i.e., hexagrams). The greatest stimulus to all the movements of the world is obtained from the *Tz'u*." (Ibid.) These passages present the contrast between the *Hsiang* and the *Tz'u*. What the *Hsiang* symbolizes are the forms and attributes representing "the complex phenomena of the world." What the *Tz'u* explains are the decisions as to what brings good fortune and what brings misfortune, in connection with "the movements of the world." Thus the *Hsiang* is static, and the *Tz'u* is dynamic; the former represents resemblance, and the latter shows the trend of development. Consequently, by the *Hsiang*, "the complex phenomena of the world" might have their representations, and by the *Tz'u,* "the movements of the world" might be comprehended. In this way, we could follow the courses that promised good fortune and avoid those that

---

[43]In the original Chinese, the word *Hsiao* should read *Tz'u,* as evidenced by the following passage.

promised misfortune, before the trend of events had actually developed.

The movements, as indicated in the "movements of the world," are taken in the sense of activities or actions. The changes and transformations of things in the world are due to these movements. As the *Hsi Tz'u* expresses it, "Good fortune and misfortune, occasion for repentance or regret, all arise from these movements." (Sec. II, Ch. 1) Also it says: "The expressions about good fortune or misfortune are used with reference to gain or loss; those about repentance or regret refer to minor faults. 'No blame' means that there is reference to repairing an error by what is good." (Sec. I, Ch. 3)

When the movement leads to "gain," there is good fortune; when the movement leads to "loss," there is misfortune. Likewise, when the movement leads to "minor faults," there is repentance or regret. Whatever exists as an event or a thing cannot divorce itself from the movement going on in the world. The hexagrams and the *hsiao* are the symbols which are applicable to "every event in past and every event in the future." As the *Hsi Tz'u* expresses it, "The *I* illuminates what has gone by and discriminates what is yet to come." (Sec. II, Ch. 6) However, the *Tz'u* attached to these symbols (i.e., the hexagrams and the *hsiao*) is the formula prognosticating the future course of development in connection with the movement, so that one may judge the best action to take. This is exactly the idea conveyed in the quotation above: "The greatest stimulus to all the movements of the world...." Because of this, the *Hsi Tz'u* says: "What the Superior Man peacefully rests in is the order shown in the *I;* and the study that gives him the greatest pleasure is that of the *Tz'u* attached to the *hsiao*." (Sec. I, Ch. 2)

Adding to the function of the *Tz'u*, we present one more passage from the *Hsi Tz'u:*

The great attribute *(te)* of Heaven and Earth is to bestow life. The great treasure of the Sage is to be on the throne. Those who guard this throne are men. That by which men are gathered together is wealth.

The administration of wealth, rectification of judgments *(Tz'u)*, restraining the people from wrong-doing — all these constitute righteousness *(yi).* (Sec. II, Ch. 1)

Thus the function of *Tz'u* is two fold: positively to stimulate "all the movements of the world," and negatively "to restrain the people from wrong-doing." This is the third fundamental concept of the *I Ching.*

These three fundamental concepts — the *I,* the *Hsiang,* and the *Tz'u* — constitute the essence of the *I Ching.* The *I* was originally used for divination, and from the *I* are evolved the three fundamental ideas, as we have seen in its appendices known as the "Ten Wings."

First, things in the universe are ever in a state of flux and change, and these changes, though endless, progress from the easy and simple to the difficult and complex. In other words, things in the universe are complex, forever changing. If we follow "the order shown in the *I,*" then among the complexities, simplicity can be found, among the changes, something unchanging. Because of this, the *Hsi Tz'u* says: "The *I* is that by which the Sages searched out the depths and investigated the hidden springs. Only through the depths could they penetrate to the views of all in the world. Only through the hidden springs could they bring to a completion all undertakings in the world." (Sec. I, Ch. 10) "To search out the depths" means "to explore what is complex, to prove what is hidden, to hook up what lies deep, and to reach what is distant." (Sec. I, Ch. 11) "To investigate the hidden springs" means to examine "the slight beginnings of movement and the earliest indications of good fortune (or misfortune)." (Sec. II, Ch. 5)

Second, the arts of civilization were inspired by the symbolic meanings of the hexagrams of the *I Ching;* that is, the *hsiang.* In other words, the *hsiang* are the "spring" of all inventions or discoveries. From these easy and simple symbols, as mentioned above, which the Sages had drawn to represent the things of the universe, they made utensils and laws for the use of the people and the benefit of the world. As the *Hsi Tz'u* says, "The sages, fully understanding the Tao of Heaven and knowing the needs of the people, thus made these mysterious things for the use of the people." (Sec. I, Ch. 11) Also it says, "In preparing things for practical use and in inventing instruments for the benefit of the world, there are none greater than the Sages." *(Ibid.)*

In addition to this, the symbols or *hsiang* may also be used as models for our conduct and can be substituted for the varied kinds of objects. In other words, if an object or idea satisfies certain conditions, it can have a *hsiang* (symbol) as its substitute. Thus, the *I,* a book of symbols, is a reflection in miniature of the whole universe. As the *Hsi Tz'u* says: "How wide is the *I,* how great! To speak of its furthest (implication), there is no limit to it; to speak of its nearest (meaning), it rests in its proper place; to speak of it in relation to all that lies between Heaven and Earth, it embraces all." (Sec. I, Ch. 6) This passage shows that the symbols of the *I* represent every kind of object or idea there is.

Third, these varied "symbolic ideas," when in movement, reveal the trend of good fortune and misfortune, or regret and repentance. All these movements and their tendencies can be explained by the *Tz'u,* that is, the judgments attached to the hexagrams and their individual lines. A hexagram or a line is the symbol of a certain type of movement, and this being so, the judgment attached to that hexagram or that line is the formula for that type of movement. Thus the symbols and their formulas, representing basic principles, are for the most part concerned with movement and change. We can look upon these principles as our guides in matters of conduct, so that "the good and the evil can be seen." Hence the *Hsi Tz'u* says: "So great is the *Tao* (principle) of the *I* that with every kind of thing it does not fail." (Sec. II, Ch. 11) Also: "The *hsiao* (lines) and *hsiang* (symbols) move within, and the good and the evil reveal themselves without. The work to be seen appears in the changes; the feelings of the Sages are seen in their judgments *(tz'u)."* (Sec. II, Ch. 1)

Accordingly, what the *I* contained was the *tz'u* attached to the hexagrams and the lines as formulae, each representing one or more *Tao* (principles), and the total of formulae being a perfect representation of all existing principles. That is what is maintained in the *I* Appendices, which we shall discuss in more detail in Part Three. One more passage from the *Hsi Tz'u* may be quoted here:

> The *I* illuminates what has gone by and discriminates what is yet to come. It makes manifest what is hidden, and brings to light what is obscure. Then it opens (its symbols) and distinguishes things by means of suitable names. In this way, all its words are correct and its judgments *(Tz'u)* are decisive; thus (the book) is complete. (Sec. II, Ch. 6)

That is to say, what is maintained in the *I* is applicable to the past as well as to the future. What is hidden and obscure is revealed, first symbolically by means of the hexagrams and the *hsiao,* then explicitly by means of the *Tz'u* — i.e., the judgments attached to the hexagrams and the *hsiao.*

PART THREE

INTERPRETATIONS OF THE "TEN WINGS"

1. Basic Rules and Principles: The *Tao*

THE SIGNIFICANCE of the *I* as a philosophical treatise is shown by the effort of the later scholars to expand and develop its original meaning in a series of appendices or "wings" into a comprehensive system of cosmology. The first two of the *I*'s eight basic trigrams, *Ch'ien* (☰) and *K'un* (☷), were equated with the *Yang* and the *Yin* as two cosmic forces, respectively representing Heaven and Earth, male and female. Their qualities are expressed in the passages quoted on pages xlii and xliii. Through the interaction of these two primal forces, all the phenomena of the universe are produced.[44] The eight trigrams, and the sixty-four hexagrams formed by their combinations, represent all the possible situations or mutations of creation, a universe in miniature. By studying these *kua* (i.e., trigrams and hexagrams) and their interpretations, one may understand the basic principles underlying all phenomenal changes, so as to take the proper course of action.

Regarding the way in which man, by means of the symbolic *kua*, knows the activties of the universe, there are two basic rules. First, the sixty-four hexagrams of the *I Ching* are forms of varied combinations of two trigrams. These two trigrams symbolize the past and the future in time, and height and depth in space. Time and space are two primary metaphysical concepts of the *I Ching*, invested with almost as profound a significance as the *Yin* and the *Yang* forces. According to the *I* Appendices, the development of a thing cannot go counter to its time and situation. That is, for a development to succeed it must be at the proper time and in the proper situation. As we have seen above, the judgments attached to the hexagrams are supposed to provide information as to how one should judge the best action to take at a given time and in a given place. According to this rule, a hexagram, as well as a *hsiao*, can represent a particular condition of time plus space.

Second, each trigram consists of three lines, and these three lines represent three different degrees in time and space. On the whole, in the first degree (i.e., the bottom line) man should adopt a cautious attitude; in the last degree (i.e., the top line) he should also be on his guard; and only in the middle degree (i.e., the middle line), should he adopt an active attitude. Regarding the hexagrams, the second and the fifth lines (counted

---

[44]This concept remained dominant in Chinese cosmological speculation down to recent times.

from the bottom) are the most significant, because they are in central positions, the second being in the center of the lower trigram and the fifth in the center of the upper; while the third and the fourth lines are variables and the first and the last lines are constants, always advising man to be cautious, as seen in the following *Ch'ien* hexagram:

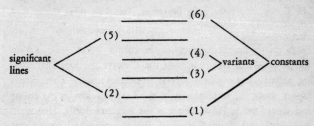

The *I*, as we have seen, was originally a book of divination. By manipulating the milfoil stalks, one finds a certain line of a certain hexagram, and then, in according with the basic rules discussed above, consults the *Tz'u* attached to that line which is supposed to provide information as to what attitude should be adopted toward a given matter at a given time and in a given place. Since these comments (*Tz'u*) are applied to various specific cases in life, they have been looked upon as formulae, representing the basic principles underlying all phenomenal changes of the universe.

We must examine these basic principles. We have seen that in the universe there are two cosmic forces, and through their interaction all phenomenal changes are produced. Let us turn to the following passages in the *Hsi Tz'u:*

Heaven is high, Earth is low; thus *Ch'ien* and *K'un* are determined. As things low and high are thus displayed, the noble and mean have their places. Movement and quiescence have their invariability. Hence comes the definite distinction between the virile and the docile.

Objects come to be aggregated through being classified; things come to be distinguished through being grouped. Hence are produced good fortune and misfortune.

In the heavens there are symbols there completed; on earth there are shapes and features there formed. In this way changes and transformations are exhibited.

Thus the virile and the docile interplay, and the Eight Trigrams act and react on each other. Things are roused by thunder and lightning; they are fertilized by wind and rain. Sun and moon revolve in their courses with a cold season and then a warm season. The *Tao* of the *Ch'ien* constitutes the male; the *Tao* of the *K'un* constitutes the female. The *Ch'ien* knows the great beginning; the *K'un* gives things their completion. (Sec. I, Ch. 1)

From this comprehensiveness of the cosmic forces — i.e., *Ch'ien* and *K'un* — the Appendices of the *I* derive the idea that there are positive and negative aspects in human affairs. The positive aspect, using the terminology of the *I* Appendices, is the strong and virile; the negative aspect is the soft and docile. Hence the undivided and divided lines of the trigrams and hexagrams, known as the *Yang*-symbol and the *Yin*-symbol, are looked upon as the symbolic representations of these aspects in human affairs.

There are, moreover, the existent conditions of the universe arising at a given time and in a given place, which should also be acknowledged in the course of development of our action. In divination, as we have seen above, one line in the hexagram indicates the degree in time and space, while the other five lines symbolize the various conditions of the universe. For the success of our action, the cooperation of these conditions is always needed, but this cooperation is beyond our control. This is a matter of *Ming*. *Ming* is often translated as Fate, Destiny, or Decree. So far as we know, to Confucius *Ming* meant the Decree of Heaven; that is, something Heaven-determined.[45] But in the Appendices it simply means that there are certain conditions in the universe which are not in man's control; in other words, there is something about which man can do nothing. What is

---

[45]Confucius often spoke of *Ming:* "If my philosophy is to prevail in the world, it is *Ming*. If my philosophy is to fail in the world, it is also *Ming*." (*Analects*, XIV, 38) He also said: "He who does not know *Ming* cannot be a Superior Man" (*ibid.*, XX, 2), and "When I was fifty years old, I knew *Ming*" (*ibid.*, II, 4).

emphasized in the Appendices is that man should do what he ought to do, regardless of the external result of his action. To act in this way is to acknowledge the existent conditions of the universe, that is, the inevitability of the universe. As a result, man will be free from anxiety as to success or fear as to failure, and will live his life in harmony with and understanding of the basic principles underlying all phenomenal changes which he has to pass.[46]

And again, there is the attitude that man should adopt after examining the positive or negative aspect of the matter as shown in the hexagram in conjunction with the existent conditions as indicated by the lines of the hexagram, and this is what is known as the *Tao*. The *Tao* given here represents one or more basic principles which govern each separate category of things, such as the *Tao* of kingliness and the *Tao* of ministership. As such this *Tao* is similar to what is known as the concept of the "universal" in Western philosophy.[47] Besides the specific multiple *Tao*, there is a general unitary *Tao* which governs the production and transformation of all things in the universe. With regard to this unitary *Tao*, there is the statement already quoted: "One *Yin* and one *Yang* constitute what is called *Tao*." The reference here is to "the *Tao* of Heaven and Earth" which everything obeys.

What exists as an event or a thing cannot divorce itself from the *Tao*, nor can it disobey the *Tao*. As we have seen, the hexagrams and their individual lines are regarded as the symbols of the various events or things in the universe. These symbols and the judgments attached to them serve as the formulae, each representing one or more *Tao* which events and things either obey or ought to obey. In terms of divination, if they obey this

[46]Thus the *I* Appendices differ from the *Tao-te Ching*. The Taoists taught the theory of "doing nothing" *(wu-wei)*, whereas the authors of the Appendices taught that of "doing for nothing." Hence, in doing one must exert himself and consciously does something for nothing; he must enjoy the doing itself, and so disregards the external result. This is exactly the idea conveyed in the passage quoted above on page 1: "The Superior Man ... nerves himself to ceaseless activity."

[47]See Fung Yu-lan, *A Short History of Chinese Philosophy*, I, 167.

Tao, that is good fortune; if not, that is bad fortune. In terms of moral teaching, if they obey this *Tao*, that is right; if not, that is wrong. That is the position which the *Hsi Tz'u* maintains: "There is a similarity here with Heaven and Earth, and hence the *I* must not be disobeyed. The knowledge (in the *I*) embraces all things, and the *Tao* is of assistance to all things in the world. As a result, there are no defects in the *I*." (Sec. I, Ch. 4)

Now let us turn to the first two hexagrams, *Ch'ien* and *K'un*, which are supposed to be the symbols of virility and docility. As is said in the *Shuo Kua*, "*Ch'ien* is (the symbol of) virility; *K'un* is (the symbol of) docility." (Ch. 7) Thus anything which satisfies the condition of being virile can have the *Ch'ien* hexagram as its substitute. Likewise, anything which satisfies the condition of being docile can have the *K'un* hexagram as its substitute. Hence the judgments attached to the *Ch'ien* hexagram and its individual lines represent the *Tao* for what is virile; those attached to the *K'un* hexagram and its individual lines represent the *Tao* for what is docile. In the *Wen Yen*, the section dealing with the *K'un* says:

Although the *Yin* has excellent qualities, it keeps under restraint in its service to the king, and dares not aim at its own achievement. This is the *Tao* of Earth, the *Tao* of wifeliness, the *Tao* of ministership. The *Tao* of Earth is not to aim at its own achievement, but on another's behalf to bring things to their proper issue.

The opposite to the *K'un* hexagram is the *Ch'ien* hexagram. Just as the *K'un* hexagram is the symbol of Earth, of a wife, of a minister, so the *Ch'ien* hexagram is the symbol of Heaven, of a husband, of a sovereign. With regard to the Ch'ien hexagram, the *Wen Yen* says: "How great indeed is *Ch'ien!* It is strong and virile, moderate and correct, pure, unmixed, and exquisite!"

Hence if one wants to know how to be a true sovereign or a true husband, one has to consult the judgments attached to the *Ch'ien* hexagram and its lines, but if one wants to know how to be a true minister or a true wife, one has to consult the judgments attached to the *K'un* hexagram and its lines. Each hexagram in the *I* represents more than one class of object, and the judgments attached to each hexagram and its lines represent one or more *Tao*. Since its symbols and formulae are the substitutes for any and every class of object, the *I* is not subject to a rigid rule of interpretation. The rule of interpretation varies according to circumstances. As the *Hsi Tz'u* says:

> The *I*, as a book, must not be out of the mind. Its *Tao* is based on frequent change (of its lines). (These lines) move and change without staying (in one place), flowing about into any of the six places of the hexagram. They ascend and descend without being fixed. The strong (i.e., undivided line) and the weak (i.e., divided line) change places, so that no rigid rule can be derived from them. It must vary as their changes indicate. (Sec. II, Ch. 8)

In short, the *Tao* of the *I*, formed of its symbols and formulae, tells the people how to find the right path amid the complexity of the universe, so that they will act in accordance with it. It is also the principle of social structure and social control, which delimits one's status and defines one's relationship with others. For instance, the *Ch'ien* is supposed to be "master," while the *K'un* is supposed to be "subordinate," ruled from above. Hence, as the *T'uan* puts it, "If the *K'un* leads, it goes astray and loses its *Tao*. If the *K'un* follows, it attains to its right path." For long this has been held in China as the *Tao* of wifeliness.

In the *T'uan* on the *Chia Jen* (Members of a Family) hexagram, there is a discussion of the proper position of man and wife, expressed as follows:

> In the *Chia Jen* hexagram, the wife has her right position within, and the husband has his right position outside. For men and women to be in the right position is the great justice of Heaven and Earth. In *Chia Jen*, there is sovereign headship, that is, the parentship. Let the father be a father, the son be a son; then let the elder brother be an elder brother, the younger brother be a younger brother; let the husband be a husband, the wife be a wife; then the *Tao* of the family is rectified. When the family is rectified, the world will be stabilized.

This is exactly what Confucius taught in his theory called the Rectification of Names *(Cheng Ming):* "Let the ruler be a ruler, the minister a minister; let the father be a father, the son a son." (*Analects,* XII, 11) The underlying idea in this statement is status, or *ming-fen*,[48] which gives every man and every woman a proper position in society and defines his or her relationships with others. In conformity with the humanist ideal of "everything in its place," the social ideal is also that of "every man in his position." For the ruler and the minister, the parents and children, and the husband and the wife to be truly rectified is for each to be in his or her proper position. If every man knows his place and acts in accordance with his position, social order will be ensured. Such is the implication of the theory of *Cheng Ming.* However, in the teachings of Confucius, this was only an ethical theory, whereas in the Appendices it becomes metaphysical as well. Hence the position and relationship of *Ch'ien* and *K'un* in the universe as established in the Appendices serve as a metaphysical and ethical interpretation of the relationship between members of the family in the world. Originally the *I,* as a Chou treatise on divination, contained considerable superstition and dogma. However, the authors of the Appendices purified and ethicized it, thus changing it from a book of divination into a work of ethical and metaphysical significance. Moreover, the ethical teachings of the *I* as elaborated in its Appendices are not restricted to private life, but can be applied to public affairs as well. This "ethicization" of life is one of the main characteristics of Chinese civilization.[49]

II. The Cosmic Conception of the *I*

Though the *I* was originally written to be used as a means of divination, it was later developed by Han thinkers into a cos-

---

[48]*Ming* means "names," and *fen* means "duties." A name designates a title, representing a man's status in the society. Without a name, he would not know his duties.

[49]See Ch'u Chai and Winberg Chai, *The Changing Society of China* (New York: New American Library, 1962), Ch. III.

mological system[50] which would lighten for the mass of mankind the burden of the mystery of the universe. Let us first take a brief glance at the salient characteristics of its cosmic conception as illustrated in the *I* Appendices. Philosophical thinking is no exception to the general rule that the distinctive characteristics of any domain of thought are determined by its first assumption. We find when we come to examine it that the cosmic conception of the *I* is based on the assumption that all that happens in the universe, natural and human, is a continuous whole, like a chain of natural sequences.

In the *I*, the *Hsu Kua* (Sequence of the Hexagrams), one of the "Ten Wings," interprets the order of the hexagrams, which is supposed to represent the natural process of the evolution of the universe. The *I* was originally divided into two sections, one dealing with Heaven and Earth or the Universe, and the other dealing with "all under the sky" or the world of man.[51] In the introductory remarks to the *Hsu Kua*, there is the statement, "Following the existence of Heaven and Earth, there is the production or existence of all things." The point is that the universe is a united whole, and this basic assumption leads inevitably to the following characteristics of the cosmic conception.

First, in the *I* Heaven and Earth denote the great whole of the universe — the transcendent sphere in which all is but a transitional process, with no fixed substance for its substratum. The universe is thus supposed to have no reality of its own, outside and independent of its phenomena. The *I* is at work in the great as well as in the small, and it embraces all natural happenings as well as all human affairs. Hence the universe is often identified with the *I* — thus emphasizing that all things in the

---

[50]The cosmological system of the *I* later became the foundation of the metaphysics and cosmology of the Sung thinkers.

[51]The Chinese expression for the universe is *Tien Ti* (Heaven and Earth) and for the world of man is *Tien hsia* (all below the sky). The difference between these two expressions should be noted, with regard to the "*Tao* of Heaven and Earth," and the "*Tao* in the World." See above, p. lxvii-lxviii.

universe are ever in a state of flux and change. As the *Hsi Tz'u* says:

> The *I* includes within its scope all the transformations in Heaven and Earth without any defect. In multifarious ways it completes all things, leaving out none. It penetrates the *Tao* of day and night with understanding. Therefore the spirit is bound to no place, nor the *I* to any form. (Sec. I, Ch. 4)

The *I* may be described as transcending shapes and features, for it "dovetails with Heaven and Earth" and "completely interweaves the *Tao* of Heaven and Earth." (Sec. I, Ch. 4) Here the "*Tao* of Heaven and Earth," referring to the principle which everything obeys and also known as "one *Yin* and one *Yang*," may also be described as transcending shapes and features. Hence, as the *Hsi Tz'u* puts it, "That which is above shapes and features is called the *Tao;* that which is within shapes and features is called the vessel." The *Tao* is different from the vessel.

In this connection, we present two more selected passages from the *Hsi Tz'u:*

> Therefore, in the *I*, there is the Supreme Ultimate, which produced the Two Modes. The Two Modes produced the Four *Hsiang*, which in turn produced the Eight Trigrams.[52] (Sec. I, Ch. 11)

> The *I* has no thought, no action. It is still, and without movement; but, when acted on, it penetrates forthwith to all phenomena and events in the world. If it were not the great mystery in the world, how could it be found doing this? (Sec. I, Ch. 10)

We find similar passages in the *Lao Tzu:*

> Out of the *Tao*, One is born;
> Out of One, Two;
> Out of Two, Three;
> Out of Three, the myriad things. (Ch. XLII)
> There is a Thing evolved from the chaos,
> Which existed before Heaven-and-Earth.
> Formless and Boundless,
> It stands alone and never changes;
> It pervades and endures.
> It may be conceived as the mother of the world. (Ch. XXV)

---

[52] This passage does not refer to the universe, but rather to the symbols, along with which go a number of formulae to which the *Tao* corresponds. However, the symbols and formulae have their counterparts in the universe itself.

These passages make clear two points, which we need only to mention briefly: First, in the universe there is a cosmic force that is the source of life. The cosmic force is the *I* or the *Tao* of the Taoists, which generates One, or the Supreme Ultimate; and One or the Supreme Ultimate produces in turn the *Yin* and the *Yang* — a kind of dualism, as designated by Two, or the Two Modes. From the interaction of the *Yin* and *Yang* springs life, as symbolized by Three, or the Four Forms, out of which arise all things, as symbolized by the Eight Trigrams. Hence "one *Yin* and one *Yang*" which equals the *Tao* constitutes the formula for the production of all things. And second, the Heaven-and-Earth with which the *I* dovetails is a Heaven-and-Earth which may be described as the Nature, i.e., "the Great Whole," "the Spontaneity," "the life," and "the *Tao*." What is called Heaven and Earth in the *I* is not "Heaven with a divine power,"[53] but the Universe with a cosmic force—i.e., "the unceasing movement going on in the Universe," which "stimulates all creatures without causing the anxieties which the Sages endured." Things in the Universe are not static; they are all part of "unceasing movement." As the *Hsi Tz'u* says, "The great attribute of Heaven and Earth is to produce," and "Production and reproduction are what the *I* represents." This of course does not mean that the *I* can produce, but that in the *I* there is the *Tao*, as represented by the symbols and formulae, in accordance with which producing and reproducing go on unceasingly.

This conception of the universe as a transitional process originates in the basic assumption that the universe is a united whole. From the standpoint of the *I*, all things in the universe are subject to the transitional process and are all part of, not units apart from, the "unceasing movements."

Then we approach the second characteristic of its cosmic conception; that is, the principle that the universe does not proceed onward, but revolves in an endless cycle. Things in the universe are ever changing according to this cosmic cycle, as

---

[53]This is the Heaven to which Confucius often refers.

we see in the succession of day and night, the periodical ebb and flow of the tide, the disappearance and return of planets, and other sequential phenomena. As the *Hsi Tz'u* says:

> When the sun goes, the moon comes; and when the moon goes, the sun comes. Thus the sun and moon give way to each other, and light continues in existence. When the winter goes, the summer comes; and when the summer goes, the winter comes. Thus winter and summer give way to each other, and the year is completed. That which goes wanes; that which comes waxes. Waxing and waning have a mutual influence, and beneficial results accrue. (Sec. II, Ch. 5)

This constant round of the sun and moon constitutes the law of nature underlying all phenomenal changes. As is said in the *T'uan* (Judgment) of the *Ku* hexagram (18): "Where there is an end, there is a beginning. Such is the course of Heaven." The name *I*, as we have seen above, primarily means "transformation and change." The Appendices emphasize that all things in the universe are ever in a process of change. In the third-line judgment of the eleventh hexagram, *T'ai*, we find: "There is no level place without a bank, no going away without returning *(fu)*." This is "the course of Heaven," according to which things in the universe undergo change and transformation. Hence there is a *Fu* hexagram (24), and in the *T'uan* (Judgment) we find: "Its *Tao* is one of reversion *(fan)* and return *(fu)*; in seven days comes its return. This is the course of Heaven. . . . Does not the *Fu* hexagram reveal the mind of Heaven and Earth?"

"The meaning of *fu* is a reverse movement back to the origin, and the reference to the mind of Heaven and Earth is to the original root."[54] Here again, we find similar passages in the *Lao Tzu:*

> While all things are together in action,
> I only look into their Return:
> For all things have been flourishing,
> And yet each returns to its Root. (Ch. 16)
> Reversion *(fan)* is the motion of the *Tao*. (Ch. 40)

[54] See Wang Pi's (226-49) *Commentary on the I.*

The *Hsu Kua*, in the interpretation of the order of hexagrams, offers a good illustration of this theory of reversion, by showing how each hexagram is followed by another which is opposite in character. For instance, "the *P'o* hexagram symbolizes decay and overthrow. Things cannot be entirely obliterated. When the process of decay and overthrow is ended, the reverse process begins. Hence this is followed by the *Fu* hexagram." This Appendix provides the principal argument for the general law that anything, when it develops to its extreme, invariably reverts to its opposite; that is, to borrow an expression from Hegel, everything involves its own negation — though according to Hegel, when a thing is negated a new thing commences on a higher level, whereas according to the *Lao Tzu* and the *I* Appendices, when a thing is negated, the new thing simply repeats the old.

This theory of reversion or returning is prominent in the writings of the ancient philosophers. Here is a statement from the *Lao Tzu:*

> The *Tao* of Heaven is like the stretching of a bow!
> It brings down what is high;
> It lifts up what is low.
> It depletes what is abundant;
> It augments what is deficient.
> Such is the *Tao* of Heaven:
> It depletes the abundant and augments the deficient. (Ch. 77)

This is the normal rhythm of nature. Were the universe to reverse the normal rhythm, it would cease to function. Similarly the *T'uan* (Judgment) of the *Feng* hexagram (55) says: "When the sun has reached its meridian height, it begins to decline. When the moon has become full, it begins to wane. Heaven and Earth are now full, now empty, according to the flow and ebb of the season."

The *Lao Tzu* and the *I* Appendices agree in considering the theory that everything involves its own negation as the general law of transformation. The content of the course of transformation in the universe is a process of construction (i.e., the *Yang* element) and destruction (i.e., the *Yin* element), as discovered by the Sung Neo-Confucianists. Thus, the first line of the hexagram *Fu* (☷☳) shows the beginning of construction and in the hexagram *Ch'ien* (☰☰) we find the completion of construction. The first line of the hexagram *Kou* (☴☰) shows the beginning of destruction and in the hexagram *K'un* (☷☷) we find the completion of destruction. The *Hsi Tz'u* identifies this process of construction-plus-destruction with that of "one opening-plus-one shutting" referred to in the interpretation of the *Ch'ien* and the *K'un*,[55] at the same time equating the constructive phase of this process with the "returning" and the destructive phase with the "going away." The complement to "going away" is "returning"; the unceasing process — from going to returning and vice versa — is designated as transformation. This going and returning has no end; in other words, there is no returning without going and no going without returning. As is said, "Between Heaven and Earth nothing goes away that does not return."[56] This also suggests the theory that everything involves its own negation.

This process of the universe as a cyclic process, like that of the universe as a transitional process, originates in the basic assumption that the universe is a united whole. The universe is composed of pairs of opposites, such as good and evil, right and wrong, subjective and objective, positive and negative. The content of the course of transformation in the universe is a process of evolution in which every phenomenon involves its own nega-

---

[55]See the *Hsi Tz'u*, Sec. I, Ch. 11.

[56]This is the *Hsiang* (Judgment) concerning the third line of the *T'ai* hexagram.

tion. The phenomenon and its negation are necessary parts making up the whole. We cannot have, for instance, a positive without a negative, or vice versa. They are correlatives which involve each other. Thus the universe proceeds in cyclic recurrence, without beginning, without end.

And finally, the third characteristic of the *I*'s cosmic conception is that in the process of the cosmic transformation "there can never be an end of things." The things in the universe are never absolutely completed or finished; they follow a definite order according to which they move everlastingly. As we have seen above, Heaven and Earth are the physical representations of the *Ch'ien* and the *K'un*, the *Yang* and the *Yin*. Themselves springing from the Supreme Ultimate, these two cosmic forces by their interaction operate to produce all the phenomena of the universe, and these in their turn produce and reproduce, so that transformation and change continue without end. Hence the *Hsi Tz'u* says:

> May we not say that the *Ch'ien* and the *K'un* are the secret and substance of the *I*? Inasmuch as the *Ch'ien* and the *K'un* are established in their several places, the *I* between them is also posited. If the *Ch'ien* and the *K'un* were taken away, there would be no means of seeing the *I*; and if the *I* were not seen, the *Ch'ien* and the *K'un* would almost cease to act. (Sec. I, Ch. 2)
>
> The *Tao* of Heaven and Earth is constantly to manifest themselves. The *Tao* of the sun and moon is constantly to emit their light. All movements of the world are constantly subject to one and the same rule. (Sec. II, Ch. 1)

Because of this, things in the Universe can never be exhausted. "The movement of Heaven is full of power," never ceasing to function. This may be shown by quoting the first and last passages of the *Hsü Kua*:

> Following the existence of Heaven and Earth, there is the production of all things. The space between Heaven and Earth is full of these things. Hence the *Ch'ien* and the *K'un* are followed by the *Tun*, which symbolizes fullness. The *Tun* also symbolizes things in their first pro-

duction. When so produced, things are sure to be undeveloped. Hence there follows the *Meng*. The *Meng* symbolizes things undeveloped — i.e., things in their youth.... (Sec. I)

He who stands above things attains to accomplishment. Hence there follows the *Chi Chi* (Having Accomplished). But things cannot be exhausted. Hence there follows the *Wei Chi* (Not Yet Accomplished), with which the *I* concludes. (Sec. II)

The underlying idea in these passages is that in the universe there is no end of things; there is no *summun bonum.* According to the *Hsü Kua,* the perfection of nature is not that it will produce a perfect end in the process of evolution, but is exactly that it produces an endless evolution. Its perfection is exactly its "unceasing movement going on in the Universe." The *Chung Yung* says: "To the most perfect[57] there is no rest." (Ch. 26, Sec. 1) This is exactly the idea conveyed in the quotation above: "Things cannot be exhausted." This also explains why next to the *Chi Chi* hexagram comes the *Wei Chi* hexagram, "with which the *I* concludes."

Here again, in the unceasing and continuous process of the universe, we find a reflection of the basic assumption that the universe is a united whole, undivided and indivisible. Any separate movement owes its existence to a unit that is subtracted from the whole. Anything divisible must be divided by something other than itself. Since there is nothing other than the whole, there cannot be units apart from the whole. Consequently, in the unceasing process of cosmic evolution, "transformation and change continue without end."

We see, then, that the character of the cosmic conception as illustrated in the *I* is fixed by the basic assumption that the universe is a continuous whole. There is a spirit of general elevation and enlightenment in which all alike communicate and

[57]Here the word "perfect" is the translation of the word *cheng* which literally means "sincerity," "realness," or "truth." *Cheng* represents the fullness of virtue corresponding to Confucius' concept of humanity *(jen)*. "The perfection of the self lies in the quality of *jen.*" (Ch. 25.)

to which Chinese culture owes much of its dignity and influence. This is so because all things in the universe are relative and in a state of flux: there is no absolute difference, no absolute separation; everything is constantly changing into something else, and therefore all things are one. This cosmic conception rests on the underlying idea that all that happens in the universe, natural and human, forms a continuous chain of natural sequences. This is a what is called "the Supreme Harmony in unison" in the *I* Appendices.[58]

III. The Ideal of Life

As we have seen above, the *I* Appendices emphasize that all things in the universe are ever in a process of change, and that all changes of things conform to the basic laws of nature. Among the basic laws underlying all phenomenal changes, the most fundamental is that "when a thing reaches one extreme, it reverts from it." This is one of the main theses of the *Lao Tzu* and also of the *I* as interpreted by the authors of its Appendices. The sixth Nine (i.e., the top line) of the *Ch'ien* hexagram reads: "The dragon in extreme will have cause for repentance." The comment on this line says:

> The phrase "in extreme" refers to one who knows progression but does not know (that progression involves) regression; one who knows life, but does not know (that life involves) death; one who knows possession, but does not know (that possession involves) loss. It is only the Sage who knows both progression and regression, both life and death, both possession and loss, and thus attains to the right way (*cheng*).[59] He only is the Sage. (*Wen Yen*, Sec. I, Ch. 6)

[58] See the *T'uan* (Judgment) on the *Ch'ien* hexagram.

[59] As to the meaning of *cheng* (right, proper), read the passage in the *T'uan* (Judgment) on the *Chia Jen* hexagram quoted above, pp. lxix-lxx.

This is the doctrine of the *I* and is also the doctrine of the *Lao Tzu*. In the *Lao Tzu*, there is the statement:

> Misery! Happiness leans on it!
> Happiness! Misery lurks under it!
> Who knows the end of this process?
> There is no absolute right.
> What is right turns wrong;
> What is good turns evil.
> Men have been in ignorance of this for so long a time.
> Therefore, the Sage is square but not cutting;
> He is angled but not injuring;
> He is straight but not stretching;
> He is enlightened but not dazzling. (Ch. 58)

Both the *I* Appendices and the *Lao Tzu* agree in theory that extremes produce opposite reactions, but the latter emphasizes the synthesis of extremes, while the former stresses the taking of the mean between these two extremes. According to the *Lao Tzu,* when from one extreme something moves to the opposite extreme, this is the step from thesis to antithesis, so as to accomplish a synthesis out of these extremes. For instance, it says:

> The greatest straightness looks like crookedness.
> The greatest skill appears clumsy.
> The greatest eloquence sounds like stammering. (Ch. 45)

This passage does not mean that there something emerges at a point midway betwen straightness and crookedness, skill and clumsiness, eloquence and stammering, but rather that they have been blended into a synthetic whole. That is to say, they are of a straightness which contains crookedness, of a skill which contains clumsiness, and of an eloquence which contains stammering. The *I* Appendices, on the other hand, caution men to choose a central course, a golden mean between extremes, which would not err either by excess or by defect. In this sense they attain what is called *chung* (the mean, center), neither too much nor too little. Let us first turn to the *I* Appendices' line of explanation, where the second and the fourth lines in a hexagram are *Yin*-positions and the third and the fifth lines are *Yang*-positions; the first and the sixth lines are not counted as positions. In the *Hsi Tz'u*, we find the following passage:

> The second and the fourth lines are of the same function, but are differentiated by their positions. The good (which they symbolize) is not the same. The second line designates much praise; the fourth line designates many fears, because of its nearness (to the highest position — i.e., the fifth-line position). The *Tao* of the yielding *(jou)* is that it is not advantageous to be far away. But essentially no blame accrues, because the yielding (of the second line) is in the central position.
>
> The third and the fifth lines are of the same function, but are differentiated by their positions. The third line represents many misfortunes, while the fifth line represents many achievements; this arises from their different positions, one being higher than the other. In this case, the yielding *(jou,* i.e., divided line) represents being subject to danger, while the strong *(kang,* i.e., undivided line) represents being triumphantly successful. (Sec. II, Ch. 9)

As we have seen, for a *Yin*-element (i.e., the *K'un*) to take the lead will entail "going astray, losing its way," so that "to follow is its right path." Thus the fourth line in a *Yin*-position, because of its nearness to the highest position, tries to lead and so loses its proper role. This is the reason for "many fears." The second line also in a *Yin*-position, because of its not being far from the lowest position and being in the center of the lower trigram, entails much praise. On the other hand, the fifth line, being a *Yang*-position in the center of the upper trigram, entails many achievements; however, the third line, though a *Yang*-position, is an insecure position on the boundary between two trigrams, with the result that there are many misfortunes.

The second and the fifth lines in a hexagram, as mentioned above, are the most significant lines, because of their central positions, the second being in the center of the lower trigram and the fifth in the center of the upper. Thus, since there is neither excess nor defect in these two lines, they attain the mean. This means that they attain to the right position, the right way, and hence they will give a good issue to any transaction or affair of any sort. Generally speaking, a *Yang*-line in a *Yang*-position and a *Yin*-line in a *Yin*-position are said to be in their proper positions, and a proper position, as a rule, gives a good issue. But a *Yang*-line in a *Yin*-position or a *Yin*-line in a *Yang*-position are said to be in their improper positions, and an improper position gives a bad issue. However, even in the latter case, the improper position can give a good issue if it be in a central position (i.e., in a second or fifth line). Regarding the second line of the *Wei Chi* ( ), the sixty-fourth hexagram, this line being a *Yang*-line in a *Yin*-position, we read: "The second line (undivided) shows good fortune arising from being firm and correct. It is in the central position and so its action becomes correct (*cheng*)."

Thus the theory that extremes produce opposite reactions urges men to take the mean (*chung*) between the extremes. As to the significance of the Mean, the *Hsi Tz'u* has the statement:

The *I* is a book in which the hexagrams begin with the first line and end with the last. The *hsiao* (lines) are the essential material. The six *hsiao* are interspersed according to the time and their substance. The beginning line (from the bottom upward) is difficult to know, but the top line is easy to know. For they form the beginning and the end (of the hexagram). The Judgments (*Tz'u*) on the first line are tentative, but at the last line everything is accomplished. However, if we explore things in their diverse formations for determining their qualities, and discriminate between right and wrong, we have to resort to the middle *hsiao* (line). (Sec. II, Ch. 9)

The development of a thing should be prevented from reaching its climax, so as to avoid the opposite coming into effect: if this be done, it attains to the right way (i.e., *chung*) and does not go counter to its *shih* (time, i.e., circumstance, or time-plus-environment). This mean (*chung*) of the *I* Appendices is one that is taken as a guide for human conduct and that must be timely and in accordance with the situation at the moment.

For instance, the second line of the *Chieh* hexagram (60) reads:
"Not going beyond that gate of the courtyard brings about
misfortune" The *Hsiang* on this line comment: " 'Not going
beyond that gate of the courtyard brings about misfortune' This
symbolizes the complete missing of the time *shih*." And again,
the fifth line of the *Chi Chi* hexagram (63) reads: "The neighbor in the east to slaughter an ox (for a major sacrifice) is
not so good as the neighbor in the west with a minor sacrifice
for which he receives a real blessing." On this line, the *Hsiang*
comment: "The eastern neighbor to slaughter an ox is not so
good in point of time as the western neighbor. The latter receives a real blessing: good fortune comes in great scale." This
is to show that good fortune or misfortune depends on whether
a line in a hexagram symbolizes the right *shih* or the missing
of the right *shih*.

Applying the principle of the *chung* and the *shih*, the *I*
Appendices offer various ways of dealing with human affairs,
similar to those mentioned in the *Lao Tzu*. In the *Hsi Tz'u*,
we find the following statement:

> The man who keeps danger in mind is the one who retains his
> position; the man who keeps ruin in mind is the one who preserves his
> security; the man who keeps disorder in mind is the one who maintains
> order. Therefore, the Superior Man, when resting in safety, does not
> forget danger; when preserving his security, he does not forget ruin;
> when maintaining order, he does not forget disorder. In this way, with
> his own person secure, he is able to protect the state. As the *I* says:
> "Am I to perish? Am I to perish?" (No, the situation) is bound to a
> clump of mulberry trees (i.e., in a very stable situation). (Sec. II, Ch. 5)[60]

This is what the *I* Appendices are designed to teach: not to
forget danger in time of peace so as to protect one's peace; not
to forget ruin in time of security so as to preserve that security;

---

[60]Cf. the *Lao Tzu*, Ch. 43: "Truly, lose a thing and you will gain; gain a thing and
you will lose." And also Ch. 23: "For a hurricane never lasts a whole morning, nor
does a rainstorm last a whole day."

not to forget disorder in time of order so as to guard that order.

Moreover, the *I* Appendices also teach that those who are in accord with the principle of the mean must display the quality of humbleness and modesty. On the fifteenth hexagram *Ch'ien* (symbol of modesty), the *T'uan* comment:

> It is the *Tao* of Heaven to send down its beneficial influences below, where they are brilliantly displayed. It is the *Tao* of Earth, lying low, to send its influences upward. It is the *Tao* of Heaven to diminish the full and augment the humble. It is the *Tao* of Earth to overthrow the full and replenish the humble. Spiritual beings inflict calamity on the full and bless the humble... Humility in a high position sheds a lustre on it; and in a low position no man can pass beyond it. Thus it is the final goal of the Superior Man.

Referring to the virtue of humility and modesty, the *Hsi Tz'u* says:

> "Toiling laboriously and yet humble, the Superior Man will bring things to an end, and good fortune." (On this statement) the Master said: "He toils but does not boast of it; he achieves but takes no merit to himself from it; this is the height of generous goodness, and speaks of the man who, though having merit, places himself below others. He is full of virtue and reverent in conduct. He is humble and yet most respectful, so that he is able to preserve his position. (Sec. I, 8) [61]

All these ideas are deducible from the general theory that each object or situation invariably gives birth to its opposite, the basic argument for the doctrine of the mean, favored by Confucianists and Taoists alike. According to them, to attain the mean is not simply, however, to do things no more than halfway. The real meaning of the mean *(chung)* is neither too much nor too little, that is, just right. As Chu Hsi (1130-1200), a great philosopher of the Sung Dynasty, said, "Achieving the mean is the name for not erring on one side or the other, for being neither too much or too little." This is what is meant by

---

[61] Cf. the *Lao Tzu*, Ch. 39: "It is upon humility that honor leans, and upon the low that the high rests. That is why princes and kings speak of themselves as 'the Orphan,' 'the Desolate,' and 'the Unworthy.'"

being just right. In other words, this is a way of action that avoids extremes, a state of mind in which human reasoning and feeling reach harmony. This state of mind is well illustrated in the *Chung Yung* (Doctrine of the Mean),[62] as in the following passage:

> To have no emotions of pleasure and anger and sorrow and joy welling up, this is to be described as being in a state of *chung*. To have these emotions welling up but in due proportion, this is described as being in a state of *ho* (harmony). *Chung* is the chief foundation of the world. *Ho* is the great harmony of the world. Once *chung* and *ho* are established, Heaven and Earth maintain their proper position and all creatures are nourished. (Ch. 1)

That is, when the emotions are not aroused, the mind maintains its equilibrium, going neither too far nor too little; that is, it is just right. This is the state of *chung*. And when the emotions are expressed in due proportion, this is also a state of *chung*, for harmony includes differences, and *chung* attunes all the differences to produce a state of harmony; that is, none of the differences will be either too great or too small. This is what the *I* Appendices set forth to teach, namely, not to be one-sided and extreme, but to maintain the mean (*chung*). As the *Hsi Tz'u* says:

> If good does not accumulate, it is not enough to make a name for a man. If evil does not accumulate, it is not enough to destroy a man's life. The inferior man thinks that minor goodness is of no benefit, and so neglects it. He thinks that minor evils do no harm, and so does not abstain from them. Hence his evils accumulate until they cannot be covered, and his guilt becomes so great that it cannot be pardoned. This is what the *I* says: "He wears a cangue and his ears are destroyed: there will be misfortune." (Sec. II, Ch. 5)[63]

---

[62] The *Chung Yung* has a good deal in common with the *I* Appendices, both of which came from more than one source. Because of this, it might be that one or more of the authors of the one had a hand in the other.

[63] This statement refers to the sixth Nine of *Shih Ho*, the twenty-first hexagram, symbolizing a man who is incorrigible, because he is deaf to warning.

PART FOUR

THE SPIRIT OF THE
I PHILOSOPHY

AS WE HAVE SEEN ABOVE, the authors of the *I* Appendices accepted the Confucianist tradition and emphasized a concern for human affairs. However, they were influenced by the Taoists and so were able to advance in their philosophical thinking and to attain to the sublime. We must examine this. The Chinese mind oscillated between Taoism and Confucianism for a long time. Confucianism, since it is generally regarded as the philosophy of social organization, is therefore also the philosophy of daily life. It is concerned chiefly with performing the common task, rather than attaining to the sublime.[64] This is why Confucianism appears "this-worldly" and is known as *ming chiao* (the teaching of names denoting the social relationships). Taoism, on the other hand, is the philosophy that is essentially naturalistic and antisocial. This kind of philosophy is generally concerned with the transcendent sphere and sublime life, but it is incompatible with the manner of life in the world of affairs. Because of this, Taoism appears "other-worldly" and reaches up to the sublime. These two streams of Chinese thought are somewhat like the traditions of classicism and romanticism in Western thought. They have been running counter to each other for centuries; and so they remain to this day.

We are going to study another line of thought as illustrated in the *I* Appendices. According to the *I* Appendices, all that happens in the universe, natural and human, is a continuous whole like a chain of natural sequences. This is what we have seen from the beginning of our discussion of its cosmic conception. The position of this line of thought is the mean state of

---

[64]This, of course, is only a superficial view of Confucianism. Space will not allow a more elaborate consideration.

the "naturalistic" and "humanistic" lines of thought. In this state, Taoism and Confucianism are no longer antagonistic to each other; they are simply a continuous whole. These Appendices offer a better sense of balance in regard to Taoism and Confucianism. Let us turn to Chapter II of the *Shuo Kua*:

> In ancient times when the Sages made the *I*, their aim was conformity with the principles *(li)* of the natures (which things possess) and of the different lots (which Heaven decrees). Therefore they established the *Tao* of Heaven designated as the *Yin* and the *Yang*, and the *Tao* of Earth designated as the soft and the hard, and the *Tao* of Man designated as *jen* (humanity) and *yi* (righteousness). They combined these three Powers and doubled them; hence in the *I* each *kua* was formed by six lines. Then the places were divided into the *Yin* and the *Yang*, which were variously occupied, now by the soft and now by the hard. Therefore, the *I* has six places, which constitute the linear figures.

In this passage, we see that the Confucian principles of *jen* and *yi* have been brought into harmony with the Taoist naturalness of Heaven-and-Earth. That which is in conformity with the principles of the natures and Heaven's decrees is also in conformity with Nature. *Jen* and *yi* are in the *Tao* of Man what the *Yin* and the *Yang* are in the *Tao* of Heaven and the soft and the hard in the *Tao* of Earth. This is the idea conveyed in the statement of the *Lao Tzu*:

> Man follows the ways of Earth,
> Earth follows the ways of Heaven,
> Heaven follows the ways of *Tao*,
> *Tao* follows the ways of Nature. (Ch. 25)

The significance of the *I* Appendices as a system of philosophy lies in their attempt to "attain to the sublime and yet perform the common task." As the *Shuo Kua* says:

> (The Sages) contemplated the changes in the *Yin* and the *Yang* and established the *kua* (in accordance with them). They brought about movements in the hard and the soft, and thus produced the *hsiao* (lines). They put themselves in accord with the *Tao* and its power *(te)*, and in conformity with the principles of what is right. Then they made an exhaustion of the principle *(li)* and effected the full development of

(every) nature with a view to arriving at an understanding of (Heaven's) decrees. (Ch. 1)

The *Shuo Kua* is thus concerned with *li* (principles), but it does not specify clearly what *li* is. In this connection we quote a passage from the *Han Fei Tzu* to illustrate the meaning of *li:*

> *Tao* is the way of everything, the form of every *li* (principle). *Li* is the line that completes things. *Tao* is the cause of the completion of everything. Things have their respective *li* and so cannot trespass on each other. That is why *li* becomes the determinant of things. Everything has its unique *li* and *Tao* disciplines the *li* of all things. That is why everything has to go through the process of transformation.[65]

As to the full development of nature, the *Chung Yung* offers a good illustration:

> It is only he who is most perfect *(cheng)* that can fully develop his own nature. Being able fully to develop his own nature, he can fully develop the nature of others. Being able fully to develop the nature of others, he can fully develop the nature of all things. Being able fully to develop the nature of all things, he can assist the transforming and nourishing powers of Heaven and Earth. Capable of assisting the transforming and nourishing powers of Heaven and Earth, he may, with Heaven and Earth, form a triad. (Ch. 22)

The heavenly decrees of which the *Shuo Kua* speaks may be interpreted as changes of things, changes which are beyond the limit of men's power.[66] "An understanding of (Heaven's) decrees" is something like what Mencius called "Knowing Heaven."[67] "Heaven" conceived in the *I* Appendices is a Heaven of "Nature" in the sense of the cosmic force which may be described as transcending shapes and features. This is in line with the naturalistic tendency of Taoistic thought. However, the Taoists, on the basis of the way of Nature, opposed human

[65]Ch. 20: "Commentaries on Lao Tzu's Teachings."

[66]For the meaning of *Ming*, here translated as "heavenly decrees," see above, page lxvi-lxvii.

[67]"Mencius said: 'He who has fully developed his mind knows his nature. Knowing his nature, he knows Heaven.' See the *Mencius*, VII, A, Ch. 1.

art and culture, whereas the authors of the *I* Appendices, on the basis of human art and culture, elaborated the way of Nature. This is the difference between the *Lao Tzu* and the *I* Appendices.

The *I* Appendices, on the one hand, identify the *Tao* of Man with the *Tao* of Heaven. This is, in fact, the Confucianist tradition. On the other hand, the *I* Appendices stress that the *Tao* of Man should be normalized in accordance with the *Tao* of Heaven. This is the idea borrowed from the *Lao Tzu*. However, to the *Taoists*, the *Tao* of Heaven is an all-embracing first principle underlying the changing phenomena of the universe, and when they spoke of the Tao of Heaven as transcending shapes and features, they were thinking of Non-being, the Unnameable, the formless Form, and the imageless Image. The authors of the *I* Appendices had a different approach. Although they agreed with the Taoists that the *Tao* of Heaven is the basic law underlying all phenomenal changes, yet they stressed that all the changes are subject to "the unceasing movement going on in the universe." With regard to the *Tao* of Heaven, there is the statement already quoted, "one *Yin* and one *Yang*," which "constitute the Tao." "That which is perpetuated by it is good. That which is completed by it is the nature (of men and things). As seen by the man of *jen*, it (i.e., the *Tao*) is called *jen;* as seen by the wise man, it is called wisdom. The common people have it in daily use, but are not aware of it. Thus the *Tao* of the Superior Man is seldom found." (*Hsi Tz'u*, Sec. I, Ch.5)

Now we see that the way of Nature — i.e., the *Tao* of Heaven — consists in the unceasing process of "one *Yin* and one *Yang*." In regard to the concept of this unceasing *Tao*, the Confucianists differed from the Taoists. "As seen by the man of *jen*, the *Tao* is called *jen*"; this is the Confucianist view. Hence the *Hsi Tz'u* says: "The great attribute of Heaven is to produce." Nothing produced by the *Tao* is evil, and so "that which is perpetuated by it (the *Tao*) is good." However, "as seen by the wise man, the *Tao* is called wisdom"; this is the Taoist view. Hence the *Lao Tzu* says: "Heaven-and-Earth is not benevolent;

it treats all things as straw-dogs." (Ch. 5)[68] It seems that Heaven-and-Earth is spontaneity itself, so it has no desire to be benevolent; it simply leaves all things to take their natural course, and does not interfere. Because of this difference, "the Tao of the Superior Man is seldom found." For the Tao of the Superior Man must embrace both *jen* and wisdom. To neglect one of the two aspects would not do at all. The difference between *jen* and wisdom is what we may describe as the distinction between the *Tao* of Man and the *Tao* of Heaven. As the *Hsi Tz'u* says: "It (i.e., the *Tao*) is manifested in *jen*, and conceals its functioning. It stimulates all creatures, without causing the anxieties which the Sages endured. (Sec. I, Ch. 5)

"The great attribute of Heaven is to produce," that is, to manifest *jen*. All creatures are produced and nourished by "its glorious power" and yet they are not aware of it. This is the *Tao* of Heaven. Although the *Tao* manifests itself as the force of *jen*, yet it remains in secret in regard to its functioning. Thus there are the anxieties of the Sages. This is the *Tao* of Man. The *Tao* of Man and the *Tao* of Heaven stand in contrast to each other as do realism and idealism; this is the antithesis between what we call the sublime and the common. As the sublime and the common exist with all their differences, how can they be synthesized into one whole? This is one problem which the *I* Appendices attempt to solve, and herein lies the spirit of the *I* philosophy.

As we have seen above, in the *I* Appendices, the word *I* is used interchangeably with *Tao,* since *Tao* is life, spontaneity, evolution, or, in one word, change itself. We have also seen that change is at work in the great as well as in the small, and that it can be read in the cosmic happenings of the universe as well as in the human affairs of the world. From this comprehensiveness of *I* or *Tao*, the *I* Appendices derive the idea that man is in the center of the universe; the individual who attains to

[68]Dogs made of straw were used at sacrifices and then discarded.

the sublime — the sphere of the transcendent — is on a par with the cosmic forces of Heaven and Earth. This is what is meant by the idea of identification with Heaven.

Thus then, on the basis of what has been said above, we may say that the *I* Appendices aim at a particular kind of highest life. This kind of highest life is "not divorced from daily regular activity," and yet at the same time "it goes straight to what is beyond the heavens." The first part of this expression represents the *Tao* of Man, the second part the *Tao* of Heaven. Because it is of the *Tao* of Man, it is concerned with human affairs; because it is of the *Tao* of Heaven, it reaches up to the sublime. In the *I* Appendices, the man who attains to this kind of highest life is what is called "the Sage," also what is called "the Great Man." Thus, in the *Wen Yen's* remarks on the *Ch'ien* hexagram, there is a picture of a sage:

> The Great Man, in his attributes, is in harmony with Heaven and Earth; in his brightness, with the sun and the moon; in his orderly procedure, with the four seasons; and in his relation to the good and bad issues, in harmony with the names and the spirits. When he acts before Heaven, Heaven does not go counter to him; when he acts after Heaven, he serves the timeliness of Heaven. Since Heaven does not go counter to him, how much less do his fellow men! How much less do the manes and the spirits! (Sec. I, Ch. 6)

The Sage attains to this sphere because he has the highest form of knowledge. According to the *I* Appendices, the *I* contains that by which man can attain to this kind of knowledge. As the *Hsi Tz'u* says: "How sublime is the *I*! It was by the *I* that the Sages were able to exalt their power and extend the scope of their achievements. Their knowledge was exalted, and their code of manners was yielding: being exalted after the pattern of Heaven; being yielding after the pattern of Earth." (Sec. I, Ch. 7)

The man who has reached this position may be described as being identified with Heaven. Although he may act in advance of Heaven, Heaven does not go counter to him; he may also act after Heaven and yet serve the timeliness of Heaven. Hence, although the sphere in which he lives is the transcendent one, his achievements are in the main concerned with the business of the world. This is what is taught in the *I* Appendices.

CH'U CHAI with WINBERG CHAI

TRANSLATOR'S PREFACE

I wrote out a translation of the Yî King, embracing both the Text and the Appendixes, in 1854 and 1855; and have to acknowledge that when the manuscript was completed, I knew very little about the scope and method of the book. I laid the volumes containing the result of my labour aside, and hoped, believed indeed, that the light would by and by dawn, and that I should one day get hold of a clue that would guide me to a knowledge of the mysterious classic.

Before that day came, the translation was soaked, in 1870, for more than a month in water of the Red Sea. By dint of careful manipulation it was recovered so as to be still legible; but it was not till 1874 that I began to be able to give to the book the prolonged attention necessary to make it reveal its secrets. Then for the first time I got hold, as I believe, of the clue, and found that my toil of twenty years before was of no service at all.

What had tended more than anything else to hide the nature of the book from my earlier studies was the way in which, with the Text, ordinarily and, as I think, correctly ascribed to king Wăn and his son Tan, there are interspersed, under each hexagram, the portions of the Appendixes I, II, and IV relating to it. The student at first thinks this an advantage. He believes that all the Appendixes were written by Confucius, and combine with the text to form one harmonious work; and he is glad to have the sentiments of 'the three sages' brought together. But I now perceived that the composition of the Text and of the Appendixes, allowing the Confucian authorship of the latter, was separated by about 700 years, and that their subject-matter was often incongruous. My first step towards a right understanding of the Yî was to study the Text by itself and as complete in itself. It was easy to do this because the imperial edition of 1715, with all its critical apparatus, keeps the Text and the Appendixes separate.

The wisdom of the course thus adopted became more apparent by the formation of eight different concordances, one for the Text, and one for each of the Appendixes. They showed that many characters in the Appendixes, and those especially which most readily occur to sinologists as characteristic of the Yî, are not to be found in the Text at all. A fuller acquaintance, moreover, with the tone and style of the Appendixes satisfied me that while we had sufficient evidence that the greater part of them was not from Confucius, we had no evidence that any part was his, unless it might be the paragraphs introduced by the compiler or compilers as sayings of 'the Master.'

Studying the Text in the manner thus described, I soon arrived at the view of the meaning and object of the Yî, which I have described in the second chapter of the Introduction; and I was delighted to find that there was a substantial agreement between my interpretations of the hexagrams and their several lines and those given by the most noted commentators from the Han dynasty down to the present. They have not formulated the scheme so concisely as I have done, and they were fettered by their belief in the Confucian authorship of the Appendixes; but they held the same general opinion, and were similarly controlled by it in construing the Text. Any sinologist who will examine the Yü Kih Zăh Kiang Yî King Kieh Î, prepared by one of the departments of the Han Lin college, and published in 1682, and which I have called the 'Daily Lessons,' or 'Lectures,' will see the agreement between my views and those underlying its paraphrase.

After the clue to the meaning of the Yî was discovered, there remained the difficulty of translating. The peculiarity of its style makes it the most difficult of all the Confucian classics to present in an intelligible version. I suppose that there are sinologists who will continue, for a time at least, to maintain that it was intended by its author or authors, whoever they were, merely as a book of divination; and of course the oracles of divination were designedly wrapped up in mysterious phraseology. But notwithstanding the account of the origin of the book and its composition by king Wăn and his son, which I have seen reason to adopt, they, its authors, had to write after the manner of diviners. There is hardly another work in the ancient literature of China that presents the same difficulties to the translator.

When I made my first translation of it in 1854, I endeavoured to be as concise in my English as the original Chinese was. Much of what I wrote was made up, in consequence, of so many English words, with little or no mark of syntactical connexion. I followed in this the example of P. Regis and his coadjutors (Introduction, page 9) in their Latin version. But their version is all but unintelligible, and mine was not less so. How to surmount this difficulty occurred to me after I had found the clue to the interpretation;—in a fact which I had unconsciously acted on in all my translations of other classics, namely, that the written characters of the Chinese are not representations of words, but symbols of ideas, and that the combination of them in composition is not a representation of what the writer would say, but of what he thinks. It is vain therefore for a translator to attempt a literal version. When the symbolic characters have brought his mind en rapport with that of his author, he is free to render the ideas in his own or any other speech in the best manner that he can attain to. This is the rule which Mencius followed in interpreting the old poems of his country:—
'We must try with our thoughts to meet the scope of a sentence, and then we shall apprehend it.' In the study of a Chinese classical book there is not so much an interpretation of the characters employed by the writer as a participation of his thoughts;—there is the seeing of mind to mind. The canon hence derived for a translator is not one of license. It will be his object to express the meaning of the original as exactly and concisely as possible. But it will be necessary for him to introduce a word or two

now and then to indicate what the mind of the writer
supplied for itself. What I have done in this way will
generally be seen enclosed in parentheses, though I
queried whether I might not dispense with them, as there
is nothing in the English version which was not, I believe,
present in the writer's thought. I hope, however, that I
have been able in this way to make the translation intelligible to readers. If, after all, they shall conclude that
in what is said on the hexagrams there is often 'much
ado about nothing,' it is not the translator who should be
deemed accountable for that, but his original.

I had intended to append to the volume translations of
certain chapters from *K*û Hsî and other writers of the Sung
dynasty; but this purpose could not be carried into effect
for want of space. It was found necessary to accompany
the version with a running commentary, illustrating the
way in which the teachings of king Wăn and his son are
supposed to be drawn from the figures and their several
lines; and my difficulty was to keep the single Yî within
the limits of one volume. Those intended translations
therefore are reserved for another opportunity; and indeed,
the Sung philosophy did not grow out of the Yî proper,
but from the Appendixes to it, and especially from the third
of them. It is more Tâoistic than Confucian.

When I first took the Yî in hand, there existed no translation of it in any western language but that of P. Regis
and his coadjutors, which I have mentioned above and in
various places of the Introduction. The authors were all
sinologists of great attainments; and their view of the Text
as relating to the transactions between the founders of the
*K*âu dynasty and the last sovereign of the Shang or Yin,
and capable of being illustrated historically, though too
narrow, was an approximation to the truth. The late
M. Mohl, who had edited the work in 1834, said to me
once, 'I like it; for I come to it out of a sea of mist, and
find solid ground.' No sufficient distinction was made in it,
however, between the Text and the Appendixes; and in dis-
cussing the third and following Appendixes the translators

were haunted by the name and shade of Confucius. To the excessive literalness of the version I have referred above.

In 1876 the Rev. Canon McClatchie, M.A., published a version at Shanghai with the title, 'A Translation of the Confucian Yî King, or the "Classic of Changes," with Notes and Appendix.' This embraces both the Text and the Appendixes, the first, second, and fourth of the latter being interspersed along with the Text, as in the ordinary school editions of the classic. So far as I can judge from his language, he does not appear to be aware that the first and second Appendixes were not the work of king Wăn and the duke of Kâu, but of a subsequent writer—he would say of Confucius—explaining their explanations of the entire hexagrams and their several lines. His own special object was 'to open the mysteries of the Yî by applying to it the key of Comparative Mythology.' Such a key was not necessary; and the author, by the application of it, has found sundry things to which I have occasionally referred in my notes. They are not pleasant to look at or dwell upon; and happily it has never entered into the minds of Chinese scholars to conceive of them. I have followed Canon McClatchie's translation from paragraph to paragraph and from sentence to sentence, but found nothing which I could employ with advantage in my own.

Long after my translation had been completed, and that of the Text indeed was printed, I received from Shanghai the third volume of P. Angelo Zottoli's 'Cursus Litteraturae Sinicae,' which had appeared in 1880. About 100 pages of it are occupied with the Yî. The Latin version is a great improvement on that in the work of Regis; but P. Zottoli translates only the Text of the first two hexagrams, with the portions of the first, second, and fourth Appendixes relating to them; and other six hexagrams with the explanations of king Wăn's Thwan and of the Great Symbolism. Of the remaining fifty-six hexagrams only the briefest summary is given; and then follow the Appendixes III, V, VI, and VII at length. The author has done his work well.

His general view of the Yî is stated in the following sentences:—'Ex Fû-hsî figuris, Wăn regis definitionibus, *K*âu ducis symbolis, et Confucii commentariis, Liber conficitur, qui a mutationibus, quas duo elementa in hexagrammatum compositione inducunt, Yî (M u t a t o r) vel Yî King (M u t a-t i o n u m L i b e r) appellatur. Quid igitur tandem famosus iste Yî King? Paucis accipe: ex linearum q u a l i t a t e continua vel intercisa; earumque s i t u, imo, medio, vel supremo; mutuaque ipsarum r e l a t i o n e, occursu, dissidio, convenientia; ex ipso scilicet trigrammatum corpore seu forma, tum ex trigrammatum symbolo seu imagine, tum ex trigrammatum proprietate seu virtute, tum etiam aliquando ex unius ad alterum hexagramma varietate, eruitur aliqua i m a g o, deducitur aliqua s e n t e n t i a, quoddam veluti ora-c u l u m continens, quod s o r t e etiam consulere possis ad documentum obtinendum, moderandae vitae solvendove dubio consentaneum. Ita liber juxta Confucii explica-tionem in scholis tradi solitam. Nil igitur sublime aut mysteriosum, nil foedum aut vile hìc quaeras; a r g u t u l u m potius l u s u m ibi video ad instructiones morales politicas-que eliciendas, ut ad satietatem usque in Sinicis passim classicis, obvias, planas, naturales; tantum, cum liber iste, ut integrum legenti textum facile patebit, ad sortilegii usum deductus fuerit, per ipsum jam summum homo obtinebit vitae beneficium, arcanam cum spiritibus communicationem secretamque futurorum eventuum cognitionem; theurgus igitur visus est iste liber, totus lux, totus spiritus, hominis-que vitae accommodatissimus; indeque laudes a Confucio ei tributas, prorsus exaggeratas, in hujus libri praesertim appendice videre erit, si vere tamen, ut communis fert opinio, ipse sit hujus appendicis auctor.'

There has been a report for two or three years of a new translation of the Yî, or at least of a part of it, as being in preparation by M. Terrien de Lacouperie, and Professor R. K. Douglas of the British Museum and King's College, London. I have alluded on pages 8, 9 of the Introduction to some inaccurate statements about native commentaries on the Yî and translations of it by foreigners, made in con-nexion with this contemplated version. But I did not know what the projected undertaking really was, till I read a letter from M. Terrien in the 'Athenæum' of the 21st January of this year. He there says that the joint translation 'deals only with the oldest part of the book, the short lists of characters which follow each of the sixty-four headings, and leaves entirely aside the explanations and commentaries attributed to Wen Wang, Kâu Kung, Confucius, and others, from 1200 B. C. downwards, which are commonly embodied as an integral part of the classic;' adding, 'The proportion of the primitive text to these additions is about one-sixth of the whole.' But if we take away these explanations and commentaries attributed to king Wăn, the duke of Kâu, and Confucius, we take away the whole Yî. There remain only the linear figures attributed to Fû-hsî, without any lists of characters, long or short, without a single written character of any kind whatever. The projectors have been misled somehow about the contents of the Yî; and unless they can overthrow all the traditions and beliefs about them, whether Chinese or foreign, their undertaking is more hopeless than the task laid on the children of Israel by Pharaoh, that they should make bricks without straw.

I do not express myself thus in any spirit of hostility. If, by discoveries in Accadian or any other long-buried and forgotten language, M. Terrien de Lacouperie can throw new light on the written characters of China or on its speech, no one will rejoice more than myself; but his ignorance of how the contents of the classic are made up does not give much prospect of success in his promised translation.

In the preface to the third volume of these 'Sacred Books of the East,' containing the Shû King, Shih King, and Hsiâo King, I have spoken of the Chinese terms Tî and Shang Tî, and shown how I felt it necessary to continue to render them by our word God, as I had done in all my translations of the Chinese classics since 1861. My doing so gave offence to some of the missionaries in China and others; and in June, 1880, twenty-three gentlemen addressed a letter to Professor F. Max Müller, complaining that, in such a work edited by him, he should allow me to give my own private interpretation of the name or names in question instead of translating them or transferring them. Professor Müller published the letter which he had received, with his reply to it, in the 'Times' newspaper of Dec. 30, 1880. Since then the matter has rested, and I introduce it again here in this preface, because, though we do not meet with the name in the Yî so frequently as in the Shû and Shih, I have, as before, wherever it does occur, translated it by God. Those who object to that term say that Shang Tî might be rendered by 'Supreme Ruler' or 'Supreme Emperor,' or by 'Ruler (or Emperor) on high;' but when I examined the question, more than thirty years ago, with all possible interest and all the resources at my command, I came to the conclusions that Tî, on its first employment by the Chinese fathers, was intended to express the same concept which our fathers expressed by God, and that such has been its highest and proper application ever since. There would be little if any difference in the meaning conveyed to readers by 'Supreme Ruler' and 'God;' but when I render Tî by God and Shang Tî by the Supreme God, or, for the sake of brevity, simply by God, I am translating, and not giving a private interpretation of my own. I do it not in the interests of controversy, but as the simple expression of what to me is truth; and I am glad to know that a great majority of the Protestant missionaries in China use Tî and Shang Tî as the nearest analogue for God.

It would be tedious to mention the many critical editions and commentaries that I have used in preparing the translation. I have not had the help of able native scholars, which saved time and was otherwise valuable when I was working in the East on other classics. The want of this, however, has been more than compensated in some respects by my copy of the 'Daily Lectures on the Yî,' the full title of which is given on page xiv. The friend who purchased it for me five years ago in Canton was obliged to content himself with a second-hand copy; but I found that the previous owner had been a ripe scholar who freely used his pencil in pursuing his studies. It was possible, from his punctuation, interlineations, and many marginal notes, to follow the exercises of his mind, patiently pursuing his search for the meaning of the most difficult passages. I am under great obligations to him; and also to the *K*âu Yî *K*eh *K*ung, the great imperial edition of the present dynasty, first published in 1715. I have generally spoken of its authors as the Khang-hsî editors. Their numerous discussions of the meaning, and ingenious decisions, go far to raise the interpretation of the Yî to a science.

J. L.

OXFORD
16th March, 1882

I CHING
BOOK OF CHANGES

I CHING
BOOK OF CHANGES

TRANSLATOR'S INTRODUCTION

CHAPTER I

THE YÎ KING FROM THE TWELFTH CENTURY B.C. TO THE COMMENCEMENT OF THE CHRISTIAN ERA

1. Confucius is reported to have said on one occasion, 'If some years were added to my life, I would give fifty to the study of the Yî, and might then escape falling into great errors[1].' The utterance is referred by the best critics to the closing period of Confucius' life, when he had returned from his long and painful wanderings among the States, and was settled again in his native Lû. By this time he was nearly seventy, and it seems strange, if he spoke seriously, that he should have thought it possible for his life to be prolonged other fifty years. So far as that specification is concerned, a corruption of the text is generally admitted. My reason for adducing the passage has simply been to prove from it the existence of a Yî King in the time of Confucius. In the history of him by Sze-mâ *Kh*ien it is stated that, in the closing years of his life, he became fond of the Yî, and wrote various appendixes to it, that he read his copy of it so much that the leathern thongs (by which the tablets containing it were bound together) were thrice worn out, and that he said, 'Give me several years (more), and I should be master of the Yî[2].' The ancient books on which Confucius had delighted

There was a Yî in the time of Confucius

---

[1] Confucian Analects, VII, xvi.
[2] The Historical Records ; Life of Confucius, p. 12.

to discourse with his disciples were those of History, Poetry, and Rites and Ceremonies[1]; but ere he passed away from among them, his attention was much occupied also by the Yî as a monument of antiquity, which in the prime of his days he had too much neglected.

2. *Kh*ien says that Confucius wrote various appendixes to the Yî, specifying all but two of the treatises, which go

The Yî is now made up of the Text which Confucius saw and the Appendixes ascribed to him

by the name of 'the Ten Appendixes,' and are, with hardly a dissentient voice, attributed to the sage. They are published along with the older Text, which is based on still older lineal figures, and are received by most Chinese readers, as well as by foreign Chinese scholars, as an integral portion of the Yî King. The two portions should, however, be carefully distinguished. I will speak of them as the Text and the Appendixes.

3. The Yî happily escaped the fires of Ʒhin, which proved so disastrous to most of the ancient literature of China in

The Yî escaped the fires of Ʒhin

B.C. 213. In the memorial which the premier Lî Sze addressed to his sovereign, advising that the old books should be consigned to the flames, an exception was made of those which treated of 'medicine, divination, and husbandry[2].' The Yî was held to be a book of divination, and so was preserved.

In the catalogue of works in the imperial library, prepared by Liû Hin about the beginning of our era, there is an enumeration of those on the Yî and its Appendixes,— the books of thirteen different authors or schools, comprehended in 294 portions of larger or smaller dimensions[3]. I need not follow the history and study of the Yî into the line of the centuries since the time of Liû Hin. The imperial Khang-hsî edition of it, which appeared in 1715, contains quotations from the commentaries of 218 scholars, covering, more or less closely, the time from the second century B.C. to our seventeenth century. I may venture to say that

---

[1] Analects, VII, xvii.
[2] Legge's Chinese Classics, I, prolegomena, pp. 6–9.
[3] Books of the Earlier Han; History of Literature, pp. 1, 2.

those 218 are hardly a tenth of the men who have tried to interpret the remarkable book, and solve the many problems to which it gives rise.

4. It may be assumed then that the Yî King, properly so called, existed before Confucius, and has come down to us as correctly as any other of the ancient books of China ; and it might also be said, as correctly as any of the old monuments of Hebrew, Sanskrit, Greek, or Latin literature. The question arises of how far before Confucius we can trace its existence. Of course an inquiry into this point will not include the portions or appendixes attributed to the sage himself. Attention will be called to them by and by, when I shall consider how far we are entitled, or whether we are at all entitled, to ascribe them to him. I do not doubt, however, that they belong to what may be called the Confucian period, and were produced some time after his death, probably between B.C. 450 and 350. By whomsoever they were written, they may be legitimately employed in illustration of what were the prevailing views in that age on various points connected with the Yî. Indeed, but for the guidance and hints derived from them as to the meaning of the text, and the relation between its statements and the linear figures, there would be great difficulty in making out any consistent interpretation of it.

The Yî before Confucius, and when it was made

(i) The earliest mention of the classic is found in the Official Book of the Kâu dynasty, where it is said that, among the duties of 'the Grand Diviner,' 'he had charge of the rules for the three Yî (systems of Changes), called the Lien-shan, the Kweî-ȝhang, and the Yî of Kâu ; that in each of them the regular (or primary) lineal figures were 8, which were multiplied, in each, till they amounted to 64.' The date of the Official Book has not been exactly ascertained. The above passage can hardly be reconciled with the opinion of the majority of Chinese critics that it was the work of the duke of Kâu, the consolidator and legislator of the dynasty so called ; but I think there must have been the groundwork of it at a very early date. When that was composed or compiled, there

The Yî mentioned in the Official Book of Kâu

was existing, among the archives of the kingdom, under the charge of a high officer, 'the Yî of *K*âu,'—what constitutes the Text of the present Yî; the Text, that is, as distinguished from the Appendixes. There were two other Yî, known as the Lien-shan and the Kwei-ṣhang. It would be a waste of time to try to discover the meaning of these designations. They are found in this and another passage of the Official Book; and nowhere else. Not a single trace of what they denoted remains, while we possess 'the Yî of *K*âu' complete[1].

(ii) In the Supplement of Ṣo *K*hiû-ming to 'the Spring and Autumn,' there is abundant evidence that divination by the Yî was frequent, throughout the states of China, before the time of Confucius. There are at least eight narratives of such a practice, between the years B.C. 672 and 564, before he was born; and five times during his life-time the divining stalks and the book were had recourse to on occasions with which he had nothing to do. In all these cases the text of the Yî, as we have it now, is freely quoted. The 'Spring and Autumn' commences in B.C. 722. If it extended back to the rise of the *K*âu dynasty, we should, no doubt, find

The Yî mentioned in the Ṣo *K*hwan

---

[1] See the *K*âu Kwan (or Lî), Book XXIV, parr. 3, 4, and 27. Biot (Le Tcheou Lî, vol. ii, pp. 70, 71) translates the former two paragraphs thus :— 'Il (Le Grand Augure) est préposé aux trois methodes pour les changements (des lignes divinatoires). La première est appelée Liaison des montagnes (Lien-shan) ; la seconde, Retour et Conservation (Kwei-ṣhang) ; la troisième, Changements des *K*âu. Pour toutes il y a huit lignes symboliques sacrées, et soixante-quatre combinaisons de ces lignes.'

Some tell us that by Lien-shan was intended Fû-hsî, and by Kwei-ṣhang Hwang Tî; others, that the former was the Yî of the Hsiâ dynasty, and the latter that of Shang or Yin. A third set will have it that Lien-shan was a designation of Shǎn Nǎng, between Fû-hsî and Hwang Tî. I should say myself, as many Chinese critics do say, that Lien-shan was an arrangement of the lineal

symbols in which the first figure was the present 52nd hexagram, K̆ǎn ☶ ☶, consisting of the trigram representing mountains doubled ; and that Kwei-ṣhang was an arrangement where the first figure was the present 2nd hexagram, Khwǎn ☷ ☷, consisting of the trigram representing the earth doubled,— with reference to the disappearance and safe keeping of plants in the bosom of the earth in winter. All this, however, is only conjecture.

accounts of divination by the Yî interspersed over the long intervening period. For centuries before Confucius appeared on the stage of his country, the Yî was well known among the various feudal states, which then constituted the Middle Kingdom [1].

(iii) We may now look into one of the Appendixes for its testimony to the age and authorship of the Text. The third Appendix is the longest, and the most important [2]. In the 49th paragraph of the second Section of it it is said:—

'Was it not in the middle period of antiquity that the Yî began to flourish? Was not he who made it (or were not they who made it) familiar with anxiety and calamity?'

The highest antiquity commences, according to Chinese writers, with Fû-hsî, B.C. 3322; and the lowest with Confucius in the middle of the sixth century B.C. Between these is the period of middle antiquity, extending a comparatively short time, from the rise of the Kâu dynasty, towards the close of the twelfth century B.C., to the Confucian era. According to this paragraph it was in this period that our Yî was made.

The 69th paragraph is still more definite in its testimony:—

'Was it not in the last age of the Yin (dynasty), when the virtue of Kâu had reached its highest point, and during the troubles between king Wăn and (the tyrant) Kâu, that (the study of) the Yî began to flourish? On this account the explanations (in the book) express (a feeling of) anxious apprehension, (and teach) how peril may be turned into security, and easy carelessness is sure to meet with overthrow.'

The dynasty of Yin was superseded by that of Kâu in B.C. 1122. The founder of Kâu was he whom we call king Wăn, though he himself never occupied the throne. The

---

[1] See in the Zo Khwan, under the 22nd year of duke Kwang (B.C. 672); the 1st year of Min (661); and in his 2nd year (660); twice in the 15th year of Hsî (645); his 25th year (635); the 12th year of Hsüan (597); the 16th year of Khăng (575); the 9th year of Hsiang (564); his 25th year (548); the 5th year of Khâo (537); his 7th year (535); his 12th year (530); and the 9th year of Âi (486).

[2] That is, the third as it appears farther on in this volume in two Sections. With the Chinese critics it forms the fifth and sixth Appendixes, or 'Wings,' as they are termed.

troubles between him and the last sovereign of Yin reached
their height in B. C. 1143, when the tyrant threw him
into prison in a place called Yû-lî, identified as having
been in the present district of Thang-yin, department of
*K*ang-teh, province of Ho-nan. Wǎn was not kept long in
confinement. His friends succeeded in appeasing the
jealousy of his enemy, and securing his liberation in the
following year. It follows that the Yî, so far as we owe
it to king Wǎn, was made in the year B.C. 1143 or 1142,
or perhaps that it was begun in the former year and finished
in the latter [1].

But the part which is thus ascribed to king Wǎn is only
a small portion of the Yî. A larger share is attributed to
his son Tan, known as the duke of *K*âu, and in it we have
allusions to king Wû, who succeeded his father Wǎn, and
was really the first sovereign of the dynasty of *K*âu [2].
There are passages, moreover, which must be understood
of events in the early years of the next reign. But the
duke of *K*âu died in the year B. C. 1105, the 11th of
king *K*hǎng. A few years then before that time, in the
last decade of the twelfth century B.C., the Yî King, as it
has come down to us, was complete [3].

5. We have thus traced the text of the Yî to its authors,
the famous king Wǎn in the year 1143 B. C., and his
equally famous son, the duke of *K*âu, in between thirty and

The Yî is not
the most
ancient of
the Chinese
books

forty years later. It can thus boast of a
great antiquity; but a general opinion has
prevailed that it belonged to a period still
more distant. Only two translations of it have
been made by European scholars. The first was executed by
Regis and other Roman Catholic missionaries in the beginning of last century, though it was given to the public only

---

[1] Sze-mâ *K*hien (History of the *K*âu Dynasty, p. 3) relates that, 'when he was
confined in Yû-lî, Wǎn increased the 8 trigrams to 64 hexagrams.'

[2] E.g., hexagrams XVII, l. 6; XLVI, l. 4. Tan's authorship of the symbolism
is recognised in the 3o *K*hwan, B.C. 540.

[3] P. Regis (vol. ii, p. 379) says: 'Vel nihil vel parum errabit qui dicet opus
Yî King fuisse perfectum anno quinto *K*hǎng Wang, seu anno 1109 aut non
ultra annum 1108, ante aerae Christianae initium; quod satis in rebus non
omnino certis.' But the fifth year of king *K*hǎng was B.C. 1111.

in 1834 by the late Jules Mohl, with a title commencing 'Y-King, antiquissimus Sinarum liber[1].' The language of the other European translator of it, the Rev. Canon McClatchie of Shanghâi, whose work appeared in 1876, is still more decided. The first sentence of his Introduction contains two very serious misstatements, but I have at present to do only with the former of them;—that 'the Yî King is regarded by the Chinese with peculiar veneration, ... as being the most ancient of their classical writings.' The Shû is the oldest of the Chinese classics, and contains documents more than a thousand years earlier than king Wăn. Several pieces of the Shih King are also older than anything in the Yî; to which there can thus be assigned only the third place in point of age among the monuments of Chinese literature. Existing, however, about 3000 years ago, it cannot be called modern. Unless it be the books of the Pentateuch, Joshua, and Judges, an equal antiquity cannot be claimed for any portion of our Sacred Scriptures.

It will be well to observe here also how much older the

The Text much older than the Appendixes

Text is than the Appendixes. Supposing them to be the work of Confucius, though it will appear by and by that this assumption

---

[1] It has been suggested that 'Antiquissimus Sinarum liber' may mean only 'A very ancient book of the Chinese,' but the first sentence of the Preface to the work commences :—' Inter omnes constat librorum Sinicorum, quos classicos vocant, primum et antiquissimum esse Y-King.'

At the end of M. De Guignes' edition of P. Gaubil's translation of the Shû, there is a notice of the Yî King sent in 1738 to the Cardinals of the Congregation de Propaganda Fide by M. Claude Visdelou, Bishop of Claudiopolis. M. De Guignes says himself, 'L' Y-King est le premier des Livres Canoniques des Chinois.' But P. Visdelou writes more guardedly and correctly :—' Pour son ancienneté, s'il en faut croire les Annales des Chinois, il a été commencé quarante-six siècles avant celui-ci. Si cela est vrai, comme toute la nation l'avoue unanimement, ou peut à juste titre l'appeler le plus ancien des livres.' But he adds, 'Ce n'étoit pas proprement un livre, ni quelque chose d'approchant; c'étoit une énigme très obscure, et plus difficile cent fois à expliquer que celle du sphinx.'

P. Couplet expresses himself much to the same effect in the prolegomena (p. xviii) to the work called 'Confucius Sinarum Philosophus,' published at Paris in 1687 by himself and three other fathers of the Society of Jesus (Intorcetta, Herdritch, and Rougemont). Both they and P. Visdelou give an example of a portion of the text and its interpretation, having singularly selected the same hexagram,—the 15th, on Humility.

can be received as only partially correct, if indeed it be received at all, the sage could not have entered on their composition earlier than B.C. 483, 660 years later than the portion of the text that came from king Wăn, and nearly 630 later than what we owe to the duke of *K*âu. But during that long period of between six and seven centuries changes may have arisen in the views taken by thinking men of the method and manner of the Yî; and I cannot accept the Text and the Appendixes as forming one work in any proper sense of the term. Nothing has prevented the full understanding of both, so far as parts of the latter can be understood, so much as the blending of them together, which originated with Pî *K*ih of the first Han dynasty. The common editions of the book have five of the Appendixes (as they are ordinarily reckoned) broken up and printed side by side with the Text; and the confusion thence arising has made it difficult, through the intermixture of incongruous ideas, for foreign students to lay hold of the meaning.

6. Native scholars have of course been well aware of the difference in time between the appearance of the Text and

Labours of native scholars on the Yî the Appendixes; and in the Khang-hsî edition of them the two are printed separately. Only now and then, however, has any critic ventured to doubt that the two parts formed one homogeneous whole, or that all the appendixes were from the style or pencil of Confucius. Hundreds of them have brought a wonderful and consistent meaning out of the Text; but to find in it or in the Appendixes what is unreasonable, or any inconsistency between them, would be to impeach the infallibility of Confucius, and stamp on themselves the brand of heterodoxy.

At the same time it is an unfair description of what

An imperfect description of their labours they have accomplished to say, as has been done lately, that since the fires of Ʒhin, 'the foremost scholars of each generation have edited the Text (meaning both the Text and the Appendixes), and heaped commentary after commentary upon it; and one and all have arrived at the somewhat

lame conclusion that its full significance is past finding out[1].'
A multitude of the native commentaries are of the highest
value, and have left little to be done for the elucidation
of the Text; and if they say that a passage in an Appendix
is 'unfathomable' or 'incalculable,' it is because their authors
shrink from allowing, even to themselves, that the ancient
sages intermeddled, and intermeddled unwisely, with things
too high for them.

When the same writer who thus speaks of native
scholars goes on to say that 'in the same way a host
Erroneous account of the labours of European Chinese scholars of European Chinese scholars have made
translations of the Yî, and have, if possible,
made confusion worse confounded,' he only
shows how imperfectly he had made himself
acquainted with the subject. 'The host of European
Chinese scholars who have made translations of the Yî'
amount to two,—the same two mentioned by me above
on pp. 6, 7. The translation of Regis and his coadjutors[2]
is indeed capable of improvement; but their work as a
whole, and especially the prolegomena, dissertations, and
notes, supply a mass of correct and valuable information.
They had nearly succeeded in unravelling the confusion,
and solving the enigma of the Yî.

CHAPTER II

The Subject-matter of the Text. The Lineal Figures and the Explanation of them

1. Having described the Yî King as consisting of a text
in explanation of certain lineal figures, and of appendixes
to it, and having traced the composition of the former to

---

[1] See a communication on certain new views about the Yî in the 'Times' of
April 20, 1880; reprinted in Trübner's American, European, and Oriental
Literary Record, New Series, vol. i, pp. 125-127.

[2] Regis' coadjutors in the work were the Fathers Joseph de Mailla, who
turned the Chinese into Latin word for word, and compared the result with the
Mankâu version of the Yî; and Peter du Tartre, whose principal business was
to supply the historical illustrations. Regis himself revised all their work and
enlarged it, adding his own dissertations and notes. See Prospectus Operis,
immediately after M. Mohl's Preface.

its authors in the twelfth century B.C., and that of the latter to between six and seven centuries later at least, I proceed to give an account of what we find in the Text, and how it is deduced from the figures.

The subject-matter of the Text may be briefly repre-

The Yî con-
sists of essays
based on lineal
figures

sented as consisting of sixty-four short essays, enigmatically and symbolically expressed, on important themes, mostly of a moral, social, and political character, and based on the same number of lineal figures, each made up of six lines, some of which are whole and the others divided.

The first two and the last two may serve for the present as a specimen of those figures : ▤▤▤, ▤ ▤ ▤; and ▤▤▤, ▤▤▤[1]. The Text says nothing about their origin and formation. There they are. King Wăn takes them up, one after another, in the order that suits himself, determined, evidently, by the contrast in the lines of each successive pair of hexagrams, and gives their significance, as a whole, with some indication, perhaps, of the action to be taken in the circumstances which he supposes them to symbolise, and whether that action will be lucky or unlucky. Then the duke of Kâu, beginning with the first or bottom line, expresses, by means of a symbolical or emblematical illustration, the significance of each line, with a similar indication of the good or bad fortune of action taken in connexion with it. The king's interpretation of the whole hexagram will be found to be in harmony with the combined significance of the six lines as interpreted by his son.

Both of them, no doubt, were familiar with the practice of divination which had prevailed in China for more than a thousand years, and would copy closely its methods and style. They were not divining themselves, but their words became oracles to subsequent ages, when men divined by the hexagrams, and sought by means of what was said under them to ascertain how it would be with them in the

---

[1] See Plate I at the end of the Introduction.

future, and learn whether they should persevere in or withdraw from the courses they were intending to pursue.

2. I will give an instance of the lessons which the lineal
figures are made to teach, but before I do so, it will be
necessary to relate what is said of their origin,
and of the rules observed in studying and
interpreting them.   For information on these
points we must have recourse to the Appendixes; and in reply
to the question by whom and in what way the figures were
formed, the third, of which we made use in the last chapter,
supplies us with three different answers.

*The origin of
the lineal
figures*

(i) The 11th paragraph of Section ii says :—

'Anciently, when the rule of all under heaven was in the hands
of Pâo-hsî, looking up, he contemplated the brilliant forms exhibited
in the sky; and looking down, he surveyed the patterns shown on
the earth.   He marked the ornamental appearances on birds and
beasts, and the (different) suitabilities of the soil.   Near at hand, in
his own person, he found things for consideration, and the same
at a distance, in things in general.   On this he devised the eight
lineal figures of three lines each, to exhibit fully the spirit-like and
intelligent operations (in nature), and to classify the qualities of the
myriads of things.'

Pâo-hsî is another name for Fû-hsî, the most ancient
personage who is mentioned with any definiteness in Chinese
history, while much that is fabulous is current about him.
His place in chronology begins in B.C. 3322, 5203 years
ago.   He appears in this paragraph as the deviser of the
eight kwâ or trigrams.   The processes by which he was
led to form them, and the purposes which he intended
them to serve, are described, but in vague and general
terms that do not satisfy our curiosity.   The eight figures,
however, were ☰, ☱, ☲, ☳, ☴,
☵, ☶, and ☷; called khien, tui, lî, kǎn,
sun, khân, kǎn, and khwǎn; and representing heaven
or the sky; water, especially a collection of water as in a
marsh or lake; fire, the sun, lightning; thunder; wind and
wood; water, especially as in rain, the clouds, springs,
streams in defiles, and the moon; a hill or mountain; and
the earth.   To each of these figures is assigned a certain
attribute or quality which should be suggested by the

natural object it symbólises; but on those attributes we need not enter at present.

(ii) The 70th and 71st paragraphs of Section i give another account of the origin of the trigrams:—

'In (the system of) the Yî there is the Great Extreme, which produced the two Î (Elementary Forms). These two Forms produced the four Hsiang (Emblematic Symbols); which again produced the eight Kwâ (or Trigrams). The eight Kwâ served to determine the good and evil (issues of events), and from this determination there ensued the (prosecution of the) great business of life.'

The two elementary Forms, the four emblematic Symbols, and the eight Trigrams can all be exhibited with what may be deemed certainty. A whole line (———) and a divided (— —) were the two Î. These two lines placed over themselves, and each of them over the other, formed the four Hsiang: ═══; ══ ══; ══ ══; ═ ═. The same two lines placed successively over these Hsiang, formed the eight Kwâ, exhibited above.

Who will undertake to say what is meant by 'the Great Extreme' which produced the two elementary Forms? Nowhere else does the name occur in the old Confucian literature. I have no doubt myself that it found its way into this Appendix in the fifth (? or fourth) century B.C. from a Tâoist source. Kû Hsî, in his 'Lessons on the Yî for the Young,' gives for it the figure of a circle,—thus, ◯; observing that he does so from the philosopher Kâu (A.D. 1017–1073)[1], and cautioning his readers against thinking that such a representation came from Fû-hsî himself. To me the circular symbol appears very unsuccessful. 'The Great Extreme,' it is said, 'divided and produced two lines,—a whole line and a divided line.' But I do not understand how this could be. Suppose it possible for the circle to unroll itself;

---

[1] Kâu-ȝze, called Kâu Tun-î and Kâu Mâu-shuh, and, still more commonly, from the rivulet near which was his favourite residence, Kâu Lien-khî. Mayers (Chinese Reader's Manual, p. 23) says:—' He held various offices of state, and was for many years at the head of a galaxy of scholars who sought for instruction in matters of philosophy and research:—second only to Kû Hsi in literary repute.'

—we shall have one long line, ——————. If this divide itself, we have two whole lines; and another division of one of them is necessary to give us the whole and the divided lines of the lineal figures. The attempt to fashion the Great Extreme as a circle must be pronounced a failure.

But when we start from the two lines as bases, the formation of all the diagrams by a repetition of the process indicated above is easy. The addition to each of the trigrams of each of the two fundamental lines produces 16 figures of four lines; dealt with in the same way, these produce 32 figures of five lines; and a similar operation with these produces the 64 hexagrams, each of which forms the subject of an essay in the text of the Yî. The lines increase in an arithmetical progression whose common difference is 1, and the figures in a geometrical progression whose common ratio is 2. This is all the mystery in the formation of the lineal figures; this, I believe, was the process by which they were first formed; and it is hardly necessary to imagine them to have come from a sage like Fû-hsî. The endowments of an ordinary man were sufficient for such a work. It was possible even to shorten the operation by proceeding at once from the trigrams to the hexagrams, according to what we find in Section i, paragraph 2 :—

'A strong and a weak line were manipulated together (till there were the 8 trigrams), and those 8 trigrams were added each to itself and to all the others (till the 64 hexagrams were formed).'

It is a moot question who first multiplied the figures from the trigrams universally ascribed to Fû-hsî to the 64 hexagrams of the Yî. The more common view is that it was king Wăn; but Kû Hsî, when he was questioned on the subject, rather inclined to hold that Fû-hsî had multiplied them himself, but declined to say whether he thought that their names were as old as the figures themselves, or only dated from the twelfth century B.C.[1] I will not venture to controvert

Who first
multiplied
the figures
to 64?

---

[1] Kû-jze Khwan shû, or Digest of Works of Kû-jze, chap. 26 (the first chapter on the Yî), art. 16.

his opinion about the multiplication of the figures, but I
must think that the names, as we have them now, were
from king Wăn.

No Chinese writer has tried to explain why the framers
stopped with the 64 hexagrams, instead of going on to
128 figures of 7 lines, 256 of 8, 512 of 9, and
so on indefinitely. No reason can be given
for it, but the cumbrousness of the result, and
the impossibility of dealing, after the manner of king Wăn,
with such a mass of figures.

Why the figures were not continued after 64

(iii) The 73rd paragraph of Section i, with but one paragraph between it and the two others which we have been
considering, gives what may be considered a third account
of the origin of the lineal figures :—

'Heaven produced the spirit-like things (the tortoise and the
divining plant), and the sages took advantage of them. (The
operations of) heaven and earth are marked by so many changes
and transformations, and the sages imitated them (by means of the
Yî). Heaven hangs out its (brilliant) figures, from which are seen
good fortune and bad, and the sages made their emblematic interpretations accordingly. The Ho gave forth the scheme or map,
and the Lo gave forth the writing, of (both of) which the sages
took advantage.'

The words with which we have at present to do are—
'The Ho (that is, the Yellow River) gave forth the Map.'
This map, according to tradition and popular belief, contained a scheme which served as a model to Fû-hsî in
making his 8 trigrams. Apart from this passage in the
Yî King, we know that Confucius believed in such
a map, or spoke at least as if he did[1]. In the 'Record of
Rites' it is said that 'the map was borne by a horse[2];' and
the thing, whatever it was, is mentioned in the Shû as still
preserved at court, among other curiosities, in B.C. 1079[3].
The story of it, as now current, is this, that 'a dragon-
horse' issued from the Yellow River, bearing on its back
an arrangement of marks, from which Fû-hsî got the idea
of the trigrams.

---

[1] Analects IX, viii.   [2] Lî Kî VIII, iv, 16.   [3] Shû V, xxii, 19.

All this is so evidently fabulous that it seems a waste of time to enter into any details about it. My reason for doing so is a wish to take advantage of the map in giving such a statement of the rules observed in interpreting the figures as is necessary in this Introduction.

The map that was preserved, it has been seen, in the eleventh century B.C., afterwards perished, and though there The form of was much speculation about its form from the the River Map time that the restoration of the ancient classics was undertaken in the Han dynasty, the first delineation of it given to the public was in the reign of Hui Ȝung of the Sung dynasty (A.D. 1101–1125)[1]. The most approved scheme of it is the following :—

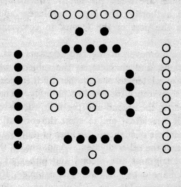

It will be observed that the markings in this scheme are small circles, pretty nearly equally divided into dark and light. All of them whose numbers are odd are light circles,— 1, 3, 5, 7, 9 ; and all of them whose numbers are even are dark,—2, 4, 6, 8, 10. This is given as the origin of what is said in paragraphs 49 and 50 of Section i about the numbers of heaven and earth. The difference in the colour of the circles occasioned the distinction of them and of what they

---

[1] See Mayers' Chinese Reader's Manual, pp. 56, 57.

signify into Yin and Yang, the dark and the bright, the
moon-like and the sun-like; for the sun is called the Great
Brightness (Thâi Yang), and the moon the Great Obscurity (Thâi Yin). I shall have more to say in the next
chapter on the application of these names. Fû-hsî in making
the trigrams, and king Wăn, if it was he who first multiplied them to the 64 hexagrams, found it convenient to
use lines instead of the circles:—the whole line (————)
for the bright circle (○), and the divided line (— —) for
the dark (●). The first, the third, and the fifth lines
in a hexagram, if they are 'correct' as it is called,
should all be whole, and the second, fourth, and sixth lines
should all be divided. Yang lines are strong (or hard),
and Yin lines are weak (or soft). The former indicate
vigour and authority; the latter, feebleness and submission. It is the part of the former to command; of the
latter to obey.

The lines, moreover, in the two trigrams that make up
the hexagrams, and characterise the subjects which they
represent, are related to one another by their position, and
have their significance modified accordingly. The first line
and the fourth, the second and the fifth, the third and the
sixth are all correlates; and to make the correlation perfect
the two members of it should be lines of different qualities,
one whole and the other divided. And, finally, the middle
lines of the trigrams, the second and fifth, that is, of the
hexagrams, have a peculiar value and force. If we have
a whole line (————) in the fifth place, and a divided line
(— —) in the second, or vice versâ, the correlation is complete. Let the subject of the fifth be the sovereign or a
commander-in-chief, according to the name and meaning of
the hexagram, then the subject of the second will be an able
minister or a skilful officer, and the result of their mutual
action will be most beneficial and successful. It is specially
important to have a clear idea of the name of the hexagram, and of the subject or state which it is intended
to denote. The significance of all the lines comes thus
to be of various application, and will differ in different
hexagrams.

I have thus endeavoured to indicate how the lineal figures were formed, and the principal rules laid down for the interpretation of them. The details are wearying, but my position is like that of one who is called on to explain an important monument of architecture, very bizarre in its conception and execution. A plainer, simpler structure might have answered the purpose better, but the architect had his reasons for the plan and style which he adopted. If the result of his labours be worth expounding, we must not grudge the study necessary to detect his processes of thought, nor the effort and time required to bring the minds of others into sympathy with his.

My own opinion, as I have intimated, is, that the second account of the origin of the trigrams and hexagrams is the true one. However the idea of the whole and divided lines arose in the mind of the first framer, we must start from them ; and then, manipulating them in the manner described, we arrive, very easily, at all the lineal figures, and might proceed to multiply them to billions. We cannot tell who devised the third account of their formation from the map or scheme on the dragon-horse of the Yellow River[1]. Its object, no doubt, was to impart a supernatural character to the trigrams and produce a religious veneration for them. It may be doubted whether the scheme as it is now fashioned be the correct one,—such as it was in the *K*âu dynasty. The paragraph where it is mentioned, goes on to say—'The Lo produced the writing.' This writing was a scheme of the same character as the Ho map, but on the back of a tortoise, which emerged from the river Lo, and showed it to the Great Yü, when he was engaged in his celebrated work of draining off the waters of the flood, as related in the Shû. To the hero sage it suggested 'the Great Plan,' an interesting but mystical document of the same classic, 'a Treatise,' according to Gaubil, 'of Physics, Astrology, Divination, Morals, Politics, and Religion,' the great model for the government of the

---

[1] Certainly it was not Confucius. See on the authorship of the Appendixes, and especially of Appendix III, in the next chapter.

kingdom. The accepted representation of this writing is the following :—

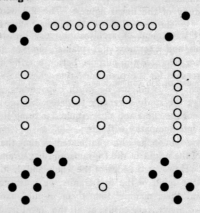

But substituting numbers for the number of marks, we have

$$4 \quad 9 \quad 2$$

$$3 \quad 5 \quad 7$$

$$8 \quad 1 \quad 6$$

This is nothing but the arithmetical puzzle, in which the numbers from 1 to 9 are arranged so as to make 15 in whatever way we add them[1]. If we had the original form of 'the River Map,' we should probably find it a numerical trifle, not more difficult, not more supernatural, than this magic square.

3. Let us return to the Yî of *K*âu, which, as I have said above on p. 10, contains, under each of the 64 hexagrams, a brief essay of a moral, social, or political character, symbolically expressed.

---

[1] For this dissection, which may also be called reductio ad absurdum, of the Lo writing, I was indebted first to P. Regis. See his Y-King I, p. 60. But *K*û Hsî also has got it in the Appendix to his 'Lessons on the Yî for the Young.'

To understand it, it will be necessary to keep in mind the circumstances in which king Wăn addressed himself to the study of the lineal figures. The kingdom, under the sovereigns of the Yin or Shang dynasty, was utterly disorganised and demoralised. A brother of the reigning king thus described its condition :—

State of the country in time of king Wăn

'The house of Yin can no longer exercise rule over the land. The great deeds of our founder were displayed in a former age, but through mad addiction to drink we have destroyed the effects of his virtue. The people, small and great, are given to highway robberies, villainies, and treachery. The nobles and officers imitate one another in violating the laws. There is no ce tainty that criminals will be apprehended. The lesser people rise up and commit violent outrages on one another. The dynasty of Yin is sinking in ruin ; its condition is like that of one crossing a large stream, who can find neither ford nor bank [1].'

This miserable state of the nation was due very much to the character and tyranny of the monarch. When the son of Wăn took the field against him, he thus denounced him in 'a Solemn Declaration' addressed to all the states :—

The character of the monarch

'Shâu, the king of Shang, treats all virtue with contemptuous slight, and abandons himself to wild idleness and irreverence. He has cut himself off from Heaven, and brought enmity between himself and the people. He cut through the leg-bones of those who were wading in a (winter-)morning ; he cut out the heart of the good man [2]. His power has been shown in killing and murdering. His honours and confidence are given to the villainous and bad. He has driven from him his instructors and guardians. He has thrown to the winds the statutes and penal laws. He neglects the sacrifices to Heaven and Earth. He has discontinued the offerings

---

[1] The Shû IV, xi, 1, 2.

[2] These were well-known instances of Shâu's wanton cruelty. Observing some people one winter's day wading through a stream, he ordered their legs to be cut through at the shank-bone, that he might see the marrow which could so endure the cold. 'The good man' was a relative of his own, called Pî-kan. Having enraged Shâu by the sternness of his rebukes, the tyrant ordered his heart to be cut out, that he might see the structure of a sage's heart.

in the ancestral temple. He makes (cruel) contrivances of wonderful device and extraordinary ingenuity to please his wife [1].—
God will no longer bear with him, but with a curse is sending down
his ruin [2].'

Such was the condition of the nation, such the character
of the sovereign. Meanwhile in the west of the kingdom,

The lords of Kâu; and especially king Wăn

in a part of what is now the province of Shen-
hsî, lay the principality of Kâu, the lords of
which had long been distinguished for their
ability and virtue. Its present chief, now known to us as
king Wăn, was Khang, who had succeeded to his father
in B.C. 1185. He was not only lord of Kâu, but had come
to be a sort of viceroy over a great part of the kingdom.
Equally distinguished in peace and war, a model of all that
was good and attractive, he conducted himself with remarkable wisdom and self-restraint. Princes and people
would have rejoiced to follow him to attack the tyrant, but
he shrank from exposing himself to the charge of being
disloyal. At last the jealous suspicion of Shâu was aroused.
Wăn, as has been already stated, was thrown into prison in
B.C. 1143, and the order for his death might arrive at any
moment. Then it was that he occupied himself with the
lineal figures.

The use of those figures—of the trigrams at least—had
long been practised for the purposes of divination. The
employment of the divining stalks is indicated in 'the
Counsels of the Great Yü,' one of the earliest Books of
the Shû [3], and a whole section in 'the Great Plan,' also a
Book of the Shû, and referred to the times of the Hsiâ
dynasty, describes how 'doubts were to be examined'
by means of the tortoise-shell and the stalks [4]. Wăn could
not but be familiar with divination as an institution of his

---

[1] We do not know what these contrivances were. But to please his wife,
the infamous Tâ-kî, Shâu had made 'the Heater' and 'the Roaster,' two
instruments of torture. The latter was a copper pillar laid above a pit of
burning charcoal, and made slippery; culprits were forced to walk along it.

[2] The Shû V, i, Sect. iii, 2, 3.

[3] Shû II, ii, 18.

[4] Shû V, iv, 20-31.

country[1]. Possibly it occurred to him that nothing was
King Wăn
in prison,
occupied with
the lineal
figures more likely to lull the suspicions of his
dangerous enemy than the study of the
figures ; and if his keepers took notice of what
he was doing, they would smile at his lines,
and the sentences which he appended to them.

I like to think of the lord of *K*âu, when incarcerated in
Yû-lî, with the 64 figures arranged before him. Each hexagram assumed a mystic meaning, and glowed with a deep
significance. He made it tell him of the qualities of various
objects of nature, or of the principles of human society,
or of the condition, actual and possible, of the kingdom. He
named the figures, each by a term descriptive of the idea
with which he had connected it in his mind, and then he proceeded to set that idea forth, now with a note of exhortation,
now with a note of warning. It was an attempt to restrict
the follies of divination within the bounds of reason. The
last but one of the Appendixes bears the name of ' Sequence
of the Diagrams.' I shall have to speak of it more at
length in the next chapter. I only remark at present that
it deals, feebly indeed, with the names of the hexagrams in
harmony with what I have said about them, and tries to
account for the order in which they follow one another. It
does all this, not critically as if it needed to be established,
but in the way of expository statement, relating that about
which there was no doubt in the mind of the author.

But all the work of prince *Kh*ang or king Wăn in the
Yî thus amounts to no more than 64 short paragraphs.
Work of the
duke of *K*âu
on the separate
lines We do not know what led his son Tan to
enter into his work and complete it as he
did. Tan was a patriot, a hero, a legislator,
and a philosopher. Perhaps he took the lineal figures
in hand as a tribute of filial duty. What had been done
for the whole hexagram he would do for each line, and
make it clear that all the six lines 'bent one way their
precious influence,' and blended their rays in the globe
of light which his father had made each figure give forth.

---

[1] In the Book of Poetry we have Wăn's grandfather (Than-fû, III, i, ode 3. 3)
divining, and his son (king Wû, III, i, ode 10. 7) doing the same.

But his method strikes us as singular. Each line seemed
to become living, and suggested some phenomenon in nature
or some case of human experience, from which the wisdom
or folly, the luckiness or unluckiness, indicated by it could
be inferred. It cannot be said that the duke carried out
his plan in a way likely to interest any one but a hsien
shăng who is a votary of divination, and admires the
style of its oracles. According to our notions, a framer of
emblems should be a good deal of a poet, but those of
the Yî only make us think of a dryasdust. Out of more
than 350, the greater number are only grotesque. We do
not recover from the feeling of disappointment till we
remember that both father and son had to write 'according
to the trick,' after the manner of diviners, as if this lineal
augury had been their profession.

4. At length I come to illustrate what I have said on the
subject-matter of the Yî by an example. It shall be the

The seventh hexagram   treatment of the seventh hexagram (☵☷),
which king Wăn named S z e, meaning Hosts.
The character is also explained as meaning 'multitudes;'
and in fact, in a feudal kingdom, the multitudes of the
people were all liable to become its army, when occasion
required, and the 'host' and the 'population' might be
interchangeable terms. As Froude expresses it in the
introductory chapter to his History of England, 'Every man
was regimented somewhere.'

The hexagram S z e is composed of the two trigrams
Khan (☵) and Khwăn (☷), exhibiting waters
collected on the earth; and in other symbolisms besides
that of the Yî, waters indicate assembled multitudes of
men. The waters on which the mystical Babylon sits in
the Apocalypse are explained as 'peoples and multitudes
and nations and tongues.' I do not positively affirm
that it was by this interpretation of the trigrams that
king Wăn saw in ☵☷ the feudal hosts of his country
collected, for neither from him nor his son do we learn, by
their direct affirmation, that they had any acquaintance
with the trigrams of Fû-hsî. The name which he gave

the figure shows, however, that he saw in it the feudal hosts in the field. How shall their expedition be conducted that it may come to a successful issue?

Looking again at the figure, we see that it is made up of five divided lines, and of one undivided. The undivided line occupies the central place in the lower trigram,—the most important place, next to the fifth, in the whole hexagram. It will represent, in the language of the commentators, 'the lord of the whole figure;' and the parties represented by the other lines may be expected to be of one mind with him or obedient to him. He must be the leader of the hosts. If he were on high, in the fifth place, he would be the sovereign of the kingdom. This is what king Wăn says:—

'Sze indicates how (in the case which it supposes), with firmness and correctness, and (a leader of) age and experience, there will be good fortune and no error.'

This is a good auspice. Let us see how the duke of Kâu expands it.

He says:—

'The first line, divided, shows the host going forth according to the rules (for such a movement). If those (rules) be not good, there will be evil.'

We are not told what the rules for a military expedition were. Some commentators understand them of the reasons justifying the movement,—that it should be to repress and punish disorder and rebellion. Others, with more likelihood, take them to be the discipline or rules laid down to be observed by the troops. The line is divided, a weak line in a strong place, 'not correct:' this justifies the caution given in the duke's second sentence.

The Text goes on :—

'The second line, undivided, shows (the leader) in the midst of the hosts. There will be good fortune and no error. The king has thrice conveyed to him his charge.'

This does not need any amplification. The duke saw in the strong line the symbol of the leader, who enjoyed the full confidence of his sovereign, and whose authority admitted of no opposition.

On the third line it is said :—

'The third line, divided, shows how the hosts may possibly have many commanders :—(in such a case) there will be evil.'

The third place is odd, and should be occupied by a strong line, instead of which we have a weak line in it. But it is at the top of the lower trigram, and its subject should be in office or activity. There is suggested the idea that its subject has vaulted over the second line, and wishes to share in the command and honour of him who has been appointed sole commander-in-chief. The lesson in the previous line is made of none effect. We have a divided authority in the expedition. The result can only be evil.

On the fourth line the duke wrote :—

'The fourth line, divided, shows the hosts in retreat : there is no error.'

The line is also weak, and victory cannot be expected ; but in the fourth place a weak line is in its correct position, and its subject will do what is right in his circumstances. He will retreat, and a retreat is for him the part of wisdom. When safely affected, where advance would be disastrous, a retreat is as glorious as victory.

Under the fifth line we read :—

'The fifth line, divided, shows birds in the fields which it is advantageous to seize (and destroy). There will be no error. If the oldest son lead the host, and younger men be (also) in command, however firm and correct he may be, there will be evil.'

We have an intimation in this passage that only defensive war, or war waged by the rightful authority to put down rebellion and lawlessness, is right. The 'birds in the fields' are emblematic of plunderers and invaders, whom it will be well to destroy. The fifth line symbolises the chief authority, but here he is weak or humble, and has given all power and authority to execute judgment into the hands of the commander-in-chief, who is the oldest son ; and in the subject of line 3 we have an example of the younger men who would cause evil if allowed to share his power.

Finally, on the sixth line the duke wrote:—

'The topmost line, divided, shows the great ruler delivering his charges (to the men who have distinguished themselves), appointing some to be rulers of states, and others to be chiefs of clans. But small men should not be employed (in such positions).'

The action of the hexagram has been gone through. The expedition has been conducted to a successful end. The enemy has been subdued. His territories are at the disposal of the conqueror. The commander-in-chief has done his part well. His sovereign, 'the great ruler,' comes upon the scene, and rewards the officers who have been conspicuous by their bravery and skill, conferring on them rank and lands. But he is warned to have respect in doing so to their moral character. Small men, of ordinary or less than ordinary character, may be rewarded with riches and certain honours; but land and the welfare of its population should not be given into the hands of any who are not equal to the responsibility of such a trust.

The above is a specimen of what I have called the essays that make up the Yî of Kâu. So would king Wăn and his son have had all military expeditions conducted in their country 3000 years ago. It seems to me that the principles which they lay down might find a suitable application in the modern warfare of our civilised and Christian Europe. The inculcation of such lessons cannot have been without good effect in China during the long course of its history.

Sze is a fair specimen of its class. From the other 63 hexagrams lessons are deduced, for the most part equally good and striking. But why, it may be asked, why should they be conveyed to us by such an array of lineal figures, and in such a farrago of emblematic representations? It is not for the foreigner to insist on such a question. The Chinese have not valued them the less because of the antiquated dress in which their lessons are arrayed. Hundreds of their commentators have evolved and developed their meaning with a minuteness of detail and felicity of illustration that leave nothing to be desired. It is for foreign students of Chinese to gird up their loins for the mastery of the book instead of talking about it as mysterious and all but inexplicable.

Granting, however, that the subject-matter of the Yî is what has been described, very valuable for its practical wisdom, but not drawn up from an abysmal deep of philosophical speculation, it may still be urged, 'But in all this we find nothing to justify the name of the book as Yî King, the "Classic of Changes." Is there not something more, higher or deeper, in the Appendixes that have been ascribed to Confucius, whose authority is certainly not inferior to that of king Wăn, or the duke of *K*âu?' To reply fully to this question will require another chapter.

CHAPTER III

THE APPENDIXES

1. Two things have to be considered in this chapter:—the authorship of the Appendixes, and their contents. The

Subjects of the chapter

Text is ascribed, without dissentient voice, to king Wăn, the founder of the *K*âu dynasty, and his son Tan, better known as the duke of *K*âu; and I have, in the preceding chapters, given reasons for accepting that view. As regards the portion ascribed to king Wăn, the evidence of the third of the Appendixes and the statement of Sze-mâ *K*hien are as positive as could be desired; and as regards that ascribed to his son, there is no ground for calling in question the received tradition. The Appendixes have all been ascribed to Confucius, though not with entirely the same unanimity. Perhaps I have rather intimated my own opinion that this view cannot be sustained. I have pointed out that, even if it be true, between six and seven centuries elapsed after the Text of the classic appeared before the Appendixes were written; and I have said that, considering this fact, I cannot regard its two parts as a homogeneous whole, or as constituting one book in the ordinary acceptation of that name. Before entering on the question of the authorship, a very brief statement of the nature and number of the Appendixes will be advantageous.

2. They are reckoned to be ten, and called the Shih Yî or 'Ten Wings.' They are in reality not so many; but the

Number and nature of the Appendixes

Text is divided into two sections, called the Upper and Lower, or, as we should say, the first and second, and then the commentary on each section is made to form a separate Appendix. I have found it more convenient in the translation which follows to adopt a somewhat different arrangement.

My first Appendix, in two sections, embraces the first and second 'wings,' consisting of remarks on the paragraphs by king Wăn in the two parts of the Text.

My second Appendix, in two sections, embraces the third and fourth 'wings,' consisting of remarks on the symbolism of the duke of *K*âu in his explanation of the individual lines of the hexagrams.

My third Appendix, in two sections, embraces the fifth and sixth 'wings,' which bear the name in Chinese of 'Appended Sentences,' and constitute what is called by many 'the Great Treatise.' Each wing has been divided into twelve chapters of very different length, and I have followed this arrangement in my sections. This is the most important Appendix. It has less of the nature of commentary than the previous four wings. While explaining much of what is found in the Text, it diverges to the origin of the trigrams, the methods pursued in the practice of divination, the rise of many arts in the progress of civilisation, and other subjects.

My fourth Appendix, also in two sections, forms the seventh 'wing.' It is confined to an amplification of the expositions of the first and second hexagrams by king Wăn and his son, purporting to show how they may be interpreted of man's nature and doings.

My fifth Appendix is the eighth 'wing,' called 'Discourses on the Trigrams.' It treats of the different arrangement of these in respect of the seasons of the year and the cardinal points by Fû-hsî and king Wăn. It contains also one paragraph, which might seem to justify the view that there is a mythology in the Yî.

My sixth Appendix, in two sections, is the ninth 'wing,'—

'a Treatise on the Sequence of the Hexagrams,' intended to trace the connexion of meaning between them in the order in which they follow one another in the Text of king Wăn.

My seventh Appendix is the tenth 'wing,' an exhibition of the meaning of the 64 hexagrams, not taken in succession, but promiscuously and at random, as they approximate to or are opposed to one another in meaning.

3. Such are the Appendixes of the Yî King. We have

The authorship of the Appendixes

to enquire next who wrote them, and especially whether it be possible to accept the dictum that they were all written by Confucius. If they have come down to us, bearing unmistakeably the stamp of the mind and pencil of the great sage, we cannot but receive them with deference, not to say with reverence. If, on the contrary, it shall appear that with great part of them he had nothing to do, and that it is not certain that any part of them is from him, we shall feel entirely at liberty to exercise our own judgment on their contents, and weigh them in the balances of our reason.

None of the Appendixes, it is to be observed, bear the

There is no superscription of Confucius on any of the Appendixes

superscription of Confucius. There is not a single sentence in any one of them ascribing it to him. I gave in the first chapter, on p. 2, the earliest testimony that these treatises were produced by him. It is that of Sze-mâ *Kh*ien, whose 'Historical Records' must have appeared about the year 100 before our era. He ascribes all the Appendixes, except the last two of them, which he does not mention at all, expressly to Confucius; and this, no doubt, was the common belief in the fourth century after the sage's death.

But when we look for ourselves into the third and fourth Appendixes—the fifth, sixth, and seventh 'wings'—both

The third and fourth Appendixes evidently not from Confucius

of which are specified by *Kh*ien, we find it impossible to receive his statement about them. What is remarkable in both parts of the third is, the frequent occurrence of the formula, 'The Master said,' familiar to all readers of the Confucian Analects. Of course, the sentence following that formula, or the paragraph covered by it, was, in the judgment of the writer, in the language of Confucius; but what shall we say of the portions preceding and following? If he were the author of them, he would not thus be distinguishing himself from himself. The formula occurs in the third Appendix at least twenty-three times. Where we first meet with it, Kû Hsî has a note to the effect that 'the Appendixes having been all made by Confucius, he ought not to be himself introducing the formula, "The Master said;" and that it may be presumed, wherever it occurs, that it is a subsequent addition to the Master's text.' One instance will show the futility of this attempt to solve the difficulty. The tenth chapter of Section i commences with the 59th paragraph:—

'In the Yî there are four things characteristic of the way of the sages. We should set the highest value on its explanations, to guide us in speaking; on its changes, for the initiation of our movements; on its emblematic figures, for definite action, as in the construction of implements; and on its prognostications, for our practice of divination.'

This is followed by seven paragraphs expanding its statements, and we come to the last one of the chapter which says,—'The Master said, "Such is the import of the statement that there are four things in the Yî, characteristic of the way of the sages."' I cannot understand how it could be more fully conveyed to us that the compiler or compilers of this Appendix were distinct from the Master whose words they quoted, as it suited them, to confirm or illustrate their views.

In the fourth Appendix, again, we find a similar occurrence of the formula of quotation. It is much shorter than the third, and the phrase, 'The Master said,' does not come before us so frequently; but in the thirty-six paragraphs that compose the first section we meet with it six times.

Moreover, the first three paragraphs of this Appendix are older than its compilation, which could not have taken place till after the death of Confucius, seeing it professes to quote his words. They are taken in fact from a narrative of the 3o Kwan, as having been spoken by a marchioness-dowager of Lû fourteen years before Confucius was born. To account for this is a difficult task for the orthodox critics among the Chinese literati. *K*û Hsî attempts to perform it in this way:—that anciently there was the explanation given in these paragraphs of the four adjectives employed by king Wăn to give the significance of the first hexagram; that it was employed by Mû *K*iang of Lû; and that Confucius also availed himself of it, while the chronicler used, as he does below, the phraseology of 'The Master said,' to distinguish the real words of the sage from such ancient sayings. But who was 'the chronicler?' No one can tell. The legitimate conclusion from *K*û's criticism is, that so much of the Appendix as is preceded by 'The Master said' is from Confucius,—so much and no more. I am thus obliged to come to the conclusion that Confucius had nothing to do with the composition of these two Appendixes, and that they were not put together till after his death. I have no pleasure in differing from the all but unanimous opinion of Chinese critics and commentators. What is called 'the destructive criticism' has no attractions for me; but when an opinion depends on the argument adduced to support it, and that argument turns out to be of no weight, you can no longer set your seal to this, that the opinion is true. This is the position in which an examination of the internal evidence as to the authorship of the third and fourth Appendixes has placed me. Confucius could not be their author. This conclusion weakens the

Bearing of the conclusion as to the third and fourth on the other Appendixes

confidence which we have been accustomed to place in the view that 'the ten wings' were to be ascribed to him unhesitatingly. The view has broken down in the case of three of them;—possibly there is no sound reason for holding the Confucian origin of the other seven.

I cannot henceforth maintain that origin save with bated breath. This, however, can be said for the first two Appendixes in my arrangement, that there is no evidence against their being Confucian like the fatal formula, 'The Master said.' So it is with a good part of my fifth Appendix; but the concluding paragraphs of it, as well as the seventh

Appendix, and the sixth also in a less degree, seem too trivial to be the production of the great man. As a translator of every sentence both in the Text and the Appendixes, I confess my sympathy with P. Regis, when he condenses the fifth Appendix into small space, holding that the 8th and following paragraphs are not worthy to be translated. 'They contain,' he says, 'nothing but the mere enumeration of things, some of which may be called Yang, and others Yin, without any other cause for so thinking being given. Such a method of procedure would be unbecoming any philosopher, and it cannot be denied to be unworthy of Confucius, the chief of philosophers [1].'

I could not characterise Confucius as 'the chief of philosophers,' though he was a great moral philosopher, and has been since he went out and in among his disciples, the best teacher of the Chinese nation. But from the first time my attention was directed to the Yî, I regretted that he had stooped to write the parts of the Appendixes now under remark. It is a relief not to be obliged to receive them as his. Even the better treatises have no other claim to that character besides the voice of tradition, first heard nearly 400 years after his death.

4. I return to the Appendixes, and will endeavour to give a brief, but sufficient, account of their contents.

The first bears in Chinese the name of Thwan *K*wan, 'Treatise on the Thwan,' thwan being the name given

The first Appendix

to the paragraphs in which Wăn expresses his sense of the significance of the hexagrams. He does not tell us why he attaches to each hexagram such and such a meaning, nor why he predicates good fortune or bad fortune in connexion with it, for he speaks oracularly, after the manner of a diviner. It is the object of the writer of this Appendix to show the processes of king Wăn's thoughts in these operations, how he looked at the component trigrams with their symbolic intimations, their attributes and qualities, and their linear composition, till he could not think otherwise of the figures than he did. All these considerations are sometimes taken into account,

---

[1] Regis' Y-King. vol. ii, p. 576.

and sometimes even one of them is deemed sufficient. In this way some technical characters appear which are not found in the Text. The lines, for instance, and even whole trigrams are distinguished as kang and ɀâu, 'hard or strong' and 'weak or soft.' The phrase Kwei-shăn, 'spirits,' or 'spiritual beings,' occurs, but has not its physical signification of 'the contracting and expanding energies or operations of nature.' The names Yin and Yang, mentioned above on pp. 15, 16, do not present themselves.

I delineated, on p. 11, the eight trigrams of Fû-hsî, and gave their names, with the natural objects they are said to represent, but did not mention the attributes, the virtutes, ascribed to them. Let me submit here a table of them, with those qualities, and the points of the compass to which they are referred. I must do this because king Wăn made a change in the geographical arrangement of them, to which reference is made perhaps in his text and certainly in this treatise. He also is said to have formed an entirely different theory as to the things represented by the trigrams, which it will be well to give now, though it belongs properly to the fifth Appendix.

FÛ-HSÎ'S TRIGRAMS

1	2	3	4	5	6	7	8
khien	*tui*	*lî*	*kăn*	*sun*	*khân*	*kăn*	*khwăn*
Heaven, the sky.	Water, collected as in a marsh or lake.	Fire, as in lightning; the sun.	Thunder.	The wind; wood.	Water, as in rain, clouds, springs, streams, and defiles. The moon.	Hills, or mountains.	The earth.
S.	S.E.	E.	N.E.	S.W.	W.	N.W.	N.
Untiring strength; power.	Pleasure; complacent satisfaction.	Brightness; elegance.	Moving, exciting power.	Flexibility; penetration.	Peril; difficulty.	Resting; the act of arresting.	Capaciousness; submission.

The natural objects and phenomena thus represented are found up and down in the Appendixes. It is impossible to believe that the several objects were assigned to the several figures on any principles of science, for there is no indication of science in the matter: it is difficult even to suppose that they were assigned on any comprehensive scheme of thought. Why are tui and khân used to represent water in different conditions, while khân, moreover, represents the moon? How is sun set apart to represent things so different as wind and wood? At a very early time the Chinese spoke of 'the five elements,' meaning water, fire, wood, metal, and earth; but the trigrams were not made to indicate them, and it is the general opinion that there is no reference to them in the Yî [1].

Again, the attributes assigned to the trigrams are learned mainly from this Appendix and the fifth. We do not readily get familiar with them, nor easily accept them all. It is impossible for us to tell whether they were a part of the jargon of divination before king Wăn, or had grown up between his time and that of the author of the Appendixes.

King Wăn altered the arrangement of the trigrams so that not one of them should stand at the same point of the compass as in the ancient plan. He made them also representative of certain relations among themselves, as if they composed a family of parents and children. It will be sufficient at present to give a table of his scheme.

KING WĂN'S TRIGRAMS

1	2	3	4	5	6	7	8
lî	sun	kăn	kăn	khân	khien	tui	khwăn
Second daughter.	Oldest daughter.	Oldest son.	Youngest son.	Second son.	Father.	Youngest daughter.	Mother.
S.	S.E.	E.	N.E.	N.	N.W.	W.	S.W.

[1] See Kâo Yî's Hâi Yü Zhung Khâo, Book I, art. 3 (1790).

[16]

There is thus before us the apparatus with which the writer of the Appendix accomplishes his task. Let me select one of the shortest instances of his work. The fourteenth hexagram is ≣≣, called Tâ Yû, and meaning 'Possessing in great abundance.' King Wăn saw in it the symbol of a government prosperous and realising all its proper objects; but all that he wrote on it was 'Tâ Yû (indicates) great progress and success.' Unfolding that view of its significance, the Appendix says :—

'In Tâ Yû the weak (line) has the place of honour, is grandly central, and (the strong lines) above and below respond to it. Hence comes its name of "Possession of what is great." The attributes (of its constituent trigrams, *kh*ien and lî) are strength and vigour, elegance and brightness. (The ruling line in it) responds to (the ruling line in the symbol of) heaven, and its actings are (consequently all) at the proper times. Thus it is that it is said to indicate great progress and success.'

In a similar way the paragraphs on all the other 63 hexagrams are gone through ; and, for the most part, with success. The conviction grows upon the student that the writer has on the whole apprehended the mind of king Wăn.

I stated, on p. 32, that the name kwei-shăn occurs in this Appendix. It has not yet, however, received the semi-physical, semi-metaphysical signification which the comparatively modern scholars of the Sung dynasty give to it. There are two passages where it is found ;—the second paragraph on *Kh*ien, the fifteenth hexagram, and the third on Făng, the fifty-fifth. By consulting them the reader will be able to form an opinion for himself. The term kwei denotes specially the human spirit disembodied, and shăn is used for spirits whose seat is in heaven. I do not see my way to translate them, when used binomially together, otherwise than by spiritual beings or spiritual agents.

*K*û Hsî once had the following question suggested by the second of these passages put to him :—'Kwei-shăn is a name for the traces of making and transformation ; but when it is said that (the interaction of) heaven and earth is now vigorous and abundant, and now dull and void, growing and diminishing according to the seasons, that constitutes the traces of making and transformation; why should the writer further speak of the Kwei-shǎn?' He replied, 'When he uses the style of "heaven and earth," he is speaking of the result generally; but in ascribing it to the Kwei-shǎn, he is representing the traces of their effective interaction, as if there were men (that is, some personal agency) bringing it about[1].' This solution merely explains the language away. When we come to the fifth Appendix, we shall understand better the views of the period when these treatises were produced.

The single character shǎn is used in explaining the thwan on Kwân, the twentieth hexagram, where we read :—

'In Kwân we see the spirit-like way of heaven, through which the four seasons proceed without error. The sages, in accordance with (this) spirit-like way, laid down their instructions, and all under heaven yield submission to them.'

The author of the Appendix delights to dwell on the changing phenomena taking place between heaven and earth, and which he attributes to their interaction; and he was penetrated evidently with a sense of the harmony between the natural and spiritual worlds. It is this sense, indeed, which vivifies both the thwan and the explanation of them.

5. We proceed to the second Appendix, which professes to do for the duke of Kâu's symbolical exposition of the several lines what the Thwan Kwan does for the entire

The second Appendix

figures. The work here, however, is accomplished with less trouble and more briefly. The whole bears the name of Hsiang Kwan, 'Treatise on the Symbols' or 'Treatise on the Symbolism (of the Yî).'

---

[1] See the 'Collected Comments' on hexagram 55 in the Khang-hsî edition of the Yî (App. I). 'The traces of making and transformation' mean the ever-changing phenomena of growth and decay. Our phrase 'Vestiges of Creation' might be used to translate the Chinese characters. See the remarks of the late Dr. Medhurst on the hexagrams 15 and 55 in his 'Dissertation on the Theology of the Chinese,' pp. 107–112. In hexagram 15, Canon McClatchie for kwei-shǎn gives 'gods and demons;' in hexagram 55, 'the Demon-gods.'

If there were reason to think that it came in any way from
Confucius, I should fancy that I saw him sitting with a
select class of his disciples around him. They read the
duke's Text column after column, and the master drops now
a word or two, and now a sentence or two, that illuminate
the meaning. The disciples take notes on their tablets, or
store his remarks in their memories, and by and by they
write them out with the whole of the Text or only so much
of it as is necessary. Whoever was the original lecturer,
the Appendix, I think, must have grown up in this way.

It would not be necessary to speak of it at greater length,
if it were not that the six paragraphs on the symbols of
the duke of Kâu are always preceded by one which is
called 'the Great Symbolism,' and treats of the trigrams
composing the hexagram, how they go together to form
the six-lined figure, and how their blended meaning
appears in the institutions and proceedings of the great
men and kings of former days, and of the superior men
of all time. The paragraph is for the most part, but by no
means always, in harmony with the explanation of the
hexagram by king Wăn, and a place in the Thwan Kwan
would be more appropriate to it. I suppose that, because
it always begins with the mention of the two symbolical
trigrams, it is made, for the sake of the symmetry, to form
a part of the treatise on the Symbolism of the Yî.

I will give a few examples of the paragraphs of the
Great Symbolism. The first hexagram ☰☰ is formed

The Great
Symbolism
by a repetition of the trigram Khien ☰,
representing heaven, and it is said on it:—
'Heaven in its motion (gives) the idea of strength. The
superior man, in accordance with this, nerves himself to
ceaseless activity.'

The second hexagram ☷☷ is formed by a repetition
of the trigram Khwăn ☷ ☷, representing the earth, and
it is said on it:—'The capacious receptivity of the earth
is what is denoted by Khwăn. The superior man, in
accordance with this, with his large virtue, supports men
and things.'

The forty-fourth hexagram, called Kâu ䷫, is formed by the trigrams Sun ☴, representing wind, and Khien ☰, representing heaven or the sky, and it is said on it:—'(The symbol of) wind, beneath that of the sky, forms Kâu. In accordance with this, the sovereign distributes his charges, and promulgates his announcements throughout the four quarters (of the kingdom).'

The fifty-ninth hexagram, called Hwân ䷺, is formed by the trigrams Khân ☵, representing water, and Sun ☴, representing wind, and it is said on it:—'(The symbol of) water and (that of wind) above it form Hwân. The ancient kings, in accordance with this, presented offerings to God, and established the ancestral temple.' The union of the two trigrams suggested to king Wăn the idea of dissipation in the alienation of men from the Supreme Power, and of the minds of parents from their children; a condition which the wisdom of the ancient kings saw could best be met by the influences of religion.

One more example. The twenty-sixth hexagram, called Tâ Khû ䷙, is formed of the trigrams Khien, representing heaven or the sky, and Kân ☶, representing a mountain, and it is said on it:—'(The symbol of) heaven in the midst of a mountain forms Tâ Khû. The superior man, in accordance with this, stores largely in his memory the words of former men and their conduct, to subserve the accumulation of his virtue.' We are ready to exclaim and ask, 'Heaven, the sky, in the midst of a mountain! Can there be such a thing?' and Kû Hsî will tell us in reply, 'No, there cannot be such a thing in reality; but you can conceive it for the purpose of the symbolism.'

From this and the other examples adduced from the Great Symbolism, it is clear that, so far as its testimony bears on the subject, the trigrams of Fû-hsî did not receive their form and meaning with a deep intention that they should serve as the basis of a philosophical scheme concerning the constitution of heaven and earth and all that

is in them.   In this Appendix they are used popularly, just
as one

> 'Finds tongues in trees, books in the running brooks,
>   Sermons in stones, and good in everything.'

The writer moralises from them in an edifying manner.
There is ingenuity, and sometimes instruction also, in what
he says, but there is no mystery.   Chinese scholars and
gentlemen, however, who have got some little acquaintance
with western science, are fond of saying that all the truths
of electricity, heat, light, and other branches of European
physics, are in the eight trigrams.   When asked how then
they and their countrymen have been and are ignorant of
those truths, they say that they have to learn them first
from western books, and then, looking into the Yî, they see
that they were all known to Confucius more than 2000 years
ago.   The vain assumption thus manifested is childish;
and until the Chinese drop their hallucination about the
Yî as containing all things that have ever been dreamt of
in all philosophies, it will prove a stumbling-block to them,
and keep them from entering on the true path of science.

6. We go on to the third Appendix in two sections, being
the fifth and sixth 'wings,' and forming what is called 'The
Great Treatise.'   It will appear singular to the
reader, as it has always done to myself, that
neither in the Text, nor in the first two Appendixes, does
the character called Yî, which gives its name to the classic,
once appear.   It is the symbol of 'change,' and is formed
from the character for 'the sun' placed over that for 'the
moon[1].'   As the sun gives place to the moon, and the
moon to the sun, so is change always proceeding in the
phenomena of nature and the experiences of society.   We
meet with the character nearly fifty times in this Appendix;
—applied most commonly to the Text of our classic, so that
Yî King or Yî Shû is 'the Classic or Book of Changes.'
It is also applied often to the changes in the lines of the

The third
Appendix

---

[1] 易 = 日, the sun, placed over 勿, a form of the old 𝔇 (= 月), the
moon.

figures, made by the manipulations of divination, apart
from any sentence or oracle concerning them delivered
by king Wăn or his son. There is therefore the system
of the Yî as well as the book of the Yî. The definition
of the name which is given in one paragraph will suit them
both :—' Production and reproduction is what is called (the
process of) change[1].' In nature there is no vacuum. When
anything is displaced, what displaces it takes the empty
room. And in the lineal figures, the strong and the weak
lines push each other out.

Now the remarkable thing asserted is, that the
changes in the lines of the figures and
the changes of external phenomena show
a wonderful harmony and concurrence. We
read :—

Harmony between the lines ever changing and the changes in external phenomena

' The Yî was made on a principle of accordance with heaven
and earth, and shows us therefore, without rent or confusion, the
course (of things) in heaven and earth [2].'

' There is a similarity between the sage and heaven and earth ;
and hence there is no contrariety in him to them. His knowledge
embraces all things, and his course is intended to be helpful to
all under the sky ; and therefore he falls into no error. He acts
according to the exigency of circumstances, without being carried
away by their current ; he rejoices in Heaven, and knows its ordinations ; and hence he has no anxieties. He rests in his own
(present) position, and cherishes the spirit of generous benevolence ;
and hence he can love (without reserve)[3].'

' (Through the Yî) he embraces, as in a mould or enclosure, the
transformations of heaven and earth without any error ; by an ever-
varying adaptation he completes (the nature of) all things without
exception ; he penetrates to a knowledge of the course of day and
night (and all other correlated phenomena). It is thus that his
operation is spirit-like, unconditioned by place, while the changes
(which he produces) are not restricted to any form.'

One more quotation :—

' The sage was able to survey all the complex phenomena under
the sky. He then considered in his mind how they could be

----

[1] III, i, 29 (chap. 5. 6).   [2] III, i, 20 (chap. 4. 1).
[3] III, i, 22.

figured, and (by means of the diagrams) represented their material forms and their character ¹.'

All that is thus predicated of the sage, or ancient sages, though the writer probably had Fû-hsî in his mind, is more than sufficiently extravagant, and reminds us of the language in 'the Doctrine of the Mean,' that 'the sage, able to assist the transforming and nourishing powers of heaven and earth, may with heaven and earth form a ternion ².'

I quoted largely, in the second chapter, from this Appendix the accounts which it gives of the formation of the lineal figures. There is no occasion to return to that subject. Let us suppose the figures formed. They seem to have

Divination
the significance, when looked at from certain points of view, which have been determined for us by king Wăn and the duke of *K*âu. But this does not amount to divination. How can the lines be made to serve this purpose? The Appendix professes to tell us.

Before touching on the method which it describes, let me observe that divination was practised in China from

Ancient divination
a very early time. I will not say 5,200 years ago, in the days of Fû-hsî, for I cannot repress doubts of his historical personality; but as soon as we tread the borders of something like credible history, we find it existing. In the Shû King, in a document that purports to be of the twenty-third century B.C.³, divination by means of the tortoise-shell is mentioned; and somewhat later we find that method continuing, and also divination by the lineal figures, manipulated by means of the stalks of a plant ⁴, the Ptarmica Sibirica ⁵, which is still cultivated on and about the grave of Confucius, where I have myself seen it growing.

The object of the divination, it should be acknowledged,

Object of the divination
was not to discover future events absolutely, as if they could be known beforehand ⁶, but

---

¹ III, i, 38 (chap. 8. 1).   ² Doctrine of the Mean, chap. xxii.
³ The Shû II, ii, 18.   ⁴ The Shû V, iv, 20, 31.
⁵ See Williams' Syllabic Dictionary on the character 蓍.

⁶ Canon McClatchie (first paragraph of his Introduction) says:—' The Yî is regarded by the Chinese with peculiar veneration .... as containing a mine of

to ascertain whether certain schemes, and conditions of events contemplated by the consulter, would turn out luckily or unluckily. But for the actual practice the stalks of the plant were necessary; and I am almost afraid to write that this Appendix teaches that they were produced by Heaven of such a nature as to be fit for the purpose. 'Heaven,' it says, in the 73rd paragraph of Section i, quoted above on p. 14, 'Heaven produced the spirit-like things.' The things were the tortoise and the plant, and in paragraph 68, the same quality of being shăn, or 'spirit-like,' is ascribed to them. Occasionally, in the field of Chinese literature, we meet with doubts as to the efficacy of divination, and the folly of expecting any revelation of the character of the future from an old tortoise-shell and a handful of withered twigs [1]; but when this Appendix was made, the writer had not attained to so much common sense. The stalks were to him 'spirit-like,' possessed of

---

knowledge, which, if it were possible to fathom it thoroughly, would, in their estimation, enable the fortunate possessor to foretell all future events.' This misstatement does not surprise me so much as that Morrison, generally accurate on such points, should say (Dictionary, Part II, i, p. 1020, on the character 易):—

' Of the odd and even numbers, the kwâ or lines of Fû-hsî are the visible signs; and it being assumed that these signs answer to the things signified, and from a knowledge of all the various combinations of numbers, a knowledge of all possible occurrences in nature may be previously known.' The whole article from which I take this sentence is inaccurately written. The language of the Appendix on the knowledge of the future given by the use of the Yî is often incautious, and a cursory reader may be misled; to a careful student, however, the meaning is plain. The second passage of the Shû, referred to above, treats of 'the Examination of Doubts,' and concludes thus:—' When the tortoise-shell and the stalks are both opposed to the views of men, there will be good fortune in stillness, and active operations will be unlucky.'

[1] A remarkable instance is given by Liû Kî (of the Ming dynasty, in the fifteenth century) in a story about Shâo Phing, who had been marquis of Tungling in the time of Zhin, but was degraded under Han. Having gone once to Sze-mâ Ki-kû, one of the most skilful diviners of the country, and wishing to know whether there would be a brighter future for him, Sze-mâ said, 'Ah! is it the way of Heaven to love any (partially)? Heaven loves only the virtuous. What intelligence is possessed by spirits? They are intelligent (only) by their connexion with men. The divining stalks are so much withered grass; the tortoise-shell is a withered bone. They are but things, and man is more intelligent than things. Why not listen to yourself instead of seeking (to learn) from things?' The whole piece is in many of the collections of Kû Wăn, or Elegant Writing.

a subtle and invisible virtue that fitted them for use in divining.

Given the stalks with such virtue, the process of mani-

Formation of the lineal figures by the divining stalks pulating them so as to form the lineal figures is described (Section i, chap. 9, parr. 49–58), but it will take the student much time and thought to master the various operations. Forty-nine stalks were employed, which were thrice manipulated for each line, so that it took eighteen manipulations to form a hexagram. The lines were determined by means of the numbers derived from the River Map or scheme. Odd numbers gave strong or undivided lines, and even numbers gave the weak or divided. An important part was played in combining the lines, and forming the hexagrams by the four emblematic symbols, to which the numbers 9, 8, 7, 6 were appropriated[1]. The figures having been formed, recourse was had for their interpretation to the thwan of king Wăn, and the emblematic sentences of the duke of Kâu. This was all the part which numbers played in the divination by the Yî, helping the operator to make up his lineal figure. An analogy has often been asserted between the numbers of the Yî and the numbers of Pythagoras; and certainly we might make ten, and more than ten, antinomies from these Appendixes in startling agreement with the ten principia of the Pythagoreans. But if Aristotle was correct in holding that Pythagoras regarded numbers as entities, and maintained that Number was the Beginning (Principle, ἀρχή) of things, the cause of their material existence, and of their

---

[1] These numbers are commonly derived from the River Scheme, in the outer sides of which are the corresponding marks :— ●●●●●, opposite to ●●; ○○○○○○○, opposite to ○; ●●●●●●●●, opposite to ●●●●; and ○○○○○○○○○, opposite to ○○○. Hence the number 6 is assigned to ▬▬ ▬▬, 7 to ▬▬▬▬, 8 to ▬▬▬ ▬▬▬, and 9 to ▬▬▬▬▬▬. Hence also, in connexion with the formation of the figures by manipulation of the stalks, 9 becomes the number symbolical of the undivided line, as representing Khien ▬▬▬▬▬▬, and 6 of the divided line, as representing Khwăn ▬▬ ▬▬ ▬▬ ▬▬. But the late delineation of the map, as given on p. 15, renders all this uncertain, so far as the scheme is concerned. The numbers of the hsiang, however, may have been fixed, must have been fixed indeed, at an early period.

modifications and different states, then the doctrine of the philosopher of Samos was different from that of the Yî[1], in which numbers come in only as aids in divining to form the hexagrams. Of course all divination is vain, nor is the method of the Yî less absurd than any other. The Chinese themselves have given it up in all circles above those of the professional quacks, and yet their scholars continue to maintain the unfathomable science and wisdom of these appended treatises!

It is in this Appendix that we first meet with the names yin and yang[2], of which I have spoken briefly on pp. 15, 16. Up to this point, instead of them, the names for the two elementary forms of the lines have been kang and sâu, which I have translated by 'strong and weak,' and which also occur here ten times. The following attempt to explain these different names appears in the fifth Appendix, paragraph 4 :—

The names Yin and Yang

'Anciently when the sages made the Yî, it was with the design that its figures should be in conformity with the principles underlying the natures (of men and things), and the ordinances appointed (for them by Heaven). With this view they exhibited in them the way of heaven, calling (the lines) yin and yang; the way of earth, calling them the strong (or hard) and the weak (or soft); and the way of man, under the names of benevolence and righteousness. Each (trigram) embraced those three Powers, and being repeated, its full form consisted of six lines.'

However difficult it may be to make what is said here intelligible, it confirms what I have affirmed of the significance of the names yin and yang, as meaning bright and dark, derived from the properties of the sun and moon. We may use for these adjectives a variety of others, such as active and inactive, masculine and feminine, hot and cold, more or less analogous to them; but there arise the important questions,—Do we find yang and yin not merely used to indicate the quality of what they are applied

[1] See the account of Pythagoras and his philosophy in Lewes' History of Philosophy, pp. 18-38 (1871).
[2] See Section i, 24, 32, 35; Section ii, 28, 29, 30, 35.

to, but at the same time with substantival force, denoting
what has the quality which the name denotes? Had the
doctrine of a primary matter of an ethereal nature, now
expanding and showing itself full of activity and power
as yang, now contracting and becoming weak and inactive
as yin:—had this doctrine become matter of speculation
when this Appendix was written? The Chinese critics
and commentators for the most part assume that it had.
P. Regis, Dr. Medhurst, and other foreign Chinese scholars
repeat their statements without question. I have sought
in vain for proof of what is asserted. It took more than
a thousand years after the closing of the Yî to fashion in
the Confucian school the doctrine of a primary matter. We
do not find it fully developed till the era of the Sung
dynasty, and in our eleventh and twelfth centuries[1]. To
find it in the Yî is the logical, or rather illogical, error of
putting 'the last first.' Neither creation nor cosmogony
was before the mind of the author whose work I am
analysing. His theme is the Yî,—the ever-changing phenomena of nature and experience. There is nothing but
this in the 'Great Treatise' to task our powers;—nothing
deeper or more abstruse.

---

[1] As a specimen of what the ablest Sung scholars teach, I may give the
remarks (from the 'Collected Comments') of Kû Kän (of the same century as
Kû Hsî, rather earlier) on the 4th paragraph of Appendix V:—' In the Yî there
is the Great Extreme. When we speak of the yin and yang, we mean the air
(or ether) collected in the Great Void. When we speak of the Hard and Soft,
we mean that ether collected, and formed into substance. Benevolence and
righteousness have their origin in the great void, are seen in the ether sub-
stantiated, and move under the influence of conscious intelligence. Looking at
the one origin of all things we speak of their nature ; looking at the endowments
given to them, we speak of the ordinations appointed (for them). Looking at
them as (divided into) heaven, earth, and men, we speak of their principle.
The three are one and the same. The sages wishing that (their figures)
should be in conformity with the principles underlying the natures (of men and
things) and the ordinances appointed (for them), called them (now) yin and
yang, (now) the hard and the soft, (now) benevolence and righteousness, in
order thereby to exhibit the ways of heaven, earth, and men; it is a view of them
as related together. The trigrams of the Yî contain the three Powers ; and
when they are doubled into hexagrams, there the three Powers unite and are
one. But there are the changes and movements of their (several) ways, and
therefore there are separate places for the yin and yang, and reciprocal uses
of the hard and the soft.'

As in the first Appendix, so in this, the name kwei-shăn occurs twice; in paragraghs 21 and 50 of Section i. In the former instance, each part of the name has its significance. Kwei denotes the animal soul or nature, and Shăn, the intellectual soul, the union of which constitutes the living rational man. I have translated them, it will be seen, by 'the anima and the animus.' Canon McClatchie gives for them 'demons and gods;' and Dr. Medhurst said on the passage, 'The kwei-shăns are evidently the expanding and contracting principles of human life. . . . . The kwei-shăns are brought about by the dissolution of the human frame, and consist of the expanding and ascending shăn, which rambles about in space, and of the contracted and shrivelled kwei, which reverts to earth and nonentity [1].'

The name Kwei-shăn

This is pretty much the same view as my own, though I would not here use the phraseology of 'expanding and contracting.' Canon McClatchie is consistent with himself, and renders the characters by 'demons and gods.'

In the latter passage it is more difficult to determine the exact meaning. The writer says, that 'by the odd numbers assigned to heaven and the even numbers assigned to earth, the changes and transformations are effected, and the spirit-like agencies kept in movement;' meaning that by means of the numbers the spirit-like lines might be formed on a scale sufficient to give a picture of all the changing phenomena, taking place, as if by a spiritual agency, in nature. Medhurst contents himself on it with giving the explanation of Kû Hsî, that 'the kwei-shăns refer to the contractions and expandings, the recedings and approachings of the productive and completing powers of the even and odd numbers [2].' Canon McClatchie does not follow his translation of the former passage and give here 'demons and gods,' but we have 'the Demon-god (i.e. Shang Tî) [3].' I shall refer to this version when considering the fifth Appendix.

---

[1] Dissertation on the Theology of the Chinese, pp. 111, 112.
[2] Theology of the Chinese, p. 122.
[3] Translation of the Yî King, p. 312.

The single character shăn occurs more than twenty
times;—used now as a substantive, now as an adjective,

Shan alone   and again as a verb. I must refer the reader
to the translation and notes for its various
significance, subjoining in a note a list of the places where
it occurs [1].

Much more might be said on the third Appendix, for
the writer touches on many other topics, antiquarian and
speculative, but a review of them would help us little in
the study of the leading subject of the Yî. In passing on
to the next treatise, I would only further say that the
style of this and the author's manner of presenting his
thoughts often remind the reader of 'the Doctrine of the
Mean.' I am surprised that 'the Great Treatise' has
never been ascribed to the author of that Doctrine, Ȝze-
sze, the grandson of Confucius, whose death must have
taken place between B.C. 400 and 450.

7. The fourth Appendix, the seventh 'wing' of the Yî,
need not detain us long. As I stated on p. 27, it is con-

The fourth   fined to an exposition of the Text on the first
Appendix   and second hexagrams, being an attempt to
show that what is there affirmed of heaven and earth may
also be applied to man, and that there is an essential
agreement between the qualities ascribed to them, and the
benevolence, righteousness, propriety, and wisdom, which are
the four constituents of his moral and intellectual nature.

It is said by some of the critics that Confucius would
have treated all the other hexagrams in a similar way, if
his life had been prolonged, but we found special grounds
for denying that Confucius had anything to do with the
composition of this Appendix; and, moreover, I cannot
think of any other figure that would have afforded to the
author the same opportunity of discoursing about man.
The style and method are after the manner of 'the Doctrine
of the Mean' quite as much as those of 'the Great Treatise.'
Several paragraphs, moreover, suggest to us the magniloquence of Mencius. It is said, for instance, by Ȝze-sze, of

---

[1] Section i, 23, 32, 57, 58, 62, 64, 67, 68, 69, 73, 76, 81; Section ii, 11, 15,
33, 34, 41, 45.

the sage, that 'he is the equal or correlate of Heaven [1],' and in this Appendix we have the sentiment expanded into the following:—

'The great man is he who is in harmony in his attributes with heaven and earth; in his brightness with the sun and moon; in his orderly procedure with the four seasons; and in his relation to what is fortunate and what is calamitous with the spiritual agents. He may precede Heaven, and Heaven will not act in opposition to him; he may follow Heaven, but will act only as Heaven at the time would do. If Heaven will not act in opposition to him, how much less will man! how much less will the spiritual agents [2]!'

One other passage may receive our consideration :—

'The family that accumulates goodness is sure to have super-abundant happiness, and the family that accumulates evil is sure to have superabundant misery [3].'

The language makes us think of the retribution of good and evil as taking place in the family, and not in the in-dividual; the judgment is long deferred, but it is inflicted at last, lighting, however, not on the head or heads that most deserved it. Confucianism never falters in its affirma-tion of the difference between good and evil, and that each shall have its appropriate recompense; but it has little to say of the where and when and how that recompense will be given. The old classics are silent on the subject of any other retribution besides what takes place in time. About the era of Confucius the view took definite shape that, if the issues of good and evil, virtue and vice, did not take effect in the experience of the individual, they would certainly do so in that of his posterity. This is the prevailing doctrine among the Chinese at the present day; and one of the earliest expressions, perhaps the earliest expression, of it was in the sentence under our notice that has been copied from this Appendix into almost every moral treatise that circulates in China. A wholesome and an important truth it is, that 'the sins of parents are visited

---

[1] *K*ung-yung xxxi, 4.
[2] Section i, 34. This is the only paragraph where kwei-shăn occurs. Section ii, 5.

on their children;' but do the parents themselves escape the curse? It is to be regretted that this short treatise, the only 'wing' of the Yî professing to set forth its teachings concerning man as man, does not attempt any definite reply to this question. I leave it, merely observing that it has always struck me as the result of an after-thought, and a wish to give to man, as the last of 'the Three Powers,' a suitable place in connexion with the Yî. The doctrine of 'the Three Powers' is as much out of place in Confucianism as that of 'the Great Extreme.' The treatise contains several paragraphs interesting in themselves, but it adds nothing to our understanding of the Text, or even of the object of the appended treatises, when we try to look at them as a whole.

8. It is very different with the fifth of the Appendixes, which is made up of 'Remarks on the Trigrams.' It is shorter than the fourth, consisting of only 22 paragraphs, in some of which the author rises to a height of thought reached nowhere else in these treatises, while several of the others are so silly and trivial, that it is difficult, not to say impossible, to believe that they are the production of the same man. We find in it the earlier and later arrangement of the trigrams,—the former, that of Fû-hsî, and the latter, that of king Wǎn; their names and attributes; the work of God in nature, described as a progress through the trigrams; and finally a distinctive, but by no means exhaustive, list of the natural objects, symbolised by them.

The fifth Appendix

It commences with the enigmatic declaration that 'Anciently, when the sages made the Yî,' (that is, the lineal figures, and the system of divination by them), 'in order to give mysterious assistance to the spiritual Intelligences, they produced (the rules for the use of) the divining plant.' Perhaps this means no more than that the lineal figures were made to 'hold the mirror up to nature,' so that men by the study of them would understand more of the unseen and spiritual operations, to which the phenomena around them were owing, than they could otherwise do.

First paragraph

The author goes on to speak of the Fû-hsî trigrams, and passes from them to those of king Wăn in paragraph 8. That and the following two are very remarkable; but before saying anything of them, I will go on to the 14th, which is the only passage that affords any ground for saying that there is a mythology in the Yî. It says:—

'*Kh*ien is (the symbol of) heaven, and hence is styled father. Khwăn is (the symbol of) earth, and hence is

Mythology of
the Yî styled mother. *K*ăn (shows) the first application (of khwăn to *kh*ien), resulting in getting (the first of) its male (or undivided lines), and hence we call it the oldest son. Sun (shows) a first application (of *kh*ien to khwăn), resulting in getting (the first of) its female (or divided lines), and hence we call it the oldest daughter. Khăn (shows) a second application (of khwăn to *kh*ien), and Lî a second (of *kh*ien to khwăn), resulting in the second son and second daughter. In *K*ăn and Tui we have a third application (of khwăn to *kh*ien and of *kh*ien to khwăn), resulting in the youngest son and youngest daughter.'

From this language has come the fable of a marriage between *Kh*ien and Khwăn, from which resulted the six other trigrams, considered as their three sons and three daughters; and it is not to be wondered at, if some men of active and ill-regulated imaginations should see Noah and his wife in those two primary trigrams, and in the others their three sons and the three sons' wives. Have we not in both cases an ogdoad? But I have looked in the paragraph in vain for the notion of a marriage-union between heaven and earth.

It does not treat of the genesis of the other six trigrams by the union of the two, but is a rude attempt to explain their forms when they were once existing[1]. According to the idea of changes, *Kh*ien and Khwăn are continually varying their forms by their interaction. As here represented, the

---

[1] This view seems to be in accordance with that of Wû *Kh*ăng (of the Yüan dynasty), as given in the 'Collected Comments' of the Khang-hsî edition. The editors express their approval of it in preference to the interpretation of *K*û Hsî, who understood the whole to refer to the formation of the lineal figures, the 'application' being 'the manipulation of the stalks to find the proper line.'

other trigrams are not 'produced[1]' by a marriage-union, but from the application, literally the seeking, of one of them—of Khwăn as much as of *Khien*—addressed to the other[2].

This way of speaking of the trigrams, moreover, as father and mother, sons and daughters, is not so old as Fû-hsî; nor have we any real proof that it originated with king Wăn. It is not of 'the highest antiquity.' It arose some time in 'middle antiquity,' and was known in the era of the Appendixes; but it had not prevailed then, nor has it prevailed since, to discredit and supersede the older nomenclature. We are startled when we come on it in the place which it occupies. And there it stands alone. It is not entitled to more attention than the two paragraphs that precede it, or the eight that follow it, none of which were thought by P. Regis worthy to be translated. I have just said that it stands 'alone.' Its existence, however, seems to me to be supposed in the fourth chapter, paragraphs 28–30, of the third Appendix, Section ii; but there only the trigrams of 'the six children' are mentioned, and nothing is said of 'the parents.' *Kăn*, khân, and kăn are referred to as being yang, and sun, lî, and tui as being yin. What is said about them is trifling and fanciful.

Leaving the question of the mythology of the Yî, of which I am myself unable to discover a trace, I now call attention to paragraphs 8–10, where the author speaks of the work of God in nature in all the year as a progress through the trigrams, and as being effected by His Spirit. The description assumes the peculiar arrangement of the trigrams, ascribed to king Wăn, and which I have exhibited above, on page 33[3]. Father Regis adopts the general view

Operation of God in nature throughout the year

---

[1] But the Chinese term Shăng 生, often rendered 'produced,' must not be pressed, so as to determine the method of production, or the way in which one thing comes from another.

[2] The significance of the mythological paragraph is altogether lost in Canon McClatchie's version:—'*Khien* is Heaven, and hence he is called Father; Khwăn is Earth, and hence she is called Mother; *Kăn* is the first male, and hence he is called the eldest son,' &c. &c.

[3] The reader will understand the difference in the two arrangements better by a reference to the circular representations of them on Plate III.

of Chinese critics that Wăn purposely altered the earlier and established arrangement, as a symbol of the disorganisation and disorder into which the kingdom had fallen[1]. But it is hard to say why a man did something more than 3000 years ago, when he has not himself said anything about it. So far as we can judge from this Appendix, the author thought that king Wăn altered the existing order and position of the trigrams with regard to the cardinal points, simply for the occasion,—that he might set forth vividly his ideas about the springing, growth, and maturity in the vegetable kingdom from the labours of spring to the cessation from toil in winter. The marvel is that in doing this he brings God upon the scene, and makes Him in the various processes of nature the 'all and in all.'

The 8th paragraph says :—

'God comes forth in *K*ăn (to his producing work) ; He brings (His processes) into full and equal action in Sun ; they are manifested to one another in Lî ; the greatest service is done for Him in Khwăn ; He rejoices in Tui ; He struggles in *K*hien ; He is comforted and enters into rest in Khân ; and he completes (the work of) the year in Kăn.'

God is here named Tî, for which P. Regis gives the Latin 'Supremus Imperator,' and Canon McClatchie, after him, 'the Supreme Emperor.' I contend that 'God' is really the correct translation in English of Tî ; but to render it here by 'Emperor' would not affect the meaning of the paragraph. *K*û Hsî says that 'by Tî is intended the Lord and Governor of heaven ;' and Khung Ying-tâ, about five centuries earlier than *K*û, quotes Wang Pî, who died A.D.

---

[1] E. g. I, 23, 24 :—' Observant etiam philosophi (lib. 15 Sinicae philosophiae Sing-lî) principem Wăn-wang antiquum octo symbolorum, unde aliae figurae omnes pendent, ordinem invertisse ; quo ipsa imperii suis temporibus subversio graphice exprimi poterat, mutatis e naturali loco, quem genesis dederat, iis quatuor figuris, quae rerum naturalium pugnis ac dissociationibus, quas posterior labentis anni pars afferre solet, velut in antecessum, repraesentandis idoneae videbantur ; v. g. si symbolum ☲ Lî, ignis, supponatur loco symboli ☵ Khân, aquae, utriusque elementi inordinatio principi visa est non minus apta ad significandas ruinas et clades reipublicae male ordinatae, quam naturales ab hieme aut imminente aut saeviente rerum generatarum corruptiones.' See also pp. 67, 68.

249, to the effect that 'Tî is the lord who produces (all) things, the author of prosperity and increase.'

I must refer the reader to the translation in the body of the volume for the 9th paragraph, which is too long to be introduced here. As the 8th speaks directly of God, the 9th, we are told, 'speaks of all things following Him, from spring to winter, from the east to the north, in His progress throughout the year.'   In words strikingly like those of the apostle Paul, when writing his Epistle to the Romans, Wan Kℏung-ᴣung (of the Khang-hsî period) and his son, in their admirable work called, 'A New Digest of Collected Explanations of the Yî King,' say :—'God (Himself) cannot be seen ; we see Him in the things (which He produces).' The first time I read these paragraphs with some understanding, I thought of Thomson's Hymn on the Seasons, and I have thought of it in connexion with them a hundred times since. Our English poet wrote :—

> 'These, as they change, Almighty Father, these
> Are but the varied God.   The rolling year
> Is full of Thee.   Forth in the pleasing spring
> Thy beauty walks, Thy tenderness and love.
> Then comes Thy glory in the summer months,
> With light and heat refulgent.   Then Thy sun
> Shoots full perfection through the swelling year.
> Thy bounty shines in autumn unconfined,
> And spreads a common feast for all that lives.
> In winter awful Thou!'

Prudish readers have found fault with some of Thomson's expressions, as if they savoured of pantheism.   The language of the Chinese writer is not open to the same captious objection.   Without poetic ornament, or swelling phrase of any kind, he gives emphatic testimony to God as renewing the face of the earth in spring, and not resting till He has crowned the year with His goodness.

And there is in the passage another thing equally wonderful.   The 10th paragraph commences:—'When we speak of Spirit, we mean the subtle presence (and operation of God) with all things ;' and the writer goes on to illustrate this sentiment from the action and influences symbolised

by the six 'children,' or minor trigrams,—water and fire,
thunder and wind, mountains and collections of water. *Kû*
Hsî says, that there is that in the paragraph which he does
not understand.   Some Chinese scholars, however, have
not been far from descrying the light that is in it.   Let
Liang Yin, of our fourteenth century, be adduced as an
example of them.   He says:—'The spirit here simply
means God.   God is the personality (literally, the body
or substantiality) of the Spirit; the Spirit is God in operation.   He who is lord over and rules all things is God;
the subtle presence and operation of God with all things
is by His Spirit.'   The language is in fine accord with the
definition of shăn or spirit, given in the 3rd Appendix,
Section i, 32.

I wish that the Treatise on the Trigrams had ended with the
10th paragraph.   The writer had gradually risen to a noble
   Concluding   elevation of thought from which he plunges
   paragraphs   into a slough of nonsensical remarks which
it would be difficult elsewhere to parallel.   I have referred
on p. 31 to the judgment of P. Regis about them.   He could
not receive them as from Confucius, and did not take the
trouble to translate them, and transfer them to his own pages.
My plan required me to translate everything published in
China as a part of the Yî King; but I have given my reasons for doubting whether any portion of these Appendixes
be really from Confucius.   There is nothing that could
better justify the supercilious disregard with which the
classical literature of China is frequently treated than to
insist on the concluding portion of this treatise as being
from the pencil of its greatest sage.   I have dwelt at some
length on the 14th paragraph, because of its mythological
semblance; but among the eight paragraphs that follow it,
it would be difficult to award the palm for silliness.   They
are descriptive of the eight trigrams, and each one enu-
merates a dozen or more objects of which its subject is
symbolical.   The writer must have been fond of and familiar
with horses. *Kh*ien, the symbol properly of heaven, suggests
to him the idea of a good horse; an old horse; a lean horse;
and a piebald. *Kă*n, the symbol of thunder, suggests the

idea of a good neigher; of the horse with white hind-legs; of the prancing horse; and of one with a white star in his forehead. Khân, the symbol of water, suggests the idea of the horse with an elegant spine; of one with a high spirit; of one with a drooping head; and of one with a shambling step. The reader will think he has had enough of these symbolisings of the trigrams. I cannot believe that the earlier portions and this concluding portion of the treatise were by the same author. If there were any evidence that paragraphs 8 to 10 were by Confucius, I should say that they were worthy, even more than worthy, of him; what follows is mere drivel. Horace's picture faintly pourtrays the inconsistency between the parts :—

'Desinit in piscem mulier formosa superne.'

In reviewing the second of these Appendixes, I was led to speak of the original significance of the trigrams, in opposition to the views of some Chinese who pretend that they can find in them the physical truths discovered by the researches of western science. May I not say now, after viewing the phase of them presented in these paragraphs, that they were devised simply as aids to divination, and partook of the unreasonableness and uncertainty belonging to that?

9. The sixth Appendix is the Treatise on the Sequence of the Hexagrams, to which allusion has been made more

The sixth Appendix than once. It is not necessary to dwell on it at length. King Wăn, it has been seen, gave a name to each hexagram, expressive of the idea— some moral, social, or political truth—which he wished to set forth by means of it; and this name enters very closely into its interpretation. The author of this treatise endeavours to explain the meaning of the name, and also the sequence of the figures, or how it is that the idea of the one leads on to that of the next. Yet the reader must not expect to find in the 64 a chain 'of linked sweetness long drawn out.' The connexion between any two is generally sufficiently close; but on the whole the essays, which I have said they form, resemble 'a heap of orient pearls at random strung.' The changeableness of human affairs is a topic never long absent from the writer's mind. He is firmly persuaded that 'the fashion of the world passeth away.' Union is sure to give place to separation, and by and by that separation will issue in re-union.

There is nothing in the treatise to suggest anything about its authorship; and as the reader will see from the notes, we are perplexed occasionally by meanings given to the names that differ from the meanings in the Text.

10. The last and least Appendix is the seventh, called 3â Kwâ *K*wan, or 'Treatise on the Lineal Figures taken promiscuously,'—not with regard to any sequence, but as they approximate, or are opposed, to one another in meaning. It is in rhyme, moreover, and this, as much as the meaning, determined, no doubt, the grouping of the hexagrams. The student will learn nothing of value from it; it is more a 'jeu d'esprit' than anything else.

I CHING
BOOK OF CHANGES

TEXT SECTION I

I THE *KHIEN* HEXAGRAM

 CH'IEN

Explanation of the entire figure by king Wăn

*Kh*ien (represents) what is great and originating, penetrating, advantageous, correct and firm.

Explanation of the separate lines by the duke of *K*âu.

1. In the first (or lowest) NINE, undivided, (we see its subject as) the dragon lying hid (in the deep). It is not the time for active doing.

2. In the second NINE, undivided, (we see its subject as) the dragon appearing in the field. It will be advantageous to meet with the great man.

3. In the third NINE, undivided, (we see its subject as) the superior man active and vigilant all the day, and in the evening still careful and apprehensive. (The position is) dangerous, but there will be no mistake.

4. In the fourth NINE, undivided, (we see its subject as the dragon looking) as if he were leaping up, but still in the deep. There will be no mistake.

5. In the fifth NINE, undivided, (we see its subject as) the dragon on the wing in the sky. It will be advantageous to meet with the great man.

6. In the sixth (or topmost) NINE, undivided, (we see its subject as) the dragon exceeding the proper limits. There will be occasion for repentance.

7. (The lines of this hexagram are all strong and undivided, as appears from) the use of the number NINE. If the host of dragons (thus) appearing were to divest themselves of their heads, there would be good fortune.

The Text under each hexagram consists of one paragraph by king Wăn, explaining the figure as a whole, and of six (in the case of hexagrams 1 and 2, of seven) paragraphs by the duke of *K*âu, explaining the individual lines. The explanatory notices introduced above to this effect will not be repeated. A double space will be used to mark off the portion of king Wăn from that of his son.

Each hexagram consists of two of the trigrams of Fû-hsî, the lower being called 'the inner,' and the one above 'the outer.' The lines, however, are numbered from one to six, commencing with the lowest. To denote the number of it and of the sixth line, the terms for 'commencing' and 'topmost' are used. The intermediate lines are simply 'second,' 'third,' &c. As the lines must be either whole or divided, technically called strong and weak, yang and yin, this distinction is indicated by the application to them of the numbers nine and six. All whole lines are nine, all divided lines, six.

Two explanations have been proposed of this application of these numbers. The *K*hien trigram, it is said, contains 3 strokes (━━━━━), and the Khwăn 6 (━━ ━━). But the yang contains the yin in itself, and its representative number will be $3+6=9$, while the yin, not containing the yang, will only have its own number or 6. This explanation, entirely arbitrary, is now deservedly abandoned. The other is based on the use of the 'four Hsiang,' or emblematic figures (━━━━━ the great or old yang, ━━ ━━ the young yang, ━━ ━━ the old yin, and ━━━━━ the young yin). To these are assigned (by what process is unimportant for our present purpose) the numbers 9, 8, 7, 6. They were 'the old yang,' represented by 9, and 'the old yin,' represented by 6, that, in the manipulation of the stalks to form new diagrams, determined the changes of figure; and so 9 and 6 came to be used as the

II THE KHWĂN HEXAGRAM

K'UN

Khwăn (represents) what is great and originating, penetrating, advantageous, correct and having the firmness of a mare.   When the superior man (here

---

names of a yang line and a yin line respectively. This explanation is now universally acquiesced in. The nomenclature of first nine, nine two, &c., or first six, six two, &c., however, is merely a jargon ; and I have preferred to use, instead of it, in the translation, in order to describe the lines, the names 'undivided' and 'divided.'

I. Does king Wăn ascribe four attributes here to *Kh*ien, or only two? According to Appendix IV, always by Chinese writers assigned to Confucius, he assigns four, corresponding to the principles of benevolence, righteousness, propriety, and knowledge in man's nature. *K*'û Hsî held that he assigned only two, and that we should translate, 'greatly penetrating,' and 'requires to be correct and firm,' two responses in divination. Up and down throughout the Text of the 64 hexagrams, we often find the characters thus coupled together. Both interpretations are possible. I have followed what is accepted as the view of Confucius. It would take pages to give a tithe of what has been written in justification of it, and to reconcile it with the other.

'The dragon' is the symbol employed by the duke of *K*âu to represent 'the superior man' and especially 'the great man,' exhibiting the virtues or attributes characteristic of heaven. The creature's proper home is in the water, but it can disport itself on the land, and also fly and soar aloft. It has been from the earliest time the emblem with the Chinese of the highest dignity and wisdom, of sovereignty and sagehood, the combination of which constitutes 'the great man.' One emblem runs through the lines of many of the hexagrams as here.

But the dragon appears in the sixth line as going beyond the proper limits. The ruling-sage has gone through all the sphere in which he is called on to display his attributes ; it is time for him to relax. The line should not be always pulled tight ; the bow should not be always kept drawn. The unchanging use

intended) has to make any movement, if he take the
initiative, he will go astray; if he follow, he will find
his (proper) lord. The advantageousness will be
seen in his getting friends in the south-west, and
losing friends in the north-east. If he rest in correctness and firmness, there will be good fortune.

1. In the first SIX, divided, (we see its subject)
treading on hoarfrost. The strong ice will come
(by and by).

2. The second SIX, divided, (shows the attribute
of) being straight, square, and great. (Its operation), without repeated efforts, will be in every
respect advantageous.

3. The third SIX, divided, (shows its subject)
keeping his excellence under restraint, but firmly
maintaining it. If he should have occasion to engage in the king's service, though he will not claim
the success (for himself), he will bring affairs to a
good issue.

4. The fourth SIX, divided, (shows the symbol
of) a sack tied up. There will be no ground for
blame or for praise.

5. The fifth SIX, divided, (shows) the yellow
lower garment. There will be great good fortune.

---

of force will give occasion for repentance. The moral meaning
found in the line is that 'the high shall be abased.'

The meaning given to the supernumerary paragraph is the opposite
of that of paragraph 6. The 'host of dragons without their heads'
would give us the next hexagram, or Khwăn, made up of six divided
lines. Force would have given place to submission, and haughtiness
to humility; and the result would be good fortune. Such at least
is the interpretation of the paragraph given in a narrative of the
Ʒo-Kwan under B.C. 513. For further explanation of the duke of
Kâu's meaning, see Appendixes II and IV.

6. The sixth SIX, divided (shows) dragons fighting in the wild. Their blood is purple and yellow.

7. (The lines of this hexagram are all weak and divided, as appears from) the use of the number SIX. If those (who are thus represented) be perpetually correct and firm, advantage will arise.

II. The same attributes are here ascribed to Khwăn, as in the former hexagram to *Kh*ien;—but with a difference. The figure, made up of six divided lines, expresses the ideal of subordination and docility. The superior man, represented by it, must not take the initiative; and by following he will find his lord,—the subject, that is of *Kh*ien. Again, the correctness and firmness is defined to be that of 'a mare,' 'docile and strong,' but a creature for the service of man. That it is not the sex of the animal which the writer has chiefly in mind is plain from the immediate mention of the superior man, and his lord.

That superior man will seek to bring his friends along with himself to serve his ruler. But according to the arrangement of the trigrams by king Wăn, the place of Khwăn is in the south-west, while the opposite quarter is occupied by the yang trigram Kăn, as in Figure 2, Plate III. All that this portion of the Thwan says is an instruction to the subject of the hexagram to seek for others of the same principles and tendencies with himself to serve their common lord. But in quietness and firmness will be his strength.

The symbolism of the lines is various. Paragraph 2 presents to us the earth itself, according to the Chinese conception of it, as a great cube. To keep his excellence under restraint, as in paragraph 3, is the part of a minister or officer, seeking not his own glory, but that of his ruler. Paragraph 4 shows its subject exercising a still greater restraint on himself than in paragraph 3. There is an interpretation of the symbolism of paragraph 5 in a narrative of the 3o *K*wan, under the 12th year of duke *Kh*âo, B.C. 530. 'Yellow' is one of the five 'correct' colours, and the colour of the earth. 'The lower garment' is a symbol of humility. The fifth line is the seat of honour. If its occupant possess the qualities indicated, he will be greatly fortunate.

See the note on the sixth line of hexagram 1. What is there said to be 'beyond the proper limits' takes place here 'in the wild.' The humble subject of the divided line is transformed into a

III   The *K*un Hexagram

CHUN

*K*un (indicates that in the case which it pre-supposes) there will be great progress and success, and the advantage will come from being correct and firm. (But) any movement in advance should not be (lightly) undertaken. There will be advantage in appointing feudal princes.

1. The first NINE, undivided, shows the difficulty (its subject has) in advancing. It will be advantageous for him to abide correct and firm; advantageous (also) to be made a feudal ruler.

2. The second SIX, divided, shows (its subject) distressed and obliged to return; (even) the horses of her chariot (also) seem to be retreating. (But) not by a spoiler (is she assailed), but by one who seeks her to be his wife. The young lady maintains her firm correctness, and declines a union. After ten years she will be united, and have children.

3. The third SIX, divided, shows one following the deer without (the guidance of) the forester, and only finding himself in the midst of the forest. The superior man, acquainted with the secret risks, thinks it better to give up the chase. If he went forward, he would regret it.

---

dragon, and fights with the true dragon, the subject of the undivided line. They fight and bleed, and their blood is of the colour proper to heaven or the sky, and the colour proper to the earth. Paragraph 7 supposes that the hexagram Khwăn should become changed into *Kh*ien ;—the result of which would be good.

4. The fourth SIX, divided, shows (its subject as a lady), the horses of whose chariot appear in retreat. She seeks, however, (the help of) him who seeks her to be his wife. Advance will be fortunate; all will turn out advantageously.

5. The fifth NINE, undivided, shows the difficulties in the way of (its subject's) dispensing the rich favours that might be expected from him. With firmness and correctness there will be good fortune in small things; (even) with them in great things there will be evil.

6. The topmost SIX, divided, shows (its subject) with the horses of his chariot obliged to retreat, and weeping tears of blood in streams.

III. The character called *K*un is pictorial, and was intended to show us how a plant struggles with difficulty out of the earth, rising gradually above the surface. This difficulty, marking the first stages in the growth of a plant, is used to symbolise the struggles that mark the rise of a state out of a condition of disorder, consequent on a great revolution. The same thing is denoted by the combination of the trigrams that form the figure;—as will be seen in the notes on it under Appendix II.

I have introduced within parentheses, in the translation, the words 'in the case which the hexagram presupposes.' It is necessary to introduce them. King Wăn and his son wrote, as they did in every hexagram, with reference to a particular state of affairs which they had in mind. This was the unspoken text which controlled and directed all their writing; and the student must try to get hold of this, if he would make his way with comfort and success through the Yî. Wăn saw the social and political world around him in great disorder, hard to be remedied. But he had faith in himself and the destinies of his House. Let there be prudence and caution, with unswerving adherence to the right; let the government of the different states be entrusted to good and able men:—then all would be well.

The first line is undivided, showing the strength of its subject. He will be capable of action, and his place in the trigram of mobility will the more dispose him to it. But above him is the

IV THE MĂNG HEXAGRAM

MÊNG

Măng (indicates that in the case which it pre-
supposes) there will be progress and success. I do
not (go and) seek the youthful and inexperienced,

trigram of peril; and the lowest line of that, to which especially he
must look for response and co-operation, is divided and weak.
Hence arise the ideas of difficulty in advancing, the necessity of
caution, and the advantage of his being clothed with authority.

To the subject of the second line, divided, advance is still more
difficult. He is weak in himself; he is pressed by the subject of
the strong line below him. But happily that subject, though strong,
is correct; and above in the fifth line, in the place of authority, is
the strong one, union with whom and the service of whom should
be the objects pursued. All these circumstances suggested to the
duke of Kâu the idea of a young lady, sought in marriage by a
strong wooer, when marriage was unsuitable, rejecting him, and
finally, after ten years, marrying a more suitable, the only suitable,
match for her.

The third line is divided, not central, and the number of its
place is appropriate to the occupancy of a strong line. All these
things should affect the symbolism of the line. But the outcome
of the whole hexagram being good, the superior man sees the immediate danger and avoids it.

The subject of the fourth line, the first of the upper trigram, has
recourse to the strong suitor of line 1, the first of the lower trigram;
and with his help is able to cope with the difficulties of the position,
and go forward.

The subject of the fifth line is in the place of authority, and
should show himself a ruler, dispensing benefits on a great scale.
But he is in the very centre of the trigram denoting perilousness,
and line 2, which responds to 5, is weak. Hence arises the symbolism, and great things should not be attempted.

The sixth line is weak; the third responding to it is also weak;
it is at the extremity of peril; the game is up. What can remain
for its subject in such a case but terror and abject weeping?

but he comes and seeks me. When he shows (the sincerity that marks) the first recourse to divination, I instruct him. If he apply a second and third time, that is troublesome; and I do not instruct the troublesome. There will be advantage in being firm and correct.

1. The first SIX, divided, (has respect to) the dispelling of ignorance. It will be advantageous to use punishment (for that purpose), and to remove the shackles (from the mind). But going on in that way (of punishment) will give occasion for regret.

2. The second NINE, undivided, (shows its subject) exercising forbearance with the ignorant, in which there will be good fortune; and admitting (even the goodness of women, which will also be fortunate. (He may be described also as) a son able to (sustain the burden of) his family.

3. The third SIX, divided, (seems to say) that one should not marry a woman whose emblem it might be, for that, when she sees a man of wealth, she will not keep her person from him, and in no wise will advantage come from her.

4. The fourth SIX, divided, (shows its subject as if) bound in chains of ignorance. There will be occasion for regret.

5. The fifth SIX, divided, shows its subject as a simple lad without experience. There will be good fortune.

6. In the topmost NINE, undivided, we see one smiting the ignorant (youth). But no advantage

will come from doing him an injury. Advantage
would come from warding off injury from him.

IV. As *K*un shows us plants struggling from beneath the surface, Măng suggests to us the small and undeveloped appearance
which they then present; and hence it came to be the symbol of
youthful inexperience and ignorance. The object of the hexagram
is to show how such a condition should be dealt with by the parent
and ruler, whose authority and duty are represented by the second
and sixth, the two undivided lines. All between the first and last
sentences of the Thwan must be taken as an oracular response
received by the party divining on the subject of enlightening the
youthful ignorant. This accounts for its being more than usually
enigmatical, and for its being partly rhythmical. See Appendix I,
in loc.

The subject of the first line, weak, and at the bottom of the
figure, is in the grossest ignorance. Let him be punished. If
punishment avail to loosen the shackles and manacles from the
mind, well; if not, and punishment be persevered with, the effect
will be bad.

On the subject of the second line, strong, and in the central
place, devolves the task of enlightening the ignorant; and we have
him discharging it with forbearance and humility. In proof of his
generosity, it is said that 'he receives,' or learns from, even weak
and ignorant women. He appears also as 'a son' taking the place
of his father.

The third line is weak, and occupies an odd place belonging
properly to an undivided line; nor is its place in the centre. All
these things give the subject of it so bad a character.

The fourth line is far from both the second and sixth, and can
get no help from its correlate,—the first line, weak as itself. What
good can be done with or by the subject of it?

The fifth line is in the place of honour, and has for its correlate
the strong line in the second place. Being weak in itself, it is
taken as the symbol of a simple lad, willing to be taught.

The topmost line is strong, and in the highest place. It is
natural, but unwise, in him to use violence in carrying on his
educational measures. A better course is suggested to him.

V THE HSÜ HEXAGRAM

HSÜ

Hsü intimates that, with the sincerity which is declared in it, there will be brilliant success. With firmness there will be good fortune; and it will be advantageous to cross the great stream.

1. The first NINE, undivided, shows its subject waiting in the distant border. It will be well for him constantly to maintain (the purpose thus shown), in which case there will be no error.

2. The second NINE, undivided, shows its subject waiting on the sand (of the mountain stream). He will (suffer) the small (injury of) being spoken (against), but in the end there will be good fortune.

3. The third NINE, undivided, shows its subject in the mud (close by the stream). He thereby invites the approach of injury.

4. The fourth SIX, divided, shows its subject waiting in (the place of) blood. But he will get out of the cavern.

5. The fifth NINE, undivided, shows its subject waiting amidst the appliances of a feast. Through his firmness and correctness there will be good fortune.

6. The topmost SIX, divided, shows its subject entered into the cavern. (But) there are three guests coming, without being urged, (to his help).

If he receive them respectfully, there will be good
fortune in the end.

V. Hsü means waiting. Strength confronted by peril might be
expected to advance boldly and at once to struggle with it; but it
takes the wiser plan of waiting till success is sure. This is the
lesson of the hexagram. That 'sincerity is declared in it' is proved
from the fifth line in the position of honour and authority, central,
itself undivided and in an odd place. In such a case, nothing but
firm correctness is necessary to great success.

'Going through a great stream,' an expression frequent in the Yî,
may mean undertaking hazardous enterprises, or encountering
great difficulties, without any special reference; but more natural
is it to understand by 'the great stream' the Yellow river, which the
lords of *K*âu must cross in a revolutionary movement against the
dynasty of Yin and its tyrant. The passage of it by king Wû, the
son of Wăn in B.C. 1122, was certainly one of the greatest deeds in
the history of China. It was preceded also by long 'waiting,' till
the time of assured success came.

'The border' under line 1 means the frontier territory of the
state. There seems no necessity for such a symbolism. 'The sand'
and 'the mud' are appropriate with reference to the watery defile;
but it is different with 'the border.' The subject of the line appears
at work in his distant fields, not thinking of anything but his daily
work; and he is advised to abide in that state and mind.

'The sand' of paragraph 2 suggests a nearer approach to the
defile, but its subject is still self-restrained and waiting. I do
not see what suggests the idea of his suffering from 'the strife of
tongues.'

In paragraph 3 the subject is on the brink of the stream. His
advance to that position has provoked resistance, which may result
in his injury.

Line 4 has passed from the inner to the upper trigram, and
entered on the scene of danger and strife;—'into the place of blood.'
Its subject is 'weak and in the correct place for him;' he therefore
retreats and escapes from the cavern, where he was engaged with
his enemy.

Line 5 is strong and central, and in its correct place, being that
of honour. All good qualities therefore belong to the subject of
it, who has triumphed, and with firmness will triumph still more.

Line 6 is weak, and has entered deeply into the defile and its
caverns. What will become of its subject? His correlate is the

VI The Sung Hexagram

SUNG

Sung intimates how, though there is sincerity in one's contention, he will yet meet with opposition and obstruction; but if he cherish an apprehensive caution, there will be good fortune, while, if he must prosecute the contention to the (bitter) end, there will be evil. It will be advantageous to see the great man; it will not be advantageous to cross the great stream.

1. The first six, divided, shows its subject not perpetuating the matter about which (the contention is). He will suffer the small (injury) of being spoken against, but the end will be fortunate.

2. The second nine, undivided, shows its subject unequal to the contention. If he retire and keep concealed (where) the inhabitants of his city are (only) three hundred families, he will fall into no mistake.

3. The third six, divided, shows its subject keeping in the old place assigned for his support, and firmly correct. Perilous as the position is, there will be good fortune in the end. Should he per-

---

strong line 3 below, which comes with its two companions to his help. If they are respectfully received, that help will prove effectual. P. Regis tries to find out a reference in these 'three guests' to three princes who distinguished themselves by taking part with K͏͏̄au in its struggle with Yin or Shang; see vol. i, pp. 279–282. I dare not be so confident of any historical reference.

chance engage in the king's business, he will not (claim the merit of) achievement.

4. The fourth NINE, undivided, shows its subject unequal to the contention. He returns to (the study of Heaven's) ordinances, changes (his wish to contend), and rests in being firm and correct. There will be good fortune.

5. The fifth NINE, undivided, shows its subject contending;—and with great good fortune.

6. The topmost NINE, undivided, shows how its subject may have the leathern belt conferred on him (by the sovereign), and thrice it shall be taken from him in a morning.

VI. We have strength in the upper trigram, as if to regulate and control the lower, and peril in that lower as if looking out for an opportunity to assail the upper; or, as it may be represented, we have one's self in a state of peril matched against strength from without. All this is supposed to give the idea of contention or strife. But the undivided line in the centre of Khân is emblematic of sincerity, and gives a character to the whole figure. An individual, so represented, will be very wary, and have good fortune; but strife is bad, and if persevered in even by such a one, the effect will be evil. The fifth line, undivided, in an odd place, and central, serves as a representative of 'the great man,' whose agency is sure to be good; but the topmost line being also strong, and with its two companions, riding as it were, on the trigram of peril, its action is likely to be too rash for a great enterprise. See the treatise on the Thwan, in loc.

The subject of line 1 is weak and at the bottom of the figure. He may suffer a little in the nascent strife, but will let it drop; and the effect will be good.

Line 2 represents one who is strong, and has the rule of the lower trigram;—he has the mind for strife, and might be expected to engage in it. But his strength is weakened by being in an even place, and he is no match for his correlate in line 5, and therefore retreats. A town or city with only three hundred families is said

VII THE SZE HEXAGRAM

 SHIH

Sze indicates how, in the case which it supposes, with firmness and correctness, and (a leader of) age

to be very small. That the subject of the line should retire to so insignificant a place is further proof of his humility.

Line 3 is weak and in an odd place. Its subject therefore is not equal to strive, but withdraws from the arena. Even if forced into it, he will keep himself in the background;—and be safe. 'He keeps in the old place assigned for his support' is, literally, 'He eats his old virtue;' meaning that he lives in and on the appanage assigned to him for his services.

Line 4 is strong, and not in the centre; so that we are to conceive of its subject as having a mind to strive. But immediately above it is line 5, the symbol of the ruler, and with him it is hopeless to strive; immediately below is 3, weak, and out of its proper place, incapable of maintaining a contention. Its proper correlate is the lowest line, weak, and out of its proper place, from whom little help can come. Hence its subject takes the course indicated, which leads to good fortune.

Line 5 has every circumstance in favour of its subject.

Line 6 is strong and able to contend successfully; but is there to be no end of striving? Persistence in it is sure to end in defeat and disgrace. The contender here might receive a reward from the king for his success; but if he received it thrice in a morning, thrice it would be taken from him again. As to the nature of the reward here given, see on the Lî Kî, X, ii, 32.

P. Regis explains several of the expressions in the Text, both in the Thwan and the Hsiang, from the history of king Wăn and his son king Wû. Possibly his own circumstances may have suggested to Wăn some of the Thwan; and his course in avoiding a direct collision with the tyrant Shâu, and Wû's subsequent exploits may have been in the mind of the duke of Kâu. Some of the sentiments, however, cannot be historically explained. They are general protests against all contention and strife.

and experience, there will be good fortune and no error.

1. The first SIX, divided, shows the host going forth according to the rules (for such a movement). If these be not good, there will be evil.

2. The second NINE, undivided, shows (the leader) in the midst of the host. There will be good fortune and no error. The king has thrice conveyed to him the orders (of his favour).

3. The third SIX, divided, shows how the host may, possibly, have many inefficient leaders. There will be evil.

4. The fourth SIX, divided, shows the host in retreat. There is no error.

5. The fifth SIX, divided, shows birds in the fields, which it will be advantageous to seize (and destroy). In that case there will be no error. If the oldest son leads the host, and younger men (idly occupy offices assigned to them), however firm and correct he may be, there will be evil.

6. The topmost SIX, divided, shows the great ruler delivering his charges, (appointing some) to be rulers of states, and others to undertake the head-ship of clans; but small men should not be employed (in such positions).

VII. The conduct of military expeditions in a feudal kingdom, and we may say, generally, is denoted by the hexagram Sze. Referring to Appendixes I and II for an explanation of the way in which the combination of lines in it is made out to suggest the idea of an army, and that idea being assumed, it is easy to see how the undivided line in the second place should be interpreted of the general, who is responded to by the divided line in the fifth and royal place. Thus entire trust is reposed in him. He is strong

VIII   THE PĬ HEXAGRAM

PĬ

PĬ indicates that (under the conditions which it supposes) there is good fortune. But let (the principal party intended in it) re-examine himself, (as if)

and correct, and his enterprises will be successful. He is denominated *k*ang *z*ăn, 'an old, experienced man.'

'The rules,' it is said, 'are twofold;—first, that the war be for a righteous end; and second, that the manner of conducting it, especially at the outset, be right.' But how this and the warning in the conclusion should both follow from the divided line being in the first place, has not been sufficiently explained.

How line 2 comes to be the symbol of the general in command of the army has been shown above on the Thwan. The orders of the king thrice conveyed to him are to be understood of his appointment to the command, and not of any rewards conferred on him as a tribute to his merit. Nor is stress to be laid on the 'thrice.' 'It does not mean that the appointment came to him three times; but that it was to him exclusively, and with the entire confidence of the king.'

The symbolism of line 3 is very perplexing. P. Regis translates it:—'Milites videntur deponere sarcinas in curribus. Male.' Canon McClatchie has:—'Third-six represents soldiers as it were lying dead in their baggage carts, and is unlucky.' To the same effect was my own translation of the paragraph, nearly thirty years ago. But the third line, divided, cannot be forced to have such an indication. The meaning I have now given is more legitimate, taken character by character, and more in harmony with the scope of the hexagram. The subject of line 2 is the one proper leader of the host. But line 3 is divided and weak, and occupies the place of a strong line, as if its subject had perversely jumped over two, and perched himself above it to take the command. This interpretation also suits better in the 5th paragraph.

Line 4 is weak and not central; and therefore 'to retreat' is

by divination, whether his virtue be great, unintermitting, and firm. If it be so, there will be no error. Those who have not rest will then come to him; and with those who are (too) late in coming it will be ill.

1. The first SIX, divided, shows its subject seeking by his sincerity to win the attachment of his object. There will be no error. Let (the breast) be full of sincerity as an earthenware vessel is of its contents, and it will in the end bring other advantages.

2. In the second SIX, divided, we see the movement towards union and attachment proceeding from the inward (mind). With firm correctness there will be good fortune.

3. In the third SIX, divided, we see its subject seeking for union with such as ought not to be associated with.

4. In the fourth SIX, divided, we see its subject

---

natural for its subject. But its place is even, and proper for a divided line; and the retreat will be right in the circumstances.

In line 5 we seem to have an intimation of the important truth that only defensive war, or war waged by the rightful authority to put down rebellion and lawlessness, is right. 'The birds in the fields' symbolise parties attacking for plunder. The fifth line symbolises the chief authority,—the king, who is weak, or humble, and in the centre, and cedes the use of all his power to the general symbolised by line 2. The subject of 2 is 'the oldest son.' Those of three and four are supposed to be 'the younger brother and son,' that is, the younger men, who would cause evil if admitted to share the command.

The lesson on the topmost line is true and important, but the critics seem unable to deduce it from the nature of the line, as divided and in the sixth place.

seeking for union with the one beyond himself. With firm correctness there will be good fortune.

5. The fifth NINE, undivided, affords the most illustrious instance of seeking union and attachment. (We seem to see in it) the king urging his pursuit of the game (only) in three directions, and allowing the escape of all the animals before him, while the people of his towns do not warn one another (to prevent it). There will be good fortune.

6. In the topmost SIX, divided, we see one seeking union and attachment without having taken the first step (to such an end). There will be evil.

VIII. The idea of union between the different members and classes of a state, and how it can be secured, is the subject of the hexagram Pî. The whole line occupying the fifth place, or that of authority, in the hexagram, represents the ruler to whom the subjects of all the other lines offer a ready submission. According to the general rules for the symbolism of the lines, the second line is the correlate of the fifth; but all the other lines are here made subject to that fifth;—which is also a law of the Yî, according to the 'Daily Lecture.' To me it has the suspicious look of being made for the occasion. The harmony of union, therefore, is to be secured by the sovereign authority of one; but he is warned to see to it that his virtue be what will beseem his place, and subjects are warned not to delay to submit to him.

Where does the 'sincerity' predicated of the subject of line 1 come from? The 'earthenware vessel' is supposed to indicate its plain, unadorned character; but there is nothing in the position and nature of the line, beyond the general idea in the figure, to suggest the attribute.

Line 2 is the proper correlate of 5. Its position in the centre of the inner or lower trigram agrees with the movement of its subject as proceeding from the inward mind.

Line 3 is weak, not in the centre, nor in its correct place. The lines above and below it are both weak. All these things are supposed to account for what is said on it.

'The one beyond himself' in line 4 is the ruler or king, who is

IX   THE HSIÂO *KHÛ* HEXAGRAM

HSIAO CH'U

Hsiâo *Khû* indicates that (under its conditions) there will be progress and success. (We see) dense clouds, but no rain coming from our borders in the west.

1. The first NINE, undivided, shows its subject returning and pursuing his own course. What mistake should he fall into? There will be good fortune.

2. The second NINE, undivided, shows its subject, by the attraction (of the former line), returning (to the proper course). There will be good fortune.

---

the subject of 5, and with whom union ought to be sought. The divided line, moreover, is in a place proper to it. If its subject be firm and correct, there will be good fortune.

The subject of line 5 is the king, who must be the centre of union. The ancient kings had their great hunting expeditions in the different seasons; and that of each season had its peculiar rules. But what is stated here was common to all. When the beating was completed, and the shooting was ready to commence, one side of the enclosure into which the game had been driven was left open and unguarded;—a proof of the royal benevolence, which did not want to make an end of all the game. So well known and understood is this benevolence of the model king of the hexagram, that all his people try to give it effect. Thus the union contemplated is shown to be characterised by mutual confidence and appreciation in virtue and benevolence.

A weak line being in the 6th place, which is appropriate to it, its subject is supposed to be trying to promote union among and with the subjects of the lines below. It is too late. The time is past. Hence it is symbolised as 'without a head,' that is, as not having taken the first step, from which its action should begin, and go on to the end.

3. The third NINE, undivided, suggests the idea of a carriage, the strap beneath which has been removed, or of a husband and wife looking on each other with averted eyes.

4. The fourth SIX, divided, shows its subject possessed of sincerity. The danger of bloodshed is thereby averted, and his (ground for) apprehension dismissed. There will be no mistake.

5. The fifth NINE, undivided, shows its subject possessed of sincerity, and drawing others to unite with him. Rich in resources, he employs his neighbours (in the same cause with himself).

6. The topmost NINE, undivided, shows how the rain has fallen, and the (onward progress) is stayed; —(so) must we value the full accumulation of the virtue (represented by the upper trigram). But a wife (exercising restraint), however firm and correct she may be, is in a position of peril, (and like) the moon approaching to the full. If the superior man prosecute his measures (in such circumstances), there will be evil.

IX. The name Hsiâo *Khû* is interpreted as meaning 'small restraint.' The idea of 'restraint' having once been determined on as that to be conveyed by the figure, it is easily made out that the restraint must be small, for its representative is the divided line in the fourth place; and the check given by that to all the undivided lines cannot be great. Even if we suppose, as many critics do, that all the virtue of that upper trigram Sun is concentrated in its first line, the attribute ascribed to Sun is that of docile flexibility, which cannot long be successful against the strength emblemed by the lower trigram *Kh*ien. The restraint therefore is small, and in the end there will be 'progress and success.'

The second sentence of the Thwan contains indications of the place, time, and personality of the writer which it seems possible to ascertain. The fief of *K*âu was the western portion of the

X THE LÎ HEXAGRAM

LÜ

(Lî suggests the idea of) one treading on the tail of a tiger, which does not bite him. There will be progress and success.

---

kingdom of Yin or Shang, the China of the twelfth century B.C., the era of king Wǎn. Rain coming and moistening the ground is the cause of the beauty and luxuriance of the vegetable world, and the emblem of the blessings flowing from good training and good government. Here therefore in the west, the hereditary territory of the house of *K*âu, are blessings which might enrich the whole kingdom; but they are somehow restrained. The dense clouds do not empty their stores.

P. Regis says:—' To declare openly that no rain fell from the heavens long covered with dense clouds over the great tract of country, which stretched from the western border to the court and on to the eastern sea, was nothing else but leaving it to all thoughtful minds to draw the conclusion that the family of Wǎn was as worthy of the supreme seat as that of Shâu, the tyrant, however ancient, was unworthy of it (vol. i, p. 356).' The intimation is not put in the Text, however, so clearly as by P. Regis.

Line 1 is undivided, the first line of *Kh*ien, occupying its proper place. Its subject, therefore, notwithstanding the check of line 4, resumes his movement, and will act according to his strong nature, and go forward.

Line 2 is also strong, and though an even place is not appropriate to it, that place being central, its subject will make common cause with the subject of line 1; and there will be good fortune.

Line 3, though strong, and in a proper place, yet not being in the centre, is supposed to be less able to resist the restraint of line 4; and hence it has the ill omens that are given.

The subject of line 4, one weak line against all the strong lines of the hexagram, might well expect wounds, and feel apprehension in trying to restrain the others; but it is in its proper place; it is the first line also of Sun, whose attribute is docile flexibility.

1. The first NINE, undivided, shows its subject treading his accustomed path. If he go forward, there will be no error.

2. The second NINE, undivided, shows its subject treading the path that is level and easy;—a quiet and solitary man, to whom, if he be firm and correct, there will be good fortune.

3. The third SIX, divided, shows a one-eyed man (who thinks he) can see; a lame man (who thinks he) can walk well; one who treads on the tail of a tiger and is bitten. (All this indicates) ill fortune. We have a (mere) bravo acting the part of a great ruler.

4. The fourth NINE, undivided, shows its subject treading on the tail of a tiger. He becomes full of apprehensive caution, and in the end there will be good fortune.

5. The fifth NINE, undivided, shows the resolute tread of its subject. Though he be firm and correct, there will be peril.

6. The sixth NINE, undivided, tells us to look at (the whole course) that is trodden, and examine the

---

The strong lines are moved to sympathy and help, and 'there is no mistake.'

Line 5 occupies the central place of Sun, and converts, by the sincerity of its subject, 4 and 6 into its neighbours, who suffer themselves to be used by it, and effect their common object.

In line 6, the idea of the hexagram has run its course. The harmony of nature is restored. The rain falls, and the onward march of the strong lines should now stop. But weakness that has achieved such a result, if it plume itself on it, will be in a position of peril; and like the full moon, which must henceforth wane. Let the superior man, when he has attained his end, remain in quiet.

presage which that gives. If it be complete and without failure, there will be great good fortune.

X. The character giving its name to the hexagram plays an important part also in the symbolism; and this may be the reason why it does not, as the name, occupy the first place in the Thwan. Looking at the figure, we see it is made up of the trigrams Tui, representing a marsh, and Khien, representing the sky. Tui is a yin trigram, and its top line is divided. Below Khien, the great symbol of strength, it may readily suggest the idea of treading on a tiger's tail, which was an old way of expressing what was hazardous (Shû V, xxv, 2). But what suggests the statement that 'the tiger does not bite the treader?' The attribute of Tui is pleased satisfaction. Of course such an attribute could not be predicated of one who was in the fangs of a tiger. The coming scatheless out of such danger further suggests the idea of 'progress and success' in the course which king Wǎn had in his mind. And according to Appendix VI, that course was 'propriety,' the observance of all the rules of courtesy. On these, as so many stepping-stones, one may tread safely amid scenes of disorder and peril.

Line 1 is an undivided line in an odd place; giving us the ideas of activity, firmness, and correctness. One so characterised will act rightly.

Line 2 occupies the middle place of the trigram, which is supposed to symbolise a path cut straight and level along the hill-side, or over difficult ground. Line 5 is not a proper correlate, and hence the idea of the subject of 2 being 'a quiet and solitary man.'

Line 3 is neither central nor in an even place, which would be proper to it. But with the strength of will which the occupant of an odd place should possess, he goes forward with the evil results so variously emblemed. The editors of the imperial edition, in illustration of the closing sentence, refer to Analects VII, x.

Line 4 is in contiguity with 5, whose subject is in the place of authority; but he occupies the place proper to a weak or divided line, and hence he bethinks himself, and goes softly.

Beneath the symbolism under line 5, lies the principle that the most excellent thing in 'propriety' is humility. And the subject of the line, which is strong and central, will not be lacking in this, but bear in mind that the higher he is exalted, the greater may be his fall.

XI   THE THÂI HEXAGRAM

T'AI

In Thâi (we see) the little gone and the great come. (It indicates that) there will be good fortune, with progress and success.

1. The first NINE, undivided, suggests the idea of grass pulled up, and bringing with it other stalks with whose roots it is connected. Advance (on the part of its subject) will be fortunate.

2. The second NINE, undivided, shows one who can bear with the uncultivated, will cross the Ho without a boat, does not forget the distant, and has no (selfish) friendships. Thus does he prove himself acting in accordance with the course of the due Mean.

3. The third NINE, undivided, shows that, while there is no state of peace that is not liable to be disturbed, and no departure (of evil men) so that they shall not return, yet when one is firm and correct, as he realises the distresses that may arise, he will commit no error. There is no occasion for sadness at the certainty (of such recurring changes); and in this mood the happiness (of the present) may be (long) enjoyed.

4. The fourth SIX, divided, shows its subject fluttering (down);—not relying on his own rich

---

What is said on line 6 is good, but is only a truism. The whole course has been shown; if every step has been right and appropriate, the issue will be very good.

resources, but calling in his neighbours. (They all come) not as having received warning, but in the sincerity (of their hearts).

5. The fifth SIX, divided, reminds us of (king) Tî-yî's (rule about the) marriage of his younger sister. By such a course there is happiness and there will be great good fortune.

6. The sixth SIX, divided, shows us the city wall returned into the moat. It is not the time to use the army. (The subject of the line) may, indeed, announce his orders to the people of his own city; but however correct and firm he may be, he will have cause for regret.

XI. The language of the Thwan has reference to the form of Thâi, with the three strong lines of *Khien* below, and the three weak lines of Khwăn above. The former are 'the great,' active and vigorous; the latter are 'the small,' inactive and submissive. But where have the former 'come' from, and whither are the latter 'gone?' In many editions of the Yî beneath the hexagram of Thâi here, there appears that of Kwei Mei, the 54th in order (☰☱), which becomes Thâi, if the third and fourth lines exchange places. But in the notes on the Thwan, in the first Appendix, on hexagram 6, I have spoken of the doctrine of 'changing figures,' and intimated my disbelief of it. The different hexagrams arose necessarily by the continued manipulation of the undivided and divided lines, and placing them each over itself and over the other. When king Wăn wrote these Thwan, he was taking the 64 hexagrams, as they were ready to his hand, and not forming one from another by any process of divination. The 'gone' and 'come' are merely equivalent to 'below' and 'above,' in the lower trigram or in the upper.

A course in which the motive forces are represented by the three strong, and the opposing by the three weak lines, must be progressive and successful. Thâi is called the hexagram of the first month of the year, the first month of the natural spring, when for six months, through the fostering sun and genial skies, the processes of growth will be going on.

XII   THE PHÎ HEXAGRAM

P'I

In Phî there is the want of good understanding between the (different classes of) men, and its indication is unfavourable to the firm and correct

The symbolism of paragraph 1 is suggested by the three strong lines of *Kh*ien all together, and all possessed by the same instinct to advance. The movement of the first will be supported by that of the others, and be fortunate.

The second line is strong, but in an even place. This is supposed to temper the strength of its subject; which is expressed by the first of his characteristics. But the even place is the central; and it is responded to by a proper correlate in the fifth line above. Hence come all the symbolism of the paragraph and the auspice of good fortune implied in it.

Beneath the symbolism in paragraph 3 there lies the persuasion of the constant change that is taking place in nature and in human affairs. As night succeeds to day, and winter to summer, so calamity may be expected to follow prosperity, and decay the flourishing of a state. The third is the last of the lines of *Kh*ien, by whose strength and activity the happy state of Thâi has been produced. Another aspect of things may be looked for; but by firmness and correctness the good estate of the present may be long continued.

According to the treatise on the Thwan, the subjects of the fourth and other upper lines are not 'the small returning' as opponents of the strong lines below, as is generally supposed; but as the correlates of those lines, of one heart and mind with them to maintain the state of Thâi, and giving them, humbly but readily, all the help in their power.

Tî-yî, the last sovereign but one of the Yin dynasty, reigned from B.C. 1191 to 1155; but what was the history of him and his sister here referred to we do not know. P. Regis assumes that he gave his sister in marriage to the lord of *K*âu, known in subse-

course of the superior man.   We see in it the great
gone and the little come.

1. The first SIX, divided, suggests the idea of
grass pulled up, and bringing with it other stalks
with whose roots it is connected.   With firm correctness (on the part of its subject), there will be
good fortune and progress.

2. The second SIX, divided, shows its subject
patient and obedient.   To the small man (comporting himself so) there will be good fortune.   If the
great man (comport himself) as the distress and obstruction require, he will have success.

3. The third SIX, divided, shows its subject
ashamed of the purpose folded (in his breast).

4. The fourth NINE, undivided, shows its subject
acting in accordance with the ordination (of Heaven),
and committing no error.   His companions will come
and share in his happiness.

5. In the fifth NINE, undivided, we see him who

quent time as king Wăn, and that she was the famous Thai-sze ;—
contrary to all the evidence I have been able to find on the subject.
According to Khăng-ʒze, Ti-yî was the first to enact a law that
daughters of the royal house, in marrying princes of the states, should
be in subjection to them, as if they were not superior to them in
rank.   Here line 5, while occupying the place of dignity and authority in the hexagram, is yet a weak line in the place of a strong
one ; and its subject, accordingly, humbly condescends to his
strong and proper correlate in line 2.

The course denoted by Thâi has been run ; and will be followed by one of a different and unhappy character.   The earth dug
from the moat had been built up to form a protecting wall ; but it
is now again fallen into the ditch.   War will only aggravate the
evil ; and however the ruler may address good proclamations to
himself and the people of his capital, the coming evil cannot be
altogether averted.

brings the distress and obstruction to a close,—the great man and fortunate. (But let him say), 'We may perish! We may perish!' (so shall the state of things become firm, as if) bound to a clump of bushy mulberry trees.

6. The sixth NINE, undivided, shows the overthrow (and removal of) the condition of distress and obstruction. Before this there was that condition. Hereafter there will be joy.

XII. The form of Phî, it will be seen, is exactly the opposite of that of Thâi. Much of what has been said on the interpretation of that will apply to this, or at least assist the student in making out the meaning of its symbolism. Phî is the hexagram of the seventh month. Genial influences have done their work, the processes of growth are at an end. Henceforth increasing decay must be looked for.

Naturally we should expect the advance of the subject of the first of the three weak lines to lead to evil; but if he set himself to be firm and correct, he will bring about a different issue.

Patience and obedience are proper for the small man in all circumstances. If the great man in difficulty yet cherish these attributes, he will soon have a happy issue out of the distress.

The third line is weak. Its place is odd, and therefore for it incorrect. Its subject would vent his evil purpose, but has not strength to do so. He is left therefore to the shame which he ought to feel without a word of warning. Does the ming of the fourth line mean 'the ordination of Heaven,' as Kû Hsî thinks; or the orders of the ruler, as Khang-ȝze says? Whichever interpretation be taken (and some critics unite the two), the action of the subject of the line, whose strength is tempered by the even position, will be good and correct, and issue in success and happiness.

The strong line in the fifth, (its correct), place, brings the distress and obstruction to a close. Yet its subject—the ruler in the hexagram—is warned to continue to be cautious in two lines of rhyme:—

'And let him say, "I die! I die!"
So to a bushy clump his fortune he shall tie.'

There is an end of the condition of distress. It was necessary that condition should give place to its opposite; and the strong line in the topmost place fitly represents the consequent joy.

XIII   THE THUNG ZĂN HEXAGRAM

T'UNG JÊN

Thung Zăn (or 'Union of men') appears here (as we find it) in the (remote districts of the) country, indicating progress and success. It will be advantageous to cross the great stream. It will be advantageous to maintain the firm correctness of the superior man.

1. The first NINE, undivided, (shows the representative of) the union of men just issuing from his gate. There will be no error.

2. The second SIX, divided, (shows the representative of) the union of men in relation with his kindred. There will be occasion for regret.

3. The third NINE, undivided, (shows its subject) with his arms hidden in the thick grass, and at the top of a high mound. (But) for three years he makes no demonstration.

4. The fourth NINE, undivided, (shows its subject) mounted on the city wall; but he does not proceed to make the attack (he contemplates). There will be good fortune.

5. In the fifth NINE, undivided, (the representative of) the union of men first wails and cries out, and then laughs. His great host conquers, and he (and the subject of the second line) meet together.

6. The topmost NINE, undivided, (shows the repre-

sentative of) the union of men in the suburbs. There
will be no occasion for repentance.

XIII. Thung Zăn describes a condition of nature and of the
state opposite to that of Phî. There was distress and obstruction;
here is union. But the union must be based entirely on public
considerations, without taint of selfishness.

The strong line in the fifth, its correct, place, occupies the most
important position, and has for its correlate the weak second line,
also in its correct place. The one divided line is naturally sought
after by all the strong lines. The upper trigram is that of heaven,
which is above; the lower is that of fire, whose tendency is to mount
upwards. All these things are in harmony with the idea of union.
But the union must be free from all selfish motives, and this is
indicated by its being in the remote districts of the country, where
people are unsophisticated, and free from the depraving effects
incident to large societies. A union from such motives will cope
with the greatest difficulties; and yet a word of caution is added.

Line 1 emblems the first attempts at union. It is strong, but in
the lowest place; and it has no proper correlate above. There is,
however, no intermixture of selfishness in it.

Lines 2 and 5 are proper correlates, which fact suggests in this
hexagram the idea of their union being limited and partial, and
such as may afford ground for blame.

Line 3 is strong, and in an odd place; but it has not a proper correlate in 6. This makes its subject more anxious to unite with 2;
but 2 is devoted to its proper correlate in 5, of whose strength 3 is
afraid, and takes the measures described. His abstaining so long,
however, from any active attempt, will save him from misfortune.

Line 4 is strong, but in an even place, which weakens its subject.
He also would fain make an attempt on 2; but he is afraid, and
does not carry his purpose into effect.

Line 5 is strong, in an odd, and the central place; and would fain
unite with 2, which indeed is the proper correlate of its subject.
But 3 and 4 are powerful foes that oppose the union. Their
opposition makes him weep; but he collects his forces, defeats
them, and effects his purpose.

The union reaches to all within the suburbs, and is not yet universal; but still there is no cause for repentance.

XIV   THE TÂ YÛ HEXAGRAM

TA YU

Tâ Yû indicates that, (under the circumstances which it implies), there will be great progress and success.

1. In the first NINE, undivided, there is no approach to what is injurious, and there is no error. Let there be a realisation of the difficulty (and danger of the position), and there will be no error (to the end).

2. In the second NINE, undivided, we have a large waggon with its load. In whatever direction advance is made, there will be no error.

3. The third NINE, undivided, shows us a feudal prince presenting his offerings to the Son of Heaven. A small man would be unequal (to such a duty).

4. The fourth NINE, undivided, shows its subject keeping his great resources under restraint. There will be no error.

5. The fifth SIX, divided, shows the sincerity of its subject reciprocated by that of all the others (represented in the hexagram). Let him display a proper majesty, and there will be good fortune.

6. The topmost NINE, undivided, shows its subject with help accorded to him from Heaven. There will be good fortune, advantage in every respect.

XIV. Tâ Yû means 'Great Havings;' denoting in a kingdom a state of prosperity and abundance, and in a family or individual, a

XV   THE *KHIEN* HEXAGRAM

   CH'IEN

*Khi*en indicates progress and success. The superior man, (being humble as it implies), will have a (good) issue (to his undertakings).

1. The first SIX, divided, shows us the superior man who adds humility to humility. (Even) the great

---

state of opulence. The danger threatening such a condition arises from the pride which it is likely to engender. But everything here is against that issue. Apart from the symbolism of the trigrams, we have the place of honour occupied by a weak line, so that its subject will be humble; and all the other lines, strong as they are, will act in obedient sympathy. There will be great progress and success.

Line 1, though strong, is at the lowest part of the figure, and has no correlate above. No external influences have as yet acted injuriously on its subject. Let him do as directed, and no hurtful influence will ever affect him.

The strong line 2 has its proper correlate in line 5, the ruler of the figure, and will use its strength in subordination to his humility. Hence the symbolism.

Line 3 is strong, and in the right (an odd) place. The topmost line of the lower trigram is the proper place for a feudal lord. The subject of this will humbly serve the condescending ruler in line 5. A small man, having the place without the virtue, would give himself airs.

Line 4 is strong, but the strength is tempered by the position, which is that of a weak line. Hence he will do no injury to the mild ruler, to whom he is so near.

Line 5 symbolises the ruler. Mild sincerity is good in him, and affects his ministers and others. But a ruler must not be without an awe-inspiring majesty.

Even the topmost line takes its character from 5. The strength of its subject is still tempered, and Heaven gives its approval.

stream may be crossed with this, and there will be good fortune.

2. The second SIX, divided, shows us humility that has made itself recognised. With firm correctness there will be good fortune.

3. The third NINE, undivided, shows the superior man of (acknowledged) merit. He will maintain his success to the end, and have good fortune.

4. The fourth SIX, divided, shows one, whose action would be in every way advantageous, stirring up (the more) his humility.

5. The fifth SIX, divided, shows one who, without being rich, is able to employ his neighbours. He may advantageously use the force of arms. All his movements will be advantageous.

6. The sixth SIX, divided, shows us humility that has made itself recognised. The subject of it will with advantage put his hosts in motion; but (he will only) punish his own towns and state.

XV. An essay on humility rightly follows that on abundant possessions. The third line, which is a whole line amid five others divided, occupying the topmost place in the lower trigram, is held by the Khang-hsî editors and many others to be 'the lord of the hexagram,' the representative of humility, strong, but abasing itself. There is nothing here in the text to make us enter farther on the symbolism of the figure. Humility is the way to permanent success.

A weak line, at the lowest place of the figure, is the fitting symbol of the superior man adding humility to humility.

Line 2 is weak, central, and in its proper place, representing a humility that has 'crowed;' that is, has proclaimed itself.

Line 3 is strong, and occupies an odd (its proper) place. It is 'the lord of the hexagram,' to whom all represented by the lines above and below turn.

Line 4 is weak and in its proper position. Its subject is sure to

XVI   The Yü Hexagram

YÜ

Yü indicates that, (in the state which it implies), feudal princes may be set up, and the hosts put in motion, with advantage.

1. The first SIX, divided, shows its subject proclaiming his pleasure and satisfaction. There will be evil.

2. The second SIX, divided, shows one who is firm as a rock. (He sees a thing) without waiting till it has come to pass; with his firm correctness there will be good fortune.

3. The third SIX, divided, shows one looking up (for favours), while he indulges the feeling of pleasure and satisfaction. If he would understand!— If he be late in doing so, there will indeed be occasion for repentance.

4. The fourth NINE, undivided, shows him from whom the harmony and satisfaction come. Great

---

be successful and prosperous, but being so near the fifth line, he should still use the greatest precaution.

All men love and honour humility, in itself and without the adjuncts which usually command obedience and respect. Hence his neighbours follow the ruler in the fifth line, though he may not be very rich or powerful. His humility need not keep him from asserting the right, even by force of arms.

The subject of the sixth line, which is weak, is outside the game, so to speak, that has been played out. He will use force, but only within his own sphere and to assert what is right. He will not be aggressive.

is the success which he obtains. Let him not allow suspicions to enter his mind, and thus friends will gather around him.

5. The fifth six, divided, shows one with a chronic complaint, but who lives on without dying.

6. The topmost six, divided, shows its subject with darkened mind devoted to the pleasure and satisfaction (of the time); but if he change his course even when (it may be considered as) completed, there will be no error.

XVI. The Yü hexagram denoted to king Wăn a condition of harmony and happy contentment throughout the kingdom, when the people rejoiced in and readily obeyed their sovereign. At such a time his appointments and any military undertakings would be hailed and supported. The fourth line, undivided, is the lord of the figure, and being close to the fifth or place of dignity, is to be looked on as the minister or chief officer of the ruler. The ruler gives to him his confidence; and all represented by the other lines yield their obedience.

Line 1 is weak, and has for its correlate the strong 4. Its subject may well enjoy the happiness of the time. But he cannot contain himself, and proclaims, or boasts of, his satisfaction;—which is evil.

Line 2, though weak, is in its correct position, the centre, more-over, of the lower trigram. Quietly and firmly its subject is able to abide in his place, and exercise a far-seeing discrimination. All is indicative of good fortune.

Line 3 is weak, and in an odd place. Immediately below line 4, its subject keeps looking up to the lord of the figure, and depends on him, thinking of doing nothing, but how to enjoy himself. The consequence will be as described, unless he speedily change.

The strong subject of line 4 is the agent to whom the happy condition is owing; and it is only necessary to caution him to main-tain his confidence in himself and his purpose, and his adherents and success will continue.

Line 5 is in the ruler's place; but it is weak, and he is in danger of being carried away by the lust of pleasure. Moreover, proximity to the powerful minister represented by 4 is a source of danger.

XVII   THE SUI HEXAGRAM

SUI

Sui indicates that (under its conditions) there will be great progress and success. But it will be advantageous to be firm and correct. There will (then) be no error.

1. The first NINE, undivided, shows us one changing the object of his pursuit; but if he be firm and correct, there will be good fortune. Going beyond (his own) gate to find associates, he will achieve merit.

2. The second SIX, divided, shows us one who cleaves to the little boy, and lets go the man of age and experience.

3. The third SIX, divided, shows us one who cleaves to the man of age and experience, and lets go the little boy. Such following will get what it seeks; but it will be advantageous to adhere to what is firm and correct.

4. The fourth NINE, undivided, shows us one followed and obtaining (adherents). Though he be firm and correct, there will be evil. If he be sincere (however) in his course, and make that evident, into what error will he fall?

Hence he is represented as suffering from a chronic complaint, but nevertheless he does not die. See Appendix II on the line.

Line 6, at the very top or end of the hexagram, is weak, and its subject is all but lost. Still even for him there is a chance of safety, if he will but change.

5. The fifth NINE, undivided, shows us (the ruler) sincere in (fostering all) that is excellent. There will be good fortune.

6. The topmost SIX, divided, shows us (that sincerity) firmly held and clung to, yea, and bound fast. (We see) the king with it presenting his offerings on the western mountain.

XVII. Sui symbolises the idea of following. It is said to follow Yü, the symbol of harmony and satisfaction. Where there are these conditions men are sure to follow; nor will they follow those in whom they have no complacency. The hexagram includes the cases where one follows others, and where others follow him; and the auspice of great progress and success is due to this flexibility and applicability of it. But in both cases the following must be guided by a reference to what is proper and correct. See the notes on the Thwan and the Great Symbolism.

Line 1 is strong, and lord of the lower trigram. The weak lines ought to follow it; but here it is below them, in the lowest place of the figure. This gives rise to the representation of one changing his pursuit. Still through the native vigour indicated by the line being strong, and in its correct place, its subject will be fortunate. Going beyond his gate to find associates indicates his public spirit, and superiority to selfish considerations.

Line 2 is weak. Its proper correlate is the strong 5; but it prefers to cleave to the line below, instead of waiting to follow 5. Hence the symbolism of the text, the bad omen of which needs not to be mentioned.

Line 3 is also weak, but it follows the strong line above it and leaves line 1, reversing the course of 2;—with a different issue. It is weak, however, and 4 is not its proper correlate; hence the conclusion of the paragraph is equivalent to a caution.

Line 4 is strong, and in the place of a great minister next the ruler in 5. But his having adherents may be injurious to the supreme and sole authority of that ruler, and only a sincere loyalty will save him from error and misfortune.

Line 5 is strong, and in its correct place, with 2 as its proper correlate; thus producing the auspicious symbolism.

The issue of the hexagram is seen in line 6; which represents the ideal of following, directed by the most sincere adherence to

XVIII   THE KÛ HEXAGRAM

KU

Kû indicates great progress and success (to him who deals properly with the condition represented by it). There will be advantage in (efforts like that of) crossing the .great stream. (He should weigh well, however, the events of) three days before the turning point, and those (to be done) three days after it.

1. The first SIX, divided, shows (a son) dealing with the troubles caused by his father. If he be an (able) son, the father will escape the blame of having erred. The position is perilous, but there will be good fortune in the end.

2. The second NINE, undivided, shows (a son) dealing with the troubles caused by his mother. He should not (carry) his firm correctness (to the utmost).

3. The third NINE, undivided, shows (a son) dealing with the troubles caused by his father. There may be some small occasion for repentance, but there will not be any great error.

4. The fourth SIX, divided, shows (a son) viewing

what is right. This influence not only extends to men, but also to spiritual beings. 'The western hill' is mount Khi, at the foot of which was the original settlement of the house of Kâu, in B.C. 1325. The use of the name 'king' here brings us down from Wǎn into the time of king Wû at least.

indulgently the troubles caused by his father.   If he
go forward, he will find cause to regret it.

5. The fifth SIX, divided, shows (a son) dealing
with the troubles caused by his father.   He obtains
the praise of using (the fit instrument for his work).

6. The sixth NINE, undivided, shows us one who
does not serve either king or feudal lord, but in a
lofty spirit prefers (to attend to) his own affairs.

XVIII. In the 6th Appendix it is said, 'They who follow another
are sure to have services (to perform), and hence Sui is followed
by Kû.' But Kû means the having painful or troublesome services
to do. It denotes here a state in which things are going to ruin,
as if through poison or venomous worms; and the figure is supposed to describe the arrest of the decay and the restoration to
soundness and vigour, so as to justify its auspice of great progress
and success. To realise such a result, however, great efforts will
be required, as in crossing the great stream; and a careful consideration of the events that have brought on the state of decay,
and the measures to be taken to remedy it is also necessary. See
Appendix I on the 'three days.'

The subject of line 1, and of all the other lines, excepting perhaps 6, appears as a son. Yet the line itself is of the yin nature,
and the trigram in which it plays the principal part is also yin.
Line 2 is strong, and of the yang nature, with the yin line 5 as
its proper correlate. In line 2, 5 appears as the mother; but its subject there is again a son, and the upper trigram altogether is yang.
I am unable to account for these things. As is said in the note of
Regis on line 2 :—'Haec matris filiique denominatio ad has lineas
mere translatitia est, et, ut ait commentarius vulgaris, ad explicatio-
nem sententiarum eas pro matre et filio supponere dicendum
est. Nec ratio reddetur si quis in utroque hoc nomine mysterium
quaerat. Cur enim aliis in figuris lineae nunc regem, nunc vasal-
lum, jam imperii administrum, mox summum armorum
praefectum referre dicantur? Accommodantur scilicet lineae ad
verba sententiae et verba sententiae ad sensum, quemadmodum faci-
endum de methodis libri Shih King docet Mencius, V, i, ode 4. 2.'

We must leave this difficulty. Line 1 is weak, and its correlate
4 is also weak. What can its subject do to remedy the state of
decay? But the line is the first of the figure, and the decay is not

XIX   THE LIN HEXAGRAM

LIN

Lin (indicates that under the conditions supposed in it) there will be great progress and success, while it will be advantageous to be firmly correct. In the eighth month there will be evil.

1. The first NINE, undivided, shows its subject advancing in company (with the subject of the

---

yet great. By giving heed to the cautions in the Text, he will accomplish what is promised.

The ruler in line 5 is represented by a weak line, while 2 is strong. Thus the symbolism takes the form of a son dealing with the prevailing decay induced somehow by his mother. But a son must be very gentle in all his intercourse with his mother, and especially so, when constrained by a sense of duty to oppose her course. I do not think there is anything more or better to be said here. The historical interpretation adopted by Regis and his friends, that the father here is king Wǎn, the mother Thâi-sze, and the son king Wû, cannot be maintained. I have searched, but in vain, for the slightest Chinese sanction of it, and it would give to Kû the meaning of misfortunes endured, instead of troubles caused.

Line 3 is strong, and not central, so that its subject might well go to excess in his efforts. But this tendency is counteracted by the line's place in the trigram Sun, often denoting lowly submission.

Line 4 is weak, and in an even place, which intensifies that weakness. Hence comes the caution against going forward.

The weak line 5, as has been said, is the seat of the ruler; but its proper correlate is the strong 2, the strong siding champion minister, to whom the work of the hexagram is delegated.

Line 6 is strong, and has no proper correlate below. Hence it suggests the idea of one outside the sphere of action, and taking no part in public affairs, but occupied with the culture of himself.

second line). Through his firm correctness there will be good fortune.

2. The second NINE, undivided, shows its subject advancing in company (with the subject of the first line). There will be good fortune; (advancing) will be in every way advantageous.

3. The third SIX, divided, shows one well pleased (indeed) to advance, (but whose action) will be in no way advantageous. If he become anxious about it (however), there will be no error.

4. The fourth SIX, divided, shows one advancing in the highest mode. There will be no error.

5. The fifth SIX, divided, shows the advance of wisdom, such as befits the great ruler. There will be good fortune.

6. The sixth SIX, divided, shows the advance of honesty and generosity. There will be good fortune, and no error.

XIX. In Appendix VI Lin is explained as meaning 'great.' The writer, having misunderstood the meaning of the previous Kû, subjoins—'He who performs such services may become "great."' But Lin denotes the approach of authority,—to inspect, to comfort, or to rule. When we look at the figure, we see two strong undivided lines advancing on the four weak lines above them, and thence follows the assurance that their action will be powerful and successful. That action must be governed by rectitude, however, and by caution grounded on the changing character of all conditions and events. The meaning of the concluding sentence is given in Appendix I as simply being—that, 'the advancing power will decay in no long time.' Lû Kǎn-khî (Ming dynasty) says:—'The sun (or the day) is the symbol of what is Yang; and the moon is the symbol of what is Yin. Eight is the number of the second of the four emblematic figures (the smaller Yin), and seven is the number of the third of them (the smaller Yang). Hence to indicate the period of the coming of what is Yin, we use the phrase, "the eighth month;" and to indicate the period of the coming of what is

XX   THE KWÂN HEXAGRAM

KUAN

Kwân shows (how he whom it represents should be like) the worshipper who has washed his hands, but not (yet) presented his offerings ;—with sincerity

---

Yang, we use the phrase, "the seventh day."' The Khang-hsî editors say that this is the best explanation of the language of the Text that can be given :—'The Yang numbers culminate in 9, the influence then receding and producing the 8 of the smaller Yin. The Yin numbers culminate in 6, and the next advance produces the 7 of the smaller Yang; so that 7 and 8 are the numbers indicating the first birth of what is Yin and what is Yang.' 'If we go to seek,' they add, 'any other explanation of the phraseology of the Text, and such expressions as "3 days," "3 years," "10 years," &c., we make them unintelligible.' Lin is the hexagram of the twelfth month.

Line 1 is a strong line in its proper place. The danger is that its subject may be more strong than prudent, hence the caution in requiring firm correctness.

Line 2, as strong, should be in an odd place ; but this is more than counterbalanced by the central position, and its correlate in line 5.

Line 3 is weak, and neither central, nor in its correct position. Hence its action will not be advantageous; but being at the top of the trigram Tui, which means being pleased, its subject is represented as 'well pleased to advance.' Anxious reflection will save him from error.

Line 4, though weak, is in its proper place, and has for its correlate the strong 1. Hence its advance is 'in the highest style.'

Line 5 is the position of the ruler. It is weak, but being central, and having for its correlate the strong and central 2, we have in it a symbol of authority distrustful of itself, and employing fit agents;—characteristic of the wise ruler.

Line 6 is the last of the trigram Khwăn, the height therefore of docility. Line 2 is not its correlate, but it belongs to the Yin to seek for the Yang ; and it is so emphatically in this case. Hence the characteristic and issue as assigned.

and an appearance of dignity (commanding reverent regard).

1. The first SIX, divided, shows the looking of a lad;—not blamable in men of inferior rank, but matter for regret in superior men.

2. The second SIX, divided, shows one peeping out from a door. It would be advantageous if it were (merely) the firm correctness of a female.

3. The third SIX, divided, shows one looking at (the course of) his own life, to advance or recede (accordingly).

4. The fourth SIX, divided, shows one contemplating the glory of the kingdom. It will be advantageous for him, being such as he is, (to seek) to be a guest of the king.

5. The fifth NINE, undivided, shows its subject contemplating his own life(-course). A superior man, he will (thus) fall into no error.

6. The sixth NINE, undivided, shows its subject contemplating his character to see if it be indeed that of a superior man. He will not fall into error.

XX. The Chinese character Kwân, from which this hexagram is named, is used in it in two senses. In the Thwan, the first paragraph of the treatise on the Thwan, and the paragraph on the Great Symbolism, it denotes showing, manifesting; in all other places it denotes contemplating, looking at. The subject of the hexagram is the sovereign and his subjects, how he manifests himself to them, and how they contemplate him. The two upper, undivided, lines belong to the sovereign; the four weak lines below them are his subjects,—ministers and others who look up at him. Kwân is the hexagram of the eighth month.

In the Thwan king Wăn symbolises the sovereign by a worshipper when he is most solemn in his religious service, at the commencement of it, full of sincerity and with a dignified carriage.

Line 1 is weak, and in the lowest place, improper also for it;—

XXI THE SHIH HO HEXAGRAM

SHIH HO

Shih Ho indicates successful progress (in the condition of things which it supposes). It will be advantageous to use legal constraints.

1. The first NINE, undivided, shows one with his feet in the stocks and deprived of his toes. There will be no error.

2. The second SIX, divided, shows one biting through the soft flesh, and (going on to) bite off the nose. There will be no error.

---

the symbol of a thoughtless lad, who cannot see far, and takes only superficial views.

Line 2 is also weak, but in its proper place, showing a woman, living retired, and only able to peep as from her door at the subject of the fifth line. But ignorance and retirement are proper in a woman.

Line 3, at the top of the lower trigram Khwăn, and weak, must belong to a subject of the utmost docility, and will wish to act only according to the exigency of time and circumstances.

Line 4, in the place proper to its weakness, is yet in immediate proximity to 5, representing the sovereign. Its subject is moved accordingly, and stirred to ambition.

Line 5 is strong, and in the place of the ruler. He is a superior man, but this does not relieve him from the duty of self-contemplation or examination.

There is a slight difference in the 6th paragraph from the 5th, which can hardly be expressed in a translation. By making a change in the punctuation, however, the different significance may be brought out. Line 6 is strong, and should be considered out of the work of the hexagram, but its subject is still possessed by the spirit of its idea, and is led to self-examination.

3. The third SIX, divided, shows one gnawing dried flesh, and meeting with what is disagreeable. There will be occasion for some small regret, but no (great) error.

4. The fourth NINE, undivided, shows one gnawing the flesh dried on the bone, and getting the pledges of money and arrows. It will be advantageous to him to realise the difficulty of his task and be firm,— in which case there will be good fortune.

5. The fifth SIX, divided, shows one gnawing at dried flesh, and finding the yellow gold. Let him be firm and correct, realising the peril (of his position). There will be no error.

6. The sixth NINE, undivided, shows one wearing the cangue, and deprived of his ears. There will be evil.

XXI. Shih Ho means literally 'Union by gnawing.' We see in the figure two strong lines in the first and last places, while all the others, with the exception of the fourth, are divided. This suggests the idea of the jaws and the mouth between them kept open by something in it. Let that be gnawed through and the mouth will close and the jaws come together. So in the body politic. Remove the obstacles to union, and high and low will come together with a good understanding. And how are those obstacles to be removed? By force, emblemed by the gnawing; that is, by legal constraints. And these are sure to be successful. The auspice of the figure is favourable. There will be success.

Lines 1 and 6 are much out of the game or action described in the figure. Hence they are held to represent parties receiving punishment, while the other lines represent parties inflicting it. The punishment in line 1 is that of the stocks, administered for a small offence, and before crime has made much way. But if the 'depriving' of the toes is not merely keeping them in restraint, but cutting them off, as the Chinese character suggests, the punishment appears to a western reader too severe.

Line 2 is weak, appropriately therefore in an even place, and it is central besides. The action therefore of its subject should

XXII   THE PÎ HEXAGRAM

PI

Pî indicates that there should be free course (in what it denotes). There will be little advantage (however) if it be allowed to advance (and take the lead).

---

be effective; and this is shown by the 'biting through the soft flesh,' an easy thing. Immediately below, however, is a strong offender represented by the strong line, and before he will submit it is necessary to 'bite off his nose;' for punishment is the rule;—it must be continued and increased till the end is secured.

Line 3 is weak, and in an even place. The action of its subject will be ineffective; and is emblemed by the hard task of gnawing through dried flesh, and encountering, besides, what is distasteful and injurious in it. But again comes in the consideration that here punishment is the rule, and the auspice is not all bad.

Of old, in a civil case, both parties, before they were heard, brought to the court an arrow (or a bundle of arrows), in testimony of their rectitude, after which they were heard; in a criminal case, they in the same way deposited each thirty pounds of gold, or some other metal. See the Official Book of *K*au, 27. 14, 15. The subject of the fourth line's getting those pledges indicates his exercising his judicial functions; and what he gnaws through indicates their difficulty. Moreover, though the line is strong, it is in an even place; and hence comes the lesson of caution.

The fifth line represents 'the lord of judgment.' As it is a weak line, he will be disposed to leniency; and his judgments will be correct. This is declared by his finding the 'yellow metal;' for yellow is one of the five 'correct' colours. The position is in the centre and that of rule; but the line being weak, a caution is given, as under the previous line.

The action of the figure has passed, and still we have, in the subject of line 6, one persisting in wrong, a strong criminal, wearing the cangue, and deaf to counsel. Of course the auspice is evil.

1. The first NINE, undivided, shows one adorning (the way of) his feet. He can discard a carriage and walk on foot.

2. The second SIX, divided, shows one adorning his beard.

3. The third NINE, undivided, shows its subject with the appearance of being adorned and bedewed (with rich favours). But let him ever maintain his firm correctness, and there will be good fortune.

4. The fourth SIX, divided, shows one looking as if adorned, but only in white. As if (mounted on) a white horse, and furnished with wings, (he seeks union with the subject of the first line), while (the intervening third pursues), not as a robber, but intent on a matrimonial alliance.

5. The fifth SIX, divided, shows its subject adorned by (the occupants of) the heights and gardens. He bears his roll of silk, small and slight. He may appear stingy; but there will be good fortune in the end.

6. The sixth NINE, undivided, shows one with white as his (only) ornament. There will be no error.

XXII. The character Pî is the symbol of what is ornamental and of the act of adorning. As there is ornament in nature, so should there be in society; but its place is secondary to that of what is substantial. This is the view of king Wǎn in his Thwan. The symbolism of the separate lines is sometimes fantastic.

Line 1 is strong, and in an odd place. It is at the very bottom of the hexagram, and is the first line of Lî, the trigram for fire or light, and suggesting what is elegant and bright. Its subject has nothing to do but to attend to himself. Thus he cultivates—adorns—himself in his humble position; but if need be, righteousness requiring it, he can give up every luxury and indulgence.

XXIII   THE PO HEXAGRAM

 PO

Po indicates that (in the state which it symbolises) it will not be advantageous to make a movement in any direction whatever.

Line 2 is weak and in its proper place, but with no proper correlate above. The strong line 3 is similarly situated. These two lines therefore keep together, and are as the beard and the chin. Line 1 follows 2. What is substantial commands and rules what is merely ornamental.

Line 3 is strong, and between two weak lines, which adorn it, and bestow their favours on it. But this happy condition is from the accident of place. The subject of the line must be always correct and firm to ensure its continuance.

Line 4 has its proper correlate in 1, from whose strength it should receive ornament, but 2 and the strong 3 intervene and keep them apart, so that the ornament is only white, and of no bright colour. Line 4, however, is faithful to 1, and earnest for their union. And finally line 3 appears in a good character, and not with the purpose to injure, so that the union of 1 and 4 takes place. All this is intended to indicate how ornament recognises the superiority of solidity. Compare the symbolism of the second line of *K*un (3), and that of the topmost line of Khwei (38).

Line 5 is in the place of honour, and has no proper correlate in 2. It therefore associates with the strong 6, which is symbolised by the heights and gardens round a city, and serving both to protect and to beautify it. Thus the subject of the line receives adorning from without, and does not of itself try to manifest it. Moreover, in his weakness, his offerings of ceremony are poor and mean. But, as Confucius said, 'In ceremonies it is better to be sparing than extravagant.' Hence that stinginess does not prevent a good auspice.

Line 6 is at the top of the hexagram. Ornament has had its course, and here there is a return to pure, 'white,' simplicity. Substantiality is better than ornament.

1. The first SIX, divided, shows one overturning the couch by injuring its legs. (The injury will go on to) the destruction of (all) firm correctness, and there will be evil.

2. The second SIX, divided, shows one over-throwing the couch by injuring its frame. (The injury will go on to) the destruction of (all) firm correctness, and there will be evil.

3. The third SIX, divided, shows its subject among the overthrowers; but there will be no error.

4. The fourth SIX, divided, shows its subject having overthrown the couch, and (going to injure) the skin (of him who lies on it). There will be evil.

5. The fifth SIX, divided, shows (its subject leading on the others like) a string of fishes, and (obtaining for them) the favour that lights on the inmates of the palace. There will be advantage in every way.

6. The topmost NINE, undivided, shows its subject (as) a great fruit which has not been eaten. The superior man finds (the people again) as a chariot carrying him. The small men (by their course) overthrow their own dwellings.

XXIII. Po is the symbol of falling or of causing to fall, and may be applied, both in the natural and political world, to the process of decay, or that of overthrow. The figure consists of five divided lines, and one undivided, which last thus becomes the prominent and principal line in the figure. Decay or overthrow has begun at the bottom of it, and crept up to the top. The hexagram is that of the ninth month, when the beauty and glory of summer have disappeared, and the year is ready to fall into the arms of sterile winter. In the political world, small men have gradually displaced good men and great, till but one remains; and the lesson for him is to wait. The power operating against him is

XXIV   THE FÛ HEXAGRAM

FU

Fû indicates that there will be free course and progress (in what it denotes). (The subject of it) finds no one to distress him in his exits and

too strong; but the fashion of political life passes away. If he wait, a change for the better will shortly appear.

The lesser symbolism is chiefly that of a bed or couch with its occupant. The idea of the hexagram requires this occupant to be overthrown, or at least that an attempt be made to overthrow him. Accordingly the attempt in line 1 is made by commencing with the legs of the couch. The symbolism goes on to explain itself. The object of the evil worker is the overthrow of all firm correctness. Of course there will be evil.

Line 2 is to the same effect as 1; only the foe has advanced from the legs to the frame of the couch.

Line 3 also represents an overthrower; but it differs from the others in being the correlate of 6. The subject of it will take part with him. His association is with the subject of 6, and not, as in the other weak lines, with one of its own kind.

From line 4 the danger is imminent. The couch has been overthrown. The person of the occupant is at the mercy of the destroyers.

With line 5 the symbolism changes. The subject of 5 is 'lord of all the other weak lines,' and their subjects are at his disposal. He and they are represented as fishes, following one another as if strung together. All fishes come under the category of yin. Then the symbolism changes again. The subject of 5, representing and controlling all the yin lines, is loyal to the subject of the yang sixth line. He is the rightful sovereign in his palace, and 5 leads all the others there to enjoy the sovereign's favours.

We have still different symbolism under line 6. Its strong subject, notwithstanding the attempts against him, survives, and acquires fresh vigour. The people again cherish their sovereign, and the plotters have wrought to their own overthrow.

entrances; friends come to him, and no error is committed. He will return and repeat his (proper) course. In seven days comes his return. There will be advantage in whatever direction movement is made.

1. The first NINE, undivided, shows its subject returning (from an error) of no great extent, which would not proceed to anything requiring repentance. There will be great good fortune.

2. The second SIX, divided, shows the admirable return (of its subject). There will be good fortune.

3. The third SIX, divided, shows one who has made repeated returns. The position is perilous, but there will be no error.

4. The fourth SIX, divided, shows its subject moving right in the centre (among those represented by the other divided lines), and yet returning alone (to his proper path).

5. The fifth SIX, divided, shows the noble return of its subject. There will be no ground for repentance.

6. The topmost SIX, divided, shows its subject all astray on the subject of returning. There will be evil. There will be calamities and errors. If with his views he put the hosts in motion, the end will be a great defeat, whose issues will extend to the ruler of the state. Even in ten years he will not be able to repair the disaster.

XXIV. Fû symbolises the idea of returning, coming back or over again. The last hexagram showed us inferior prevailing over superior men, all that is good in nature and society yielding before what is bad. But change is the law of nature and society. When decay has reached its climax, recovery will begin to take place. In Po we had one strong topmost line, and five weak lines below

XXV   THE WÛ WANG HEXAGRAM

WU WANG

Wû Wang indicates great progress and success, while there will be advantage in being firm and

---

it; here we have one strong line, and five weak lines above it. To illustrate the subject from what we see in nature,—Po is the hexagram of the ninth month, in which the triumph of cold and decay in the year is nearly complete. It is complete in the tenth month, whose hexagram is Khwăn ▤ ▤; then follows our hexagram Fû, belonging to the eleventh month, in which was the winter solstice when the sun turned back in his course, and moved with a constant regular progress towards the summer solstice. In harmony with these changes of nature are the changes in the political and social state of a nation. There is nothing in the Yî to suggest the hope of a perfect society or kingdom that cannot be moved.

The strong bottom line is the first of Kăn, the trigram of movement, and the upper trigram is Khwăn, denoting docility and capacity. The strong returning line will meet with no distressing obstacle, and the weak lines will change before it into strong, and be as friends. The bright quality will be developed brighter and brighter from day to day, and month to month.

The sentence, 'In seven days comes his return,' occasions some perplexity. If the reader will refer to hexagrams 44, 33, 12, 20, 23, and 2, he will see that during the months denoted by those figures, the 5th, 6th, 7th, 8th, 9th, and 10th, the yin lines have gradually been prevailing over the yang, until in Khwăn (2) they have extruded them entirely from the lineal figure. Then comes our Fû, as a seventh figure, in which the yang line begins to reassert itself, and from which it goes on to extrude the yin lines in their turn. Explained therefore of the months of the year, we have to take a day for a month. And something analogous—we cannot say exactly what—must have place in society and the state.

correct. If (its subject and his action) be not correct, he will fall into errors, and it will not be advantageous for him to move in any direction.

1. The first NINE, undivided, shows its subject free from all insincerity. His advance will be accompanied with good fortune.

2. The second SIX, divided, shows one who reaps without having ploughed (that he might reap), and gathers the produce of his third year's fields without having cultivated them the first year for that end. To such a one there will be advantage in whatever direction he may move.

3. The third SIX, divided, shows calamity happening to one who is free from insincerity;—as in

---

The concluding auspice or oracle to him who finds this Fû by divination is what we might expect.

The subject of line 1 is of course the undivided line, meaning here, says Khäng-ze, 'the way of the superior man.' There must have been some deviation from that, or 'returning' could not be spoken of.

Line 2 is in its proper place, and central; but it is weak. This is more than compensated for, however, by its adherence to line 1, the fifth line not being a proper correlate. Hence the return of its subject is called excellent or admirable.

Line 3 is weak, and in the uneven place of a strong line. It is the top line, moreover, of the trigram whose attribute is movement. Hence the symbolism; but any evil issue may be prevented by a realisation of danger and by caution.

Line 4 has its proper correlate in 1; different from all the other weak lines; and its course is different accordingly.

Line 5 is in the central place of honour, and the middle line of Khwăn, denoting docility. Hence its auspice.

Line 6 is weak; and being at the top of the hexagram, when its action of returning is all concluded, action on the part of its subject will lead to evils such as are mentioned. 'Ten years' seems to be a round number, signifying a long time, as in hexagram 3. 2.

the case of an ox that has been tied up. A passer
by finds it (and carries it off), while the people in the
neighbourhood have the calamity (of being accused
and apprehended).

4. The fourth NINE, undivided, shows (a case) in
which, if its subject can remain firm and correct,
there will be no error.

5. The fifth NINE, undivided, shows one who is
free from insincerity, and yet has fallen ill. Let
him not use medicine, and he will have occasion for
joy (in his recovery).

6. The topmost NINE, undivided, shows its subject
free from insincerity, yet sure to fall into error, if
he take action. (His action) will not be advantageous in any way.

XXV. Wang is the symbol of being reckless, and often of being
insincere; Wû Wang is descriptive of a state of entire freedom from
such a condition ; its subject is one who is entirely simple and sincere. The quality is characteristic of the action of Heaven, and of
the highest style of humanity. In this hexagram we have an essay
on this noble attribute. An absolute rectitude is essential to it. The
nearer one comes to the ideal of the quality, the more powerful
will be his influence, the greater his success. But let him see to it
that he never swerve from being correct.

The first line is strong; at the commencement of the inner
trigram denoting movement, the action of its subject will very much
characterise all the action set forth, and will itself be fortunate.

Line 2 is weak, central, and in its correct place. The quality
may be predicated of it in its highest degree. There is an entire
freedom in its subject from selfish or mercenary motive. He is
good simply for goodness' sake. And things are so constituted
that his action will be successful.

But calamity may also sometimes befal the best, and where there
is this freedom from insincerity ; and line 3 being weak, and in the
place of an even line, lays its subject open to this misfortune. 'The
people of the neighbourhood' are of course entirely innocent.

Line 4 is the lowest in the trigram of strength, and 1 is not a

XXVI   THE TÂ *KHÛ* HEXAGRAM

TA CH'U

Under the conditions of Tâ *Khû* it will be advantageous to be firm and correct. (If its subject do not seek to) enjoy his revenues in his own family (without taking service at court), there will be good fortune. It will be advantageous for him to cross the great stream.

1. The first NINE, undivided, shows its subject in a position of peril. It will be advantageous for him to stop his advance.

2. The second NINE, undivided, shows a carriage with the strap under it removed.

3. The third NINE, undivided, shows its subject urging his way with good horses. It will be advantageous for him to realise the difficulty (of his course), and to be firm and correct, exercising himself daily in his charioteering and methods of defence;

---

proper correlate, nor is the fourth the place for a strong line. Hence the paragraph must be understood as a caution.

Line 5 is strong, in the central place of honour, and has its proper correlate in 2. Hence its subject must possess the quality of the hexagram in perfection. And yet he shall be sick or in distress. But he need not be anxious. Without his efforts a way of escape for him will be opened.

Line 6 is at the top of the hexagram, and comes into the field when the action has run its course. He should be still, and not initiate any fresh movement.

then there will be advantage in whatever direction
he may advance.

4. The fourth SIX, divided, shows the young bull,
(and yet) having the piece of wood over his horns.
There will be great good fortune.

5. The fifth SIX, divided, shows the teeth of a
castrated hog. There will be good fortune.

6. The sixth NINE, undivided, shows its subject
(as) in command of the firmament of heaven. There
will be progress.

XXVI. *Khû* has two meanings. It is the symbol of restraint,
and of accumulation. What is repressed and restrained accumulates its strength and increases its volume. Both these meanings
are found in the treatise on the Thwan; the exposition of the
Great Symbolism has for its subject the accumulation of virtue. The
different lines are occupied with the repression or restraint of movement. The first three lines receive that repression, the upper three
exercise it. The accumulation to which all tends is that of virtue;
and hence the name of Tâ *Khû*, 'the Great Accumulation.'

What the Thwan teaches, is that he who goes about to
accumulate his virtue must be firm and correct, and may then,
engaging in the public service, enjoy the king's grace, and undertake the most difficult enterprises.

Line 1 is subject to the repression of 4, which will be increased
if he try to advance. It is better for him to halt.

Line 2 is liable to the repression of 5, and stops its advance of
itself, its subject having the wisdom to do so through its position in
the central place. The strap below, when attached to the axle,
made the carriage stop; he himself acts that part.

Line 3 is the last of *Khien*, and responds to the sixth line, the
last of Kǎn, above. But as they are both strong, the latter does
not exert its repressive force. They advance rapidly together;
but the position is perilous for 3. By firmness and caution, however, its subject will escape the peril, and the issue will be good.

The young bull in line 4 has not yet got horns. The attaching
to their rudiments the piece of wood to prevent him from goring is
an instance of extraordinary precaution; and precaution is always
good.

XXVII   The Î Hexagram

Î indicates that with firm correctness there will be good fortune (in what is denoted by it). We must look at what we are seeking to nourish, and by the exercise of our thoughts seek for the proper aliment.

1. The first NINE, undivided, (seems to be thus addressed), 'You leave your efficacious tortoise, and look at me till your lower jaw hangs down.' There will be evil.

2. The second SIX, divided, shows one looking downwards for nourishment, which is contrary to what is proper; or seeking it from the height (above), advance towards which will lead to evil.

3. The third SIX, divided, shows one acting contrary to the method of nourishing. However firm he may be, there will be evil. For ten years let him not take any action, (for) it will not be in any way advantageous.

A boar is a powerful and dangerous animal. Let him be castrated, and though his tusks remain, he cares little to use them. Here line 5 represents the ruler in the hexagram, whose work is to repress the advance of evil. A conflict with the subject of the strong second line in its advance would be perilous; but 5, taking early precaution, reduces it to the condition of the castrated pig. Not only is there no evil, but there is good fortune.

The work of repression is over, and the strong subject of line 6 has now the amplest scope to carry out the idea of the hexagram in the accumulation of virtue.

4. The fourth SIX, divided, shows one looking downwards for (the power to) nourish. There will be good fortune. Looking with a tiger's downward unwavering glare, and with his desire that impels him to spring after spring, he will fall into no error.

5. The fifth SIX, divided, shows one acting contrary to what is regular and proper; but if he abide in firmness, there will be good fortune. He should not, (however, try to) cross the great stream.

6. The sixth NINE, undivided, shows him from whom comes the nourishing. His position is perilous, but there will be good fortune. It will be advantageous to cross the great stream.

XXVII. Î is the symbol of the upper jaw, and gives name to the hexagram; but the whole figure suggests the appearance of the mouth. There are the two undivided lines at the bottom and top, and the four divided lines between them. The first line is the first in the trigram Kăn, denoting movement; and the sixth is the third in Kăn, denoting what is solid. The former is the lower jaw, part of the mobile chin; and the other the more fixed upper jaw. The open lines are the cavity of the mouth. As the name of the hexagram, Î denotes nourishing,—one's body or mind, one's self or others. The nourishment in both the matter and method will differ according to the object of it; and every one must determine what to employ and do in every case by exercising his own thoughts, only one thing being premised,—that in both respects the nourishing must be correct, and in harmony with what is right. The auspice of the whole hexagram is good.

The first line is strong, and in its proper place; its subject might suffice for the nourishing of himself, like a tortoise, which is supposed to live on air, without more solid nourishment. But he is drawn out of himself by desire for the weak 4, his proper correlate, at whom he looks till his jaw hangs down, or, as we say, his mouth waters. Hence the auspice is bad. The symbolism takes the form of an expostulation addressed, we must suppose, by the fourth line to the first.

The weak 2, insufficient for itself, seeks nourishment first from

XXVIII   The Tâ Kwo Hexagram

TA KUO

Tâ Kwo suggests to us a beam that is weak. There will be advantage in moving (under its conditions) in any direction whatever; there will be success.

1. The first six, divided, shows one placing mats of the white mâo grass under things set on the ground. There will be no error.

2. The second NINE, undivided, shows a decayed

the strong line below, which is not proper, and then from the strong 6, not its proper correlate, and too far removed. In either case the thing is evil.

Line 3 is weak, in an odd place; and as it occupies the last place in the trigram of movement, all that quality culminates in its subject. Hence he considers himself sufficient for himself, without any help from without, and the issue is bad.

With line 4 we pass into the upper trigram. It is next to the ruler's place in 5 moreover, and bent on nourishing and training all below. Its proper correlate is the strong 1; and though weak in himself, its subject looks with intense desire to the subject of that for help; and there is no error.

The subject of line 5 is not equal to the requirements of his position; but with a firm reliance on the strong 6, there will be good fortune. Let him not, however, engage in the most difficult undertakings.

The topmost line is strong, and 5 relies on its subject; but being penetrated with the idea of the hexagram, he feels himself in the position of master or tutor to all under heaven. The task is hard and the responsibility great; but realising these things, he will prove himself equal to them.

willow producing shoots, or an old husband in possession of his young wife. There will be advantage in every way.

3. The third NINE, undivided, shows a beam that is weak. There will be evil.

4. The fourth NINE, undivided, shows a beam curving upwards. There will be good fortune. If (the subject of it) looks for other (help but that of line one), there will be cause for regret.

5. The fifth NINE, undivided, shows a decayed willow producing flowers, or an old wife in possession of her young husband. There will be occasion neither for blame nor for praise.

6. The topmost SIX, divided, shows its subject with extraordinary (boldness) wading through a stream, till the water hides the crown of his head. There will be evil, but no ground for blame.

XXVIII. Very extraordinary times require very extraordinary gifts in the conduct of affairs in them. This is the text on which king Wăn and his son discourse after their fashion in this hexagram. What goes, in their view, to constitute anything extraordinary is its greatness and difficulty. There need not be about it what is not right.

Looking at the figure we see two weak lines at the top and bottom, and four strong lines between them, giving us the idea of a great beam unable to sustain its own weight. But the second and fifth lines are both strong and in the centre; and from this and the attributes of the component trigrams a good auspice is obtained.

Line 1 being weak, and at the bottom of the figure, and of the trigram Sun, which denotes flexibility and humility, its subject is distinguished by his carefulness, as in the matter mentioned; and there is a good auspice.

Line 2 has no proper correlate above. Hence he inclines to the weak 1 below him; and we have the symbolism of the line. An

XXIX THE KHAN HEXAGRAM

K'AN

Khan, here repeated, shows the possession of
sincerity, through which the mind is penetrating.
Action (in accordance with this) will be of high
value.

1. The first six, divided, shows its subject in the
double defile, and (yet) entering a cavern within it.
There will be evil.

2. The second NINE, undivided, shows its subject

old husband with a young wife will yet have children; the action
of the subject of 2 will be successful.

Line 3 is strong, and in an odd place. Its subject is confident
in his own strength, but his correlate in 6 is weak. Alone, he is
unequal to the extraordinary strain on him, and has for his symbol
the weak beam.

Line 4 is near 5, the ruler's place. On its subject devolves the
duty of meeting the extraordinary exigency of the time; but he is
strong; and, the line being in an even place, his strength is tempered. He will be equal to his task. Should he look out for the
help of the subject of 1, that would affect him with another element
of weakness; and his action would give cause for regret.

Line 5 is strong and central. Its subject should be equal to
achieve extraordinary merit. But he has no proper correlate below,
and as 2 inclined to 1, so does this to 6. But here the willow
only produces flowers, not shoots;—its decay will soon reappear.
An old wife will have no children. If the subject of the line is not
to be condemned as that of 3, his action does not deserve praise.

The subject of 6 pursues his daring course, with a view to
satisfy the extraordinary exigency of the time, and benefit all under
the sky. He is unequal to the task, and sinks beneath it; but his
motive modifies the judgment on his conduct.

in all the peril of the defile. He will, however, get a little (of the deliverance) that he seeks.

3. The third SIX, divided, shows its subject, whether he comes or goes (= descends or ascends), confronted by a defile. All is peril to him and unrest. (His endeavours) will lead him into the cavern of the pit. There should be no action (in such a case).

4. The fourth SIX, divided, shows its subject (at a feast), with (simply) a bottle of spirits, and a subsidiary basket of rice, while (the cups and bowls) are (only) of earthenware. He introduces his important lessons (as his ruler's) intelligence admits. There will in the end be no error.

5. The fifth NINE, undivided, shows the water of the defile not yet full, (so that it might flow away); but order will (soon) be brought about. There will be no error.

6. The topmost SIX, divided, shows its subject bound with cords of three strands or two strands, and placed in the thicket of thorns. But in three years he does not learn the course for him to pursue. There will be evil.

XXIX. The trigram Khan, which is doubled to form this hexagram, is the lineal symbol of water. Its meaning, as a character, is 'a pit,' 'a perilous cavity, or defile;' and here and elsewhere in the Yî it leads the reader to think of a dangerous defile, with water flowing through it. It becomes symbolic of danger, and what the authors of the Text had in mind was to show how danger should be encountered, its effect on the mind, and how to get out of it.

The trigram exhibits a strong central line, between two divided lines. The central represented to king Wăn the sincere honesty and goodness of the subject of the hexagram, whose mind was sharpened and made penetrating by contact with danger, and who

XXX　The Lî Hexagram

Lî indicates that, (in regard to what it denotes), it will be advantageous to be firm and correct, and that thus there will be free course and success.

---

acted in a manner worthy of his character. It is implied, though the Thwan does not say it, that he would get out of the danger.

Line 1 is weak, at the bottom of the figure, and has no correlate above, no helper, that is, beyond itself. All these things render the case of its subject hopeless. He will by his efforts only involve himself more deeply in danger.

Line 2 is strong, and in the centre. Its subject is unable, indeed, to escape altogether from the danger; but he does not involve himself more deeply in it like the subject of 1, and obtains some ease.

Line 3 is weak, and occupies the place of a strong line. Its subject is in an evil case.

Line 4 is weak, and will get no help from its correlate in 1. Its subject is not one who can avert the danger threatening himself and others. But his position is close to that of the ruler in 5, whose intimacy he cultivates with an unostentatious sincerity, symbolled by the appointments of the simple feast, and whose intelligence he cautiously enlightens. In consequence, there will be no error.

The subject of line 5 is on the eve of extrication and deliverance. The waters of the defile will ere long have free vent and disappear, and the ground will be levelled and made smooth. The line is strong, in a proper place, and in the place of honour.

The case of the subject of line 6 is hopeless. When danger has reached its highest point, there he is, represented by a weak line, and with no proper correlate below. The 'thicket of thorns' is taken as a metaphor for a prison; but if the expression has a history, I have been unable to find it.

Let (its subject) also nourish (a docility like that of) the cow, and there will be good fortune.

1. The first NINE, undivided, shows one ready to move with confused steps. But he treads at the same time reverently, and there will be no mistake.

2. The second SIX, divided, shows its subject in his place in yellow. There will be great good fortune.

3. The third NINE, undivided, shows its subject in a position like that of the declining sun. Instead of playing on his instrument of earthenware, and singing to it, he utters the groans of an old man of eighty. There will be evil.

4. The fourth NINE, undivided, shows the manner of its subject's coming. How abrupt it is, as with fire, with death, to be rejected (by all)!

5. The fifth SIX, divided, shows its subject as one with tears flowing in torrents, and groaning in sorrow. There will be good fortune.

XXX. Lî is the name of the trigram representing fire and light, and the sun as the source of both of these. Its virtue or attribute is brightness, and by a natural metaphor intelligence. But Lî has also the meaning of inhering in, or adhering to, being attached to. Both these significations occur in connexion with the hexagram, and make it difficult to determine what was the subject of it in the minds of the authors. If we take the whole figure as expressing the subject, we have, as in the treatise on the Thwan, 'a double brightness,' a phrase which is understood to denominate the ruler. If we take the two central lines as indicating the subject, we have weakness, dwelling with strength above and below. In either case there are required from the subject a strict adherence to what is correct, and a docile humility. On the second member of the Thwan *Kh*äng-ze says:—' The nature of the ox is docile, and that of the cow is much more so. The subject of the hexagram adhering closely to

6. The topmost NINE, undivided, shows the king employing its subject in his punitive expeditions. Achieving admirable (merit), he breaks (only) the chiefs (of the rebels). Where his prisoners were not their associates, he does not punish. There will be no error.

---

what is correct, he must be able to act in obedience to it, as docile as a cow, and then there will be good fortune.'

Line 1 is strong, and at the bottom of the trigram for fire, the nature of which is to ascend. Its subject therefore will move upwards, and is in danger of doing so coarsely and vehemently. But the lowest line has hardly entered into the action of the figure, and this consideration operates to make him reverently careful of his movements; and there is no error.

Line 2 is weak, and occupies the centre. Yellow is one of the five correct colours, and here symbolises the correct course to which the subject of the line adheres.

Line 3 is at the top of the lower trigram, whose light may be considered exhausted, and suggests the symbol of the declining sun. The subject of the line should accept the position, and resign himself to the ordinary amusements which are mentioned, but he groans and mourns instead. His strength interferes with the lowly contentment which he should cherish.

The strength of line 4, and its being in an even place, make its subject appear in this unseemly manner, disastrous to himself.

Line 5 is in the place of honour, and central. But it is weak, as is its correlate. Its position between the strong 4 and 6 fills its subject with anxiety and apprehension, that express themselves as is described. But such demonstrations are a proof of his inward adherence to right and his humility. There will be good fortune.

Line 6, strong and at the top of the figure, has the intelligence denoted by its trigrams in the highest degree, and his own proper vigour. Through these his achievements are great, but his generous consideration is equally conspicuous, and he falls into no error.

TEXT   SECTION II

XXXI   THE HSIEN HEXAGRAM

HSIEN

Hsien indicates that, (on the fulfilment of the conditions implied in it), there will be free course and success.   Its advantageousness will depend on the being firm and correct, (as) in marrying a young lady.   There will be good fortune.

1. The first SIX, divided, shows one moving his great toes.

2. The second SIX, divided, shows one moving the calves of his leg.   There will be evil.   If he abide (quiet in his place), there will be good fortune.

3. The third NINE, undivided, shows one moving his thighs, and keeping close hold of those whom he follows.   Going forward (in this way) will cause regret.

4. The fourth NINE, undivided, shows that firm correctness which will lead to good fortune, and prevent all occasion for repentance.   If its subject be unsettled in his movements, (only) his friends will follow his purpose.

5. The fifth NINE, undivided, shows one moving the flesh along the spine above the heart.   There will be no occasion for repentance.

6. The sixth SIX, divided, shows one moving his jaws and tongue.

XXXI. With the 31st hexagram commences the Second Section of the Text. It is difficult to say why any division of the hexagrams should be made here, for the student tries in vain to discover any continuity in the thoughts of the author that is now broken. The First Section does not contain a class of subjects different from those which we find in the Second. That the division was made, however, at a very early time, appears from the sixth Appendix on the Sequence of the Hexagrams, where the writer sets forth an analogy between the first and second figures, representing heaven and earth, as the originators of all things, and this figure and the next, representing (each of them) husband and wife, as the originators of all the social relations. This, however, is far from carrying conviction to my mind. The division of the Text of the Yî into two sections is a fact of which I am unable to give a satisfactory account.

Hsien, as explained in the treatise on the Thwan, has here the meaning of mutual influence, and the duke of Kâu, on the various lines, always uses Kan for it in the sense of 'moving' or 'influencing to movement or action.' This is to my mind the subject of the hexagram considered as an essay,—'Influence; the different ways of bringing it to bear, and their issues.'

The Chinese character called hsien is 咸, the graphic symbol for 'all, together, jointly.' Kan, the symbol for 'influencing,' has hsien in it as its phonetic constituent (though the changes in pronunciation make it hard for an English reader to appreciate this), with the addition of hsin, the symbol for 'the heart.' Thus 感 kan, 'to affect or influence,' = 咸 + 心; and it may have been that while the name or word was used with the significance of 'influencing,' the 心 was purposely dropt from it, to indicate the most important element in the thing,—the absence of all purpose or motive. I venture to think that this would have been a device worthy of a diviner.

With regard to the idea of husband and wife being in the teaching of the hexagram, it is derived from the more recent symbolism of the eight trigrams ascribed to king Wăn, and exhibited on p. 33 and plate III. The more ancient usage of them is given in the paragraph on the Great Symbolism of Appendix II. The figure consists of Kăn (☵), 'the youngest son,' and over it Tui (☱), 'the youngest daughter.' These are in 'happy union.'

XXXII   THE HĂNG HEXAGRAM

HÊNG

Hăng indicates successful progress and no error (in what it denotes). But the advantage will come from being firm and correct; and movement in any direction whatever will be advantageous.

1. The first SIX, divided, shows its subject deeply (desirous) of long continuance. Even with firm

---

No influence, it is said, is so powerful and constant as that between husband and wife; and where these are young, it is especially active. Hence it is that Hsien is made up of Kăn and Tui. All this is to me very doubtful. I can dimly apprehend why the whole line (———) was assumed as the symbol of strength and authority, and the broken line as that of weakness and submission. Beyond this I cannot follow Fû-hsî in his formation of the trigrams; and still less can I assent to the more recent symbolism of them ascribed to king Wăn.

Coming now to the figure, and its lines, the subject is that of mutual influence; and the author teaches that that influence, correct in itself, and for correct ends, is sure to be effective. He gives an instance,—the case of a man marrying a young lady, the regulations for which have been laid down in China from the earliest times with great strictness and particularity. Such influence will be effective and fortunate.

Line 1 is weak, and at the bottom of the hexagram. Though 4 be a proper correlate, yet the influence indicated by it must be ineffective. However much a man's great toes may be moved, that will not enable him to walk.

The calves cannot move of themselves. They follow the moving of the feet. The moving of them indicates too much anxiety to move. Line 2, moreover, is weak. But it is also the central line, and if its subject abide quiet, till he is acted on from above, there will be good fortune.

Neither can the thighs move of themselves. The attempt to

correctness there will be evil; there will be no advantage in any way.

2. The second NINE, undivided, shows all occasion for repentance disappearing.

3. The third NINE, undivided, shows one who does not continuously maintain his virtue. There are those who will impute this to him as a disgrace. However firm he may be, there will be ground for regret.

4. The fourth NINE, undivided, shows a field where there is no game.

5. The fifth SIX, divided, shows its subject continuously maintaining the virtue indicated by it. In a wife this will be fortunate; in a husband, evil.

6. The topmost SIX, divided, shows its subject exciting himself to long continuance. There will be evil.

---

move them is inauspicious. Its subject, however, the line being strong, and in an odd place, will wish to move, and follows the subject of 4, which is understood to be the seat of the mind. He exercises his influence therefore with a mind and purpose, which is not good.

Line 4 is strong, but in an even place. It is the seat of the mind. Its subject therefore is warned to be firm and correct in order to a good issue. If he be wavering and uncertain, his influence will not extend beyond the circle of his friends.

The symbolism of line 5 refers to a part of the body behind the heart, and is supposed therefore to indicate an influence, ineffective indeed, but free from selfish motive, and not needing to be repented of.

Line 6 is weak, and in an even place. It is the topmost line also of the trigram of satisfaction. Its influence by means of speech will only be that of loquacity and flattery, the evil of which needs not to be pointed out.

XXXII. The subject of this hexagram may be given as perseverance in well doing, or in continuously acting out the law of one's

XXXIII THE THUN HEXAGRAM

TUN

Thun indicates successful progress (in its circumstances). To a small extent it will (still) be advantageous to be firm and correct.

1. The first SIX, divided, shows a retiring tail. The position is perilous. No movement in any direction should be made.

being. The sixth Appendix makes it a sequel of the previous figure. As that treats, it is said, of the relation between husband and wife, so this treats of the continuous observance of their respective duties. Hsien, we saw, is made up of Kăn, the symbol of the youngest son, and Tui, the symbol of the youngest daughter, attraction and influence between the sexes being strongest in youth. Hăng consists of Sun, 'the oldest daughter,' and Kăn, the oldest son. The couple are more staid. The wife occupies the lower place; and the relation between them is marked by her submission. This is sound doctrine, especially from a Chinese point of view; but I doubt whether such application of his teaching was in the mind of king Wăn. Given two parties, an inferior and superior in correlation. If both be continuously observant of what is correct, the inferior being also submissive, and the superior firm, good fortune and progress may be predicated of their course.

Line 1 has a proper correlate in 4; but between them are two strong lines; and it is itself weak. These two conditions are against its subject receiving much help from the subject of 4. He should be quiet, and not forward for action.

Line 2 is strong, but in the place of a weak line. Its position, however, being central, and its subject holding fast to the due mean, the unfavourable condition of an even place is more than counteracted.

Line 3 is strong, and in its proper place; but being beyond the centre of the trigram, its subject is too strong, and coming under

2. The second SIX, divided, shows its subject holding (his purpose) fast as if by a (thong made from the) hide of a yellow ox, which cannot be broken.

3. The third NINE, undivided, shows one retiring but bound,—to his distress and peril. (If he were to deal with his binders as in) nourishing a servant or concubine, it would be fortunate for him.

4. The fourth NINE, undivided, shows its subject retiring notwithstanding his likings. In a superior man this will lead to good fortune; a small man cannot attain to this.

5. The fifth NINE, undivided, shows its subject retiring in an admirable way. With firm correctness there will be good fortune.

6. The sixth NINE, undivided, shows its subject retiring in a noble way. It will be advantageous in every respect.

---

the attraction of his correlate in 6, he is supposed to be ready to abandon his place and virtue. He may try to be firm and correct, but circumstances are adverse to him.

Line 4 is strong in the place of a weak line, and suggests the symbolism of the duke of *K*âu.

The weak 5th line responds to the strong 2nd, and may be supposed to represent a wife conscious of her weakness, and docilely submissive; which is good. A husband, however, and a man generally, has to assert himself, and lay down the rule of what is right.

In line 6 the principle of perseverance has run its course; the motive power of *K*ăn is exhausted. The line itself is weak. The violent efforts of its subject can only lead to evil.

XXXIII. Thun is the hexagram of the sixth month; the yin influence is represented by two weak lines, and has made good its footing in the year. The figure thus suggested to king Wăn the growth of small and unprincipled men in the state, before whose advance superior men were obliged to retire. This is the theme of his essay,—how, 'when small men multiply and increase in power,

XXXIV   THE TÂ *K*WANG HEXAGRAM

TA CHUANG

Tâ *K*wang indicates that (under the conditions which it symbolises) it will be advantageous to be firm and correct.

---

the necessity of the time requires superior men to withdraw before them.' Yet the auspice of Thun is not all bad. By firm correctness the threatened evil may be arrested to a small extent.

'A retiring tail' seems to suggest the idea of the subject of the lines hurrying away, which would only aggravate the evil and danger of the time.

'His purpose' in line 2 is the purpose to withdraw. The weak 2 responds correctly to the strong 5, and both are central. The purpose therefore is symbolled as in the text. The 'yellow' colour of the ox is introduced because of its being 'correct,' and of a piece with the central place of the line.

Line 3 has no proper correlate in 6; and its subject allows himself to be entangled and impeded by the subjects of 1 and 2. He is too familiar with them, and they presume, and fetter his movements ;—compare Analects, 17. 25. He should keep them at a distance.

Line 4 has a correlate in 1, and is free to exercise the decision belonging to its subject. The line is the first in *Kh*ien, symbolic of strength.

In the Shû IV, v, Section 2. 9, the worthy Î Yin is made to say, 'The minister will not for favour or gain continue in an office whose work is done ;' and the Khang-hsî editors refer to his words as an illustration of what is said on line 5. It has its correlate in 2, and its subject carries out the purpose to retire 'in an admirable way.'

Line 6 is strong, and with no correlate to detain it in 3. Its subject vigorously and happily carries out the idea of the hexagram.

1. The first NINE, undivided, shows its subject manifesting his strength in his toes. But advance will lead to evil,—most certainly.

2. The second NINE, undivided, shows that with firm correctness there will be good fortune.

3. The third NINE, undivided, shows, in the case of a small man, one using all his strength; and in the case of a superior man, one whose rule is not to do so. Even with firm correctness the position would be perilous. (The exercise of strength in it might be compared to the case of) a ram butting against a fence, and getting his horns entangled.

4. The fourth NINE, undivided, shows (a case in which) firm correctness leads to good fortune, and occasion for repentance disappears. (We see) the fence opened without the horns being entangled. The strength is like that in the wheel-spokes of a large waggon.

5. The fifth SIX, divided, shows one who loses his ram(-like strength) in the ease of his position. (But) there will be no occasion for repentance.

6. The sixth SIX, divided, shows (one who may be compared to) the ram butting against the fence, and unable either to retreat, or to advance as he would fain do: There will not be advantage in any respect; but if he realise the difficulty (of his position), there will be good fortune.

XXXIV. The strong lines predominate in Tâ Kwang. It suggested to king Wăn a state or condition of things in which there was abundance of strength and vigour. Was strength alone enough for the conduct of affairs? No. He saw also in the figure that which suggested to him that strength should be held in subordination to the idea of right, and exerted only in harmony with it.

XXXV   THE ӠIN HEXAGRAM

CHIN

In Ӡin we see a prince who secures the tranquillity (of the people) presented on that account with numerous horses (by the king), and three times in a day received at interviews.

This is the lesson of the hexagram, as sententiously expressed in the Thwan.

Line 1 is strong, in its correct place, and also the first line in *Kh*ien, the hexagram of strength, and the first line in Tâ *Kw*ang. The idea of the figure might seem to be concentrated in it; and hence we have it symbolised by 'strength in the toes,' or 'advancing.' But such a measure is too bold to be undertaken by one in the lowest place, and moreover there is no proper correlate in 4. Hence comes the evil auspice.

Line 2 is strong, but the strength is tempered by its being in an even place, instead of being excited by it, as might be feared. Then the place is that in the centre. With firm correctness there will be good fortune.

Line 3 is strong, and in its proper place. It is at the top moreover of *Kh*ien. A small man so symbolled will use his strength to the utmost; but not so the superior man. For him the position is beyond the safe middle, and he will be cautious; and not injure himself, like the ram, by exerting his strength.

Line 4 is still strong, but in the place of a weak line; and this gives occasion to the cautions with which the symbolism commences. The subject of the line going forward thus cautiously, his strength will produce good effects, such as are described.

Line 5 is weak, and occupies a central place. Its subject will cease therefore to exert his strength; but this hexagram does not forbid the employment of strength, but would only control and

1. The first SIX, divided, shows one wishing to advance, and (at the same time) kept back. Let him be firm and correct, and there will be good fortune. If trust be not reposed in him, let him maintain a large and generous mind, and there will be no error.

2. The second SIX, divided, shows its subject with the appearance of advancing, and yet of being sorrowful. If he be firm and correct, there will be good fortune. He will receive this great blessing from his grandmother.

3. The third SIX, divided, shows its subject trusted by all (around him). All occasion for repentance will disappear.

4. The fourth NINE, undivided, shows its subject with the appearance of advancing, but like a marmot. However firm and correct he may be, the position is one of peril.

5. The fifth SIX, divided, shows how all occasion for repentance disappears (from its subject). (But) let him not concern himself about whether he shall fail or succeed. To advance will be fortunate, and in every way advantageous.

6. The topmost NINE, undivided, shows one advancing his horns. But he only uses them to punish the (rebellious people of his own) city. The position

direct it. All that is said about him is that he will give no occasion for repentance.

Line 6 being at the top of K'ăn, the symbol of movement, and at the top of Tâ Kwang, its subject may be expected to be active in exerting his strength; and through his weakness, the result would be as described. But he becomes conscious of his weakness, reflects and rests, and good fortune results, as he desists from the prosecution of his unwise efforts.

is perilous, but there will be good fortune. (Yet) however firm and correct he may be, there will be occasion for regret.

XXXV. The Thwan of this hexagram expresses its subject more fully and plainly than that of any of the previous thirty-four. It is about a feudal prince whose services to the country have made him acceptable to his king. The king's favour has been shown to him by gifts and personal attentions such as form the theme of more than one ode in the Shih; see especially III, iii, 7. The symbolism of the lines dimly indicates the qualities of such a prince. 3in means 'to advance.' Hexagrams 46 and 53 agree with this in being called by names that indicate progress and advance. The advance in 3in is like that of the sun, 'the shining light, shining more and more to the perfect day.'

Line 1 is weak, and in the lowest place, and its correlate in 4 is neither central nor in its correct position. This indicates the small and obstructed beginnings of his subject. But by his firm correctness he pursues the way to good fortune; and though the king does not yet believe in him, he the more pursues his noble course.

Line 2 is weak, and its correlate in 5 is also weak. Its subject therefore has still to mourn in obscurity. But his position is central and correct, and he holds on his way, till success comes ere long. The symbolism says he receives it 'from his grandmother;' and readers will be startled by the extraordinary statement, as I was when I first read it. Literally the Text says 'the king's mother,' as P. Regis rendered it,—'Istam magnam felicitatem a matre regis recipit.' He also tries to give the name a historical reference;—to Thâi-Kiang, the grandmother of king Wăn; Thâi-Zăn, his mother; or to Thâi-sze, his wife, and the mother of king Wû and the duke of Kâu, all famous in Chinese history, and celebrated in the Shih. But 'king's father' and 'king's mother' are well-known Chinese appellations for 'grandfather' and 'grandmother.' This is the view given on the passage, by Khăng-ȝze, Kû Hsî, and the Khang-hsî editors, the latter of whom, indeed, account for the use of the name, instead of 'deceased mother,' which we find in hexagram 62, by the regulations observed in the ancestral temple. These authorities, moreover, all agree in saying that the name points us to line 5, the correlate of 2, and 'the lord of the hexagram.' Now the subject of line 5 is the sovereign, who at length acknowledges the worth of the feudal lord, and gives him

XXXVI   THE MING Î HEXAGRAM

MING I

Ming Î indicates that (in the circumstances which it denotes) it will be advantageous to realise the

the great blessing. The 'New Digest of Comments on the Yî (1686),' in its paraphrase of the line, has, 'He receives at last this great blessing from the mild and compliant ruler.' I am not sure that 'motherly king' would not be the best and fairest translation of the phrase.

Canon McClatchie has a very astonishing note on the name, which he renders 'Imperial Mother' (p. 164):—'That is, the wife of Imperial Heaven (Juno), who occupies the "throne of the diagram," viz. the fifth stroke, which is soft and therefore feminine. She is the Great Ancestress of the human race. See Imp. Ed. vol. iv, Sect. v, p. 25, Com.' Why such additions to the written word?

Line 3 is weak, and in an odd place; but the subjects of 1 and 2 are possessed by the same desire to advance as the subject of this. A common trust and aim possess them; and hence the not unfavourable auspice.

Line 4 is strong, but it is in an even place, nor is it central. It suggests the idea of a marmot (? or rat), stealthily advancing. Nothing could be more opposed to the ideal of the feudal lord in the hexagram.

In line 5 that lord and his intelligent sovereign meet happily. He holds on his right course, indifferent as to results, but things are so ordered that he is, and will continue to be, crowned with success.

Line 6 is strong, and suggests the idea of its subject to the last continuing his advance, and that not only with firm correctness, but with strong force. The 'horns' are an emblem of threatening strength, and though he uses them only in his own state, and against the rebellious there, that such a prince should have any occasion to use force is matter for regret.

difficulty (of the position), and maintain firm correctness.

1. The first NINE, undivided, shows its subject, (in the condition indicated by) Ming Î, flying, but with drooping wings. When the superior man (is revolving) his going away, he may be for three days without eating. Wherever he goes, the people there may speak (derisively of him).

2. The second SIX, divided, shows its subject, (in the condition indicated by) Ming Î, wounded in the left thigh. He saves himself by the strength of a (swift) horse; and is fortunate.

3. The third NINE, undivided, shows its subject, (in the condition indicated by) Ming Î, hunting in the south, and taking the great chief (of the darkness). He should not be eager to make (all) correct (at once).

4. The fourth SIX, divided, shows its subject (just) entered into the left side of the belly (of the dark land). (But) he is able to carry out the mind appropriate (in the condition indicated by) Ming Î, quitting the gate and courtyard (of the lord of darkness).

5. The fifth SIX, divided, shows how the count of Kî fulfilled the condition indicated by Ming Î. It will be advantageous to be firm and correct.

6. The sixth SIX, divided, shows the case where there is no light, but (only) obscurity. (Its subject) had at first ascended to (the top of) the sky; his future shall be to go into the earth.

XXXVI. In this hexagram we have the representation of a good and intelligent minister or officer going forward in the service of his country, notwithstanding the occupancy of the throne by a weak

XXXVII   THE *K*iâ *Z*ăn HEXAGRAM

CHIA JÊN

For (the realisation of what is taught in) *K*iâ *Z*ăn, (or for the regulation of the family), what is

---

and unsympathising sovereign. Hence comes its name of Ming Î, or 'Intelligence Wounded,' that is, injured and repressed. The treatment of the subject shows how such an officer will conduct himself, and maintain his purpose. The symbolism of the figure is treated of in the same way in the first and second Appendixes. Appendix VI merely says that the advance set forth in 35 is sure to meet with wounding, and hence ℨin is followed by Ming Î.

Line 1 is strong, and in its right place;—its subject should be going forward. But the general signification of the hexagram supposes him to be wounded. The wound, however, being received at the very commencement of its action, is but slight. And hence comes the emblem of a bird hurt so as to be obliged to droop its wings. The subject then appears directly as 'the superior man.' He sees it to be his course to desist from the struggle for a time, and is so rapt in the thought that he can fast for three days and not think of it. When he does withdraw, opposition follows him; but it is implied that he holds on to his own good purpose.

Line 2 is weak, but also in its right place, and central; giving us the idea of an officer, obedient to duty and the right. His wound in the left thigh may impede his movements, but does not disable him. He finds means to save himself, and maintains his good purpose.

Line 3, strong and in a strong place, is the topmost line of the lower trigram. It responds also to line 6, in which the idea of the sovereign, emblemed by the upper trigram, is concentrated. The lower trigram is the emblem of light or brightness, the idea of which again is expressed by the south, to which we turn when we look at the sun in its meridian height. Hence the subject of the

most advantageous is that the wife be firm and correct.

1. The first NINE, undivided, shows its subject establishing restrictive regulations in his household. Occasion for repentance will disappear.

2. The second SIX, divided, shows its subject taking nothing on herself, but in her central place attending to the preparation of the food. Through her firm correctness there will be good fortune.

3. The third NINE, undivided, shows its subject (treating) the members of the household with stern severity. There will be occasion for repentance, there will be peril, (but) there will (also) be good fortune. If the wife and children were to be smirking and chattering, in the end there would be occasion for regret.

4. The fourth SIX, divided, shows its subject

---

line becomes a hunter pursuing his game, and successfully. The good officer will be successful in his struggle; but let him not be over eager to put all things right at once.

Line 4 is weak, but in its right place. Kû Hsî says he does not understand the symbolism, as given in the Text. The translation indicates the view of it commonly accepted. The subject of the line evidently escapes from his position of danger with little damage.

Line 5 should be the place of the ruler or sovereign in the hexagram; but 6 is assigned as that place in Ming Î. The officer occupying 5, the centre of the upper trigram, and near to the sovereign, has his ideal in the count of Kî, whose action appears in the Shû, III, pp. 123, 127, 128. He is a historical personage.

Line 6 sets forth the fate of the ruler, who opposes himself to the officer who would do him good and intelligent service. Instead of becoming as the sun, enlightening all from the height of the sky, he is as the sun hidden below the earth. I can well believe that the writer had the last king of Shang in his mind.

enriching the family. There will be great good fortune.

5. The fifth NINE, undivided, shows the influence of the king extending to his family. There need be no anxiety; there will be good fortune.

6. The topmost NINE, undivided, shows its subject possessed of sincerity and arrayed in majesty. In the end there will be good fortune.

XXXVII. Kiâ Zăn, the name of the hexagram, simply means 'a household,' or 'the members of a family.' The subject of the essay based on the figure, however, is the regulation of the family, effected mainly by the co-operation of husband and wife in their several spheres, and only needing to become universal to secure the good order of the kingdom. The important place occupied by the wife in the family is seen in the short sentence of the Thwan. That she be firm and correct, and do her part well, is the first thing necessary to its regulation.

Line 1 is strong, and in a strong place. It suggests the necessity of strict rule in governing the family. Regulations must be established, and their observance strictly insisted on.

Line 2 is weak, and in the proper place for it,—the centre, moreover, of the lower trigram. It fitly represents the wife, and what is said on it tells us of her special sphere and duty; and that she should be unassuming in regard to all beyond her sphere; always being firm and correct. See the Shih, III, 350.

Line 3 is strong, and in an odd place. If the place were central, the strength would be tempered; but the subject of the line, in the topmost place of the trigram, may be expected to exceed in severity. But severity is not a bad thing in regulating a family;—it is better than laxity and indulgence.

Line 4 is weak, and in its proper place. The wife is again suggested to us, and we are told, that notwithstanding her being confined to the internal affairs of the household, she can do much to enrich the family.

The subject of the strong fifth line appears as the king. This may be the husband spoken of as also a king; or the real king whose merit is revealed first in his family, as often in the Shih, where king Wăn is the theme. The central place here tempers the display of the strength and power.

XXXVIII   THE *KH*WEI HEXAGRAM

K'UEI

Khwei indicates that, (notwithstanding the condition of things which it denotes), in small matters there will (still) be good success.

1. The first NINE, undivided, shows that (to its subject) occasion for repentance will disappear. He has lost his horses, but let him not seek for them; —they will return of themselves. Should he meet with bad men, he will not err (in communicating with them).

2. The second NINE, undivided, shows its subject happening to meet with his lord in a bye-passage. There will be no error.

3. In the third SIX, divided, we see one whose carriage is dragged back, while the oxen in it are pushed back, and he is himself subjected to the shaving of his head and the cutting off of his nose. There is no good beginning, but there will be a good end.

4. The fourth NINE, undivided, shows its subject solitary amidst the (prevailing) disunion. (But) he meets with the good man (represented by the first

---

Line 6 is also strong, and being in an even place, the subject of it might degenerate into stern severity, but he is supposed to be sincere, complete in his personal character and self-culture, and hence his action will only lead to good fortune.

line), and they blend their sincere desires together. The position is one of peril, but there will be no mistake.

5. The fifth SIX, divided, shows that (to its subject) occasion for repentance will disappear. With his relative (and minister he unites closely and readily) as if he were biting through a piece of skin. When he goes forward (with this help), what error can there be?

6. The topmost NINE, undivided, shows its subject solitary amidst the (prevailing) disunion. (In the subject of the third line, he seems to) see a pig bearing on its back a load of mud, (or fancies) there is a carriage full of ghosts. He first bends his bow against him, and afterwards unbends it, (for he discovers) that he is not an assailant to injure, but a near relative. Going forward, he shall meet with (genial) rain, and there will be good fortune.

XXXVIII. Khwei denotes a social state in which division and mutual alienation prevail, and the hexagram teaches how in small matters this condition may be healed, and the way prepared for the cure of the whole system. The writer or writers of Appendixes I and II point out the indication in the figure of division and disunion according to their views. In Appendix VI those things appear as a necessary sequel to the regulation of the family; while it is impossible to discover any allusion to the family in the Text.

Line 1 is strong, and in an odd place. A successful course might be auspiced for its subject; but the correlate in line 4 is also strong; and therefore disappointment and repentance are likely to ensue. In the condition, however, indicated by Khwei, where people have a common virtue, they will help one another. Through the good services of 4, the other will not have to repent. His condition may be emblemed by a traveller's loss of his horses, which return to him of themselves.

Should he meet with bad men, however, let him not shrink from them. Communication with them will be of benefit. His good

XXXIX   THE *K*IEN HEXAGRAM

CHIEN

In (the state indicated by) *K*ien advantage will be found in the south-west, and the contrary in the north-east.   It will be advantageous (also) to meet

---

may overcome their evil, and at least it will help to silence their slanderous tongues.

Line 5 is weak, and its subject is the proper correlate of the strong 2.   They might meet openly; but for the separation and disunion that mark the time.   A casual, as it were a stolen, inter-view, as in a bye-lane or passage, however will be useful, and may lead on to a better understanding.

Line 3 is weak, where it ought to be strong.   Its correlate, how-ever, in 6 is strong, and the relation between them might seem what it ought to be.   But the weak 3 is between the strong lines in 2 and 4; and in a time of disunion there ensue the checking and repulsion emblemed in the Text.   At the same time the subject of line 6 inflicts on that of 3 the punishments which are mentioned. It is thus bad for 3 at first, but we are told that in the end it will be well with him ; and this will be due to the strength of the sixth line. The conclusion grows out of a conviction in the mind of the author that what is right and good is destined to triumph over what is wrong and bad.   Disorder shall in the long run give place to order, and disunion to union.

Line 4 has no proper correlate, and might seem to be solitary. But, as we saw on line 1, in this hexagram, correlates of the same class help each other.   Hence the subjects of 4 and 1, meeting together, work with good will and success.

The place of 5 is odd, but the line itself is weak, so that there might arise occasion for repentance.   But the strong 2 is a proper correlate to the weak 5.   Five being the sovereign's place, the sub-ject of 2 is styled the sovereign's relative, of the same surname with the great man. (In these circumstances), with firmness and correctness, there will be good fortune.

1. From the first SIX, divided, we learn that advance (on the part of its subject) will lead to (greater) difficulties, while remaining stationary will afford ground for praise.

2. The second SIX, divided, shows the minister of the king struggling with difficulty on difficulty, and not with a view to his own advantage.

3. The third NINE, undivided, shows its subject advancing, (but only) to (greater) difficulties. He remains stationary, and returns (to his former associates).

4. The fourth SIX, divided, shows its subject advancing, (but only) to (greater) difficulties. He remains stationary, and unites (with the subject of the line above).

5. The fifth NINE, undivided, shows its subject struggling with the greatest difficulties, while friends are coming to help him.

6. The topmost SIX, divided, shows its subject going forward, (only to increase) the difficulties,

---

with him, and head of some branch of the descendants of the royal house. It is as easy for 5, so supported, to deal with the disunion of the time, as to bite through a piece of skin.

Line 6 is an even place, and yet the line is strong;—what can its subject effect? He looks at 3, which, as weak, is a proper correlate; but he looks with the evil eye of disunion. The subject of 3 appears no better than a filthy pig, nor more real than an impossible carriage-load of ghosts. He bends his bow against him, but he unbends it, discovering a friend in 3, as 1 did in 4, and 5 in 2. He acts and with good luck, comparable to the falling rain, which results from the happy union of the yang and yin in nature.

while his remaining stationary will be (productive of) great (merit). There will be good fortune, and it will be advantageous to meet with the great man.

XXXIX. *K*ien is the symbol for incompetency in the feet and legs, involving difficulty in walking; hence it is used in this hexagram to indicate a state of the kingdom which makes the government of it an arduous task. How this task may be successfully performed, now by activity on the part of the ruler, and now by a discreet inactivity:—this is what the figure teaches, or at least gives hints about. For the development of the meaning of the symbolic character from the structure of the lineal figure, see Appendixes I and II.

The Thwan seems to require three things—attention to place, the presence of the great man, and the firm observance of correctness—in order to cope successfully with the difficulties of the situation. The first thing is enigmatically expressed, and the language should be compared with what we find in the Thwan of hexagrams 2 and 40. Referring to Figure 2, in Plate III, we find that, according to Wăn's arrangement of the trigrams, the southwest is occupied by Khwăn (☷), and the north-east by *K*ăn (☶). The former represents the champaign country; the latter, the mountainous region. The former is easily traversed and held; the latter, with difficulty. The attention to place thus becomes transformed into a calculation of circumstances; those that promise success in an enterprise, which should be taken advantage of, and those that threaten difficulty and failure, which should be shunned.

This is the generally accepted view of this difficult passage. The Khang-hsî editors have a view of their own. I have been myself inclined to find less symbolism in it, and to take the southwest as the regions in the south and west of the kingdom, which we know from the Shih were more especially devoted to Wăn and his house, while the strength of the kings of Shang lay in the north and east.

' The idea of " the great man," Mencius's " minister of Heaven," ' is illustrated by the strong line in the fifth place, having for its correlate the weak line in 2. But favourableness of circumstances and place, and the presence of the great man do not dispense from the observance of firm correctness. Throughout these essays of the Yî this is always insisted on.

XL THE *K*IEH HEXAGRAM

CHIEH

In (the state indicated by) *K*ieh advantage will be found in the south-west. If no (further) operations be called for, there will be good fortune in coming back (to the old conditions). If some operations be called for, there will be good fortune in the early conducting of them.

1. The first SIX, divided, shows that its subject will commit no error.

Line 1 is weak, whereas it ought to be strong as being in an odd place. If its subject advance, he will not be able to cope with the difficulties of the situation, but be overwhelmed by them. Let him wait for a more favourable time.

Line 2 is weak, but in its proper place. Its correlation with the strong 5, and consequent significance, are well set forth.

Line 3 is strong, and in a place of strength; but its correlate in 6 is weak, so that the advance of its subject would be unsupported. He waits therefore for a better time, and cherishes the subjects of the two lines below, who naturally cling to him.

Line 4 is weak, and, though in its proper place, its subject could do little of himself. He is immediately below the king or great man, however, and cultivates his loyal attachment to him, waiting for the time when he shall be required to act.

Line 5 is the king, the man great and strong. He can cope with the difficulties, and the subjects of 2 and the other lines of the lower trigram give their help.

The action of the hexagram is over; where can the weak 6 go forward to? Let him abide where he is, and serve the great man immediately below him. So shall he also be great;—in meritorious action at least.

2. The second NINE, undivided, shows its subject catch, in hunting, three foxes, and obtain the yellow (=golden) arrows. With firm correctness there will be good fortune.

3. The third SIX, divided, shows a porter with his burden, (yet) riding in a carriage. He will (only) tempt robbers to attack him. However firm and correct he may (try to) be, there will be cause for regret.

4. (To the subject of) the fourth NINE, undivided, (it is said), 'Remove your toes. Friends will (then) come, between you and whom there will be mutual confidence.'

5. The fifth SIX, divided, shows (its subject), the superior man (=the ruler), executing his function of removing (whatever is injurious to the idea of the hexagram), in which case there will be good fortune, and confidence in him will be shown even by the small men.

6. In the sixth SIX, divided, we see a feudal prince (with his bow) shooting at a falcon on the top of a high wall, and hitting it. (The effect of his action) will be in every way advantageous.

XL. *K*ieh is the symbol of loosing,—untying a knot or unravelling a complication; and as the name of this hexagram, it denotes a condition in which the obstruction and difficulty indicated by the preceding *K*ien have been removed. The object of the author is to show, as if from the lines of the figure, how this new and better state of the kingdom is to be dealt with. See what is said on the Thwan of *K*ien for 'the advantage to be found in the south-west.' If further active operations be not necessary to complete the subjugation of the country, the sooner things fall into their old channels the better. The new masters of the kingdom should not be anxious to change all the old manners and ways. Let them do, as the duke of *K*âu actually did do with the subjugated people of Shang. If

XLI   THE SUN HEXAGRAM

SUN

In (what is denoted by) Sun, if there be sincerity
(in him who employs it), there will be great good
fortune :—freedom from error ; firmness and correctness that can be maintained ; and advantage in every

further operations be necessary, let them be carried through without delay. Nothing is said in the Thwan about the discountenancing
and removal of small men,—unworthy ministers or officers ; but
that subject appears in more than one of the lines.

There is a weak line, instead of a strong, in the first place ; but
this is compensated for by its strong correlate in 4.

Kû Hsî says he does not understand the symbolism under line 2.
The place is even, but the line itself is strong ; the strength therefore is modified or tempered. And 2 is the correlate of the ruler
in 5. We are to look to its subject therefore for a minister striving
to realise the idea of the hexagram, and pacify the subdued kingdom. He becomes a hunter, and disposes of unworthy men,
represented by 'the three foxes.' He also gets the yellow arrows,—
the instruments used in war or in hunting, whose colour is ' correct,'
and whose form is ' straight.' His firm correctness will be good.

Line 3 is weak, when it should be strong; and occupying, as
it does, the topmost place of the lower trigram, it suggests the
symbolism of a porter in a carriage. People will say, ' How did
he get there ? The things cannot be his own.' And robbers will
attack and plunder him. The subject of the line cannot protect
himself, nor accomplish anything good.

What is said on the fourth line appears in the form of an address
to its subject. The line is strong in an even place, and 1, its correlate, is weak in an odd place. Such a union will not be productive
of good. In the symbolism 1 becomes the toe of the subject of 4.
How the friend or friends, who are to come to him on the removal
of this toe, are represented, I do not perceive.

Line 5 is weak in an odd place ; but the place is that of the
ruler, to whom it belongs to perfect the idea of the hexagram by

movement that shall be made. In what shall this (sincerity in the exercise of Sun) be employed? (Even) in sacrifice two baskets of grain, (though there be nothing else), may be presented.

1. The first NINE, undivided, shows its subject suspending his own affairs, and hurrying away (to help the subject of the fourth line). He will commit no error, but let him consider how far he should contribute of what is his (for the other).

2. The second NINE, undivided, shows that it will be advantageous for its subject to maintain a firm correctness, and that action on his part will be evil. He can give increase (to his correlate) without taking from himself.

3. The third SIX, divided, shows how of three men walking together, the number is diminished by one; and how one, walking, finds his friend.

4. The fourth SIX, divided, shows its subject diminishing the ailment under which he labours by making (the subject of the first line) hasten (to his help), and make him glad. There will be no error.

5. The fifth SIX, divided, shows parties adding to (the stores of) its subject ten pairs of tortoise shells, and accepting no refusal. There will be great good fortune.

---

removing all that is contrary to the peace and good order of the kingdom. It will be his duty to remove especially all the small men represented by the divided lines, which he can do with the help of his strong correlate in 2. Then even the small men will change their ways, and repair to him.

Line 6 is the highest line in the figure, but not the place of the ruler. Hence it appears as occupied by a feudal duke, who carries out the idea of the figure against small men, according to the symbolism employed.

6. The topmost NINE, undivided, shows its subject giving increase to others without taking from himself. There will be no error. With firm correctness there will be good fortune. There will be advantage in every movement that shall be made. He will find ministers more than can be counted by their clans.

XLI. The interpretation of this hexagram is encompassed with great difficulties. Sun is the symbol for the idea of diminishing or diminution; and what is said in Appendix I has made it to be accepted as teaching the duty of the subject to take of what is his and contribute to his ruler, or the expenses of the government under which he lives; in other words, readily and cheerfully to pay his taxes. P. Regis says, 'Sun seu (vectigalis causa) minuere . . . . est valde utile;' and Canon McClatchie in translating Appendix I has:—' Diminishing (by taxation for instance) . . . . is very lucky.' Possibly, king Wăn may have seen in the figures the subject of taxation; but the symbolism of his son takes a much wider range. My own reading of the figure and Text comes near to the view of Khăng-ṣze, that ' every diminution and repression of what we have in excess to bring it into accordance with right and reason is comprehended under Sun.'

Let there be sincerity in doing this, and it will lead to the happiest results. It will lead to great success in great things; and if the correction, or it may be a contribution towards it, appear to be very small, yet it will be accepted;— as in the most solemn religious service. This is substantially the view of the hexagram approved by the Khang-hsî editors.

Line 1 is strong, and its correlate in 4 is weak. Its subject will wish to help the subject of 4; but will not leave anything of his own undone in doing so. Nor will he diminish of his own for the other without due deliberation.

Line 2 is strong, and in the central place. But it is in the place of a weak line, and its subject should maintain his position without moving to help his correlate in 5. Maintaining his own firm correctness is the best way to help him.

Paragraph 3 is to my mind full of obscurity. Kû Hsî, adopting the view in Appendix I, says that the lower trigram was originally Khien, three undivided lines, like ' three men walking together,'

XLII   The Yî Hexagram

Yî indicates that (in the state which it denotes) there will be advantage in every movement which shall be undertaken, that it will be advantageous (even) to cross the great stream.

1. The first NINE, undivided, shows that it will be advantageous for its subject in his position to make

---

and that the third line, taken away and made to be the topmost line, or the third, in what was originally Khwăn, three divided lines, was 'the putting away of one man;' and that then the change of place by 3 and 6, while they continued their proper correlation, was, one going away, and finding his friend. I cannot lay hold of any thread of reason in this.

Line 4 is weak, and in an even place; like an individual ailing and unable to perform his proper work. But the correlate in 1 is strong; and is made to hasten to its relief. The 'joy' of the line shows the desire of its subject to do his part in the work of the hexagram.

Line 5 is the seat of the ruler, who is here humble, and welcomes the assistance of his correlate, the subject of 2. He is a ruler whom all his subjects of ability will rejoice to serve in every possible way; and the result will be great good fortune.

Line 6 has been changed from a weak into a strong line from line 3; has received therefore the greatest increase, and will carry out the idea of the hexagram in the highest degree and style. But he can give increase to others without diminishing his own resources, and of course the benefit he will confer will be incalculable. Ministers will come to serve him; and not one from each clan merely, but many. Such is the substance of what is said on this last paragraph. I confess that I only discern the meaning darkly.

a great movement. If it be greatly fortunate, no blame will be imputed to him.

2. The second SIX, divided, shows parties adding to the stores of its subject ten pairs of tortoise shells whose oracles cannot be opposed. Let him persevere in being firm and correct, and there will be good fortune. Let the king, (having the virtues thus distinguished), employ them in presenting his offerings to God, and there will be good fortune.

3. The third SIX, divided, shows increase given to its subject by means of what is evil, so that he shall (be led to good), and be without blame. Let him be sincere and pursue the path of the Mean, (so shall he secure the recognition of the ruler, like) an officer who announces himself to his prince by the symbol of his rank.

4. The fourth SIX, divided, shows its subject pursuing the due course. His advice to his prince is followed. He can with advantage be relied on in such a movement as that of removing the capital.

5. The fifth NINE, undivided, shows its subject with sincere heart seeking to benefit (all below). There need be no question about it; the result will be great good fortune. (All below) will with sincere heart acknowledge his goodness.

6. In the sixth NINE, undivided, we see one to whose increase none will contribute, while many will seek to assail him. He observes no regular rule in the ordering of his heart. There will be evil.

XLII. Yî has the opposite meaning to Sun, and is the symbol of addition or increasing. What king Wǎn had in his mind, in connexion with the hexagram, was a ruler or a government operating

XLIII   The Kwâi Hexagram

KUAI

Kwâi requires (in him who would fulfil its meaning) the exhibition (of the culprit's guilt) in the royal court, and a sincere and earnest appeal (for sym-

so as to dispense benefits to, and increase the resources of all the people.   Two indications are evident in the lines;—the strong line in the ruler's seat, or the fifth line, and the weak line in the correlative place of 2.   Whether there be other indications in the figure or its component trigrams will be considered in dealing with the Appendixes.   The writer might well say, on general grounds, of the ruler whom he had in mind, that he would be successful in his enterprises and overcome the greatest difficulties.

Line 1 is strong, but its low position might seem to debar its subject from any great enterprise.   Favoured as he is, however, according to the general idea of the hexagram, and specially responding to the proper correlate in 4, it is natural that he should make a movement; and great success will make his rashness be forgotten.

With paragraph 2 compare paragraph 5 of the preceding hexagram.   Line 2 is weak, but in the centre, and is the correlate of 5. Friends give its subject the valuable gifts mentioned; 'that is,' says Kwo Yung (Sung dynasty), 'men benefit him; the oracles of the divination are in his favour,—spirits, that is, benefit him; and finally, when the king sacrifices to God, He accepts.   Heaven confers benefit from above.'

Line 3 is weak, neither central, nor in its correct position.   It would seem therefore that its subject should have no increase given to him.   But it is the time for giving increase, and the idea of his receiving it by means of evil things is put into the line.   That such things serve for reproof and correction is well known to Chinese moralists.   But the paragraph goes on also to caution and admonish.

Line 4 is the place for a minister, near to that of the ruler.   Its subject is weak, but his place is appropriate, and as he follows the

pathy and support), with a consciousness of the peril (involved in cutting off the criminal). He should (also) make announcement in his own city, and show that it will not be well to have recourse at once to arms. (In this way) there will be advantage in whatever he shall go forward to.

1. The first NINE, undivided, shows its subject in (the pride of) strength advancing with his toes. He goes forward, but will not succeed. There will be ground for blame.

2. The second NINE, undivided, shows its subject full of apprehension and appealing (for sympathy and help). Late at night hostile measures may be (taken against him), but he need not be anxious about them.

3. The third NINE, undivided, shows its subject (about to advance) with strong (and determined) looks. There will be evil. (But) the superior man, bent on cutting off (the criminal), will walk alone and encounter the rain, (till he be hated by his proper associates) as if he were contaminated (by the others). (In the end) there will be no blame against him.

---

due course, his ruler will listen to him, and he will be a support in the most critical movements. Changing the capital from place to place was frequent in the feudal times of China. That of Shang, which preceded *K*âu, was changed five times.

Line 5 is strong, in its fitting position, and central. It is the seat of the ruler, who has his proper correlate in 2. Everything good, according to the conditions of the hexagram, therefore, may be said of him ;—as is done.

Line 6 is also strong; but it should be weak. Occupying the topmost place of the figure, its subject will concentrate his powers in the increase of himself, and not think of benefiting those below him ; and the consequence will be as described.

4. The fourth NINE, undivided, shows one from whose buttocks the skin has been stripped, and who walks slowly and with difficulty. (If he could act) like a sheep led (after its companions), occasion for repentance would disappear. But / though he hear these words, he will not believe them.

5. The fifth NINE, undivided, shows (the small men like) a bed of purslain, which ought to be uprooted with the utmost determination. (The subject of the line having such determination), his action, in harmony with his central position, will lead to no error or blame.

6. The sixth SIX, divided, shows its subject without any (helpers) on whom to call. His end will be evil.

XLIII. In Kwâi we have the hexagram of the third month, when the last remnant, cold and dark, of winter, represented by the sixth line, is about to disappear before the advance of the warm and bright days of the approaching summer. In the yin line at the top king Wăn saw the symbol of a small or bad man, a feudal prince or high minister, lending his power to maintain a corrupt government, or, it might be, a dynasty that was waxen old and ready to vanish away; and in the five undivided lines he saw the representatives of good order, or, it might be, the dynasty which was to supersede the other. This then is the subject of the hexagram,—how bad men, statesmen corrupt and yet powerful, are to be put out of the way. And he who would accomplish the task must do so by the force of his character more than by force of arms, and by producing a general sympathy on his side.

The Thwan says that he must openly denounce the criminal in the court, seek to awaken general sympathy, and at the same time go about his enterprise, conscious of its difficulty and danger. Among his own adherents, moreover, as if it were in his own city, he must make it understood how unwillingly he takes up arms. Then let him go forward, and success will attend him.

Line 1 is strong, the first line of that trigram, which expresses the idea of strength. But it is in the lowest place. The stage of

XLIV THE KÂU HEXAGRAM

KOU

Kâu shows a female who is bold and strong.   It
will not be good to marry (such) a female.

---

the enterprise is too early, and the preparation too small to make
victory certain.   Its subject had better not take the field.

Line 2 is strong, and central, and its subject is possessed with
the determination to do his part in the work of removal.   But his
eagerness is tempered by his occupancy of an even place ; and he
is cautious, and no attempts, however artful, to harm him will take
effect.

Line 3 is strong, and its subject displays his purpose too eagerly.
Being beyond the central position, moreover, gives an indication of
evil.   Lines 3 and 6 are also proper correlates; and, as elsewhere in
the Yî, the meeting of yin and yang lines is associated with falling
rain.   The subject of 3, therefore, communicates with 6, in a way
that annoys his associates ; but nevertheless he commits no error,
and, in the end, incurs no blame.

Line 4 is not in the centre, nor in an odd place, appropriate to it
as undivided.   Its subject therefore will not be at rest, nor able to
do anything to accomplish the idea of the hexagram.   He is symbolised by a culprit, who, according to the ancient and modern
custom of Chinese courts, has been bastinadoed till he presents the
appearance in the Text.   Alone he can do nothing ; if he could
follow others, like a sheep led along, he might accomplish something, but he will not listen to advice.

Purslain grows in shady places, and hence we find it here in
close contiguity to the topmost line, which is yin.   As 5 is the
ruler's seat, evil may come to him from such contiguity, and
strenuous efforts must be made to prevent such an evil.   The
subject of the line, the ruler in the central place, will commit no
error.   It must be allowed that the symbolism in this line is
not easily managed.

The subject of the 6th line, standing alone, may be easily disposed of.

1. The first six, divided, shows how its subject should be kept (like a carriage) tied and fastened to a metal drag, in which case with firm correctness there will be good fortune. (But) if he move in any direction, evil will appear. He will be (like) a lean pig, which is sure to keep jumping about.

2. The second NINE, undivided, shows its subject with a wallet of fish. There will be no error. But it will not be well to let (the subject of the first line) go forward to the guests.

3. The third NINE, undivided, shows one from whose buttocks the skin has been stripped so that he walks with difficulty. The position is perilous, but there will be no great error.

4. The fourth NINE, undivided, shows its subject with his wallet, but no fish in it. This will give rise to evil.

5. The fifth NINE, undivided, (shows its subject as) a medlar tree overspreading the gourd (beneath it). If he keep his brilliant qualities concealed, (a good issue) will descend (as) from Heaven.

6. The sixth NINE, undivided, shows its subject receiving others on his horns. There will be occasion for regret, but there will be no error.

XLIV. The single, divided, line at the top of Kwâi, the hexagram of the third month, has been displaced, and *Kh*ien has ruled over the fourth month of the year. But the innings of the divided line commence again; and here we have in Kâu the hexagram of the fifth month, when light and heat are supposed both to begin to be less.

In that divided line Wăn saw the symbol of the small or unworthy man, beginning to insinuate himself into the government

XLV   THE 3HUI HEXAGRAM

TS'UI

In (the state denoted by) 3hui, the king will
repair to his ancestral temple. It will be advan-

---

of the country. His influence, if unchecked, would go on to grow,
and he would displace one good man after another, and fill the
vacant seats with others like-minded with himself. The object of
Wăn in his Thwan, therefore, was to enjoin resistance to the
encroachment of this bad man.

Kâu is defined as giving the idea of suddenly and casually
encountering or meeting with. So does the divided line appear
all at once in the figure. And this significance of the name rules
in the interpretation of the lines, so as to set on one side the more
common interpretation of them according to the correlation;
showing how the meaning of the figures was put into them from the
minds of Wăn and Tan in the first place. The sentiments of the
Text are not learned from them; but they are forced and twisted,
often fantastically, and made to appear to give those sentiments
forth of themselves.

Here the first line, divided, where it ought to be the contrary,
becomes the symbol of a bold, bad woman, who appears unexpectedly on the scene, and wishes to subdue or win all the five
strong lines to herself. No one would contract a marriage with such
a female; and every good servant of his country will try to repel
the entrance into the government of every officer who can be so
symbolised.

Line 1 represents the bête noire of the figure. If its subject
can be kept back, the method of firm government and order will
proceed. If he cannot be restrained, he will become disgusting
and dangerous. It is not enough for the carriage to be stopt
by the metal drag; it is also tied or bound to some steadfast
object. Internal and external restraints should be opposed to the
bad man.

The 'wallet of fish' under line 2 is supposed to symbolise the

tageous (also) to meet with the great man; and then there will be progress and success, though the advantage must come through firm correctness. The use of great victims will conduce to good fortune; and in whatever direction movement is made, it will be advantageous.

1. The first six, divided, shows its subject with a sincere desire (for union), but unable to carry it out, so that disorder is brought into the sphere of his union. If he cry out (for help to his proper correlate), all at once (his tears) will give place

---

subject of line 1. It has come into the possession of the subject of 2, by virtue of the meaning of the name Kâu, which I have pointed out. With his strength therefore he can repress the advance of 1. He becomes in fact 'the lord of the hexagram,' and all the other strong lines are merely guests; and especially is it important that he should prevent 1 from approaching them. This is a common explanation of what is said under this second line. It seems far-fetched; but I can neither find nor devise anything better.

With what is said on line 3, compare the fourth paragraph of the duke's Text on the preceding hexagram. Line 3 is strong, but has gone beyond the central place; has no correlate above; and is cut off from 1 by the intervening 2. It cannot do much therefore against 1; but its aim being to repress that, there will be no great error.

Line 1 is the proper correlate of 4; but it has already met and associated with 2. The subject of 4 therefore stands alone; and evil to him may be looked for.

Line 5 is strong, and in the ruler's place. Its relation to 1 is like that of a forest tree to the spreading gourd. But let not its subject use force to destroy or repress the growth of 1; but let him restrain himself and keep his excellence concealed, and Heaven will set its seal to his virtue.

The symbolism of line 6 is difficult to understand, though the meaning of what is said is pretty clear. The Khang-hsî editors observe:—'The subject of this line is like an officer who has withdrawn from the world. He can accomplish no service for the time; but his person is removed from the workers of disorder.'

to smiles. He need not mind (the temporary difficulty); as he goes forward, there will be no error.

2. The second SIX, divided, shows its subject led forward (by his correlate). There will be good fortune, and freedom from error. There is entire sincerity, and in that case (even the small offerings of) the vernal sacrifice are acceptable.

3. The third SIX, divided, shows its subject striving after union and seeming to sigh, yet nowhere finding any advantage. If he go forward, he will not err, though there may be some small cause for regret.

4. The fourth NINE, undivided, shows its subject in such a state that, if he be greatly fortunate, he will receive no blame.

5. The fifth NINE, undivided, shows the union (of all) under its subject in the place of dignity. There will be no error. If any do not have confidence in him, let him see to it that (his virtue) be great, long-continued, and firmly correct, and all occasion for repentance will disappear.

6. The topmost SIX, divided, shows its subject sighing and weeping; but there will be no error.

XLV. 3 hui denotes collecting together, or things so collected; and hence this hexagram concerns the state of the kingdom when a happy union prevails between the sovereign and his ministers, between high and low; and replies in a vague way to the question how this state is to be preserved; by the influence of religion, and the great man, who is a sage upon the throne.

He, 'the king,' will repair to his ancestral temple, and meet in spirit there with the spirits of his ancestors. Whatever he does, being correct and right, will succeed. His religious services will be distinguished by their dignity and splendour. His victims will

XLVI   The Shăng Hexagram

SHÊNG

Shăng indicates that (under its conditions) there will be great progress and success. Seeking by

---

be the best that can be obtained, and other things will be in harmony with them.

Line 1 is weak, and in the place of a strong line. It has a proper correlate in 4, but is separated from him by the intervention of two weak lines. The consequence of these things is supposed to be expressed in the first part of the symbolism; but the subject of the line is possessed by the desire for union, which is the theme of the hexagram. Calling out to his correlate for help, he obtains it, and his sorrow is turned into joy.

Line 2 is in its proper place, and responds to the strong ruler in 5, who encourages and helps the advance of its subject. He possesses also the sincerity, proper to him in his central position; and though he were able to offer only the sacrifice of the spring, small compared with the fulness of the sacrifices in summer and autumn, it would be accepted.

Line 3 is weak, in the place of a strong line, and advanced from the central place. The topmost line, moreover, is no proper correlate. But its subject is possessed by the desire for union; and though 2 and 4 decline to associate with him, he presses on to 6, which is also desirous of union. That common desire brings them together, notwithstanding 3 and 6 are both divided lines; and with difficulty the subject of 3 accomplishes his object.

[But that an ordinary rule for interpreting the lineal indications may be thus overruled by extraordinary considerations shows how much of fancy there is in the symbolism or in the commentaries on it.]

Line 4 has its correlate in 1, and is near to the ruling line in 5. We may expect a good auspice for it; but its being strong in an odd place, calls for the caution which is insinuated.

Line 5 is strong, central, and in its correct position. Through (the qualities implied in it) to meet with the great man, its subject need have no anxiety. Advance to the south will be fortunate.

1. The first SIX, divided, shows its subject advancing upwards with the welcome (of those above him). There will be great good fortune.

2. The second NINE, undivided, shows its subject with that sincerity which will make even the (small) offerings of the vernal sacrifice acceptable. There will be no error.

3. The third NINE, undivided, shows its subject ascending upwards (as into) an empty city.

4. The fourth SIX, divided, shows its subject employed by the king to present his offerings on mount *Khî*. There will be good fortune; there will be no mistake.

5. The fifth SIX, divided, shows its subject firmly correct, and therefore enjoying good fortune. He ascends the stairs (with all due ceremony).

6. The sixth SIX, divided, shows its subject advancing upwards blindly. Advantage will be found in a ceaseless maintenance of firm correctness.

---

its subject there may be expected the full realisation of the idea of the hexagram.

Line 6, weak, and at the extremity of the figure, is still anxious for union; but he has no proper correlate, and all below are united in 5. Its subject mourns his solitary condition; and his good feeling will preserve him from error and blame.

XLVI. The character Shǎng is used of advancing in an upward direction, 'advancing and ascending.' And here, as the name of the hexagram, it denotes the advance of a good officer to the highest pinnacle of distinction. The second line, in the centre of the lower trigram, is strong, but the strength is tempered by its being in an even place. As the representative of the subject of the

XLVII   THE KHWĂN HEXAGRAM

K'UN

In (the condition denoted by) Khwăn there may (yet be) progress and success. For the firm and

---

hexagram, it shows him to be possessed of modesty and force. Then the ruler's seat, the fifth place, is occupied by a divided line, indicating that he will welcome the advance of 2. The officer therefore both has the qualities that fit him to advance, and a favourable opportunity to do so. The result of his advance will be fortunate.

It is said that after he has met with the ruler, 'the great man' in 5, 'advance to the south will be fortunate.' Kû Hsî and other critics say that 'advancing to the south' is equivalent simply to 'advancing forwards.' The south is the region of brightness and warmth; advance towards it will be a joyful progress. As P. Regis explains the phrase, the traveller will proceed 'via recta simillima illi qua itur ad austrates felicesque plagas.'

Line 1 is weak, where it should be strong; its subject, that is, is humble and docile. Those above him, therefore, welcome his advance. Another interpretation of the line is suggested by Appendix I; which deserves consideration. As the first line of Sun, moreover, it may be supposed to concentrate in itself its attribute of docility, and be the lord of the trigram.

See on the second line of Zhui. Line 2 is strong, and the weak 5 is its proper correlate. We have a strong officer serving a weak ruler; he could not do so unless he were penetrated with a sincere and devoted loyalty.

Paragraph 3 describes the boldness and fearlessness of the advance of the third line. According to the Khang-hsî editors, who, I think, are right, there is a shade of condemnation in the line. Its subject is too bold.

Line 4 occupies the place of a great minister, in immediate contiguity to his ruler, who confides in him, and raises him to the highest distinction as a feudal prince. The mention of mount

correct, the (really) great man, there will be good fortune. He will fall into no error. If he make speeches, his words cannot be made good.

1. The first SIX, divided, shows its subject with bare buttocks straitened under the stump of a tree. He enters a dark valley, and for three years has no prospect (of deliverance).

2. The second NINE, undivided, shows its subject straitened amidst his wine and viands. There come to him anon the red knee-covers (of the ruler). It will be well for him (to maintain his sincerity as) in sacrificing. Active operations (on his part) will lead to evil, but he will be free from blame.

3. The third SIX, divided, shows its subject straitened before a (frowning) rock. He lays hold of thorns. He enters his palace, and does not see his wife. There will be evil.

4. The fourth NINE, undivided, shows its subject proceeding very slowly (to help the subject of the first line), who is straitened by the carriage adorned with metal in front of him. There will be occasion for regret, but the end will be good.

Khî, at the foot of which was the capital of the lords of *K*âu, seems to take the paragraph out of the sphere of symbolism into that of history. 'The king' in it is the last sovereign of Shang; the feudal prince in it is Wăn.

In line 5 the advance has reached the highest point of dignity, and firm correctness is specially called for. 'Ascending the steps of a stair' may intimate, as *K*û Hsî says, the ease of the advance; or according to others (the Khang-hsî editors among them), its ceremonious manner.

What can the subject of the hexagram want more? He has gained all his wishes, and still he is for going onwards. His advance is blind and foolish; and only the most exact correctness will save him from the consequences.

5. The fifth NINE, undivided, shows its subject with his nose and feet cut off. He is straitened by (his ministers in their) scarlet aprons. He is leisurely in his movements, however, and is satisfied. It will be well for him to be (as sincere) as in sacrificing (to spiritual beings).

6. The sixth SIX, divided, shows its subject straitened, as if bound with creepers; or in a high and dangerous position, and saying (to himself), 'If I move, I shall repent it.' If he do repent of former errors, there will be good fortune in his going forward.

XLVII. The character Khwăn presents us with the picture of a tree within an enclosure; 'a plant,' according to Williams, 'fading for want of room;' 'a tree,' according to Tai Tung, 'not allowed to spread its branches.' However this be, the term conveys the idea of being straitened and distressed; and this hexagram indicates a state of things in which the order and government that would conduce to the well-being of the country can hardly get the development, which, by skilful management on the part of 'the great man' and others, is finally secured for them.

Looking at the figure we see that the two central places are occupied by strong lines; but 2 is confined between 1 and 3, both of which are weak, and 5 (the ruler), as well as 4 (his minister), is covered by the weak 6; all which peculiarities are held to indicate the repression or straitening of good men by bad. For the way in which the same view is derived from the great symbolism, see Appendix II, in loc.

The concluding sentence of the Thwan is literally, 'If he speak, he will not be believed;' but the Khang-hsî editors give sufficient reasons for changing one character so as to give the meaning in the translation. 'Actions,' not words, are what are required in the case.

The symbolism of 'buttocks' is rather a favourite with the duke of Kâu;—'chacun à son goût.' The poor subject of line 1 sitting on a mere stump, which affords him no shelter, is indeed badly off. The line is at the bottom of the trigram indicating peril, and 4, which is its proper correlate, is so circumstanced as not to be able

XLVIII　The 3ing Hexagram

CHING

(Looking at) 3ing, (we think of) how (the site of)
a town may be changed, while (the fashion of) its

---

to render it help; hence comes the unfavourable auspice. 'Three
years' is used, as often, for a long time.

The three strong lines in the figure (2, 4, and 5) are all held to
represent 'superior men;' and their being straitened is not in their
persons or estates, but in their principles which are denied development. Hence the subject of 2 is straitened while he fares sumptu-
ously. His correlate in 5, though not quite proper, occupies the
ruler's place, and comes to his help. That it is the ruler who
comes appears from his red or vermillion knee-covers, different
from the scarlet knee-covers worn by nobles, as in paragraph 5.
Let 2 cultivate his sincerity and do the work of the hexagram as if
he were sacrificing to spiritual beings; and then, if he keep quiet,
all will be well.

For 'a full explanation' of paragraph 3 Kû Hsî refers his readers
to what Confucius is made to say on it in Appendix III, ii, 35.
The reader, however, will probably not find much light in that
passage. The Khang-hsî editors say here:—'The subjects of the
three divided lines (1, 3, and 6) are all unable to deal aright with
the straitened state indicated by the figure. The first is at the
bottom, sitting and distressed. The second, occupies the third
place, where he may either advance or retreat; and he advances
and is distressed. Wounded abroad, he returns to his family, and
finds none to receive him; so graphically is there set forth the
distress which reckless action brings.'

Line 4 is the proper correlate of 1, but it is a strong line in an
even place, and its assistance is given dilatorily. Then 1 is over-
ridden by 2, which is represented by 'a chariot of metal.' It is
difficult for the subjects of 1 and 4 to come together, and effect
much; but 4 is near 5, which is also a strong line. Through a

wells undergoes no change. (The water of a well) never disappears and never receives (any great) increase, and those who come and those who go can draw and enjoy the benefit. If (the drawing) have nearly been accomplished, but, before the rope has quite reached the water, the bucket is broken, this is evil.

1. The first SIX, divided, shows a well so muddy that men will not drink of it; or an old well to which neither birds (nor other creatures) resort.

2. The second NINE, undivided, shows a well from which by a hole the water escapes and flows away to the shrimps (and such small creatures among the grass), or one the water of which leaks away from a broken basket.

3. The third NINE, undivided, shows a well, which has been cleared out, but is not used. Our hearts are sorry for this, for the water might be drawn out and used. If the king were (only) intelligent, both he and we might receive the benefit of it.

---

common sympathy, the subject of 5 will have a measure of success. So the symbolism of this line has been explained,—not very satisfactorily.

Line 5 is repressed by 6, and pressed on by 4. Above and below its subject is wounded. Especially is he straitened by the minister in 4, with his scarlet knee-covers. But the upper trigram is Tui, with the quality of complacent satisfaction. And this indicates, it is said, that the subject of 5 gets on notwithstanding his straits, especially by his sincerity. This explanation is not more satisfactory than the last.

Line 6 is at the top of the figure, where the distress may be supposed to reach its height. Its subject appears bound and on a perilous summit. But his extremity is also his opportunity. He is moved to think of repenting; and if he do repent, and go forward, his doing so will be fortunate.

4. The fourth SIX, divided, shows a well, the lining of which is well laid. There will be no error.

5. The fifth NINE, undivided, shows a clear, limpid well, (the waters from) whose cold spring are (freely) drunk.

6. The topmost SIX, divided, shows (the water from) the well brought to the top, which is not allowed to be covered. This suggests the idea of sincerity. There will be great good fortune.

XLVIII. Ʒing, which gives its name to this hexagram, is the symbol of a well. The character originally was pictorial (井), intended to represent a portion of land, divided into nine parts, the central portion belonging to the government, and being cultivated by the joint labour of the eight families settled on the other divisions. In the centre of it, moreover, was a well, which was the joint property of all the occupants.

What is said on Ʒing might be styled 'Moralisings on a well,' or 'Lessons to be learned from a well for the good order and government of a country.' What a well is to those in its neighbourhood, and indeed to men in general, that is government to a people. If rulers would only rightly appreciate the principles of government handed down from the good ages of the past, and faithfully apply them to the regulation of the present, they would be blessed themselves and their people with them.

In the Thwan we have the well, substantially the same through many changes of society; a sure source of dependance to men, for their refreshment and for use in their cultivation of the ground. Its form is what I have seen in the plains of northern China; what may be seen among ourselves in many places in Europe. It is deep, and the water is drawn up by a vessel let down from the top; and the value of the well depends on the water being actually raised. And so the principles of government must be actually carried out.

Line 1, being weak, and at the very bottom of the figure, suggests, or is made to suggest, the symbolism of it. Many men in authority are like such a well; corrupt, useless, unregarded.

Line 2 is strong, and might very well symbolise an active spring, ever feeding the well and, through it, the ground and its cultivators; but it is in an inappropriate place, and has no proper correlate.

XLIX THE KO HEXAGRAM

KO

(What takes place as indicated by) K o is believed in only after it has been accomplished. There will be great progress and success. Advantage will come from being firm and correct. (In that case) occasion for repentance will disappear.

1. The first NINE, undivided, shows its subject (as if he were) bound with the skin of a yellow ox.

Its cool waters cannot be brought to the top. So important is it that the ministers of a country should be able and willing rightly to administer its government. In the account of the ancient Shun it is stated that he once saved his life by an opening in the lining of a well.

Line 3 is a strong line, in its proper place ; and must represent an able minister or officer. But though the well is clear, no use is made of it. I do not find anything in the figure that can be connected with this fact. The author was wise beyond his lines. After the first sentence of the paragraph, the duke of *K*âu ceases from his function of making emblems ; reflects and moralises.

Line 4 is weak, but in its proper place. Its subject is not to be condemned, but neither is he to be praised. He takes care of himself, but does nothing for others.

Line 5 is strong, and in its right place. The place is that of the ruler, and suggests the well, full of clear water, which is drawn up, and performs its useful work. Such is the good Head of government to his people.

Line 6 is in its proper place, but weak. If the general idea of the figure was different, a bad auspice might be drawn from it. But here we see in it the symbol of the water drawn up, and the top uncovered so that the use of the well is free to all. Then the mention of 'sincerity' suggests the inexhaustibleness of the elemental supply.

2. The second SIX, divided, shows its subject making his changes after some time has passed. Action taken will be fortunate. There will be no error.

3. The third NINE, undivided, shows that action taken by its subject will be evil. Though he be firm and correct, his position is perilous. If the change (he contemplates) have been three times fully discussed, he will be believed in.

4. The fourth NINE, undivided, shows occasion for repentance disappearing (from its subject). Let him be believed in; and though he change (existing) ordinances, there will be good fortune.

5. The fifth NINE, undivided, shows the great man (producing his changes) as the tiger (does when he) changes (his stripes). Before he divines (and proceeds to action), faith has been reposed in him.

6. The sixth SIX, divided, shows the superior man producing his changes as the leopard (does when he) changes (his spots), while small men change their faces (and show their obedience). To go forward (now) would lead to evil, but there will be good fortune in abiding firm and correct.

XLIX. The character called Ko or Keh is used here in the sense of changing. Originally used for the skin of an animal or bird, alive or dead, it received the significance of changing at a very early time. Its earliest appearance, indeed, in the first Book of the Shû, is in that sense. How the transition was made from the idea of a skin or hide to that of change is a subject that need not be entered on here. The author has before him the subject of changes occurring—called for—in the state of the country; it may be on the greatest scale. The necessity of them is recognised, and hints are

L   THE TING HEXAGRAM

TING

Ting gives the intimation of great progress and success.

1. The first six, divided, shows the caldron overthrown and its feet turned up.   (But) there will be

---

given as to the spirit and manner in which they should be brought about.

For the way in which the notion of change is brought out of the trigrams of the figure, see Appendixes I and II.   It is assumed in the Thwan that change is viewed by people generally with suspicion and dislike, and should not be made hastily.   When made as a necessity, and its good effects appear, the issues will be great and good.   A proved necessity for them beforehand; and a firm correctness in the conduct of them :—these are the conditions by which changes should be regulated.

Line 1, at the bottom of the figure, may be taken as denoting change made at too early a period.   It has no proper correlate or helper, moreover, above.   Hence its subject is represented as tied up, unable to take any action.

Line 2, though weak, is in its correct place.   It is in the centre also of the trigram Lî, signifying brightness and intelligence, and has a proper correlate in the strong 5.   Let its subject take action in the way of change.

The symbolism of paragraph 3 is twofold.   The line is strong, and in the correct position, but it has passed the centre of Sun and is on its outward verge.   These conditions may dispose its subject to reckless and violent changing which would be bad.   But if he act cautiously and with due deliberation, he may take action, and he will be believed in.

Line 4 is strong, but in the place of a weak line.   This might vitiate any action of its subject in the way of change, and give occasion for repentance.   But other conditions are intimated that

advantage in its getting rid of what was bad in it. (Or it shows us) the concubine (whose position is improved) by means of her son. There will be no error.

2. The second NINE, undivided, shows the caldron with the things (to be cooked) in it. (If its subject can say), 'My enemy dislikes me, but he cannot approach me,' there will be good fortune.

3. The third NINE, undivided, shows the caldron with (the places of) its ears changed. The progress (of its subject) is (thus) stopped. The fat flesh of the pheasant (which is in the caldron) will not be eaten. But the (genial) rain will come, and the grounds for repentance will disappear. There will be good fortune in the end.

4. The fourth NINE, undivided, shows the caldron with its feet broken; and its contents, designed for the ruler's use, overturned and spilt. Its subject will be made to blush for shame. There will be evil.

---

will have a contrary effect; and if he have further secured general confidence, he may proceed to the greatest changes, even to change the dynasty,—'with good fortune.' The conditions favourable to his action are said to be such as these :—The line has passed from the lower trigram into the upper; water and fire come in it into contact ; the fourth place is that of the minister immediately below the ruler's seat. All these considerations demand action from the subject of 4 in harmony with the idea of the hexagram.

Line 5 has every quality proper to 'the lord of the hexagram,' and his action will be in every way beneficial. He is symbolled by the tiger ; and the changes which he makes by the bright stripes of the tiger when he has changed his coat.

Line 6 is weak, but its subject is penetrated with the spirit of the hexagram. If its subject be a superior man, only inferior to 'the great man,' immediately below, the changes he makes will be inferior only to his. If he be a small man, he will be compliant and submissive. The lesson for him, however, is to abide firm and correct without taking any action of his own.

5. The fifth SIX, divided, shows the caldron with yellow ears and rings of metal in them.   There will be advantage through being firm and correct.

6. The sixth NINE, undivided, shows the caldron with rings of jade.   There will be great good fortune, and all action taken will be in every way advantageous.

L. Ting was originally a pictorial character, representing a caldron with three feet and two ears, used for cooking and preparing food for the table (the mat in old times) and the altar.   The picture has disappeared from the character, but it is said that in the hexagram we have an outline from which fancy may construct the vessel.   The lower line, divided, represents its feet; lines 2, 3, 4, all undivided, represent the body of it; line 5, divided, represents its two ears; and line 6, undivided, the handle by which it was carried, or suspended from a hook.   Appendix VI makes Ting follow Ko in the order of the hexagrams, because there is no changer of the appearance and character of things equal to the furnace and caldron!

Ting and Ȝing (48) are the only two hexagrams named from things in ordinary use with men; and they are both descriptive of the government's work of nourishing.   There are three hexagrams of which that is the theme, Î (27), under which we are told in Appendix I that 'the sages nourished men of worth, by means of them to reach to the myriads of the people.'   Ȝing treats of the nourishment of the people generally by the government through its agricultural and other methods; Ting treats of the nourishment of men of talents and virtue; and that being understood, it is said, without more ado, that it 'intimates great progress and success.'   The Text that follows, however, is more difficult to interpret than that of Ȝing.

Line 1 is weak, and little or nothing can be expected from its subject.   But it has a proper correlate in the strong 4; and the disastrous overthrow, causing the feet to be directed towards 4, is understood to be lucky, as accelerating the co-operation of their two lines!   The overturned caldron is thereby emptied of bad stuff that had accumulated in it!!   The writer uses another illustration, which comes to the same thing.   A concubine is less honourable than a wife,—like the overthrown caldron.   But if she have a son,

LI   The *Kăn* Hexagram

CHEN

Kăn gives the intimation of ease and development. When (the time of) movement (which it indicates) comes, (the subject of the hexagram) will be found looking out with apprehension, and yet

---

while the proper wife has none, he will be his father's heir, and the mother, the concubine, will share in the honour of his position. Thus the issue of what was so unpromising is good. At least 'there is no mistake.' The above is what is found in the best commentaries on the paragraph. I give it, but am myself dissatisfied with it.

Line 2 is strong. 'The enemy' is the first line, which solicits 1. One, however, is able to resist the solicitation; and the whole paragraph gives a good auspice. The personal pronoun seems to show that the whole was, or was intended to be, understood as an oracular response in divination. This paragraph is rhymed, moreover, as are also 1, 3, and 4 :—

> 'In the caldron is good fare,
> See my foe with angry glare;
> But touch me he does not dare.'

Line 3 is also strong, and in the proper place; and if its correlate were the divided 5, its auspice would be entirely good. But instead of 5, its correlate is the strong 6. The place of the ears at 5 has been changed. Things promise badly. The advance of 3 is stopped. The good meat in the caldron which it symbolises will not be eaten. But 3 keeping firm 5 will by and by seek its society! The yin and the yang will mingle, and their union will be followed by genial rain. The issue will be good.

Line 4 is in the place of a great minister, who is charged with the most difficult duties, which no single man can sustain. Then the strength of 4 is weakened by being in an even place, and its correlate is the weak 1 in the lowest place. Its subject is insufficient of

smiling and talking cheerfully. When the movement (like a crash of thunder) terrifies all within
a hundred lî, he will be (like the sincere worshipper)
who is not (startled into) letting go his ladle and
(cup of) sacrificial spirits.

1. The first NINE, undivided, shows its subject,
when the movement approaches, looking out and
around with apprehension, and afterwards smiling
and talking cheerfully. There will be good fortune.

2. The second SIX, divided, shows its subject,
when the movement approaches, in a position of
peril. He judges it better to let go the articles
(in his possession), and to ascend a very lofty
height. There is no occasion for him to pursue
after (the things he has let go); in seven days he
will find them.

3. The third SIX, divided, shows its subject distraught amid the startling movements going on. If
those movements excite him to (right) action, there
will be no mistake.

---

himself for his work, and he has no sufficient help; and the result
will be evil.

'Paragraph 5,' says the Daily Lecture, 'praises the ruler as condescending to the worthy with his humble virtue.' 'Yellow' has
occurred repeatedly as 'a correct colour;' and here 'the yellow
ears and strong rings of metal' are intended to intensify our appreciation of the occupant of 5. As the line is divided, a caution is
added about being firm and correct.

Line 6 is strong, but the strength is tempered by its being in an
even place. It is this which makes the handle to be of jade, which,
though very hard, is supposed to have a peculiar and rich softness
of its own. The auspice of the line is very good. 'The great
minister,' it is said, 'the subject of 6,' performs for the ruler, the
subject of 5, in helping his government and nourishing the worthy,
the part which the handle does for the caldron.

4. The fourth NINE, undivided, shows its subject, amid the startling movements, supinely sinking (deeper) in the mud.

5. The fifth SIX, divided, shows its subject going and coming amidst the startling movements (of the time), and always in peril; but perhaps he will not incur loss, and find business (which he can accomplish).

6. The topmost SIX, divided, shows its subject, amidst the startling movements (of the time), in breathless dismay and looking round him with trembling apprehension. If he take action, there will be evil. If, while the startling movements have not reached his own person and his neighbourhood, (he were to take precautions), there would be no error, though his relatives might (still) speak against him.

LI. *K*ăn among the trigrams represents thunder, and, according to Wăn's arrangement and significance of them, 'the oldest son.' It is a phonetic character in which the significant constituent is Yü, meaning rain, and with which are formed most characters that denote atmospherical phenomena. The hexagram is formed of the trigram *K*ăn redoubled, and may be taken as representing the crash or peal of thunder; but we have seen that the attribute or virtue of the trigram is 'moving, exciting power;' and thence, symbolically, the character is indicative of movement taking place in society or in the kingdom. This is the meaning of the hexagram; and the subject is the conduct to be pursued in a time of movement—such as insurrection or revolution—by the party promoting, and most interested in, the situation. It is shown how he ought to be aware of the dangers of the time, and how by precaution and the regulation of himself he may overcome them.

The indication of a successful issue given by the figure is supposed to be given by the undivided line at the bottom of the trigram. The subject of it must be superior to the subjects of the two divided lines above. It is in the idea of the hexagram that he should be moving and advancing;—and what can his movement be but successful?

LII   THE KĂN HEXAGRAM

KÊN

When one's resting is like that of the back, and he loses all consciousness of self; when he walks

---

The next sentence shows him sensible of the danger of the occasion, but confident and self-possessed. The concluding sentence shows him rapt in his own important affairs, like a sincere worshipper, thinking only of the service in which he is engaged. Such a symbol is said to be suggested by Wăn's significance of *K*ăn as 'the oldest son (page 33).' It is his to succeed to his father, and the hexagram, as following Ting, shows him presiding over the sacrifices that have been prepared in the caldron. This is too fanciful.

What is said on line 1 is little more than a repetition of the principal part of the Thwan. The line is undivided, and gives the auspice of good fortune.

'The position of peril' to the subject of line 2 is suggested, as Appendix II says, by its position, immediately above 1. But the rest of the symbolism is obscure, and *K*û Hsî says he does not understand it. The common interpretation appears in the version. The subject of the line does what he can to get out of danger; and finally, as is signified by the central position of the line, the issue is better than could have been expected. On the specification of 'seven days,' see what is said in the treatise on the Thwan of hexagram 24. On its use here *Kh*ăng-ʒze says:—'The places of a diagram amount to 6. The number 7 is the first of another. When the movement symbolised by *K*ăn is gone by, things will be as they were before.'

Line 3 is divided, and where an undivided line should be; but if its subject move on to the fourth place, which would be right for him, the issue will not be bad.

The 4th line, however, has a bad auspice of its own. It is undivided in an even place, and it is pressed by the divided line on

in his courtyard, and does not see any (of the persons) in it,—there will be no error.

1. The first SIX, divided, shows its subject keeping his toes at rest. There will be no error; but it will be advantageous for him to be persistently firm and correct.

2. The second SIX, divided, shows its subject keeping the calves of his legs at rest. He cannot help (the subject of the line above) whom he follows, and is dissatisfied in his mind.

3. The third NINE, undivided, shows its subject keeping his loins at rest, and separating the ribs (from the body below). The situation is perilous, and the heart glows with suppressed excitement..

4. The fourth SIX, divided, shows its subject keeping his trunk at rest. There will be no error.

5. The fifth SIX, divided, shows its subject keeping his jawbones at rest, so that his words are (all) orderly. Occasion for repentance will disappear.

6. The sixth NINE, undivided, shows its subject

---

either side, hence its subject is represented as supinely sinking in the mud.

Line 5 is divided, in an odd place, and that in which the action of the hexagram may be supposed to be concentrated. Hence its subject is always in peril; but his central position indicates safety in the end.

Line 6 is weak, and has to abide the concluding terrors of the movement. Action on the part of its subject is sure to be evil. If, however, he were to take precautions, he might escape with only the censures of his relatives. But I do not see anything in the figure to indicate this final symbolism. The writer, probably, had a case in his mind, which it suited; but what that was we do not know.

devotedly maintaining his restfulness.   There will
be good fortune.

LII.   The trigram Kăn represents a mountain.   Mountains rise
up grandly from the surface of the earth, and their masses rest on it
in quiet and solemn majesty; and they serve also to arrest the onward progress of the traveller.   Hence the attribute ascribed to Kăn
is twofold; it is both active and passive—resting and arresting.
The character is used in this hexagram with both of those significations.   As the name of the figure, it denotes the mental characteristic of resting in what is right; especially resting, as it is
expressed by Chinese critics, 'in principle,'—that which is right,
on the widest scale, and in the absolute conception of the mind;
and that which is right in every different position in which a man
can be placed.   We find this treated of in the Great Learning
(Commentary, chapter 3), and in the Doctrine of the Mean,
chapter 14, and other places.   This is the theme of the hexagram; and the symbolism of it is all taken from different parts
of the human body, as in hexagram 31, and the way in which
they are dealt with.   Several of the paragraphs are certainly not
easy to translate and interpret.

The other parts of the body, such as the mouth, eyes, and ears,
have their appetencies, which lead them to what is without themselves.   The back alone has nothing to do with anything beyond
itself—hardly with itself even; all that it has to do is to stand
straight and strong.   So should it be with us, resting in principle,
free from the intrusion of selfish though s and external objects.
Amidst society, he who realises the idea of the hexagram is still
alone, and does not allow himself to be distracted from the contemplation and following of principle.   He is not a recluse, however, who keeps aloof from social life; but his distinction is that
he maintains a supreme regard to principle, when alone, and when
mingling with others.

In the symbolism the author rises from one part of the body to
the other.   The first line at the bottom of the figure fitly suggests
' the toes.'   The lesson is that from the first men should rest in,
and be anxious to do, what is right in all their affairs.   The
weakness of the line and its being in an odd place give occasion
for the caution, with which the paragraph concludes.

Above the toes are the calves, represented by the second line,
weak, but in its proper place.   Above this, again, are the loins,
represented by 3, strong, and in danger of being violent.   Line 2

LIII   THE *K*IEN HEXAGRAM

CHIEN

*K*ien suggests to us the marriage of a young lady, and the good fortune (attending it). There will be advantage in being firm and correct.

1. The first SIX, divided, shows the wild geese gradually approaching the shore. A young officer (in similar circumstances) will be in a position of danger, and be spoken against; but there will be no error.

---

follows 3, and should help it; but is unable to do so; and there results dissatisfaction.

When the calves are kept at rest, advance is stopped, but no other harm ensues. Not so when the loins are kept at rest, and unable to bend, for the connexion between the upper and lower parts of the body is then broken. The dissatisfaction increases to an angry heat. Paragraph 3 is unusually difficult. For 'loins' P. Regis has scapulae, and for ribs renes; Canon McClatchie says:—' Third Nine is stopping at a limit, and separating what is in continued succession (i. e. the backbone); thus the mind,' &c.

Line 4 is a weak line resting in a proper place; hence it gives a good auspice. The Khang-hsî editors, however, call attention to the resting of the trunk as being inferior to the resting of the back in the Thwan.

The place of the weak fifth line is not proper for it; and this accounts for the mention of its subject 'repenting,' for which, however, there is not occasion.

The third line of the trigrams, and the sixth of the hexagram, is what makes Kǎn what it is,—the symbol of a mountain. The subject of it therefore will carry out the resting required by the whole figure in the highest style.

2. The second SIX, divided, shows the geese gradually approaching the large rocks, where they eat and drink joyfully and at ease. There will be good fortune.

3. The third NINE, undivided, shows them gradually advanced to the dry plains. (It suggests also the idea of) a husband who goes on an expedition from which he does not return, and of a wife who is pregnant, but will not nourish her child. There will be evil. (The case symbolised) might be advantageous in resisting plunderers.

4. The fourth SIX, divided, shows the geese gradually advanced to the trees. They may light on the flat branches. There will be no error.

5. The fifth NINE, undivided, shows the geese gradually advanced to the high mound. (It suggests the idea of) a wife who for three years does not become pregnant; but in the end the natural issue cannot be prevented. There will be good fortune.

6. The sixth NINE, undivided, shows the geese gradually advanced to the large heights (beyond). Their feathers can be used as ornaments. There will be good fortune.

LIII. *K*ien is ordinarily used in the sense of gradually; but there is connected with that the idea also of progress or advance. The element of meaning in the character is the symbol of water; and the whole of it denotes gradual advance, like the soaking in of water. Three hexagrams contain in them the idea of advance,— 3in (35), Shăng (46), and this *K*ien; but each has its peculiarity of meaning, and that of *K*ien is the gradual manner in which the advance takes place. The subject then of the hexagram is the advance of men to offices in the state, how it should take place gradually and by successive steps, as well as on certain other

LIV   THE KWEI MEI HEXAGRAM

KUEI MEI

Kwei Mei indicates that (under the conditions which it denotes) action will be evil, and in no wise advantageous.

---

conditions that may be gathered from the Text. P. Regis gives this exposition of the subject, as taken by him from the symbolism, which he ascribes to Confucius :—' Viri probi, seu republica digni, in virtutis soliditate instituendi sunt a sapiente, bonisque regulis ut altis radicibus firmandi, nec alii ad rempublicam tractandam promovendi, nisi qui paulatim per varios minoresque gradus ad magnum hoc regimen periculo facto ascendere digni sint.' He then illustrates this sentiment by the words of Pliny :—' Eligetur multis experimentis eruditus, et qui futura possit ex praeteritis praevidere.'

But how does the lineal figure give the idea of a gradual advance? We shall see how it is attempted in the Great Symbolism to get this from the component trigrams. The account there is not satisfactory ; and still less so is what else I have been able to find on the subject. E. g., the trigrams were originally Khwăn and *Kh*ien; but the third line of Khwăn and the first of *Kh*ien have changed places ; and the trigrams now denote 'the youngest son,' and 'the eldest daughter.' If all this, which is a mere farrago, were admitted, it would not help us to the idea of an advance.

Again, the lines 2, 3, 4, 5 are all in the places proper to them as strong or weak ; we ascend by them as by regular steps to the top of the hexagram ; and this, it is said, gives the notion of the gradual steps of the advance. But neither does this carry conviction with it to the mind. We must leave the question. King Wăn, for reasons which we cannot discover, or without such reasons, determined that the hexagram *Kh*ien should denote the gradual advance of men to positions of influence and office.

The marriage of a young lady is mentioned in the Thwan as an illustration of an important event taking place with various

1. The first NINE, undivided, shows the younger sister married off in a position ancillary to the real wife. (It suggests the idea of) a person lame on

---

preliminary steps, continued from its initiation to its consummation. But all must be done in an orderly and correct manner. And so must it be with the rise of a man in the service of the state.

The goose from the most ancient times played an important part in the marriage ceremonies of the Chinese; and this may have suggested the use of it in the symbolism of the different lines. Its habits as a bird of passage, and flying in processional order, admirably suited the writer's purpose. In paragraph 1 it appears for the first time in the season approaching the shore. Then comes the real subject of the line; and the facts of its being weak, and without a proper correlate, agree with, if they do not suggest, what is said about him, and the caution added.

The geese have advanced in line 2, and so has the officer, though he is not mentioned. The line is weak or humble, and central, and has a proper correlate in 5. Hence comes the good auspice.

Line 3 is strong, and has passed the central place, to the top of the lower trigram, and has not a proper correlate in 6. Its subject is likely to be violent and at the same time unsuccessful in his movements. He is like a husband who does not care for his wife, or a wife who does not care for her child. But in the case supposed, his strength in the end would be useful.

The web-footed goose is not suited for taking hold on the branches; but on flat branches it can rest. Line 4, weak, but in an even place, does not promise a good auspice for its subject; but it is the first line in the trigram of humility, and it is concluded that he will not fall into error.

Line 5 is a strong line in the ruler's seat; and yet it appears here as the symbol of a wife. Somehow its subject has been at variance with, and kept in disgrace by, calumniating enemies such as the plunderers of paragraph 3; but things come right in the end. The wife, childless for three years, becomes at last a mother; and there is good fortune.

The subject of line 6 has reached the top of the hexagram. There is no more advance for him; and he has no correlate. But he may still do some good work for the state, and verify the auspice derived from the ornamental plumes of the geese.

one leg who yet manages to tramp along. Going forward will be fortunate.

2. The second NINE, undivided, shows her blind of one eye, and yet able to see. There will be advantage in her maintaining the firm correctness of a solitary widow.

3. The third SIX, divided, shows the younger sister who was to be married off in a mean position. She returns and accepts an ancillary position.

4. The fourth NINE, undivided, shows the younger sister who is to be married off protracting the time. She may be late in being married, but the time will come.

5. The fifth SIX, divided, reminds us of the marrying of the younger sister of (king) Tĭ-yĭ, when the sleeves of her the princess were not equal to those of the (still) younger sister who accompanied her in an inferior capacity. (The case suggests the thought of) the moon almost full. There will be good fortune.

6. The sixth SIX, divided, shows the young lady bearing the basket, but without anything in it, and the gentleman slaughtering the sheep, but without blood flowing from it. There will be no advantage in any way.

LIV. Mei Kwei is a common way of saying that a young lady is married, or, literally, 'is going home.' If the order of the characters be reversed, the verb kwei will be transitive, and the phrase will signify 'the marrying away of a daughter,' or 'the giving the young lady in marriage.' In the name of this hexagram, Kwei is used with this transitive force. But Mei means 'a younger sister,' and not merely a young lady or a daughter. Kwei Mei might be equivalent to our 'giving in marriage;' but we shall find

LV   THE FĂNG HEXAGRAM

FÊNG

Făng intimates progress and development. When a king has reached the point (which the name denotes)

that the special term has a special appropriateness. The Thwan makes the hexagram give a bad auspice concerning its subject; and for this the following reasons are given :—According to Wăn's symbolism of the trigrams, Tui, the lower trigram here, denotes the youngest daughter, and Kăn, the upper trigram, the oldest son. And as the action of the hexagram begins with that of the lower trigram, we have in the figure two violations of propriety. First, the marriage represented is initiated by the lady and her friends. She goes to her future home instead of the bridegroom coming to fetch her. Second, the parties are unequally matched. There ought not to be such disparity of age between them. Another reason assigned for the bad auspice is that lines 2, 3, 4, and 5 are all in places not suited to them, quite different from the corresponding lines in the preceding hexagram.

Is then such a marriage as the above, or marriage in general, the theme of the hexagram? I think not. The marriage comes in, as in the preceding essay, by way of illustration. With all the abuses belonging to it as an institution of his country, as will immediately appear, the writer acknowledged it without saying a word in deprecation or correction of those abuses; but from the case he selected he wanted to set forth some principles which should obtain in the relation between a ruler and his ministers. This view is insisted on in Wan King's 'New Collection of Comments on the Yî (A. D. 1686).'

A feudal prince was said to marry nine ladies at once. The principal of them was the bride who was to be the proper wife, and she was attended by two others, virgins from her father's harem; a cousin, and a half-sister, a daughter of her father by another mother of inferior rank. Under line 1 the younger sister

there is no occasion to be anxious (through fear of a change).   Let him be as the sun at noon.

---

of the hexagram appears in the inferior position of this half-sister. But the line is strong, indicative in a female of firm virtue. The mean condition and its duties are to be deplored, and give the auspice of lameness; but notwithstanding, the secondary wife will in a measure discharge her service. There will be good fortune. Notwithstanding apparent disadvantages, an able officer may do his ruler good service.

Line 2 is strong, and in the centre. The proper correlate is 5, which, however, is weak, and in the place of a strong line. With such a correlate, the able lady in 2 cannot do much in the discharge of her proper work. But if she think only of her husband, like the widow who will die rather than marry again, such devotion will have its effect and its reward. Though blind of one eye, she yet manages to see. And so devoted loyalty in an officer will compensate for many disadvantages.

Line 3 is weak, where it should be strong; and the attribute of pleased satisfaction belonging to Tui culminates in its subject. She turns out to be of so mean a character and such a slave of passion that no one will marry her. She returns and accepts the position of a concubine.

Line 4 is strong, where it should be weak; but in the case of a female the indication is not bad. The subject of the line, however, is in no haste. She waits, and the good time will come.

King Tî-yî has been already mentioned under the fifth line of hexagram 11, and in connexion with some regulation which he made about the marriage of daughters of the royal house. His sister here is honourably mentioned, so as to suggest that the adorning which she preferred was 'the ornament of the hidden man of the heart.' The comparison of her to 'the moon almost full' I am ready to hail as an instance where the duke of *K*âu is for once poetical. *Kh*ăng-ȝze, however, did not see poetry, but a symbol in it. 'The moon is not full,' he says, 'but only nearly full. A wife ought not to eclipse her husband!' However, the sister of Tî-yî gets happily married, as she deserved to do, being represented by the line in the place of honour, having its proper correlate in 2.

Line 6 is weak, at the top of the hexagram, and without a proper correlate. Hence its auspice is evil. The marriage-contract is broken, according to *K*û Hsî, and does not take effect. The

1. The first NINE, undivided, shows its subject meeting with his mate. Though they are both of the same character, there will be no error. Advance will call forth approval.

2. The second SIX, divided, shows its subject surrounded by screens so large and thick that at midday he can see from them the constellation of the Bushel. If he go (and try to enlighten his ruler who is thus emblemed), he will make himself to be viewed with suspicion and dislike. Let him cherish his feeling of sincere devotion that he may thereby move (his ruler's mind), and there will be good fortune.

3. The third NINE, undivided, shows its subject with an (additional) screen of a large and thick banner, through which at midday he can see (the small) Mei star. (In the darkness) he breaks his right arm; but there will be no error.

4. The fourth NINE, undivided, shows its subject in a tent so large and thick that at midday he can see from it the constellation of the Bushel. But he meets with the subject of the (first) line, undivided like himself. There will be good fortune.

5. The fifth SIX, divided, shows its subject bringing around him the men of brilliant ability. There will be occasion for congratulation and praise. There will be good fortune.

6. The topmost SIX, divided, shows its subject

---

parties mentioned in the paragraph appear engaged in the temple, offering or sacrificing to the spirits of their ancestors. But the woman's basket which should contain her offerings (The Shih, I, ii, ode 4) is empty, and the man attempts to perform his part in slaying the victim (The Shih, II, vi. ode 6. 5) without effect.

with his house made large, but only serving as a
screen to his household. When he looks at his door,
it is still, and there is nobody about it. For three
years no one is to be seen. There will be evil.

LV. The character Făng is the symbol of being large and
abundant, and, as the name of this hexagram, denotes a condition of
abundant prosperity. In the changes of human affairs a condition
of prosperity has often given place to one of an opposite character.
The lesson of the hexagram is to show to rulers how they may
preserve the prosperity of their state and people. The component
trigrams have the attributes of intelligence and of motive force, and
the second is under the direction of the first. A ruler with these
attributes is not likely to fail in maintaining his crown and prosperity, and it may well be said that the figure intimates progress
and development. The king is told not to be anxious, but to study
how he may always be like the sun in his meridian height, cheering
and enlightening all.

The explanation of the Thwan is thus natural and easy. It will
be found that a change is introduced in explaining the symbolism
of the lines, which it is as well to point out here. Thus far
we have found that to constitute a proper correlation between two
lines, one of them must be whole, and the other divided. Here
two undivided lines make a correlation. The law, evidently
made for the occasion, goes far to upset altogether the doctrine of
correlated lines. I have been surprised that the rules about the
lines stated in the Introduction, pp. 15, 16, have held good so often.
There have been various deviations from them, but none so gross
as that in this hexagram.

Line 1 is strong, and in an odd place. Its correlate is 4, which
would in other figures be deemed unfortunate. But here even the
Text calls 4 (for the reference must be to it) the mate of 1, and
makes their belonging to different categories of no account. The
lesson taught is that mutual helpfulness is the great instrument for
the maintenance of prosperity. The subject of line 1 is encouraged
to go forward.

Line 2 is divided, and in its proper place. Occupying the centre
of the trigram of brightness, the intelligence of it should be concentrated in its subject; but his correlate is the weak 5, weak and
in an improper place, so that he becomes the benighted ruler, and
darkness is shed from him down on 2, which is strangely symbolised.

LVI   THE LÜ HEXAGRAM

LÜ

Lü intimates that (in the condition which it denotes) there may be some little attainment and progress. If the stranger or traveller be firm and correct as he ought to be, there will be good fortune.

1. The first SIX, divided, shows the stranger mean and meanly occupied. It is thus that he brings on himself (further) calamity.

The subject of 2 therefore, if he advance, will not be acceptable to his ruler, and will not be employed. The only way in which he can be useful by developing the light that is in him is pointed out in the conclusion. The constellation of the Bushel corresponds to our Ursa Major, or perhaps part of Sagittarius.

Line 3 is strong, in its proper place. It is the last line more-over of the trigram of Brightness. All these conditions are favourable to the employment of its subject; but its correlate is the weak 6, which is at the extremity of the trigram of movement. There is no more power therefore in 6, and the subject of 3 has no one to co-operate with him. His symbolism and auspice are worse than those of 2; but his own proper goodness and capacity will save him from error. Mei is a small star in or near the Bushel.

The symbolism of line 4 is the same as that of 2, till we come to the last sentence. Then there is the strange correlation of the two strong lines in 4 and 1; and the issue is good.

The subject of line 5 is in the ruler's place, himself weak, but 'the lord' of the trigram of movement. He can do little unhelped, but if he can bring into the work and employ in his service the talents of 1, 3, and 4, and even of 2, his correlate, the results will be admirable. Nothing consolidates the prosperity of a country so much as the co-operation of the ruler and able ministers.

All the conditions of line 6 are unfavourable, and its subject is left to himself without any helpers. He is isolated for long, and undone. The issue is only evil.

2. The second SIX, divided, shows the stranger, occupying his lodging-house, carrying with him his means of livelihood, and provided with good and trusty servants.

3. The third NINE, undivided, shows the stranger, burning his lodging-house, and having lost his servants. However firm and correct he (try to) be, he will be in peril.

4. The fourth NINE, undivided, shows the traveller in a resting-place, having (also) the means of livelihood and the axe, (but still saying), 'I am not at ease in my mind.'

5. The fifth SIX, divided, shows its subject shooting a pheasant. He will lose his arrow, but in the end he will obtain praise and a (high) charge.

6. The sixth NINE, undivided, suggests the idea of a bird burning its nest. The stranger, (thus represented), first laughs and then cries out. He has lost his ox(-like docility) too readily and easily. There will be evil.

LVI. The name Lü denotes people travelling abroad, and is often translated by 'strangers.' As early as the time of king Wăn, there was a class of men who went about from one state to another, pursuing their business as pedlars or travelling merchants; but in Mencius II, i, chap. 5. 3, it is used for travellers generally, whatever it was that took them out of their own states. Confucius himself is adduced as a travelling stranger; and in this hexagram king Wăn is supposed to have addressed himself to the class of such men, and told them how they ought to comport themselves. They ought to cultivate two qualities,—those of humility and integrity (firm correctness). By means of these they would escape harm, and would make some little attainment and progress. Their rank was too low to speak of great things in connexion with them. It is interesting to find travellers, strangers in a strange land, having thus a place in the Yî.

For the manner in which the component trigrams are supposed

LVII   The Sun Hexagram

SUN

Sun intimates that (under the conditions which it denotes) there will be some little attainment and progress. There will be advantage in movement

---

to give the idea that is in Lü, see Appendix II. In Appendix I there is an endeavour to explain the Thwan by means of the lines and their relation to one another.

Line 1 is weak, in an odd place, and at the very bottom or commencement of the hexagram, These conditions are supposed to account for the unfavourable symbolism and auspice.

Line 2 is weak, but in its proper place. That place, moreover, is the central. Hence the traveller—and he might here very well be a travelling merchant—is represented in the symbolism as provided with everything he can require ; and though the auspice is not mentioned, we must understand it as being good.

Line 3 is strong, and in an even place. But it occupies the topmost place in the lower trigram; and its strength may be expected to appear as violence. So it does in the symbolism, and extraordinary violence as well. It seems unreasonable to suppose, as in the conclusion, that one so described could be in any way correct. The Khang-hsî editors remark that the subjects of 2 and 3 are represented as having 'lodging-houses,' and not any of those of the other lines, because these are the only two lines in the places proper to them !

Line 4 is strong, but in an even place. Hence its subject has not ' a lodging-house ;' but has found a situation where he has shelter, though he is exposed to perils. Hence he is represented as having an axe, which may be available for defence. Still he is not at peace in his mind. The Khang-hsî editors observe well that the mention of an axe makes us think of caution as a quality desirable in a traveller.

Line 5, though weak, is in the centre of the upper trigram, which

onward in whatever direction. It will be advantageous (also) to see the great man.

1. The first SIX, divided, shows its subject (now) advancing, (now) receding. It would be advantageous for him to have the firm correctness of a brave soldier.

2. The second NINE, undivided, shows the representative of Sun beneath a couch, and employing diviners and exorcists in a way bordering on confusion. There will be good fortune and no error.

3. The third NINE, undivided, shows its subject penetrating (only) by violent and repeated efforts. There will be occasion for regret.

4. The fourth SIX, divided, shows all occasion for repentance (in its subject) passed away. He takes game for its threefold use in his hunting.

5. The fifth NINE, undivided, shows that with firm correctness there will be good fortune (to its

---

has the quality of brightness and elegance. It is held to be the lord of the trigram Lî; and lines 4 and 6 are on either side in loyal duty to defend and help. Then the shooting a pheasant is supposed to be suggested; an elegant bird,—by the trigram of elegance. When an officer was travelling abroad in ancient times, his gift of introduction at any feudal court was a pheasant. The traveller here emblemed is praised by his attached friends, and exalted to a place of dignity by the ruler to whom he is acceptable. It will be seen how the idea of the fifth line being the ruler's seat is dropt here as being alien from the idea of the hexagram, so arbitrary is the interpretation of the symbolism.

Line 6 is strong, in an even place, at the extremity of Lî and of the whole hexagram. Its subject will be arrogant and violent; the opposite of what a traveller should be; and the issue will be evil. The symbolism must be allowed to be extravagant. What bird ever burned its nest? And the character for 'ox' is strangely used for 'ox-like docility.'

subject). All occasion for repentance will disappear, and all his movements will be advantageous. There may have been no (good) beginning, but there will be a (good) end. Three days before making any changes, (let him give notice of them); and three days after, (let him reconsider them). There will (thus) be good fortune.

6. The sixth NINE, undivided, shows the representative of penetration beneath a couch, and having lost the axe with which he executed his decisions. However firm and correct he may (try to) be, there will be evil.

LVII. With Sun as the fifth of the Fû-hsî trigrams we have become familiar. It symbolises both wind and wood; and has the attributes of flexibility (nearly allied to docility) and penetration. In this hexagram we are to think of it as representing wind with its penetrating power, finding its way into every corner and cranny.

Confucius once said (Analects 12. 19) :—' The relation between superiors and inferiors is like that between the wind and the grass. The grass must bend when the wind blows upon it.' In accordance with this, the subject of the hexagram must be understood as the influence and orders of government designed to remedy what is wrong in the people. The 'Daily Lecture' says that the upper trigram denotes the orders issuing from the ruler, and the lower the obedience rendered to them by the people; but this view is hardly borne out by the Text.

But how is it that the figure represents merely ' some little attainment?' This is generally explained by taking the first line of the trigram as indicating what the subject of it can do. But over the weak first line are two strong lines, so that its subject can accomplish but little. The Khang-hsî editors, rejecting this view, contend that, the idea of the whole figure being penetration, line 1, the symbol of weakness and what is bad, will not be able to offer much resistance to the subjects of the other lines, which will enter and dispel its influence. They illustrate this from processes of nature, education, and politics ; the effect they say is described as small, because the process is not to revolutionise or renew, but only to

LVIII   THE TUI HEXAGRAM

TUI

Tui intimates that (under its conditions) there will be progress and attainment. (But) it will be advantageous to be firm and correct.

---

correct and improve. Such as it is, however, it requires the operation of the strong and virtuous, 'the great man.' Even all this criticism is not entirely satisfactory.

Line 1 is weak, where it should be strong. The movements of its subject are expressive of perplexity. He wants vigour and decision.

Line 2 is strong, and in the right place, and has a good auspice. Things are placed or hidden beneath a couch or bed; and the subject of the line appears as searching for them. He calls in divination to assist his judgment, and exorcists to expel for him what is bad. The work is great and difficult, so that he appears almost distracted by it; but the issue is good. For this successful explanation of the line, I am indebted to the Khang-hsî editors. The writer of the Text believed of course in divination and exorcism; which was his misfortune rather than his fault or folly.

Line 3 is in the right place for a strong line. But its position at the top of the lower trigram is supposed to indicate the restlessness, and here the vehemence, of its subject. And 6 is no proper correlate. All the striving is ineffective, and there is occasion for regret.

Line 4 is weak, as is its correlate in 1. But 4 is a proper place for a weak line, and it rests under the shadow of the strong and central 5. Hence the omens of evil are counteracted; and a good auspice is obtained. The game caught in hunting was divided into three portions:—the first for use in sacrifices; the second for the entertainment of visitors; and the third for the kitchen generally. A hunt which yielded enough for all these purposes was deemed very successful.

On line 5 Khăng-ʒze says:—'It is the seat of honour, and the

1. The first NINE, undivided, shows the pleasure of (inward) harmony. There will be good fortune.

2. The second NINE, undivided, shows the pleasure arising from (inward) sincerity. There will be good fortune. Occasion for repentance will disappear.

3. The third SIX, divided, shows its subject bringing round himself whatever can give pleasure. There will be evil.

4. The fourth NINE, undivided, shows its subject deliberating about what to seek his pleasure in, and not at rest. He borders on what would be injurious, but there will be cause for joy.

5. The fifth NINE, undivided, shows its subject trusting in one who would injure him. The situation is perilous.

6. The topmost SIX, divided, shows the pleasure of its subject in leading and attracting others.

---

place for the lord of Sun, from whom there issue all charges and commands. It is central and correct; we must find in its subject the qualities denoted by Sun in their greatest excellence. But those qualities are docility and accordance with what is right; and the advantage of firm correctness is insisted on. With this all will be right.' With the concluding sentence compare the conclusion of the Thwan of hexagram 18.

The evil that paragraph 6 concludes with would arise from the quality of Sun being carried to excess. I have followed the Khang-hsî editors in adopting a change of one character in the received Text.

LVIII. The trigram Tui symbolises water as collected in a marsh or lake; and its attribute or virtus is pleasure or complacent satisfaction. It is a matter of some difficulty to determine in one's mind how this attribute came to be connected with the trigram. The Khang-hsî editors say:—'When the airs of spring begin to blow, from the collections of water on the earth the moistening vapours rise up (and descend again); so, when the breath of health is vigorous in a man's person, the hue of it is

LIX The Hwân Hexagram

HUAN

Hwân intimates that (under its conditions) there will be progress and success. The king goes to his ancestral temple; and it will be advantageous to

---

displayed in his complexion. Akin to this is the significance of the hexagram Tui representing a marsh, as denoting pleasure. Although the yin lines give it its special character they owe their power and effect to the yang; so when the qualities of mildness and harmony prevail in a man, without true-heartedness and integrity to control and direct them, they will fail to be correct, and may degenerate into what is evil. Hence it is said that it will be advantageous to be firm and correct!'

The feeling then of pleasure is the subject of this hexagram. The above quotation sufficiently explains the concluding characters of the Thwan; but where is the intimation in Tui of progress and attainments? It is supposed to be in the one weak line surmounting each trigram and supported by the two strong lines. Fancy sees in that mildness and benignity energised by a double portion of strength.

Line 1, strong in the place of strength, with no proper correlate above, is thus confined to itself. But its subject is sufficient for himself. There will be good fortune.

Line 2, by the rule of place, should be weak, but it is strong. Without any proper correlate, and contiguous to the weak 3, the subject of it might be injuriously affected, and there would be cause for repentance. But the sincerity natural in his central position counteracts all this.

The view of the third paragraph that appears in the translation is derived from the Khang-hsî editors. The evil threatened in it would be a consequence of the excessive devotion of its subject to pleasure.

'The bordering on what is injurious' in paragraph 4 has reference to the contiguity of line 4 to the weak 3. That might have

cross the great stream.   It will be advantageous to
be firm and correct.

1. The first SIX, divided, shows its subject engaged in rescuing (from the impending evil) and
having (the assistance of) a strong horse.   There
will be good fortune.

2. The second NINE, undivided, shows its subject,
amid the dispersion, hurrying to his contrivance
(for security).   All occasion for repentance will
disappear.

3. The third SIX, divided, shows its subject
discarding any regard to his own person.   There
will be no occasion for repentance.

4. The fourth SIX, divided, shows its subject
scattering the (different) parties (in the state); which
leads to great good fortune.   From the dispersion
(he collects again good men standing out, a crowd)
like a mound, which is what ordinary men would
not have thought of.

5. The fifth NINE, undivided, shows its subject
amidst the dispersion issuing his great announcements as the perspiration (flows from his body).

---

an injurious effect; but the subject of 4 reflects and deliberates
before he will yield to the seduction of pleasure, and there is cause
for joy.

The danger to the subject of line 5 is from the weak 6 above, in
whom he is represented as 'trusting.' Possibly his own strength
and sincerity of mind may be perverted into instruments of evil;
but possibly, they may operate beneficially.

The symbolism of paragraph 6 is akin to that of 3, though no
positive auspice is expressed. The subject of line 3 attracts others
round itself for the sake of pleasure; the subject of this leads them
to follow himself in quest of it.

He scatters abroad (also) the accumulations in the
royal granaries.   There will be no error.

6. The topmost NINE, undivided, shows its subject
disposing of (what may be called) its bloody wounds,
and going and separating himself from its anxious
fears.   There will be no error.

LIX. Hwân, the name of this hexagram, denotes a state of
dissipation or dispersion.   It is descriptive primarily of men's
minds alienated from what is right and good.   This alienation
is sure to go on to disorder in the commonwealth; and an attempt
is made to show how it should be dealt with and remedied.

The figure is made up of one of the trigrams for water and over
it that for wind.   Wind moving over water seems to disperse it, and
awakes naturally in the beholder the idea of dissipation.

The intimation of progress and success is supposed to be given
by the strong lines occupying the central places.   The king goes
to the ancestral temple, there to meet with the spirits of his
ancestors.   His filial piety moves them by the sincerity of its
manifestation.   Those spirits come and are present.   Let filial
piety—in our language, let sincere religion—rule in men's minds,
and there will be no alienation in them from what is right and good
or from one another.   And if the state of the country demand a
great or hazardous enterprise, let it be undertaken.   But whatever
is done, must be done with due attention to what is right, firmly
and correctly.

Line 1, at the commencement of the hexagram, tells us that the
evil has not yet made great progress, and that dealing with it will
be easy.   But the subject of the line is weak, and in an odd place.
He cannot cope with the evil himself.   He must have help, and he
finds that in a strong horse, which description is understood to be
symbolical of the subject of the strong second line.

Line 2 is strong, but in an even place.   That place is, indeed,
the central, but the attribute of the lower trigram Khan is peril.
These conditions indicate evil, and action will be dangerous; but
the subject of 2 looks to 1 below him, and takes shelter in union
with its subject.   Since the commentary of Khǎng-ʓze, this has
been the interpretation of the line.

Line 3 is weak, and in an odd place.   A regard for himself that
would unfit its subject for contributing any service to the work of

LX THE KIEH HEXAGRAM

CHIEH

Kieh intimates that (under its conditions) there will be progress and attainment. (But) if the regulations (which it prescribes) be severe and difficult, they cannot be permanent.

1. The first NINE, undivided, shows its subject not

---

the hexagram might be feared; but he discards that regard, and will do nothing to be repented of. There is a change of style in the Chinese text at this point. As Wang Shăn-ɀze (Yüan dynasty) says:—'Here and henceforth the scattering is of what should be scattered, that what should not be scattered may be collected.'

Line 4, though weak, is in its correct place, and adjoins the strong 5, which is in the ruler's seat. The subject of 4, therefore, will fitly represent the minister, to whom it belongs to do a great part in remedying the evil of dispersion. And this he does. He brings dissentient partizanship to an end; and not satisfied with that, he collects multitudes of those who had been divided into a great body so that they stand out conspicuous like a hill.

Line 5 gives us the action of the ruler himself;—by his proclamations, and by his benevolence. Kû Hsî and other critics enlarge on the symbolism of the perspiration, which they think much to the point. P. Regis avoids it, translating—'Ille, magnas leges dissipans, facit ut penetrent(ur?).' Canon McClatchie has an ingenious and original, so far as my Chinese reading goes, note upon it:—'As sweat cures fevers, so do proclamations cure rebellions.' Both of these translators miss the meaning of the other instance of the king's work.

Line 6 is occupied by a strong line, which has a proper correlate in 3; but 3 is at the top of the trigram of peril. The subject of 6 hurries away from association with the subject of it, but does so in the spirit of the hexagram, so that there is no error or blame attaching to him.

quitting the courtyard outside his door. There will be no error.

2. The second NINE, undivided, shows its subject not quitting the courtyard inside his gate. There will be evil.

3. The third SIX, divided, shows its subject with no appearance of observing the (proper) regulations, in which case we shall see him lamenting. But there will be no one to blame (but himself).

4. The fourth SIX, divided, shows its subject quietly and naturally (attentive to all) regulations. There will be progress and success.

5. The fifth NINE, undivided, shows its subject sweetly and acceptably enacting his regulations. There will be good fortune. The onward progress with them will afford ground for admiration.

6. The topmost SIX, divided, shows its subject enacting regulations severe and difficult. Even with firmness and correctness there will be evil. But though there will be cause for repentance, it will (by and by) disappear.

LX. The primary application of the character *K*ieh was to denote the joints of the bamboo; it is used also for the joints of the human frame; and for the solar and other terms of the year. Whatever makes regular division may be denominated a *K*ieh; there enter into it the ideas of regulating and restraining; and the subject of this hexagram is the regulations of government enacted for the guidance and control of the people. How the constituent trigrams are supposed to suggest or indicate this meaning will be seen in Appendix II.

*K*û Hsî anticipates that symbolism in trying to account for the statement that the figure gives the promise of success and attainment; but the ground of this is generally made out by referring to the equal division of the undivided and divided lines and our having in 2 and 5, the central places, two undivided lines. An

LXI THE *K*UNG FÛ HEXAGRAM

CHUNG FU

*K*ung Fû (moves even) pigs and fish, and leads to good fortune.   There will be advantage in cross-

---

important point concerning ‘regulations’ is brought out in the conclusion of the Thwan,—that they must be adapted to circumstances, and not made too strict and severe.

Line 1 is strong, and in its correct place. Its subject therefore would not be wanting in power to make his way. But he is supposed to be kept in check by the strong 2, and the correlate 4 is the first line in the trigram of peril. The course of wisdom therefore is to keep still. The character here rendered door is that belonging to the inner apartments, leading from the hall into which entrance is found by the outer gate, mentioned under line 2. The courtyard outside the door and that inside the gate is one and the same. The ‘Daily Lecture’ says that the paragraph tells an officer not to take office rashly, but to exercise a cautious judgment in his measures.

Line 2 is strong, in the wrong place; nor has it a proper correlate. Its subject keeps still, when he ought to be up and doing. There will be evil.

Line 3 should be strong, but it is weak. It is neither central nor correct. It has no proper correlate, and it is the topmost line in the trigram of complacent satisfaction. Its subject will not receive the yoke of regulations; and he will find out his mistake, when it is too late.

Line 4 is weak, as it ought to be, and its subject has respect to the authority of the strong ruler in 5. Hence its good symbolism and auspice.

Line 5 is strong, and in its correct place. Its subject regulates himself, having no correlate; but he is lord of the hexagram, and his influence is everywhere beneficially felt.

ing the great stream. There will be advantage in being firm and correct.

1. The first NINE, undivided, shows its subject resting (in himself). There will be good fortune. If he sought to any other, he would not find rest.

2. The second NINE, undivided, shows its subject (like) the crane crying out in her hidden retirement, and her young ones responding to her. (It is as if it were said), 'I have a cup of good spirits,' (and the response were), 'I will partake of it with you.'

3. The third SIX, divided, shows its subject having met with his mate. Now he beats his drum, and now he leaves off. Now he weeps, and now he sings.

4. The fourth SIX, divided, shows its subject (like) the moon nearly full, and (like) a horse (in a chariot) whose fellow disappears. There will be no error.

5. The fifth NINE, undivided, shows its subject perfectly sincere, and linking (others) to him in closest union. There will be no error.

6. The topmost NINE, undivided, shows its subject in chanticleer (trying to) mount to heaven. Even with firm correctness there will be evil.

Line 6 is weak, in its proper place. The subject of the topmost line must be supposed to possess an exaggerated desire for enacting regulations. They will be too severe, and the effect will be evil. But as Confucius (Analects 3. 3) says, that is not so great a fault as to be easy and remiss. It may be remedied, and cause for repentance will disappear.

LXI. *K*ung Fû, the name of this hexagram, may be represented in English by 'Inmost Sincerity.' It denotes the highest quality of man, and gives its possessor power so that he prevails with spiritual beings, with other men, and with the lower creatures. It is the

LXII THE HSIÂO KWO HEXAGRAM

HSIAO KUO

Hsiâo Kwo indicates that (in the circumstances which it implies) there will be progress and attain-

---

subject of the 'Doctrine of the Mean' from the 21st chapter onwards, where Remusat rendered it by 'la perfection,' 'la perfection morale,' and Intorcetta and his coadjutors by 'vera solidaque perfectio.' The lineal figure has suggested to the Chinese commentators, from the author of the first Appendix, two ideas in it which deserve to be pointed out. There are two divided lines in the centre and two undivided below them and above them. The divided lines in the centre are held to represent the heart or mind free from all pre-occupation, without any consciousness of self; and the undivided lines, on each side of it, in the centre of the constituent trigrams are held to denote the solidity of the virtue of one so free from selfishness. There is no unreality in it, not a single flaw.

The 'Daily Lecture' at the conclusion of its paraphrase of the Thwan refers to the history of the ancient Shun, and the wonderful achievements of his virtue. The authors give no instance of the affecting of 'pigs and fishes' by sincerity, and say that these names are symbolical of men, the rudest and most unsusceptible of being acted on. The Text says that the man thus gifted with sincerity will succeed in the most difficult enterprises. Remarkable is the concluding sentence that he must be firm and correct. Here, as elsewhere throughout the Yî, there comes out the practical character which has distinguished the Chinese people and their best teaching all along the line of history.

The translation of paragraph 1 is according to the view approved by the Khang-hsî editors. The ordinary view makes the other to whom the subject of line 1 looks or might look to be the subject of 4; but they contend that, excepting in the case of 3 and 6, the force of correlation should be discarded from the study of this

ment. But it will be advantageous to be firm and correct. (What the name denotes) may be done in small affairs, but not in great affairs. (It is like) the notes that come down from a bird on the wing ;—to descend is better than to ascend. There will (in this way) be great good fortune.

1. The first six, divided, suggests (the idea of) a bird flying, (and ascending) till the issue is evil.

2. The second six, divided, shows its subject passing by his grandfather, and meeting with his

---

hexagram; for the virtue of sincerity is all centred in itself, thence derived and thereby powerful.

For paragraph 2, see Appendix III, Section i, 42. It is in rhyme, and I have there rendered it in rhyme. The 'young ones of the crane' are represented by line 1. In the third and fourth sentences we have the symbolism of two men brought together by their sympathy in virtue. The subject of the paragraph is the effect of sincerity.

The 'mate' of line 3 is 6. The principle of correlation comes in. Sincerity, not left to itself, is influenced from without, and hence come the changes and uncertainty in the state and moods of the subject of the line.

Line 4 is weak, and in its correct place. The subject of it has discarded the correlate in 1, and hastens on to the confidence of the ruler in 5, being symbolised as the moon nearly full. The other symbol of the horse whose fellow has disappeared has reference to the discarding of the subject of 1. Anciently chariots and carriages were drawn by four horses, two outsides and two insides. Lines 1 and 4 were a pair of these ; but 1 disappears here from the team, and 4 goes on and joins 5.

Line 5 is strong and central, in the ruler's place. Its subject must be the sage on the throne, whose sincerity will go forth and bind all in union with himself.

Line 6 should be divided, but is undivided ; and coming after 5, what can the subject of it do? His efforts will be ineffectual, and injurious to himself. He is symbolised by a cock—literally, ' the plumaged voice.' But a cock is not fitted to fly high, and in attempting to do so will only suffer hurt.

grandmother; not attempting anything against his ruler, but meeting him as his minister. There will be no error.

3. The third NINE, undivided, shows its subject taking no extraordinary precautions against danger; and some in consequence finding opportunity to assail and injure him. There will be evil.

4. The fourth NINE, undivided, shows its subject falling into no error, but meeting (the exigency of his situation), without exceeding (in his natural course). If he go forward, there will be peril, and he must be cautious. There is no occasion to be using firmness perpetually.

5. The fifth SIX, divided, (suggests the idea) of dense clouds, but no rain, coming from our borders in the west. It also (shows) the prince shooting his arrow, and taking the bird in a cave.

6. The sixth SIX, divided, shows its subject not meeting (the exigency of his situation), and exceeding (his proper course). (It suggests the idea of) a bird flying far aloft. There will be evil. The case is what is called one of calamity and self-produced injury.

LXII. The name Hsiâo Kwo is explained both by reference to the lines of the hexagram, and to the meaning of the characters. The explanation from the lines appears immediately on comparing them with those of Tâ Kwo, the 28th hexagram. There the first and sixth lines are divided, and between are four undivided lines; here the third and fourth lines are undivided, and outside each of them are two divided lines. The undivided or yang lines are great, the divided or yin lines are called small. In Hsiâo Kwo the divided or small lines predominate. But this peculiar structure of the figure could be of no interest to the student, if it were not for the meaning of the name, which is 'small excesses' or 'exceeding in what is small.' The author, accepted by us as king Wăn,

LXIII   THE *Kî* *Ȝî* HEXAGRAM

CHI CHI

Kî *Ȝî* intimates progress and success in small matters.   There will be advantage in being firm

---

had in his mind our distinction of essentials and non-essentials. Is it ever good to deviate from what is recognised as the established course of procedure?   The reply is—never in the matter of right ; but in what is conventional and ceremonial—in what is non-essential—the deviation may be made, and will be productive of good.   The form may be given up, but not the substance.   But the thing must be done very carefully,—humbly and reverently, and in small matters.

The symbolism of the bird is rather obscure.   The whole of it is intended to teach humility.   It is better for the bird to descend, keeping near to where it can perch and rest, than to hold on ascending into the homeless regions of the air.

Line 1 is weak, in an odd place, and possessed by the 'idea of exceeding,' which belongs to the hexagram.   Its correlate is the strong 4, belonging to the trigram *Kăn*, the attribute of which is movement.   There is nothing to repress the tendency of 1 ; rather it is stimulated ; and hence the symbolism.

Line 2 is weak, but in its proper place, and in the centre.   Its correlate is 5, which is also a weak line.   The lines 3 and 4 between them are both strong ; and are supposed to represent the father and grandfather of the subject of 2 ; but he or she goes past them, and meets with the grandmother in 5.   Again, 5 is the ruler's seat.   The subject of 2 moves on to him, but not as an enemy ; but humbly and loyally, as his minister according to the attributes of a weak line in the central place.   It must be allowed that this view of the symbolism and its interpretation is obscure and strained.

The subject of line 3 is too confident in his own strength, and too defiant of the weak and small enemies that seek his hurt.

and correct. There has been good fortune in the beginning; there may be disorder in the end.

1. The first NINE, undivided, (shows its subject as a driver) who drags back his wheel, (or as a fox) which has wet his tail. There will be no error.

2. The second SIX, divided, (shows its subject as) a wife who has lost her (carriage-)screen. There is no occasion to go in pursuit of it. In seven days she will find it.

3. The third NINE, undivided, (suggests the case of) Kâo Зung who attacked the Demon region, but was three years in subduing it. Small men should not be employed (in such enterprises).

Line 4 is also strong, but the exercise of his strength by its subject is tempered by the position in an even place. He is warned, however, to continue quiet and restrain himself.

Line 5, though in the ruler's seat, is weak, and incapable of doing anything great. Its subject is called king or duke because of the ruler's seat; and the one whom in the concluding sentence he is said to capture is supposed to be the subject of 2.

The first part of the symbolism is the same as that of the Thwan under hexagram 9, q. v. I said there that it probably gave a testimony of the merit of the house of Kâu, as deserving the throne rather than the kings of Shang. That was because the Thwan contained the sentiments of Wăn, while he was yet only lord of Kâu. But the symbolism here was the work of the duke of Kâu, after his brother king Wû had obtained the throne. How did the symbolism then occur to him? May we not conclude that at least the hsiang of this hexagram was written during the troubled period of his regency, after the accession of Wû's son, king Khăng?

The Khang-hsî editors find in the concluding symbolism an incentive to humility :—' The duke, leaving birds on the wing, is content to use his arrows against those in a cave!'

Line 6 is weak, and is at the top of the trigram of movement. He is possessed by the idea of the hexagram in an extreme degree, and is incapable of keeping himself under restraint.

4. The fourth SIX, divided, shows its subject with rags provided against any leak (in his boat), and on his guard all day long.

5. The fifth NINE, undivided, shows its subject (as) the neighbour in the east who slaughters an ox (for his sacrifice); but this is not equal to the (small) spring sacrifice of the neighbour in the west, whose sincerity receives the blessing.

6. The topmost SIX, divided, shows its subject with (even) his head immersed. The position is perilous.

LXIII. The character called *Kî* is used as a symbol of being past or completed. *Zî* denotes primarily crossing a stream, and has the secondary meaning of helping and completing. The two characters, combined, will express the successful accomplishment of whatever the writer has in his mind. In dealing with this lineal figure, king Wǎn was thinking of the condition of the kingdom, at length at rest and quiet. The vessel of the state has been brought safely across the great and dangerous stream. The distresses of the kingdom have been relieved, and its disorders have been repressed. Does anything remain to be done still? Yes, in small things. The new government has to be consolidated. Its ruler must, without noise or clamour, go on to perfect what has been wrought, with firmness and correctness, and ever keeping in mind the instability of all human affairs. That every line of the hexagram is in its correct place, and has its proper correlate is also supposed to harmonize with the intimation of progress and success.

Line 1, the first of the hexagram, represents the time immediately after the successful achievement of the enterprise it denotes;—the time for resting and being quiet. For a season, at least, all movement should be hushed. Hence we have the symbolism of a driver trying to stop his carriage, and a fox who has wet his tail, and will not tempt the stream again.

Line 2 is weak, and in its proper place. It also has the strong correlate 5; and might be expected to be forward to act. But it occupies its correct and central place, and suggests the symbol of a lady whose carriage has lost its screen. She will not advance

LXIV THE WEI 3î HEXAGRAM

WEI CHI

Wei 3î intimates progress and success (in the circumstances which it implies). (We see) a young fox that has nearly crossed (the stream), when its tail gets immersed. There will be no advantage in any way.

---

further so soon after success has been achieved; but keep herself hidden and retired. Let her not try to find the screen. When it is said that she will find this 'after seven days,' the meaning seems to be simply this, that the period of *K*î 3î will then have been exhausted, the six lines having been gone through, and a new period, when action will be proper, shall have commenced.

The strong line 3, at the top of the lower trigram, suggests for its subject one undertaking a vigorous enterprise. The writer thinks of Kâo 3ung, the sacrificial title of Wû Ting, one of the ablest sovereigns of the Shang dynasty (B. C. 1364–1324), who undertook an expedition against the barbarous hordes of the cold and bleak regions north of the Middle States. He is mentioned again under the next hexagram. He appears also in the Shû, IV, ix, and in the Shih, IV, iii, ode 5. His enterprise may have been good, and successful, but it was tedious, and the paragraph concludes with a caution.

Line 4 is weak, and has advanced into the trigram for water. Its subject will be cautious, and prepare for evil, as in the symbolism, suggested probably by the nature of the trigram.

'The neighbour in the East' is the subject of line 5, and 'the neighbour in the West' is the subject of the correlate 2, the former quarter being yang and the latter yin. Line 5 is strong, and 2 is weak; but weakness is more likely to be patient and cautious than strength. They are compared to two men sacrificing. The one presents valuable offerings; the other very poor ones. But the

1. The first SIX, divided, shows its subject (like a fox) whose tail gets immersed. There will be occasion for regret.

2. The second NINE, undivided, shows its subject dragging back his (carriage-)wheel. With firmness and correctness there will be good fortune.

3. The third SIX, divided, shows its subject, with (the state of things) not yet remedied, advancing on; which will lead to evil. But there will be advantage in (trying to) cross the great stream.

4. The fourth NINE, undivided, shows its subject by firm correctness obtaining good fortune, so that all occasion for repentance disappears. Let him stir himself up, as if he were invading the Demon region, where for three years rewards will come to him (and his troops) from the great kingdom.

5. The fifth SIX, divided, shows its subject by firm correctness obtaining good fortune, and having no occasion for repentance. (We see in him) the brightness of a superior man, and the possession of sincerity. There will be good fortune.

6. The topmost NINE, undivided, shows its subject

---

second excels in sincerity, and his small offering is the more acceptable.

The topmost line is weak, and on the outmost edge of Khân, the trigram of peril. His action is violent and perilous, like that one attempting to cross a ford, and being plunged overhead into the water.

LXIV. Wei 3î is the reverse of Kî 3î. The name tells us that the successful accomplishment of whatever the writer had in his mind had not yet been realised. The vessel of the state has not been brought across the great and dangerous stream. Some have wished that the Yî might have concluded with Kî 3î, and the last hexagram have left us with the picture of human affairs all brought to good order. But this would not have been in harmony with the

full of confidence and therefore feasting (quietly).
There will be no error. (If he) cherish this con-

idea of the Yî, as the book of change. Again and again it has
been pointed out that we find in it no idea of a perfect and abiding
state. Just as the seasons of the year change and pursue an ever-
recurring round, so is it with the phases of society. The reign of
order has been, and has terminated ; and this hexagram calls us to
see the struggle for its realisation recommenced. It treats of how
those engaged in that struggle should conduct themselves with a
view to secure the happy consummation.

How the figure sets forth the state of things by its constituent
trigrams will appear in Appendix II. A similar indication is
supposed to be given by the lines, not one of which is in the correct place ; the strong lines being all in even places, and the weak
lines in odd. At the same time each of them has a proper correlate ; and so the figure gives an intimation of some successful
progress. See also Appendix I.

The symbolism of the young fox suggests a want of caution on
the part of those, in the time and condition denoted by the hexagram, who try to remedy prevailing disorders. Their attempt is
not successful, and they get themselves into trouble and danger.
Whatever can be done must be undertaken in another way.

I suppose a fox to be intended by the symbolism of line 1,
bringing that animal on from the Thwan. Some of the commentators understand it of any animal. The line is weak, at the
bottom of the trigram of peril, and responds to the strong 4, which
is not in its correct place. Its subject attempts to be doing, but
finds cause to regret his course.

The subject of line 2, strong, and in the centre, is able to repress
himself, and keep back his carriage from advancing ; and there is
good fortune.

The Khang-hsî editors say that it is very difficult to understand
what is said under line 3 ; and many critics suppose that a negative
has dropt out, and that we should really read that 'it will not be
advantageous to try and cross the great stream.'

Line 4, though strong, is in an even place ; and this might
vitiate the endeavours of its subject to bring about a better state of
things. But he is firm and correct. He is in the fourth place moreover, and immediately above there is his ruler, represented by a weak
line, humble therefore, and prepared to welcome his endeavours.
Let him exert himself vigorously and long, as Kâo 3ung did in his

fidence, till he (is like the fox who) gets his head immersed, it will fail of what is right.

---

famous expedition (see last hexagram, line 3), and he will make progress and have success. Expeditions beyond the frontiers in those days were not very remote. Intercourse was kept up between the army and the court. Rewards, distinctions, and whatever was necessary to encourage the army, were often sent to it.

Line 5 is weak, in an odd place. But its subject is the ruler, humble and supported by the subject of the strong 2; and hence the auspice is very good.

The subject of line 6, when the work of the hexagram has been done, appears disposed to remain quiet in the confidence of his own power, but enjoying himself; and thereby he will do right. If, on the contrary, he will go on to exert his powers, and play with the peril of the situation, the issue will be bad.

THE APPENDIXES

THE APPENDIXES

APPENDIX I

Treatise on the Thwan, or king Wăn's Explanations of the entire Hexagrams

SECTION I

I. 1. Vast is the 'great and originating (power)' indicated by *Kh*ien! All things owe to it their beginning:—it contains all the meaning belonging to (the name) heaven.

2. The clouds move and the rain is distributed; the various things appear in their developed forms.

3. (The sages) grandly understand (the connexion between) the end and the beginning, and how (the indications of) the six lines (in the hexagram) are accomplished, (each) in its season. (Accordingly) they mount (the carriage) drawn by those six dragons at the proper times, and drive through the sky.

4. The method of *Kh*ien is to change and transform, so that everything obtains its correct nature as appointed (by the mind of Heaven); and (thereafter the conditions of) great harmony are preserved in union. The result is 'what is advantageous, and correct and firm.'

5. (The sage) appears aloft, high above all things, and the myriad states all enjoy repose.

The name Thwan, and the meaning of the character so-called, are sufficiently established. The Thwan are king Wăn's explanations of the entire hexagrams. It seems impossible now to

II. 1. Complete is the 'great and originating (capacity)' indicated by Khwăn! All things owe to it their birth;—it receives obediently the influences of Heaven.

2. Khwăn, in its largeness, supports and contains all things. Its excellent capacity matches the unlimited power (of *Kh*ien). Its comprehension is wide, and its brightness great. The various things obtain (by it) their full development.

3. The mare is a creature of earthly kind. Its (power of) moving on the earth is without limit; it is mild and docile, advantageous and firm :—such is the course of the superior man.

---

ascertain how the character arose, and how it was named Thwan. The treatise on the Thwan is ascribed to Confucius; and I have considered in the Introduction, p. 30, whether the tradition to this effect may to any extent be admitted.

I. The hexagram *Kh*ien is made up of six undivided lines, or of the trigram *Kh*ien, Fû-hsî's symbol for heaven, repeated. The Thwan does not dwell upon this, but starts, in its exposition, from the word 'heaven,' supposing that the hexagram represented all the meaning which had ever been intended by that term. In paragraphs 1, 2, 4 the four attributes in Wăn's Text (2 being occupied with the second, though it is not expressly named) are illustrated by the phenomena taking place in the physical world.

In paragraphs 3 and 5, the subject is the sage. He is not named indeed; and Khung Ying-tâ (A. D. 574–648) does not introduce him till paragraph 5, when the meaning necessitates the presence of a human agent, who rules in the world of men as heaven does in that of nature. The 'connexion between the end and the beginning,' which he sees, is that of cause and effect in the operations of nature and the course of human affairs. The various steps in that course are symbolised by the lines of the hexagram; and the ideal sage, conducting his ideal government, taking his measures accordingly, is represented as driving through the sky in a carriage drawn by six dragons. *K*û Hsî extravagantly says that 'the sage is Heaven, and Heaven is the sage;' but there is nothing like this in the text.

4. 'If he take the initiative, he goes astray :'—he misses, that is, his proper course. 'If he follow,' he is docile, and gets into his regular (course). 'In the south-west he will get friends :'—he will be walking with those of his own class. 'In the north-east he will lose friends :'—but in the end there will be ground for congratulation.

5. 'The good fortune arising from resting in firmness' corresponds to the unlimited capacity of the earth.

III. 1. In *K*un we have the strong (*Kh*ien) and the weak (Khwăn) commencing their intercourse, and difficulties arising.

2. Movement in the midst of peril gives rise to 'great progress and success, (through) firm correctness.'

3. By the action of the thunder and rain, (which

II. As the writer in expounding the Thwan of hexagram 1 starts from the word 'heaven,' so here he does so from the symbolic meaning attached to 'earth.' What I have said on the Text about the difference with which the same attributes are ascribed to *Kh*ien and Khwăn, appears clearly in paragraph 1. It is the difference expressed by the words that I have supplied,—'power' and 'capacity.' *Kh*ien originates; Khwăn produces, or gives birth to what has been originated.

The 'penetrating,' or developing ability of Khwăn, as displayed in the processes of growth, is the subject of paragraph 2. 'The brightness' refers to the beauty that shines forth in the vegetable and animal worlds.

Paragraph 3 treats of the symbol of the 'mare,' to lead the mind to the course of 'the superior man,' the good and faithful minister and servant.

See the note, corresponding to paragraph 4, on the Text. 'Resting in firmness' is the normal course of Khwăn. Where it is pursued, the good effect will be great, great as the unlimited capacity of the earth.

are symbols of *K*ăn and Khan), all (between heaven and earth) is filled up. But the condition of the time is full of irregularity and obscurity. Feudal princes should be established, but the feeling that rest and peace have been secured should not be indulged (even then).

IV. 1. In Măng we have (the trigram for) a mountain, and below it that of a rugged defile with a stream in it. The conditions of peril and arrest

---

III. *K*un is made up of the trigrams *K*ăn and Khan; but according to the views on king Wăn's arrangement of the trigrams, as set forth especially in Appendix V, chap. 14, the six others come from *K*hien and Khwăn, and are said to be their children. On the first application of Khwăn to *K*hien, there results *K*ăn, the first line of *K*hien taking the place of the last of Khwăn; and on the second application, there results Khan, the middle line of *K*hien taking the place of that of Khwăn. McClatchie renders here:—'The Thun (*K*un) diagram represents the hard and the soft (air) beginning to have sexual intercourse, and bringing forth with suffering!' But there is nothing in the Yî, from the beginning to the end, to justify such an interpretation. Nor do I see how, from any account of the genesis by the component trigrams, the idea of the result as signifying a state of difficulty and distress can be readily made out.

In paragraph 2 there is an attempt from the virtues or attributes assigned to the trigrams to make out the result indicated in the Thwan. To move and excite is the quality of *K*ăn; perilousness is the quality of Khan. The power to move is likely to produce great effects; to do this in perilous and difficult circumstances requires firmness and correctness. But neither is this explanation very satisfactory.

The first part of paragraph 3 depicts a condition of trouble and disorder in the natural world occasioned by the phenomena that are symbols of the significance of *K*ăn and Khan; but this is symbolical again of the disorder and distress, political and social, characteristic of the time. Good princes throughout the nation would help to remedy that; but the supreme authority should not resign itself to indifference, trusting to them.

of progress (suggested by these) give (the idea in) Măng.

2. 'Măng indicates that there will be progress and success :'—for there is development at work in it, and its time of action is exactly what is right. 'I do not seek the youthful and inexperienced ; he seeks me :'—so does will respond to will. 'When he shows (the sincerity that marks) the first recourse to divination, I instruct him :'—for possessing the qualities of the undivided line and being in the central place, (the subject of the second line thus speaks). 'A second and third application create annoyance, and I do not instruct so as to create annoyance :'—annoyance (he means) to the ignorant.

(The method of dealing with) the young and ignorant is to nourish the correct (nature belonging to them);—this accomplishes the service of the sage.

IV. The trigram Kăn has for its symbol in the natural world a mountain, which stands up frowningly, and stops or arrests the progress of the traveller. Stoppage, understood sometimes actively, and sometimes passively, is called the virtue or attribute indicated by it. Khan, as I said on p. 32, has water for its symbol, and especially in the form of rain. Here, however, the water appears as a stream in a difficult defile, such as ordinarily appears on an approach to a mountain, and suggesting perilousness as the attribute of such a position. From the combination of these symbols and their attributes the writer thinks that he gets the idea of the character (not the entire hexagram) Măng, as symbolical of ignorance and inexperience. See on 'the Great Symbolism' below.

Down to the last sentence of paragraph 2, all that is said is intended to show how it is that the figure indicates progress and success. The whole representation is grounded on the undivided line's being in the central place. It is the symbol of active effort for the teaching of the ignorant in the proper place and time ; this being responded to by the divided fifth line, representing the ignorance to be taught as docile, 'will responds to will.' But the

V. 1. Hsü denotes waiting. (The figure) shows peril in front ; but notwithstanding the firmness and strength (indicated by the inner trigram), its subject does not allow himself to be involved (in the dangerous defile);—it is right he should not be straitened or reduced to extremity.

2. When it is said that, 'with the sincerity declared in Hsü, there will be brilliant success, and with firmness there will be good fortune,' this is shown by the position (of the fifth line) in the place assigned by Heaven, and its being the correct position for it, and in the centre. 'It will be advantageous to go through the great stream ;'—that is, going forward will be followed by meritorious achievement.

---

subject of line 2 requires sincerity in the applicant for instruction, and feels that he must make his own teaching acceptable and agreeable. All this serves to bring out the idea of progress and success.

Then finally in the young and ignorant there is 'a correct nature,' a moral state made for goodness. The efficient teacher directing his efforts to bring out and nourish that, the progress and success will be 'great ;' the service done will be worthy of 'a sage.'

V. Hsü is composed of *Khien*, having the quality of strength, and of Khan, having the quality of perilousness. The strong one might readily dare the peril, but he restrains himself and waits. This is the lesson of the hexagram,—the benefit of action well considered, of plans well matured.

The fifth line, as we have observed more than once already, is the place of honour, that due to the ruler or king. It is here called 'the Heavenly or Heaven-given seat,' the meaning of which expression is clear from its occurrence in the Shih, III, i, ode 2. 1. Five is an odd number, and the fifth is therefore the 'correct' place for an undivided line; it is also the central place of the trigram, indicating how its occupant is sure to walk in the due mean. See further the notes on the Text, p. 68.

VI. 1. The upper portion of Sung is (the tri-gram representing) strength, and the lower (that representing) peril. (The coming together of) strength and peril gives (the idea in) Sung.

2. 'Sung intimates how, though there is sin-cerity in one's contention, he will yet meet with opposition and obstruction; but if he cherish an apprehensive caution, there will be good fortune:'— a strong (line) has come and got the central place (in the lower trigram).

'If he must prosecute the contention to the (bitter) end, there will be evil:'—contention is not a thing to be carried on to extremity.

'It will be advantageous to meet with the great man:'—what he sets a value on is the due mean, and the correct place.

'It will not be advantageous to cross the great stream:'—one (attempting to do so) would find himself in an abyss.

VI. Paragraph 1 here is much to the same effect as the first sentence in the notes on the Thwan of the Text. It is said, 'Strength without peril would not produce contention; peril with-out strength would not be able to contend.'

2. 'A strong line has come and got the central place:'—this sentence has given rise to a doctrine about the changes of trigrams and hexagrams, which has obscured more than anything else the interpretation of the Yî. Where has the strong second line come from? From a hundred critics we receive the answer,—'From Tun (☰☳).' The reader will see that if the second and third lines of the lower trigram there be made to change places, there results ☰☵, or Sung. The doctrine of changing the figures by the manipulation of the stalks did spring up between the time of Wăn and his son and that of the composition of the Appendixes; but there is no trace of it in the real Text of the Yî; and it renders any scheme for the interpretation of the figures impossible. The

VII. 1. '(The name) Sze describes the multitude
(of the host). The 'firmness and correctness' (which
the hexagram indicates) refer to (moral) correctness (of aim). When (the mover) is able to use the
multitude with such correctness, he may attain to the
royal sway.

2. There is (the symbol of) strength in the centre
(of the trigram below), and it is responded to (by its
proper correlate above). The action gives rise to
perils, but is in accordance (with the best sentiments
of men). (Its mover) may by such action distress
all the country, but the people will follow him ;—
there will be good fortune, and what error should
there be ?

VIII. 1. 'Pî indicates that there is good fortune :'—(the name) Pî denotes help ; (and we see
in the figure) inferiors docilely following (their
superior).

---

editors of the imperial Yî allow this, and on the present passage discard the doctrine entirely, referring to the language of the Thwan on
hexagrams 11 and 12 as fatal to it. See the notes there, and the
Introduction, pp. 11–16. 'A strong line has come' is to be taken as
equivalent simply to 'a strong line is there.'

What 'the great man sets a value on being the due mean and
the correct place,' his decision in any matter of contention is sure
to be right.

VII. That 'multitude' is given here as if it were the meaning of
the name Sze arose, probably, from there being but one undivided
line in the figure. That is the symbol of the general, all the other
lines, divided, suggest the idea of a multitude obedient to his orders.
The general's place in the centre of the lower trigram, with the
proper correlate in line 5, suggests the idea of firmness and correctness that dominates in the hexagram. But in the last sentence
it is the ruler, and not the general of the host, who is the subject.
Compare what is said of him with Mencius, I, i, chap. 3; ii, chap.
5, &c.

2. 'Let (the principal party intended in it) re-examine himself, (as if) by divination, whether his virtue be great, unintermitting, and firm;—if it be so, there will be no error:—all this follows from the position of the strong line in the centre (of the upper trigram). 'Those who have not rest will come to him:'—high and low will respond to its subject. 'With those who are (too) late in coming it will be ill:'—(for them) the way (of good fortune here indi-cated) has been exhausted.

IX. 1. In Hsiâo *Khû* the weak line occupies its (proper) position, and (the lines) above and below respond to it. Hence comes the name of Hsiâo *Khû* (Small Restraint).

2. (It presents the symbols of) strength and flexibility. Strong lines are in the central places, and the will (of their subjects) will have free course. Thus it indicates that there will be progress and success.

3. 'Dense clouds but no rain' indicate the move-ment (of the strong lines) still going forward. The

---

'Perilousness' is the attribute of Khan, the lower trigram, and 'docility,' or 'accordance with others,' that of Khwăn, the upper. War is like 'poison' to a country, injurious, and threatening ruin to it, and yet the people will endure and encounter it in behalf of the sovereign whom they esteem and love.

VIII. There is some error in the text here,—as all the critics acknowledge. I have adopted the decision of *K*û Hsî, which by a very small change makes the whole read consistently, and in harmony with other explanations of the Thwan. 'The inferiors' are the subjects of all the other lines gathering round their supe-rior, represented in the fifth line.

'The way has been exhausted:'—they do not seek to promote and enjoy union till it is too late. The sentiment is the same as that in the lines of Shakespeare about the tide in the affairs of men.

'Commencing at our western border' indicates that the (beneficial) influence has not yet been widely displayed.

X. 1. In Lî we have (the symbol of) weakness treading on (that of) strength.

2. (The lower trigram) indicates pleasure and satisfaction, and responds to (the upper) indicating strength. Hence (it is said), 'He treads on the tail of a tiger, which does not bite him; there will be progress and success.'

3. (The fifth line is) strong, in the centre, and in

IX. 'The weak line' is said to occupy 'its proper position,' because it is in the fourth,—an even place. The 'responding' on the part of all the other lines above and below is their submitting to be restrained by it; and this arises simply from the meaning which king Wăn chose to attach to the hexagram.

But the restraint can only be small. The attributes of the two parts of the figure do not indicate anything else. The undivided line represents vigour and activity, and such a line is in the middle of each trigram. There cannot but be progress and success.

It is not easy to explain the symbolism of the last paragraph in harmony with the appended explanations. What Khăng-žze, Wang Făng, and other scholars say is to this effect:—Dense clouds ought to give rain. That they exist without doing so, shows the restraining influence of the hexagram to be still at work. But the other and active influence is, according to the general idea of the figure, continuing in operation;—there will be rain ere long. And this was taking place in the western regions subject to the House of Kâu, which still was only a fief of Shang. It was not for the inferior House to rule the superior. Kâu was for a time restrained by Shang. Let their positions be reversed by Kâu superseding Shang, and the rain of beneficent government would descend on all the kingdom. This seems to be the meaning of the paragraph. This is the answer to the riddle of it. Confucius, in his treatise on the Thwan, hints at it, but no Chinese critic has the boldness to declare it fully.

its correct place. (Its subject) occupies the God-(given) position, and falls into no distress or failure;—(his) action will be brilliant.

XI. 'The little come and the great gone in Thâi, and its indication that there will be good fortune with progress and success' show to us heaven and earth in communication with each other, and all things in consequence having free course, and (also) the high and the low, (superiors and inferiors), in communication with one another, and possessed by the same aim. The inner (trigram) is made up of the strong and undivided lines, and the outer of the weak and divided; the inner is (the symbol of) strength, and the outer of docility; the inner (represents) the superior man, and the outer the small man. (Thus) the way of

---

X. '(The symbol of) weakness' in paragraph 1, according to Wang Shăn-ʒze (Yüan dynasty), is line 3, urged by the two strong lines below, and having to encounter the three strong lines above. Hû Ping-wan (also of the Yüan dynasty) says that the whole of the lower trigram, Tui, partaking of the yin nature, is the symbol of weakness, and the whole of *Kh*ien that of strength. The *Keh-Kung* editors say that, to get the full meaning, we must hold both views.

Paragraph 2 has been sufficiently explained on the Thwan itself.

Paragraph 3 has also been explained; but there remains something to be said on the Chinese text for 'occupies the God-given position,' or, literally, 'treads on the seat of Tî.' Canon McClatchie has—'The imperial throne is now occupied.' I think that 'the seat of Tî' is synonymous with the seat of Heaven,' in paragraph 2 of this treatise on hexagram 5. If Confucius, or whoever was the writer, had before him the phrase as it occurs in the Shû, I, 12, the force of Tî will depend on the meaning assigned to it in that part of the Shû. That the fifth line occupies the place of authority is here the only important point.

the superior man appears increasing, and that of the small man decreasing.

XII. 'The want of good understanding between the (different classes of) men in Phî, and its indication as unfavourable to the firm and correct course of the superior man; with the intimation that the great are gone and the little come:'—all this springs from the fact that in it heaven and earth are not in communication with each other, and all things in consequence do not have free course; and that the high and the low (superiors and inferiors) are not in communication with one another, and there are no (well-regulated) states under the sky. The inner (trigram) is made up of the weak and divided lines, and the outer of the strong and undivided: the inner is (the symbol of) weakness, and the outer of strength; the inner (represents) the small man, and the outer the superior man. Thus the way of the small man appears increasing, and that of the superior man decreasing.

XI. There is nothing to be said on the explanation of the Thwan here beyond what has been noticed on the different paragraphs of the Text. Canon McClatchie translates :—' The Thwan means that Heaven and Earth have now conjugal intercourse with each other . . . . and the upper and lower (classes) unite together.' But in both clauses the Chinese characters are the same. Why did he not go on to say—' the upper and lower classes have conjugal intercourse together;' or rather, why did he not dismiss the idea of such intercourse from his mind altogether? Why make the Yî appear to be gross, when there is not the shadow of grossness in it? The paragraph here well illustrates how the ruling idea in all the antinomies of the Yî is that of authority and strength on the one side, and of inferiority and weakness on the other.

XII. All the symbolism here springs from the trigram Khwǎn occupying in the figure the inner or lower place, and *Kh*ien the outer or upper. It is for the inner trigram to take the initiative;

XIII. 1. In Thung Zăn the weak (line) has the place (of influence), the central place, and responds to (the corresponding line in) Khien (above); hence comes its name of Thung Zăn (or 'Union of men').

2. Thung Zăn says:—

3. The language, 'Thung Zăn appears here (as we find it) in (the remote districts of) the country, indicating progress and success, and that it will be advantageous to cross the great stream,' is moulded by its containing the strength (symbolled) in Khien. (Then) we have (the trigram indicating) elegance and intelligence, supported by (that indicating) strength; with the line in the central, and its correct, position, and responding (to the corresponding line above):—(all representing) the correct course of the superior man. It is only the superior man who can comprehend and affect the minds of all under the sky.

XIV. 1. In Tâ Yû the weak (line) has the place of honour, is grandly central, and (the strong lines) above and below respond to it. Hence comes its name of Tâ Yû (Having what is Great).

---

but how can earth (symbolised by Khwăn) take the place of heaven (symbolised by Khien)? As in nature it is heaven that originates and not earth, so in a state the upper classes must take the initiative, and not the lower.

XIII. To understand the various points in this commentary, it is only necessary to refer to the Text of the hexagram. The proper correlate of line 2 is line 5, and I have said therefore that it 'responds to (the corresponding line in) Khien.' The editors of the Khang-hsî edition, however, would make the correlate to it all the lines of Khien, as being more agreeable to the idea of union.

I do not think that a second paragraph has been lost. The

2. The attributes (of its component trigrams) are strength and vigour with elegance and brightness. (The ruling line in it) responds to (the ruling line in the symbol of) heaven, and (consequently) its action is (all) at the proper times. In this way (it is said to) indicate great progress and success.

XV. 1. *Kh*ien indicates progress and success. It is the way of heaven to send down its beneficial influences below, where they are brilliantly displayed. It is the way of earth, lying low, to send its influences upwards and (there) to act.

2. It is the way of heaven to diminish the full and augment the humble. It is the way of earth to overthrow the full and replenish the humble. Spiritual Beings inflict calamity on the full and bless the humble. It is the way of men to hate the full and love the humble. Humility in a position of honour makes that still more brilliant; and in a low position men will not (seek to) pass beyond it. Thus it is that 'the superior man will have a (good) issue (to his undertakings).'

'Thung *Z*ăn says' is merely a careless repetition of the three concluding characters of paragraph 1.

XIV. The position in the fifth place indicates the dignity, and its being central, in the centre of the upper trigram, indicates the virtue, of the lord of the figure.

The strength of the lord, moreover, is directed by intelligence; and his actions are always at the proper time, like the seasons of heaven.

XV. The Thwan on this hexagram was so brief, that the writer here deals generally with the subject of humility, showing how it is valued by heaven and earth, by spirits and by men. The descent of the heavenly influences, and the low position of the earth in paragraph 1, are both emblematic of humility. The heavenly influences have their 'display' in the beauty and fertility of the earth.

XVI. 1. In Yü we see the strong (line) responded to by all the others, and the will (of him whom it represents) being carried out; and (also) docile obedience employing movement (for its purposes). (From these things comes) Yü (the Condition of harmony and satisfaction).

2. In this condition we have docile obedience employing movement (for its purposes), and therefore it is so as between heaven and earth;—how much more will it be so (among men) in 'the setting up of feudal princes and putting the hosts in motion!'

3. Heaven and earth show that docile obedience in connexion with movement, and hence the sun and moon make no error (in time), and the four seasons do not deviate (from their order). The sages show such docile obedience in connexion with their movements, and hence their punishments and penalties are entirely just, and the people acknowledge it by their submission. Great indeed are the time and significance indicated in Yü!

The way of heaven is seen, e.g. in the daily declining of the sun, and the waning of the moon after it is full; the way of earth in the fall of the year. On the meaning of 'Spiritual Beings (Kwei Shǎn),' see the Introduction, pp. 34, 35. It is difficult to say what idea the writer attached to the name. What he says of man's appreciation of humility is striking, and, I believe, correct.

XVI. What is said in paragraph 1 about the lines has been pointed out in the notes on the Text. 'Obedience' is the attribute of Khwǎn, the lower trigram, which takes the initiative in the action of the figure; and here makes use of the movement, which is the attribute of Kǎn, the upper trigram.

I can hardly trace the connexion between the different parts of paragraph 2. Does it not proceed on the harmony produced by the thunderous explosion between heaven and earth, as declared

XVII. 1. In Sui we see the strong (trigram) come and place itself under the weak; we see (in the two) the attributes of movement and pleasure :—this gives (the idea of) Sui.

2. 'There will be great progress and success; and through firm correctness no error:'—all under heaven will be found following at such a time.

3. Great indeed are the time and significance indicated in Sui.

XVIII. 1. In Kû we have the strong (trigram) above, and the weak one below; we have (below) pliancy, and (above) stopping :— these give the idea of Kû (a Troublous Condition of affairs verging to ruin).

2. 'Kû indicates great progress and success :'—(through the course shown in it), all under heaven, there will be good order. 'There will be advantage in crossing the great stream :'—he who advances will encounter the business to be done. '(He should

---

in Appendix II? Then the analogy between natural phenomena and human and social experiences comes into play.

Paragraph 3 is also tantalising. Why does the writer introduce the subject of punishments and penalties? Are they a consequence of putting the hosts in motion?

XVII. The trigrams *K*ăn and Tui are distinguished as strong and weak, *K*ăn representing, on king Wăn's scheme, 'the eldest son,' and Tui, 'the youngest daughter.' But 'the strong' here may mean the strong line, the lowest in the hexagram. As Wang Ꝫung-*k*wan (Sung dynasty) says:—'The yang and strong line should not be below a yin and weak line, as we find it here. That is, in Sui the high places himself below the low, and the noble below the mean :'—esteeming others higher than himself, and giving the idea of following. Then *K*ăn denotes the production or excitement of motion, and Tui denotes pleasure ; and the union of these things suggests the same idea.

weigh well, however, the events of) three days before (the turning-point), and those (to be done) three
days after it :'—the end (of confusion) is the beginning (of order); such is the procedure of Heaven.

XIX. 1. In Lin (we see) the strong (lines)
gradually increasing and advancing.

2. (The lower trigram is the symbol of) being
pleased, and (the upper of) being compliant. The
strong (line) is in the central position, and is properly responded to.

3. 'There is great progress and success, along with
firm correctness :'—this is the way of Heaven.

4. 'In the eighth month there will be evil :'—(the
advancing power) will decay after no long time.

XX. 1. The great Manifester occupies an upper
place (in the figure), which consists of (the trigrams

XVIII. The symbolism here is the opposite of that in Sui. The
upper trigram *K*ăn is strong, denoting, according to king Wăn,
'the youngest son ;' and the lower, Sun, is weak, denoting 'the eldest
daughter.' For the eldest daughter to be below the youngest son
is eminently correct, and helps to indicate the auspice of great
success. The attribute of Sun is pliancy, and that of *K*ăn stoppage
or arrest. The feeble pliancy confronted by the arresting mountain gives an idea of the evil state implied in Kû.

'Three days before and after the turning-point' is, literally,
'three days before and after *k*iâ,' *k*iâ being the name of the first of
the 'earthly stems' among the cyclical characters. Hence it has
the meaning of 'beginning,' and here denotes the turning-point, at
which disorder gives place to order. According to 'the procedure
of Heaven,' history is a narrative of change, one condition of affairs
constantly giving place to another and opposite. 'A kingdom that
cannot be moved' does not enter into the circle of Chinese ideas.

XIX. See what has been said on the fourth paragraph in pp. 98, 99
on the Text. The other paragraphs need no explanation beyond
what appears in the supplemented translation.

whose attributes are) docility and flexibility. He is in the central position and his correct place, and thus exhibits (his lessons) to all under heaven.

2. 'Kwan shows its subject like a worshipper who has washed his hands, but not (yet) presented his offerings;—with sincerity and an appearance of dignity (commanding reverent regard):'—(all) beneath look to him and are transformed.

3. When we contemplate the spirit-like way of Heaven, we see how the four seasons proceed without error. The sages, in accordance with (this) spirit-like way, laid down their instructions, and all under heaven yield submission to them.

XXI. 1. The existence of something between the jaws gives rise to the name Shih Ho (Union by means of biting through the intervening article).

2. The Union by means of biting through the intervening article indicates 'the successful progress (denoted by the hexagram).'

The strong and weak (lines) are equally divided (in the figure). Movement is denoted (by the lower trigram), and bright intelligence (by the upper); thunder and lightning uniting in them, and having brilliant manifestation. The weak (fifth) line is in

XX. 'The great Manifester' is the ruler, the principal subject of the hexagram, and represented by line 5, near the top of the figure. In that figure the lower trigram is Khwăn, representing the earth, with the attribute of docility, and the upper is Sun, representing wind, with the attributes of flexibility and penetration. As is the place of line 5, so are the virtues of the ruler.

'The spirit-like way of Heaven' is the invisible and unfathomable agency ever operating by general laws, and with invariable regularity, in what we call nature. Compare with this paragraph, the definition of Shăn or Spirit in Appendix III, i, 32; and the doctrine of the agency of God, taught in Appendix VI, 8, 9.

the centre, and acts in its high position. Although it is not in its proper position, this is advantageous for the use of legal constraints.

XXII. 1. (When it is said that) Pî indicates that there should be free course (in what it denotes):—

2. (We see) the weak line coming and ornamenting the strong lines (of the lower trigram), and hence (it is said that ornament) 'should have free course.' On the other hand, the strong line above ornaments the weak ones (of the upper trigram), and hence (it is said) that 'there will be little advantage, if (ornament) be allowed to advance (and take the lead).' (This is illustrated in the) appearances that ornament the sky.

3. Elegance and intelligence (denoted by the lower trigram) regulated by the arrest (denoted by the upper) suggest the observances that adorn human (society).

4. We look at the ornamental figures of the sky, and thereby ascertain the changes of the seasons. We look at the ornamental observances of society, and understand how the processes of transformation are accomplished all under heaven.

XXI. The 'equal division of the strong and weak lines' is seen by taking them in pairs, though the order in the first pair is different from that in the two others. This is supposed to indicate the intelligence of the judgments in the action of the hexagram. *Kăn*, the lower trigram, symbolises movement; Lî, the upper, intelligence. The fifth line's acting in its high position does not intimate the formation of the figure from Yî, the 42nd hexagram, but calls attention to the fact that a weak line is here 'lord of judgment.' This does not seem natural, but the effect is good;—judgment is tempered by leniency.

XXII. The first paragraph is either superfluous or incomplete. The language of paragraph 2 has naturally been pressed into the

XXIII. 1. Po denotes overthrowing or being overthrown. We see (in the figure) the weak lines (threatening to) change the (last) strong line (into one of themselves).

2. That 'it will not be advantageous to make a movement in any direction whatever' appears from the fact that the small men are (now) growing and increasing. The superior man acts according to (the exigency of the time), and stops all forward movement, looking at the (significance of the) symbolic figures (in the hexagram). He values the processes of decrease and increase, of fulness and decadence, (as seen) in the movements of the heavenly bodies.

---

service of the doctrine of changing the figures by divining manipulation; see p. 219, on paragraph 2 of the Thwan of hexagram 6. But as the Khang-hsî editors point out, 'the weak line coming and ornamenting the two strong lines' simply indicates how substantiality should have the help of ornament, and 'the strong line above (or ascending) and ornamenting the two weak lines' indicates that ornament should be restrained by substantiality. Ornament has its use, but it must be kept in check.—The closing sentence has no connexion with what precedes. Some characters are wanting, to show how the writer passes on to speak of 'the ornamental figures of the sky.' The whole should then be joined on to paragraph 3. The 'figures of the sky' are all the heavenly bodies in their relative positions and various movements, producing day and night, heat and cold, &c. The observances of society are the ceremonies and performances which regulate and beautify the intercourse of men, and constitute the transforming lessons of sagely wisdom.

XXIII. 'The symbolic figures in the hexagram' are Khwăn, below, the representative of docility, acting as circumstances require; and Kăn, the representative of a mountain, which arrests the progress of the traveller. The superior man of the topmost line thus interprets them, and acts accordingly. Yet he is not left without hope. Winter is followed by spring; night is

XXIV. 1. 'Fû indicates the free course and progress (of what it denotes):'—it is the coming back of what is intended by the undivided line.

2. (Its subject's) actions show movement directed by accordance with natural order. Hence 'he finds no one to distress him in his exits and entrances,' and 'friends come to him, and no error is committed.'

3. 'He will return and repeat his proper course; in seven days comes his return:'—such is the movement of the heavenly (revolution).

4. 'There will be advantage in whatever direction movement is made:'—the strong lines are growing and increasing.

5. Do we not see in Fû the mind of heaven and earth?

XXV. In Wû Wang we have the strong (first) line come from the outer (trigram), and become in the inner trigram lord (of the whole figure); we have (the attributes of) motive power and strength; we have the strong line (of the fifth place) in the

---

succeeded by day; the moon wanes, and then begins to wax again. So will it be in political life. As we read in the Hebrew prophet Isaiah, 'In returning and rest shall ye be saved; in quietness and in confidence shall be your strength.'

XXIV. 'The movement of the heavenly revolution' in paragraph 3 has reference to the regular alternations of darkness and light, and of cold and heat, as seen in the different months of the year. Hâu Hsing-kwo (of the Thang dynasty) refers to the expressions in the Shih, I, xv, ode 1, 'the days of (our) first (month), second (month),' &c., as illustrating the use of day for month, as we have it here; but that is to explain what is obscure by what is more so; though I believe, as stated on the Text, that 'seven days' is here equivalent to 'seven months.'

'The mind of heaven and earth' is the love of life and of all goodness that rules in the course of nature and providence.

central position, and responded to (by the weak second):—there will be 'great progress proceeding from correctness; such is the appointment of Heaven.

'If (its subject and his action) be not correct, he will fall into errors, and it will not be advantageous for him to move in any direction:'—whither can he (who thinks he is) free from all insincerity, (and yet is as here described) proceed? Can anything be done (advantageously) by him whom the (will and) appointment of Heaven do not help?

XXVI. 1. In (the trigrams composing) Tâ *Kh*û we have (the attributes) of the greatest strength and of substantial solidity, which emit a brilliant light; and indicate a daily renewal of his virtue (by the subject of it).

2. The strong line is in the highest place, and suggests the value set on talents and virtue; there is power (in the upper trigram) to keep the strongest in restraint:—all this shows 'the great correctness' (required in the hexagram).

3. 'The good fortune attached to the subject's not seeking to enjoy his revenues in his own family' shows how talents and virtue are nourished.

XXV. The advocates of one trigram's changing into another, which ought not to be admitted, we have seen, into the interpretation of the Yî, make Wû Wang to be derived from Sung (No. 6), the second line there being manipulated into the first of this; but this representation is contrary to the words of the text, which make the strong first line come from the outer trigram, i. e. from *Kh*ien. And so it does, as related, not very intelligibly, in Appendix V, 10, *K*ăn, the lower trigram here, being 'the eldest son,' resulting from the first application of Khwăn to *Kh*ien. The three peculiarities in the structure of the figure afford the auspice of progress and success; and very striking is the brief and emphatic declaration, that such progress is 'the appointment of Heaven.'

4. 'It will be advantageous to cross the great stream:'—(the fifth line, representing the ruler,) is responded to by (the second, the central line of *Kh*ien, representing) Heaven.

XXVII. 1. 'Î indicates that with firm correctness there will be good fortune:'—when the nourishing is correct, there will be good fortune. 'We must look at what we are seeking to nourish:'—we must look at those whom we wish to nourish. 'We must by the exercise of our thoughts seek the proper aliment:'—we must look to our own nourishing of ourselves.

2. Heaven and earth nourish all things. The sages nourish men of talents and virtue, by them to reach to the myriads of the people. Great is (the work intended by this) nourishing in its time!

XXVI. In paragraph 1, Tâ *Kh*û evidently means the 'grand accumulation' of virtue, indicated by the attributes of its component trigrams. 'Substantial solidity' may very well be given as the attribute of mountains.

'The strong line in the highest place' of paragraph 2 is line 6, whose subject is thus above the ruler represented by 5, and has the open firmament for his range in doing his work. This, and his ability to repress the strongest opposition, show how he is supported by all that is correct and right.

In a kingdom where the object of the government is the accumulation of virtue, good and able men will not be left in obscurity.

What will not a high and good purpose, supported by the greatest strength, be able to do?

XXVII. Many of the critics, in illustration of paragraph 1, refer appropriately to Mencius, VI, i, chap. 14.

In illustration of paragraph 2 they refer to the times and court of Yâo and Shun, sage rulers, from whose cherishing and nourishing came Yü to assuage the waters of the deluge, 3î to teach the people agriculture, Hsieh as minister of instruction, Kâo Yâo as minister of crime, and others;—all to do the work of nourishing the people.

XXVIII. 1. Tâ Kwo shows the great ones
(= the undivided lines) in excess.

2. In 'the beam that is weak' we see weakness
both in the lowest and the topmost (lines).

3. The strong lines are in excess, but (two of
them) are in the central positions. The action (of
the hexagram is represented by the symbols of)
flexibility and satisfaction. (Hence it is said),
'There will be advantage in moving in any direction
whatever; yea, there will be success.'

4. Great indeed is (the work to be done in) this
very extraordinary time.

XXIX. 1. Khan repeated shows us one defile
succeeding another.

2. This is the nature of water;—it flows on,
without accumulating its volume (so as to overflow);
it pursues its way through a dangerous defile, without losing its true (nature).

3. That 'the mind is penetrating' is indicated by
the strong (line) in the centre. That 'action (in
accordance with this) will be of high value' tells us
that advance will be followed by achievement.

4. The dangerous (height) of heaven cannot be
ascended; the difficult places of the earth are moun-

XXVIII. Paragraph 3. In the Great Symbolism 'wood' appears
as the natural object symbolised by Sun, and not 'wind,' which we
find more commonly. The attribute of 'flexibility,' however, is
the quality of Sun, whether used of wind or of wood.

Paragraph 4. Such a time, it is said, was that of Yâo and Shun,
of Thang the Successful, and of king Wû. What these heroes did,
however, was all called for by the exigency of their times, and not
by whim or principle of their own, which they wished to make
prominent.

tains, rivers, hills, and mounds. Kings and princes arrange, by means of such strengths, to maintain their territories. Great indeed is the use of (what is here) taught about seasons of peril.

XXX. 1. Lî means being attached to. The sun and moon have their place in the sky. All the grains, grass, and trees have their place on the earth. The double brightness (of the two tri-grams) adheres to what is correct, and the result is the transforming and perfecting all under the sky.

2. The weak (second line) occupies the middle and correct position, and gives the indication of 'a free and successful course;' and, moreover, 'nourishing (docility like that of) the cow' will lead to good fortune.

XXIX. On paragraph 2 Liang Yin says:—'Water stops at the proper time, and moves at the proper time. Is not this an emblem of the course of the superior man in dealing with danger?'

On paragraph 4 the Khang-hsî editors say that to exercise one's self in meeting difficulty and peril is the way to establish and strengthen the character, and that the use of such experience is seen in all measures for self-defence, there being no helmet and mail like leal-heartedness and good faith, and no shield and tower like propriety and righteousness.

XXX. 'The double brightness' in paragraph 1 has been much discussed. Some say that it means 'the ruler,' becoming brighter and brighter. Others say that it means both the ruler and his ministers, combining their brightness. The former view seems to me the better. The analogy between the natural objects and a transforming and perfecting rule is far fetched.

'The central and correct position' in paragraph 2 can be said only of the second line, and not of the fifth, where an undivided line would be more correct. The 'and moreover' of the translation is 'therefore' in the original; but I cannot make out the force and suitability of that conjunction.

SECTION II

XXXI. 1. Hsien is here used in the sense of
Kan, meaning (mutually) influencing.

2. The weak (trigram) above, and the strong
one below; their two influences moving and responding to each other, and thereby forming a union; the
repression (of the one) and the satisfaction (of the
other); (with their relative position), where the
male is placed below the female :— all these
things convey the notion of 'a free and successful
course (on the fulfilment of the conditions), while
the advantage will depend on being firm and correct,
as in marrying a young lady, and there will be good
fortune.'

3. Heaven and earth exert their influences, and
there ensue the transformation and production of
all things. The sages influence the minds of men,
and the result is harmony and peace all under the
sky. If we look at (the method and issues) of those
influences, the true character of heaven and earth
and of all things can be seen.

XXXII. 1. Hăng denotes long continuance.
The strong (trigram) is above, and the weak one
below; (they are the symbols of) thunder and wind,

XXXI. Paragraph 2. Tui, the upper trigram, is weak and
yin; and Kăn, the lower, is strong and yang; see Appendixes III,
ii, 4, and V, 10. Kăn is below Tui; whereas the subject of the
lower trigram should always take the initiative in these figures.

which are in mutual communication; (they have the qualities of) docility and motive force; their strong and weak (lines) all respond, each to the other:— these things are all found in Hăng.

2. (When it is said that) 'Hăng indicates successful progress and no error (in what it denotes); but the advantage will come from being firm and correct,' this indicates that there must be long continuance in its way of operation. The way of heaven and earth is to be long continued in their operation without stopping.

3. (When it is said that) 'Movement in any direction whatever will be advantageous,' this implies that when (the moving power) is spent, it will begin again.

4. The sun and moon, realising in themselves (the course of Heaven), can perpetuate their shining. The four seasons, by their changing and transforming, can perpetuate their production (of things). The sages persevere long in their course, and all under the sky are transformed and perfect. When we look at what they continue doing long, the natural tendencies of heaven, earth, and all things can be seen.

XXXII. All the conditions in paragraph 1 must be understood as leading to the indication of progress and success, which is explained in paragraph 2, and illustrated by the analogy of the course of heaven and earth.

'Movement in any direction,' as explained in paragraph 3, indicates the ever-occurring new modes and spheres of activity, to which he who is firm and correct is called.

Paragraph 4, and especially its concluding sentence, are of a meditative and reflective character not uncommon in the treatise on the Thwan.

XXXIII. 1. 'Thun indicates successful progress:'—that is, in the very retiring which Thun denotes there is such progress. The strong (line) is in the ruling place, (the fifth), and is properly responded to (by the second line). The action takes place according to (the requirement of) the time.

2. 'To a small extent it will (still) be advantageous to be firm and correct:'—(the small men) are gradually encroaching and advancing.

3. Great indeed is the significance of (what is required to be done in) the time that necessitates retiring.

XXXIV. 1. In Tâ *K*wang we see that which is great becoming strong. We have the (trigram) denoting strength directing that which denotes movement, and hence (the whole) is expressive of vigour.

2. 'Tâ *K*wang indicates that it will be advantageous to be firm and correct:'—that which is great (should be) correct. Given correctness and greatness (in their highest degree), and the character and tendencies of heaven and earth can be seen.

XXXIII. 'The superior man,' it is said, 'advances or withdraws according to the character of the time. The strength and correct position of the fifth line show that he is able to maintain himself; and as it is responded to by the weak second line, no opposition to what is correct in him would come from any others. He might therefore keep his place; but looking at the two weak lines, 1 and 2, he recognises in them the advance and irrepressible progress of small men, and that for a time it is better for him to give way and withdraw from the field. Thus there is successful progress even in his retiring.'

XXXIV. Paragraph 1. 'That which is great' denotes, in the first place, the group of four strong lines which strikes us on

XXXV. 1. 3in denotes advancing.

2. (In 3in we have) the bright (sun) appearing above the earth; (the symbol of) docile submission cleaving to that of the Great brightness; and the weak line advanced and moving above:—all these things give us the idea of 'a prince who secures the tranquillity (of the people), presented on that account with numerous horses (by the king), and three times in a day received at interviews.'

XXXVI. 1. (The symbol of) the Earth and that of Brightness entering into the midst of it give the idea of Ming Î (Brightness wounded or obscured).

2. The inner (trigram) denotes being accomplished and bright; the outer, being pliant and submissive. The case of king Wăn was that of one

---

looking at the figure, and then the superior man, or the strong men in positions of power, of whom these are the representatives. *Kh*ien is the trigram of strength, and *K*ăn that of movement.

Paragraph 2. 'That which is great (should be) correct:'—that the 'should be' must be supplied in the translation appears from this, that the paragraph is intended to illustrate the text that 'it will be advantageous to be firm and correct.' The power of man becomes then a reflexion of the great power which we see working in nature, 'impartially,' 'unselfishly.'

XXXV. To those who advocate the view that the hexagrams of the Yî have been formed by changes of the lines in manipulating with the divining stalks, the words of paragraph 2, that we have in the figure 'the weak line advanced and moving above,' suggest the derivation of 3in from Kwan, whose 4th and 5th lines are made to change places (☰☰). But we have seen that that view is inadmissible in the interpretation of the Yî. And a simple explanation of the language at once presents itself. As Hsiang An-shih (Sung dynasty) says, 'Of the three "daughter" trigrams it is only Lî which has its divided line occupying the central place of honour, when it is the upper trigram in a hexagram.'

who with these qualities was yet involved in great difficulties.

3. 'It will be advantageous to realise the difficulty (of the position), and maintain firm correctness:'— that is, (the individual concerned) should obscure his brightness. The case of the count of *K*î was that of one who, amidst the difficulties of his House, was able (thus) to maintain his aim and mind correct.

XXXVII. 1. In *K*iâ *Z*ăn the wife has her correct place in the inner (trigram), and the man his correct place in the outer. That man and woman occupy their correct places is the great righteousness shown (in the relation and positions of) heaven and earth.

2. In *K*iâ *Z*ăn we have the idea of an authoritative ruler;—that, namely, represented by the parental authority.

3. Let the father be indeed father, and the son son; let the elder brother be indeed elder brother, and the younger brother younger brother; let the husband be indeed husband, and the wife wife:— then will the family be in its normal state. Bring the family to that state, and all under heaven will be established.

XXXVI. The sun disappearing, as we say, 'below the earth,' or, as the Chinese writer conceives it, 'into the midst of, or within the earth,' sufficiently indicates the obscuration or wounding of brightness,—the repression and resistance of the good and bright.

King Wăn was not of the line of Shang. Though opposed and persecuted by its sovereign, he could pursue his own course, till his line came in the end to supersede the other. It could not be so with the count of *K*î, who was a member of the House of Shang. He could do nothing that would help on its downfall. γ

XXXVII. Paragraph 1 first explains the statement of the

XXXVIII. 1. In Khwei we have (the symbol of) Fire, which, when moved, tends upwards, and that of a Marsh, whose waters, when moved, tend downwards. We have (also the symbols of) two sisters living together, but whose wills do not move in the same direction.

2. (We see how the inner trigram expressive of) harmonious satisfaction is attached to (the outer expressive of) bright intelligence; (we see) the weak line advanced and acting above, and how it occupies the central place, and is responded to by the strong (line below). These indications show that 'in small matters there will (still) be good fortune.'

3. Heaven and earth are separate and apart, but the work which they do is the same. Male and female are separate and apart, but with a common will they seek the same object. There is diversity between the myriad classes of beings, but there is an analogy between their several operations. Great indeed are the phenomena and the results of this condition of disunion and separation.

Thwan, about the wife, represented by line 2; and then proceeds to the husband, represented by line 5. The two trigrams become representative of the family circle, and the wide world without it. In the reference to heaven and earth it is not supposed that they are really husband and wife; but in their relation and positions they symbolise that social relation and the individuals in it.

Paragraph 2, more closely rendered, would be—'That in *K*îa *Z*ǎn there is an authoritative ruler is a way of naming father and mother.' Does the writer mean to say that while the assertion of authority was indispensable in a family, that authority must have combined in it both force and gentleness?

XXXVIII. In paragraph 1 we have first an explanation of the meaning of Khwei from the symbolism of Fû-hsî. Then follows

XXXIX. 1. *K*ien denotes difficulty. There is (the trigram expressive of) perilousness in front. When one, seeing the peril, can arrest his steps (in accordance with the significance of the lower trigram), is he not wise ?

2. (The language of) *K*ien; that 'advantage will be found in the south-west,' refers to the (strong fifth line) advanced and in the central place. That 'there will be no advantage in the north-east,' intimates that the way (of dealing with the *K*ien state) is exhausted. That 'it will be advantageous to see the great man,' intimates that advance will lead to achievement. That the places (of the different lines after the first) are those appropriate to them indicates firm correctness and good fortune, with which the regions (of the kingdom) are brought to their normal state. Great indeed is the work to be done in the time of *K*ien!

---

an explanation from that ascribed to king Wăn, where Tui represents the youngest daughter and Lî the second. The Khang-hsî editors observe that in many hexagrams we have two daughters dwelling together, but that only in this and 49 is attention called to it. The reason, they say, is that in those two diagrams the sisters are the second and third daughters, while in the others one of them is the eldest, whose place and superiority are fixed, so that between her and either of the others there can be no division or collision.

About what is said, in paragraph 2, on the weak line, as advanced and acting above, see the note on hexagram 35.

The lesson of paragraph 3 is not unity in diversity, but union with diversity.

XXXIX. The upper or front trigram is Khân, the attribute of which is perilousness; the lower is Kăn, of which the arresting, actively or passively, of movement or advance is the attribute. We can understand how the union of these attributes gives the ideas of difficulty and prudent caution.

The explanations in paragraph 2 of the phraseology of the Thwan

XL. 1. In *K*ieh we have (the trigram expressive
of) peril going on to that expressive of movement.
By movement there is an escape from the peril :—
(this is the meaning of) *K*ieh.

2. 'In (the state indicated by) *K*ieh, advantage
will be found in the south-west :'—the movement
(thus) intimated will win all. That 'there will be
good fortune in coming back (to the old conditions)' shows that such action is that of the due
medium. That 'if some operations be necessary,
there will be good fortune in the early conducting of
them' shows that such operations will be successful.

3. When heaven and earth are freed (from the
grasp of winter), we have thunder and rain. When
these come, the buds of the plants and trees that
produce the various fruits begin to burst. Great
indeed are the phenomena in the time intimated
by *K*ieh.

---

are not all easily followed. It is said that the advantageousness
of the south-west is due to the central line in 5 ; but if we are to
look for the meaning of south-west in Khwăn, as in the diagram
of king Wăn's trigrams, there is no strong central line in it. May
Khân, as a yang trigram, be used for Khwăn?

XL. 1. The meaning of the hexagram is brought out sufficiently
well in paragraph 1 by means of the attributes of the constituent
trigrams.

2. How it is that the movement indicated in the first condition
will ' win' all does not immediately appear. The Khang-hsî editors
say that 'moving to the south and west' is the same as 'returning
back to the old conditions,' and that 'winning all' and acting 'according to the due medium' are descriptive of the effect and method
without reference to the symbolism. Another explanation might
be devised ; but I prefer to leave the matter in doubt.

3. Paragraph 3 shows the analogy of what takes place in nature
to the beneficent social and political changes described in the text,
as is done very frequently in this Appendix.

XLI. 1. In Sun (we see) the lower (trigram) diminished, and the upper added to. (But) the method (of action) implied in this operates also above (or, mounts upwards (also) and operates).

2. 'If there be sincerity in this method of diminution, there will be great good fortune; freedom from error; firmness and correctness that can be maintained; and advantage in every movement that shall be made. In what shall this (sincerity in the exercise of Sun) be employed? (Even) in sacrifice, two baskets of grain, (though there be nothing else), may be presented:'—for these two baskets there ought to be the fitting time. There is a time when the strong should be diminished, and the weak should be strengthened. Diminution and increase, overflowing and emptiness:—these take place in harmony with the conditions of the time.

XLI. 1. All that we see is two undivided lines in the lower trigram, and then a divided one, and exactly the opposite in the upper. But the whole figure could not but have this form from the process of its formation, whether by the gradual addition of the two primitive lines, or by the imposition of the whole trigrams on one another. To say that the upper lines of *Kh*ien and Khwăn changed places to express the idea of subjects contributing in taxes to the maintenance of their ruler is absurd; and if that thought were in the mind of king Wăn (which I very much doubt), it would only show how he projected his own idea, formed independently of the figure, into its lines.

On the second sentence, the Khang-hsî editors say:—'When a minister devotes his life in the service of his lord, or the people undertake their various labours in behalf of their government, these are instances of the ministering of those below to increase those above. But in this way the intercourse of the two becomes close and their aims become the same;—does not the method of action of those below communicate itself to those above?'

In paragraph 2 the subject of contribution, such as the payment of

XLII. 1. In Yî we see the upper (trigram) diminished, and the lower added to. The satisfaction of the people (in consequence of this) is without limit. What descends from above reaches to all below, so great and brilliant is the course (of its operation).

2. That 'there will be advantage in every movement which shall be undertaken' appears from the central and correct (positions of the second and fifth lines), and the (general) blessing (the dispensing of which they imply).

That 'it will be advantageous (even) to cross the great stream' appears from the action of wood (shown in the figure).

3. Yî is made up of (the trigrams expressive of) movement and docility, (through which) there is daily advancement to an unlimited extent. We have (also) in it heaven dispensing and earth producing, leading to an increase without restriction

---

taxes, passes into the background. The Khang-hsî editors say :—
'What is meant by diminishing in this hexagram is the regulation of expenditure or contribution according to the time. This would vary in a family according to its poverty or wealth; and in a state according to the abundance or scantiness of its resources. When it is said that there must be sincerity along with a diminution, it means that though such a diminution cannot be helped, yet what is given should be given sincerely. A small sacrifice sincerely offered is accepted. In the language, "There is a time when the strong should be diminished and the weak be strengthened," we are not to find the two baskets in the diminution of the strong. "The strong" is what is essential,—in this case sincerity; "The weak" is what is unimportant,—the amount and manner of the offering. If one supplement the insufficiency of his offering with the abundance of his sincerity, the insignificance of his two baskets will not be despised.'

of place.   Everything in the method of this increase
proceeds according to the requirements of the time.

XLII. 1. The process of the formation of the trigrams here is
the reverse of that in the preceding hexagram; and is open to the
remarks I have made on that. Of course the people are full of
complacency and pleasure in the labours of their ruler for their
good.

2. The mention of 'the action of wood' has reference to the
upper trigram Sun, which is the symbol both of wind and wood.
From wood boats and ships are made, on which the great stream
may be crossed. In three hexagrams, this, 59, and 61, of which
Sun is a part, we find mention made of crossing the great stream.
It is generally said that the lower trigram *K*ăn also symbolises
wood; but that is obtained by a roundabout process. *K*ăn occupies the place of the east in Wan's arrangement of the trigrams;
but the east symbolises spring, when the growth of vegetation
begins; and therefore *K*ăn may symbolise wood! It was stated
on p. 33, that the doctrine of 'the five elements' does not appear
in the Yî. *K*hăng-ʒze takes wood (木 mû), 'as a misprint for
increase (益 yî).'

3. The words 'heaven dispensing and earth producing' are
based on the fancied genesis of the figure from *K*hien and
Khwăn (☰☷), the first lines in each changing places. It
was the author of this Appendix, probably, who first introduced
that absurd notion in connexion with the formation of Sun
and Yî.

One rhyme runs through and connects these three paragraphs
thus :—

> 'Yî spoils the high, gives to the low;
> The people feel intense delight.
> Down from above to all below,
> The blessing goes, so large and bright.
> Success will every movement mark,
> Central its source, its course aright.
> The great stream even may be crossed,
> When planks of wood their strength unite.
> Yî movement shows and docile feet,
> Which progress day by day invite.
> Heaven gives; productive earth responds;
> Increase crowns every vale and height;

XLIII. 1. Kwâi is the symbol of displacing or removing. We see (in the figure) the strong (lines) displacing the weak. (We have in it the attributes of) strength and complacency. There is displacement, but harmony (continues).

2. 'The exhibition (of the criminal's guilt) in the royal courtyard' is suggested by the (one) weak (line) mounted on the five strong lines.

There 'is an earnest and sincere appeal (for sympathy and support), and a consciousness of the peril (involved in the undertaking):'—it is the realisation of this danger, which makes the method (of compassing the object) brilliant.

'He should make an announcement in his own city, and show that it will not be well to have recourse at once to arms:'—(if he have recourse to arms), what he prefers will (soon) be exhausted.

'There will be advantage in whatever he shall go forward to:'—when the growth of the strong (lines) has been completed, there will be an end (of the displacement).

And ceaselessly it hastens on,
Each season's gifts quick to requite.'

XLIII. 1. The last clause of paragraph 1 is good in itself, showing that the strong and worthy statesman in removing a bad man from the state is not actuated by any private feelings. The sentiment, however, as it is expressed, can hardly be said to follow from the symbolism.

Paragraph 2. The same may be said of all the notes appended to the different clauses of this second paragraph. Hû Ping-wăn (Yüan dynasty) says:—'If but a single small man be left, he is sufficient to make the superior man anxious; if but a single inordinate desire be left in the mind, that is sufficient to disturb the harmony of heavenly principles. The eradication in both cases must be complete, before the labour is ended.'

XLIV. 1. Kâu has the significance of unexpectedly coming on. (We see in it) the weak (line) coming unexpectedly on the strong ones.

2. 'It will not be good to marry (such) a female :'—one (so symbolised) should not be long associated with.

3. Heaven and earth meeting together (as here represented), all the variety of natural things become fully displayed.

4. When a strong (line) finds itself in the central and correct position, (good government) will greatly prevail all under the sky.

5. Great indeed is the significance of what has to be done at the time indicated by Kâu !

XLV. 1. 3hui indicates (the condition of union, or) being collected. We have in it (the symbol of) docile obedience going on to (what is expressed by that of) satisfaction. There is the strong line in the central place, and rightly responded to. Hence comes the (idea of) union.

2. ' The king will repair to his ancestral temple :'—

XLIV. On paragraph 1 the Khang-hsî editors say :—'"The weak line meets with (or comes unexpectedly on) the strong ones;"—the weak line, that is, plays the principal part. The case is like that of the minister who assumes the power of deciding for himself on all measures, or of a hen's announcing the morning;—is not the name of (shameless) boldness rightly applied to it ? Hence nothing more is said about the symbol of the bold female ; but attention is called to the second part of the Thwan.'

Paragraph 2 needs no remark. Paragraphs 3, 4, and 5 all speak of the importance of powers and parties meeting together,—in the world of nature, and in the sphere of human affairs. But I do not see how this sentiment is a natural sequel to that in 1 and 2, nor that it has any connexion with the teaching of the Thwan and Symbolism.

with the utmost filial piety he presents his offerings
(to the spirits of his ancestors).

'It will be advantageous to meet the great man,
and there will then be prosperity and success:'—
the union effected by him will be on and through
what is correct.

'The use of great victims will conduce to good
fortune; and in whatsoever direction movement is
made, it will be advantageous:'—all is done in
accordance with the ordinances of Heaven.

3. When we look at the way in which the gather-
ings (here shown) take place, the natural tendencies
(in the outward action) of heaven and earth and of
all things can be seen.

XLVI. 1. (We find) the weak (line), as it finds
the opportunity, ascending upwards.

2. We have (the attribute) of flexibility and that
of obedience; we have the strong line (below) and
its proper correlate above:—these things indicate that
there will be 'great progress and success.'

XLV. The lower trigram in Ʒhui is Khwăn, whose attribute
is docile obedience; and the upper is Tui, whose attribute is
pleased satisfaction. Then we have the strong line in 5, and
its proper correlate in 2. These things may give the idea of union.
They might also give the idea of other good things.

The Khang-hsî editors say that though 'all is done in accordance with the ordinances of Heaven' follows the concluding clauses
of the Thwan, yet the sentiment of the words must be extended
to the other clauses as well. Khăng-ʒze says that 'the ordinances of
Heaven' are simply the natural and practical outcome of 'heavenly
principle;'—in this case what should and may be done according
to the conditions and requirements of the time. So do the critics
of China try to shirk the idea of personality in 'Heaven.'

With paragraph 3, compare the concluding paragraphs of the
Thwan Kwan on hexagrams 31, 32.

3. 'Seeking (by the qualities implied in Shăng) to meet with the great man, its subject need have no anxiety:'—there will be ground for congratulation.

'Advance to the south will be fortunate:'—his aim will be carried out.

XLVII. 1. In Khwăn (we see) the strong (lines) covered and obscured (by the weak).

2. We have in it (the attribute of) perilousness going on to that of satisfaction. Who is it but the superior man that, though straitened, still does not fail in making progress to his proper end?

'For the firm and correct, the (really) great man, there will be good fortune:'—this is shown by the central positions of the strong (lines).

'If he make speeches, his words cannot be made good:'—to be fond of arguing or pleading is the way to be reduced to extremity.

XLVI. The explanation of the first paragraph has given occasion to much difference of opinion. Some will have 'the weak (line)' to be 4; some 5; and some the whole of Khwăn, the upper trigram. The advocates of 4, make it come from hexagram 40, the weak 3 of which ascends to the strong 4, displaces it, and takes its place; but we have seen repeatedly the folly of the doctrine of changing lines and figures. The great symbolism of Appendix II suggests the proper explanation. The lower trigram, Sun, represents here not wind but wood. The first line, weak, is the root of a tree planted beneath the earth. Its gradual growth symbolises the advance upwards of the subject of the hexagram, fostered, that is, by the circumstances of the time.

XLVII. 1. One sees the relative position of the strong and weak lines in the figure; but to deduce from that the idea expressed by Khwăn requires a painful straining of the imagination. That idea was in the mind, and then the lines were interpreted accordingly.

2. 'Perilousness' is the attribute of the lower trigram, and 'satisfaction' that of the upper. The superior man, however straitened,

XLVIII. 1. (We have the symbol of) wood in the water and the raising of the water; which (gives us the idea of) a well. A well supplies nourishment and is not (itself) exhausted.

2. 'The site of a town may be changed, while the fashion of its·wells undergoes no change:'— this is indicated by the central position of the strong lines (in the second and fifth places).

'The drawing is nearly accomplished, but the rope has not yet reached the water of the well:'— its service has not yet been accomplished.

'The bucket is broken:'—it is this that occasions evil.

XLIX. 1. In Ko (we see) water and fire extinguishing each other; (we see also) two daughters dwelling together, but with their minds directed to

---

remains master of himself, and pursues the proper end of principle settled in his mind.

Why should the subject of Khwăn make speeches, be fond of arguing or pleading,—as the characters say, if we could translate them literally, 'setting a value on the mouth?' The reply to this is found in the trigram denoting 'satisfaction,' or 'being pleased.' The party in the extremity of Khwăn yet wishes and tries to make men pleased with him.

XLVIII. *K*ăng Khang-*Kh*ăng says:—'Khân, the upper trigram, represents water, and Sun, the lower, wood. This wood denotes the water-wheel or pulley with its bucket, which descends into the mouth of the spring, and brings the water up to the top.' This may be a correct explanation of the figure, though the reading of it from bottom to top seems at first to be strange.

Paragraph 2. That the fashion of the well does not undergo any (great) change is dwelt upon as illustrating the unchangeableness of the great principles of human nature and of government. But that this truth may be learned from the strong and central lines only produces a smile. So do the remarks on the other two sentences of the Thwan.

different objects :—(on account of these things) it is called (the hexagram of) Change.

2. 'It is believed in (only) after it has been accomplished :'—when the change has been made, faith is accorded to it.

(We have) cultivated intelligence (as the basis of) pleased satisfaction, (suggesting) 'great progress and success,' coming from what is correct.

When change thus takes place in the proper way, 'occasion for repentance disappears.'

3. Heaven and earth undergo their changes, and the four seasons complete their functions. Thang changed the appointment (of the line of Hsiâ to the throne), and Wû (that of the line of Shang), in accordance with (the will of) Heaven, and in response to (the wishes of) men. Great indeed is what takes place in a time of change.

L. 1. In Ting we have (symbolically) the figure of a caldron. (We see) the (symbol of) wood entering into that of fire, which suggests the idea of cook-

---

XLIX. Paragraph 1. Lî, the lower trigram, represents fire, and Tui, the upper, represents water. Water will extinguish fire, and fire again will dry up water. Each, to all appearance, produces a change in the other. Again, according to king Wǎn's scheme of the trigrams, as shown on p. 33, and in Figure 1, Plate III, Lî is the second, and Tui the youngest daughter. Their wills are likely to differ in love and other things; but this symbolism does not so readily suggest the idea of change.

2. The first sentence suggests how the dislike to change on the part of people generally is overcome.

The second suggests how change proceeding from intelligence and giving general satisfaction will be successful.

Paragraph 3 tells us how the greatest natural and the greatest political changes are equally successful and admirable when conducted aright.

ing. The sages cooked their offerings in order to present them to God, and made great feasts to nourish their wise and able (ministers).

2. We have the symbol of) flexible obedience, and that (which denotes) ears quick of hearing and eyes clear-sighted. (We have also) the weak (line) advanced and acting above, in the central place, and responded to by the strong (line below). All these things give the idea of 'great progress and success.'

LI. 1. *K*ăn (gives the intimation of) ease and development.

2. 'When the (time of) movement (which it indicates) comes, (its subject) will be found looking out with apprehension:'—that feeling of dread leads to happiness. 'And yet smiling and talking cheer-fully:'—the issue (of his dread) is that he adopts (proper) laws (for his course).

'The movement (like a crash of thunder) terrifies

L. 1. See the notes on the Text of the Thwan about the figure of a caldron in Ting. Its component trigrams are Sun representing wood, and Lî representing fire; which may very well suggest the idea of cooking. The last sentence of the paragraph is entirely after the style of 'the Great Symbolism.' The Khang-hsî editors say that the distinction between Ȝing and Ting appears here very clearly, the former relating to the nourishment of the people, and the latter to the nourishing men of worth. They add that the reality of the offerings to God is such nourishing. 'God' is here Shang Tî, which Canon McClatchie translates 'the First Emperor,' adding in a note, 'The Chinese Jupiter, the Emperor of gods and men!'

2. The first sentence deduces the sentiment of the Thwan from the attributes or virtues of the trigrams with considerable amplifica-tion of the virtue of Lî. The second line of Lî, as being divided, calls forth in other hexagrams the same notice as here. It is the most important line in the figure, and being responded to by the strong 2, gives an indication of the 'great progress and success.'

all within a hundred lî:'—it startles the distant and frightens the near.

'**He will be like the sincere worshipper, who is not startled into letting go his ladle and cup of sacrificial spirits:**'—he makes his appearance, and maintains his ancestral temple and the altars of the spirits of the land and grain, as presiding at all sacrifices.

LII. 1. Kăn denotes stopping or resting;— resting when it is the time to rest, and acting when it is the time to act. When one's movements and restings all take place at the proper time for them, his way (of proceeding) is brilliant and intelligent.

2. Resting in one's resting-point is resting in one's proper place. The upper and lower (lines of the hexagram) exactly correspond to each other, but are without any interaction; hence it is said that '(the subject of the hexagram) has no consciousness of self; that when he walks in his courtyard, he does not see (any of) the persons in it; and that there will be no error.'

LI. Paragraph 1. See what is said on the Text.

2. The explanations of the Thwan here are good; but in no way deduced from the figure.

3. The portion of the text printed in a different type is supposed to have dropt out of the Chinese copies. The explanation of it that follows is based on Wăn's view of Kăn as representing the oldest son. See on the Text.

LII. 1. The Khang-hsî editors give their opinion that what is said in the first sentence of this paragraph, after the explanation of the name, illustrates the first sentence of the Thwan, and that the other sentence illustrates the rest of the Thwan. It may be so, but the whole of the Thwan appears in paragraph 2.

2. The hexagram being made up of Kăn repeated, lines 1, 2, 3 are of course the same as 4, 5, and 6. But it will be seen that there is not a proper correlation among them all. I do not see,

LIII. 1. The advance indicated by *K*ien is (like) the marrying of a young lady which is attended by good fortune.

2. (The lines) as they advance get into their correct places:—this indicates the achievements of a successful progress.

The advance is made according to correctness:— (the subject of the hexagram) might rectify his country.

3. Among the places (of the hexagram) we see the strong undivided line in the centre.

4. 'In (the attributes of) restfulness and flexible penetration we have (the assurance of) an (onward) movement that is inexhaustible.

LIV. 1. By Kwei Mei (the marrying away of a younger sister) the great and righteous relation between heaven and earth (is suggested to us). If heaven and earth were to have no intercommunication, things would not grow and flourish as they do. The marriage of a younger sister is the end (of her maidenhood) and the beginning (of her motherhood).

2. We have (in the hexagram the desire of)

---

however, that this furnishes any ground for the entire obliviousness of self, which the Thwan makes out to be in the figure.

LIII. The first sentence of paragraph 2 describes the lines from 2 to 5 all getting into their proper places, as has been pointed out on the Text, and that sentence is symbolical of what is said in the second. 'The rectification of the country' is the reality of 'the successful progress.'

'The strong undivided line' in paragraph 3 is the fifth of the figure.

Out of rest comes movement to go on for an indefinite time, and be succeeded by rest again;—as says paragraph 4.

pleasure and, on the ground of that, movement following. The marrying away is of a younger sister.

3. 'Any action will be evil:'—the places (of the lines) are not those appropriate to them.

'It will be in no wise advantageous :'— the weak (third and fifth lines) are mounted on strong lines.

LV. 1. Făng has the signification of being great. It is made up of the trigrams (representing)

LIV. 1. Kwei Mei in this Appendix has the meaning simply of marriage, and for Mei we might substitute Nü, 'daughter' or 'young lady.' This appears from the writer's going on to point out, as elsewhere, the analogy between the growth of things in nature from the interaction of heaven and earth and the increase of mankind through marriage. He does this with a delicate touch. There is no grossness in the original any more than there is in the translation.

But how are we to reconcile this reference to the action of heaven and earth with the bad auspice of the Thwan? The Khang-hsî editors felt the pressure of this difficulty, and they adduce a similar inconsistency in the account of hexagram 44 in this treatise, adding, 'From this we may say that the interaction of the yin and yang cannot be dispensed with, but that we ought to be careful about it in the beginning in order to prevent mischief in the end. This is the doctrine of the Yî.' This is very well, but it is no solution of the difficulty. The editors could not admit that the author of the Appendix did not understand or did not deal fairly with the Text; for that author, they thought, was Confucius.

2. The same editors say that paragraph 2 implies both that the desire for the marriage originated with the lady, and that she was aware that the gentleman was older than herself.

3. The position of a divided line above an undivided is always represented as an evil omen ; it is difficult to understand why. There is less of an appearance of reason about it than in some other things which are said about the lines. The lines are where they cannot but be from the way in which the figures were formed.

intelligence and movement directed by that intelligence. It is thus that it has that signification.

2. 'The king has reached the condition (denoted by Făng):'—he has still to make it greater.

'There is no occasion to be anxious. Let him be as the sun at noon :'—it is for him to cause his light to shine on all under the sky.

3. When the sun has reached the meridian height, it begins to decline. When the moon has become full, it begins to wane. The (interaction of) heaven and earth is now vigorous and abundant, now dull and scanty, growing and diminishing according to the seasons. How much more must it be so with (the operations of) men! How much more also with the spiritual agency!

LVI. 1. 'Lü indicates that there may be some small attainment and progress :'—the weak (line) occupies the central place in the outer (trigram), and is obedient to the strong (lines on either side of it). (We have also the attributes of quiet) resting closely attached to intelligence (in the com-

---

LV. The Khang-hsî editors remark that paragraph 1 is not so much explaining the meaning of the name Făng, as accounting for the hexagram, composed of Lî and Kăn, having such a meaning.

Paragraph 3 seems rather contrary to the lesson of the hexagram. According to it, prosperity cannot be maintained, any more than we can have the other seasons without winter or perpetual day without night; but the object of the essay is to exhort to the maintenance of prosperity. Is it the case that the rise of every commonwealth and cause must be followed by its decay and fall? The mind refuses to admit the changes of the seasons, &c., as a true analogy for all moral and intellectual movements. See an important remark on the concluding sentence in the Introduction, pp. 34, 35.

ponent trigrams). Hence it is said, 'There may be some small attainment and progress. If the stranger or traveller be firm and correct as he ought to be, there will be good fortune.'

2. Great is the time and great is the right course to be taken as intimated in Lü!

LVII. 1. The double Sun shows how, in accordance with it, (governmental) orders are reiterated.

2. (We see that) the strong (fifth line) has penetrated into the central and correct place, and the will (of its subject) is being carried into effect; (we see also) the weak (first and fourth lines) both obedient to the strong lines (above them). It is hence said, 'There will be some little attainment and progress. There will be advantage in movement onward in whatever direction. It will be advantageous also to see the great man.'

LVI. What is said in paragraph 1 is intended to explain the Thwan, and not to account for the meaning of the name Lü. It is assumed that Lü means a stranger; and the writer from the position of the fifth line, and from the attributes of the component trigrams, derives the ideas of humility, docility, a quiet restfulness, and intelligence as the characteristics proper to a stranger, and which are likely to lead to his attaining what he desires, and then advancing.

LVII. 1. The language of this paragraph has often occurred to me in reading commands and addresses issued by the emperors of China, such as the essays on the precepts in what is called the Sacred Edict, the reiteration employed in many of which is remarkable.

Paragraph 2. The 'obedience of the weak lines to the strong ones' grows, in a way not very perceptible, from the idea of the hexagram, and the quality of the trigram as denoting penetration and flexibility.

LVIII. 1. Tui has the meaning of pleased satisfaction.

2. (We have) the strong (lines) in the centre, and the weak (lines) on the outer edge (of the two trigrams), (indicating that) in pleasure what is most advantageous is the maintenance of firm correctness. Through this there will be found an accordance with (the will of) heaven, and a correspondence with (the feelings of) men. When (such) pleasure goes before the people, (and leads them on), they forget their toils; when it animates them in encountering difficulties, they forget (the risk of) death. How great is (the power of) this pleased satisfaction, stimulating in such a way the people!

LIX. 1. 'Hwan intimates that there will be progress and success:'—(we see) the strong line (in the second place) of the lower trigram, and not suffering any extinction there; and (also) the weak line occupying its place in the outer trigram, and uniting (its action) with that of the line above.

2. 'The king goes to his ancestral temple:'—the king's (mind) is without any deflection.

3. 'It will be advantageous to cross the great stream:'—(the subject of the hexagram) rides in

---

LVIII. The feeling of pleasure going before the people and leading them on to endure toil and encounter death must be supposed to be produced in them by the example and lessons of their ruler. Lü Faû-hsien paraphrases this portion of the text thus:—'When the sage with this precedes them, he can make them endure toil without any wish to decline it, and go with him into difficulty and danger without their having any fear.' I think this was intended to be the teaching of the hexagram, but the positive expression of it is hardly discernible.

(a vessel of) wood (over water), and will do so with success.

LX. 1. '*K*ieh intimates progress and attainment:'—the strong and weak (lines) are equally divided, and the strong lines occupy the central places.

2. 'If the regulations (which *K*ieh prescribes) be severe and difficult, they cannot be permanent:'—its course (of action) will in that case come to an end.

3. (We have the feeling of) pleasure and satisfaction directing the course amidst peril. (We have) all regulations controlled (by authority) in its proper place. (We have) free action proceeding from the central and correct position.

4. Heaven and earth observe their regular terms, and we have the four seasons complete. (If rulers) frame their measures according to (the due) regulations, the resources (of the state) suffer no injury, and the people receive no hurt.

LIX. 1. This paragraph has been partially anticipated in the notes on the Thwan. The second line is said to suffer 'no extinction,' because the lower trigram is that of peril. The Khanghsî editors say that the former part of this paragraph shows how the root of the work of the hexagram is strengthened, and the latter part how the execution of that work is secured.

The conclusion of paragraph 2 is, literally, 'The king indeed is in the middle.' This does not mean, as some say, that the king is in the middle of the temple, but that his mind or heart is exactly set on the central truth of what is right and good.

The upper trigram Sun represents both wind and wood. To explain the meaning of Hwan, the significance of wind is taken; the writer here seizes on that of wood, as furnishing materials for a boat in which the great stream can be crossed.

LX. Paragraph 1. See what is said on the Text of the Thwan.

LXI. 1. In *K*ung Fû we have the (two) weak lines in the innermost part (of the figure), and strong lines occupying the central places (in the trigrams). (We have the attributes) of pleased satisfaction and flexible penetration. Sincerity (thus symbolled) will transform a country.

2. ' Pigs and fish (are moved), and there will be good fortune :'—sincerity reaches to (and affects even) pigs and fishes.

' There will be advantage in crossing the great stream :'—(we see in the figure) one riding on (the emblem of) wood, which forms an empty boat.

3. In (the exercise of the virtue denoted by) *K*ung Fû, (it is said that) ' there will be advantage in being firm and correct :'—in that virtue indeed we have the response (of man) to Heaven.

' Its course will come to an end' is the opposite of the intimation in *K*ieh of progress and attainment.

In paragraph 3 the writer returns to this intimation of the figure :—by the attributes of the trigrams; by the appropriate positions of lines 4 and 5; and by the central and correct place of 5.

Paragraph 4 illustrates the importance of doing things according to rule by reference to the operations of nature and the enactments and institutions of sage rulers.

LXI. 1. The structure of the lineal figure which is here insisted on has been pointed out in explaining the Thwan. On what is further said as to the attributes of the trigrams and their effect, *Kh*ang-*zze* observes :—' We have in the sincerity shown in the upper trigram superiors condescending to those below them in accordance with their peculiarities, and we have in that of the lower those below delighted to follow their superiors. The combination of these two things leads to the transformation of the country and state.'

Paragraph 2. The two divided lines in the middle of the figure are supposed to give the semblance of an empty boat, and an

LXII. 1. In Hsiâo Kwo (we see) the small (lines) exceeding the others, and (giving the intimation of) progress and attainment.

2. Such 'exceeding, in order to its being advantageous, must be associated with firmness and correctness:'—that is, it must take place (only) according to (the requirements of) the time.

3. The weak (lines) are in the central places, and hence (it is said that what the name denotes) may be done in small affairs, and there will be good fortune.

4. Of the strong (lines one) is not in its proper place, and (the other) is not central, hence it is said that (what the name denotes) 'should not be done in great affairs.'

5. (In the hexagram) we have 'the symbol of a bird on the wing, and of the notes that come down from such a bird, for which it is better to descend than to ascend, thereby leading to great good fortune:'—to ascend is contrary to what is reasonable in the case, while to descend is natural and right.

---

empty boat, it is said (with doubtful truth), is not liable to be upset. The trigram Sun symbolises both wind and wood.

A good commentary on paragraph 3 is supplied in many passages of 'the Doctrine of the Mean,' e. g. chap. 20. 18 :—' Sincerity is the way of Heaven. The attainment of sincerity is the way of men.'

LXII. Paragraph 1. That the small lines exceed the others appears at a glance. The intimation of progress and attainment is less clear. Compare the first paragraph of Appendix I to hexagram 33.

'The requirements of the time' in paragraph 2 cannot make

LXIII. 1. '*Kî 3î* intimates progress and success:'—in small matters, that is, there will be that progress and success.

2. 'There will be advantage in being firm and correct:'—the strong and weak (lines) are correctly arranged, each in its appropriate place.

3. 'There has been good fortune in the beginning:'—the weak (second line) is in the centre.

4. 'In the end' there is a cessation (of effort), and 'disorder arises:'—the course (that led to rule and order) is (now) exhausted.

LXIV. 1. 'Wei 3î intimates progress and success (in the circumstances which it implies):'—the weak (fifth) line is in the centre.

2. 'The young fox has nearly crossed the stream:'—but he has not yet escaped from the midst (of the danger and calamity).

---

right wrong or wrong right; but they may modify the conventional course to be taken in any particular case.

It is easy to explain paragraphs 3 and 4, but what is said in them carries no conviction to the mind.

The sentiment of paragraph 5 is good, apart from the symbolism, which is only perplexing.

LXIII. For paragraphs 1 and 2, see the note on the Text of the Thwan.

It is difficult to see the concatenation in paragraph 3 between the sentiment of the Thwan and the nature of the second line. The Khang-hsî editors compare this hexagram and the next with 11 and 12, observing that the goodness of Thâi (11) is concentrated, as here, in the second line.

The sentiment of paragraph 4 is that which we have often met with,—that things move on with a constant process of change. Disorder succeeds to order, and again order to disorder.

'Its tail gets immersed. There will be no advantage in any way:'—there is not at the end a continuance (of the purpose) at the beginning. Although the places (of the different lines) are not those appropriate to them, yet a strong (line) and a weak (line always) respond to each other.

LXIV. Paragraph 1. The indication is derived from the fifth line, divided, which is in the ruler's place. It occupies a strong place, has for its correlate the strong 2, and is itself in the centre of the yin trigram Lî.

Paragraph 2. Line 2 represents 'the young fox.' A strong line in the midst of the trigram of peril, its subject will be restless; and responding to the ruler in 5, he will be forward and incautious in taking action. The issue will be evil, and the latter end different from the beginning. What is said in the last sentence shows further how Wei Ȝî indicates progress.

APPENDIX II

Treatise on the Symbolism of the Hexagrams, and of the duke
of *K*âu's Explanations of the several Lines

Section I

I. Heaven, in its motion, (gives the idea of)
strength. The superior man, in accordance with
this, nerves himself to ceaseless activity.

1. 'The dragon lies hid in the deep;—it is not
the time for active doing:'—(this appears from) the
strong and undivided line's being in the lowest place.

2. 'The dragon appears in the field:'—the diffusion of virtuous influence has been wide.

3. 'Active and vigilant all the day:'—(this refers
to) the treading of the (proper) path over and over
again.

4. 'He seems to be leaping up, but is still in the
deep:'—if he advance, there will be no error.

5. 'The dragon is on the wing in the sky:'—the
great man rouses himself to his work.

6. 'The dragon exceeds the proper limits;—
there will be occasion for repentance:'—a state of
fulness, that is, should not be indulged in long.

7. 'The same NINE(undivided)is used' (in all the
places of this hexagram), but the attribute of
heaven (thereby denoted) should not (always) take
the foremost place.

Like the Text under each hexagram, what is said under each in
this treatise on its symbolism is divided into two portions. The

II. The (capacity and sustaining) power of the earth is what is denoted by Khwǎn. The superior man, in accordance with this, with his large virtue supports (men and) things.

1. 'He is treading on hoarfrost;—the strong ice will come (by and by):'—the cold (air) has begun to take form. Allow it to go on quietly according to its nature, and (the hoarfrost) will come to strong ice.

2. The movement indicated by the second SIX, (divided), is 'from the straight (line) to the square.' '(Its operation), without repeated effort, in every way advantageous,' shows the brilliant result of the way of earth.

3. 'He keeps his excellence under restraint, but firmly maintains it :'—at the proper time he will manifest it. 'He may have occasion to engage in the king's service :'—great is the glory of his wisdom.

---

first is called 'the Great Symbolism,' and is occupied with the tri-grammatic composition of the hexagram, to the statement of which is always subjoined an exhibition of the use which should be, or has been, made of the lesson suggested by the meaning of the whole figure in the administration of affairs, or in self-government. If the treatise be rightly ascribed to Confucius, this practical applica-tion of the teaching of the symbols is eminently characteristic of his method in inculcating truth and duty; though we often find it difficult to trace the connexion between his premiss and conclusion. This portion of the treatise will be separated by a double space from what follows,—'the Lesser Symbolism,' in the explanations of the several lines.

I. *Kh*ien is formed by redoubling the trigram of the same name. In the case of other hexagrams of similar formation, the repetition of the trigram is pointed out. That is not done here, according to *K*û Hsî, 'because there is but one heaven.' But the motion of heaven is a complete revolution every day, resumed again the next ; so moves 'the unwearied sun from day to day,' making it a good symbol of renewed, untiring effort.

4. 'A sack tied up;—there will be no error:'—this shows how, through carefulness, no injury will be received.

5. 'The yellow lower-garment;—there will be great good fortune:'—this follows from that ornamental (colour's) being in the right and central place.

6. 'The dragons fight in the wild:'—the (on-ward) course (indicated by Khwăn) is pursued to extremity.

7. '(The lines are all weak and divided, as appears from) the use of the number SIX:'—but (those who are thus represented) becoming perpetually correct and firm, there will thereby be a great consummation.

II. Khwăn is formed by redoubling the trigram of the same name and having 'the earth for its symbol.' As in the former hexagram, the repetition is emphatic, not otherwise affecting the meaning of the hexagram. 'As there is but one heaven,' says _K_û Hsî, 'so there is but one earth.' The first part of 'the Great Symbolism' appears in Canon McClatchie's version as—'Khwăn is the generative part of earth.' By 'generative part' he probably means 'the productive or prolific faculty.' If he mean anything else, there comes out a conclusion antagonistic to his own view of the 'mythology' of the Yî. The character Shî, which he translates by 'generative part,' is defined in Dr. Williams' dictionary as 'the virility of males.' Such is the special significance of it. If it were so used here, the earth would be masculine.

It is difficult to say exactly what the writer meant by—'The superior man, in accordance with this, and with his large nature, supports (men and) things.' Lin Hsî-yüan (Ming dynasty) says :— 'The superior man, in his single person, sustains the burden of all under the sky. The common people depend on him for their rest and enjoyment. Birds and beasts and creeping things, and the tribes of the vegetable kingdom, depend on him for the fulfilment of their destined being. If he be of a narrow mind and cold virtue, how can he help them? Their hope in him would be in vain.'

'The Smaller Symbolism' is sufficiently dealt with in the notes on the Text.

III. (The trigram representing) clouds and (that representing) thunder form *K*un. The superior man, in accordance with this, (adjusts his measures of government) as in sorting the threads of the warp and woof.

1. Although 'there is a difficulty in advancing,' the mind (of the subject of the line) is set on doing what is correct. While noble, he humbles himself to the mean, and grandly gains the people.

2. The difficulty (to the subject of) the second SIX, (divided), arises from its place over the undivided line below it. 'The union and children after ten years' shows things resuming their regular course.

3. 'One pursues the deer without the (guidance of the) forester:'—(he does so) in (his eagerness to) follow the game. 'The superior man gives up the chase, (knowing that) if he go forward he will regret it:'—he would be reduced to extremity.

4. 'Going forward after such a search (for a helper)' shows intelligence.

5. 'Difficulty is experienced (by the subject of the fifth line) in bestowing his rich favours:'—the extent to which they reach will not yet be conspicuous.

6. 'He weeps tears of blood in streams:'—how can the state (thus emblemed) continue long?

III. Khan represents water, especially in the form of rain. Here its symbol is a cloud. The whole hexagram seems to place us in the atmosphere of a thunderous sky overhung with thick and gloomy clouds, when we feel oppressed and distressed. This is not a bad emblem of the political state in the mind of the writer. When the thunder has pealed, and the clouds have discharged their

IV. (The trigram representing) a mountain, and beneath it that for a spring issuing forth form Măng. The superior man, in accordance with this, strives to be resolute in his conduct and nourishes his virtue.

1. 'It will be advantageous to use punishment:'—the object being to bring under the influence of correcting law.

2. 'A son able to (sustain the burden of) his family:'—as appears from the reciprocation between this strong line and the weak (fifth line).

3. 'A woman (such as is here represented) should not be taken in marriage:'—her conduct is not agreeable to what is right.

4. 'The regret arising from ignorance bound in chains' is due to the special distance of (the subject of this line) from the solidity (shown in lines 2 and 6).

5. 'The good fortune belonging to the simple lad without experience' comes from his docility going on to humility.

---

burden of rain, the atmosphere is cleared, and there is a feeling of relief. But I fail again to discern clearly the connexion between the symbolism and the lesson about the superior man's administration of affairs.

The subject of the first line of the Smaller Symbolism is represented by the undivided line, and therefore is firm and correct. He is noble, but his place is below the divided lines, symbols of the weak and mean (see Appendix IV, i, 1).

Line 2. 'Things resume their regular course:'—the subject is now at liberty to seek a union with the subject of line 5, according to the rules of the symbolism. Lines 1 and 4, 2 and 5, 3 and 6, the corresponding lines of the trigrams, are correlates.

The subject of line 4 naturally recurs to the correlate in line 1. He is the natural helper in the case, and he has the ability.

6. 'Advantage will come from warding off injury:'—(the subject of this line) above and (the ignorant) below, all do and are done to in accordance with their nature.

V. (The trigram for) clouds ascending over that

IV. 'The spring here issuing forth' is different from the defile with a stream in it, in the explanation of the Thwan; different moreover from 'rain,' mentioned also as the phenomenon which is the natural symbol of Khan. The presence of water, however, is common to the three. But the water of the spring, or of the stream, would flow away from the hill, and not be stopped by it; as an emblem therefore of the ignorance and inexperience denoted by Măng it is not suitable. Kû Hsî says that 'the water of a spring is sure to move on and gradually advance.' This may serve as a symbol of the general process and progress of education, though it gives no account of the symbolism of the hill. It serves also to explain in part the transition of the writer to the subject of the superior man, and his dealing apparently with himself.

Does line 1 set forth the use of punishment as the dernier resort, undesirable, but possibly unavoidable, to bring men in subjection to law?

The force of line 2 comes out fully in the Thwan.

That a woman such as is represented in line 3 should not be taken in marriage is clear enough; but I do not see the bearing of the illustration on the proper lesson in the hexagram.

Line 3 separates 4 from 2, and 5 separates it from 6. Weak in itself, it is farther removed than any other from the two strong lines in the hexagram, and is represented as 'cribbed' in its ignorance.

The fifth is the most honourable place in the figure, and here is occupied by a weak line. This looks, however, to the occupant of line 2, less honourable than itself, and is marked by the two attributes that are named. Compare what is said on line 2.

A strong line in the topmost place must represent, according to the scheme of the hexagram, one who uses force in the cause of education; but the force is put forth not on the ignorant, but on those who would keep them ignorant, or increase their ignorance. The subject of this line, therefore, acts according to his nature, and the subjects of all the weak lines below are cared for as is best for them.

for the sky forms Hsü. The superior man, in accordance with this, eats and drinks, feasts and enjoys himself (as if there were nothing else to employ him).

1. 'He is waiting in the (distant) border:'—he makes no movement to encounter rashly the difficulties (of the situation). 'It will be advantageous for him constantly to maintain (the purpose thus shown), in which case there will be no error:'—he will not fail to pursue that regular course.

2. 'He is waiting on the sand:'—he occupies his position in the centre with a generous forbearance. Though 'he suffer the small injury of being spoken (against),' he will bring things to a good issue.

3. 'He is waiting in the mud:'—calamity is (close at hand, and as it were) in the outer (trigram). 'He himself invites the approach of injury:'—if he be reverent and careful, he will not be worsted.

4. 'He is waiting in (the place of) blood:'—he accommodates himself (to the circumstances of the time), and hearkens to (its requirements).

5. 'The appliances of a feast, and the good fortune through being firm and correct,' are indicated by (the position in) the central and correct place.

6. 'Guests come unurged (to give their help), and if (the subject of the line) receive them respectfully, there will be good fortune in the end:'—though the occupant and the place are not suited to each other, there has been no great failure (in what has been done).

V. 'The cloud,' it is said, 'that has risen to the top of the sky, has nothing more to do till it is called on, in the harmony of heaven

VI. (The trigram representing) heaven and (that representing) water, moving away from each other, form Sung. The superior man, in accordance with this, in the transaction of affairs takes good counsel about his first steps.

1. 'He does not perpetuate the matter about which (the contention is):'—contention should not be prolonged. Although 'he may suffer the small (injury) of being spoken against,' his argument is clear.

2. 'He is unequal to the contention; he retires and keeps concealed, stealthily withdrawing from it:'—for him from his lower place to contend with (the stronger one) above, would be to (invite) calamity, as if he brought it with his hand to himself.

3. 'He confines himself to the support assigned

---

and earth, to discharge its store of rain.' This gives to the writer the idea of waiting; and the superior man is supposed to be taught by this symbolism to enjoy his idle time, while he is waiting for the approach of danger and occasion for action.

'The regular course' of the subject of line 1 seems to be the determination to wait, at a distance from danger, the proper time to act.

The subject of line 2, which is undivided and in the centre, is thereby shown to be possessed of a large and generous forbearance.

The recognition of the circumstances of the time, and hearkening to its requirements, explain, in paragraph 4, 'the retreat from the cavern,' which is not here repeated from the Text. The line being weak and divided, its subject knows his own incompetency, and takes this prudent step.

Kû says that he does not understand what is said under line 6,—that the occupant and the place are not suited to each other, for the yin line being in the sixth, an even place, seems to be where it ought to be. We are only surprised that cases of inconsistency in these explanations are not more numerous.

to him of old:'—(thus) following those above him, he will have good fortune.

4. 'He returns to (the study of Heaven's) ordinances, changes (his wish to contend), and rests in being firm and correct:'—he does not fail (in doing what is right).

5. 'He contends;—and with great fortune:'—this is shown by his holding the due mean and being in the correct place.

6. 'He receives the robe through his contention:'—but still he is not deserving of respect.

VII. (The trigram representing) the earth and in the midst of it that representing water, form Sze. The superior man, in accordance with this, nourishes and educates the people, and collects (from among them) the multitudes (of the hosts).

1. 'The host goes forth according to the rules (for) such a movement:'—if those rules be not observed, there will be evil.

VI. The symbolism here is different from that in the Text of the Thwan. We have the visible sky ascending and water or rain descending, which indicate, one hardly sees how, opposition and contention. The lesson as to the course of the superior man is a good one, but might with equal propriety be deduced from many other hexagrams.

Hsiang An-shih (Sung dynasty) says that the first part of paragraph 2 is all to be taken as the language of the duke of Kâu, the characters being varied; the rest is the remark of the writer of this treatise.

It is observed that the returning to (the study of Heaven's) ordinances, and changing the wish to contend, in paragraph 4, are not two things, but only one; 'the ordinances (ming) meaning what is right in principle.' The wish to contend was wrong in principle, and is now abandoned.

'The robe' takes the place of 'the leathern sash' in paragraph 6; but the sash was merely an appendage of the robe.

2. 'He is in the midst of the host, and there will be good fortune:'—he has received the favour of Heaven. 'The king has thrice conveyed to him the orders (of) his favour:'—(the king) cherishes the myriad regions in his heart.

3. 'The host with the possibility of its having many idle leaders:'—great will be its want of success.

4. 'The host is in retreat; but there is no error:'—there has been no failure in the regular course.

5. 'The oldest son leads the host:'—its movements are directed by him in accordance with his position in the centre. 'Younger men idly occupy their positions:'—the employment of such men is improper.

6. 'The great ruler delivers his charges:'—thereby he rightly apportions merit. 'Small men should not be employed:'—they are sure to throw the states into confusion.

VII. 'The Great Symbolism' here is not more satisfactory than in other paragraphs of it which have already come before us. K'û Hsî says:—'As the water is not outside the earth, so soldiers are not outside the people. Therefore if (a ruler) be able to nourish the people, he can get the multitudes (of his hosts).' Is the meaning this,—that originally the people and soldiers are one body; that a portion of the people are taken out from among the mass, as occasion requires, to do the duty of soldiers; and that the nourishment and education of the people is the best way to have good soldiers ready for use on any emergency? Compare the saying of Confucius in Analects XIII, xxx.

What is said on the second line, that the general 'has received the favour of Heaven,' refers of course to the entire confidence reposed in him by the ruler or king, the subject of line 5. In this way Thien here is equal to Thien wang, so frequent in the 'Spring and Autumn,' and meaning—'King by the grace of

VIII. (The trigram representing) the earth, and over it (that representing) water, form Pî. The ancient kings, in accordance with this, established the various states and maintained an affectionate relation to their princes.

1. From 'the seeking union with its object' shown in the first SIX, (divided), there will be other advantages.

2. 'The movement towards union and attachment proceeds from the inward (mind):'—(the party concerned) does not fail in what is proper to himself.

3. 'Union is sought with such as ought not to be associated with:'—but will not injury be the result?

4. 'Union is sought (by the party intended here) with one beyond himself, and (in this case) with a worthy object:'—he is following (the ruler) above him.

5. 'The good fortune belonging to the most illustrious instance of seeking union and attachment' appears in the correct and central position (of the fifth line, undivided). (The king's) neglecting (the animals) confronting him (and then fleeing), and (only) taking those who present themselves as it were obediently, is seen in

---

Heaven.' But the great powers given to the general are from the king's wish through him to promote the good of all the nation.

In military operations there must be one ruling will and mind. A divided authority is sure to be a failure. But 'a retreat' is no evidence of failure in a campaign. When advance would lead to disaster, retreat is the regular course to pursue.

Other ways can be found to reward small men. They ought not to be placed in situations where the condition of others will depend on them.

'his allowing the escape of those in front of him.'
'That the people of his towns do not warn one
another (to prevent such escape),' shows how he, in
his high eminence, has made them pursue the due
course.

6. 'He seeks union and attachment without taking
the first (step to such an end):'—there is no possibility of a (good) issue.

IX. (The trigram representing) the sky, and that
representing wind moving above it, form Hsiâo
Khû. The superior man, in accordance with this,
adorns the outward manifestation of his virtue.

1. 'He returns and pursues his own path:'—it is
right that there should be good fortune.

2. 'By the attraction (of the subject of the former
line) he returns (to its own course),' and is in the
central place:—neither will he err in what is due
from him.

3. 'Husband and wife look on each other with
averted eyes:'—(the subject of line three is like a

VIII. 'Water upon the face of the earth' is supposed to be an
emblem of close union. Of the mere fact of close union this may
be accepted as a fair illustration, and of its completeness. Some
other symbolism might set forth better the tendency of parties to
union, and their seeking it. What is said about the ancient kings
is more pertinent to the meaning of the hexagram than in many
other applications in 'the Great Symbolism.' The king appears in
it not only as the centre, but as the cause, of union.

'The other advantages' under line 1 refer to all the benefits that
will result from sincerity and union, which are in themselves good.

It is hardly possible to make what is said under line 5, on the
royal huntings, agree with the account of them given on the same
line in the duke of Kâu's text. I suspect that there is some
corruption of the text. The two verbs 'neglecting' and 'taking'
seem to be used, the one for the other.

husband who) cannot maintain correctly his relations with his wife.

4. 'He is possessed of sincerity; his (ground for) apprehension is dismissed:'—(the subjects of the lines) above agree in aim with him.

5. 'He is possessed of sincerity, and draws others to unite with him:'—he does not use only his own rich resources.

6. 'The rain has fallen and (the onward progress) is stayed:'—the power (denoted in the figure) has accumulated to the full. 'If the superior man prosecute his measures, there will be evil:'—he will find himself obstructed.

IX. The suitability of the symbolism here is made all to turn on the wind. 'Wind,' says *Kû*, 'is simply the air, without solid substance; it can restrain, but not for long.' The wind moves in the sky for a time, and then ceases. The process of thought from the symbol to the lesson is not easily traced. Is it meant to say that virtue manifesting itself outwardly—in the carriage and speech—is, however good, but a small matter, admirable in an officer, or even a feudal lord, but that we look for more in a king, the Head of a nation?

Khăng-jze calls attention to the addition to the duke of *Kâu's* explanation in the notice on line 2, that 'it is in the central place,' adding that this explains how the subject of the line restrains himself, and does not go beyond what is due from him.

Only half of the symbolism in the Text of line 3 is taken up here. Line 1, it is said, is far from line 4, the mauvais sujet of the hexagram, and little affected by it; line 2 is nearer, but, being in the centre, suffers little; line 3 is close on it, and, not being in the centre, comes under its evil influence; while line 6 gives no help.

Line 4 is weak, and in an even place, appropriate to it; and hence its subject is said to 'have sincerity.' Being the first line, moreover, of Sun, the two others take their character from it.

Line 5, being undivided, and occupying the most important place in the figure, according to the value usually attached to the lines, is

X. (The trigram representing) the sky above, and below it (that representing the waters of) a marsh, form Lî. The superior man, in accordance with this, discriminates between high and low, and gives settlement to the aims of the people.

1. 'He treads his accustomed path and goes forward :'—singly and exclusively he carries out his (long-cherished) wishes.

2. 'A quiet and solitary man, to whom, being firm and correct, there will be good fortune :'—holding the due mean, he will not allow himself to be thrown into disorder.

3. 'A one-eyed man (who thinks that he) can see :'—he is not fit to see clearly. 'A lame man (who thinks that he can) tread well :'—one cannot walk along with him. 'The ill fortune of being bitten' arises from the place not being the proper one for him. 'A (mere) bravo acting the part of a great ruler :'—this is owing to his aims being (too) violent.

4. 'He becomes full of apprehensive caution, and in the end there will be good fortune :'—his aim takes effect.

5. 'He treads resolutely; and though he be firm and correct, there is peril :'—this is due to his being in the position that is correct and appropriate to him.

---

said 'to be rich,' or 'to have rich resources.' With these he unites with the 'subjects' of line 4 to effect their common object.

Under line 6 we are told that the restraint is at its height, and the restrained should keep still for a time. The paragraph is metrical. The paragraphs to lines 1, 2, 3, all rhyme together. So do those to 4, 5; and now under 6, we have a couplet :—

'Lo! rain, lo! rest, the power is full!
Good man! hold hard. Obstructions rule.'

6. 'There will be great good fortune,' and that in the occupancy of the topmost line :—this is great matter for congratulation.

XI. (The trigrams for) heaven and earth in communication together form Thâi. The (sage) sovereign, in harmony with this, fashions and completes (his regulations) after the courses of heaven and earth, and assists the application of the adaptations furnished by them,—in order to benefit the people.

1. 'The good fortune of advance, (as suggested by the emblem of) the grass pulled up,' arises from the will (of the party intended) being set on what is external to himself.

2. 'He bears with the uncultivated, and proves himself acting in accordance with the due mean :'—for (his intelligence is) bright and (his capacity is) great.

3. 'There is no going away so that there shall not be a return' refers to this as the point where the interaction of heaven and earth takes place.

4. 'He comes fluttering (down), not relying on

X. 'The sky above and a marsh lying below it is true,' says Khǎng-ʒze, 'in nature and reason; and so should be the rules of propriety on which men tread.' This symbolism is far-fetched; and so is the application of it, if in any way drawn from it. But it is true that the members of a community or nation must keep their several places and duties in order to its being in a state of good order.

For lines 1, 2, 3, and 4, see notes on the Text.

If we might translate the conclusion of what is said on line 5, by—'in the position that is correctly appropriate to him,' the meaning would be more clear, though still the assumption which I have pointed out on the Text would underlie the statement; and as evidently as there, what is said under line 6 is but a truism.

his own rich resources :'—both he and his neighbours are out of their real (place where they are).
'They have not received warning, but (come) in the
sincerity (of their hearts) :'—this is what they have
desired in the core of their hearts.

5. 'By such a course there is happiness, and there
will be great good fortune :'—(the subject of the
line) employs the virtue proper to his central position to carry his wishes into effect.

6. 'The city wall returned back into the moat'
shows how the (governmental) orders have (long)
been in disorder.

XII. (The trigrams of) heaven and earth, not in
intercommunication, form Phî. The superior man,
in accordance with this, restrains (the manifestation)
of) his virtue, and avoids the calamities (that threaten
him). There is no opportunity of conferring on him
the glory of emolument.

XI. It is difficult to translate the application of 'the Great Symbolism' here, so that it shall be intelligible to a reader. *Khăng-зze*
says:—'A ruler should frame his laws and regulations so that the
people may avail themselves of the seasons of heaven, and of the
advantages afforded by the earth, assisting their transforming and
nourishing services, and completing their abundant and admirable
benefits. Thus the breath of spring, calling forth all vegetable life,
gives the law for sowing and planting; the breath of autumn,
completing and solidifying all things, gives the law for ingathering
and storing,' &c.

The subject of line 1 has 'his will on what is external to himself :'—he is bent on going forward.

Khû Hsî explains what is said on paragraph 4, that the upper
lines 'are out of their real place where they are,' or, literally, 'have
lost their substantiality,' by the remark that 'their proper place, as
being weak lines, is below.' The editors of the imperial edition
prefer another explanation, on which I need not enter.

1. 'The good fortune through firm goodness, (suggested by) the pulling up of the grass,' arises from the will (of the parties intended) being bent on (serving) the ruler.

2. 'The great man, comporting himself as the distress and obstruction require, will have success:'— he does not allow himself to be disordered by the herd (of small men).

3. That 'his shame is folded in his breast' is owing to the inappropriateness of his position.

4. 'He acts in accordance with the ordination (of Heaven), and commits no error:'—the purpose of his mind can be carried into effect.

5. 'The good fortune of the great man' arises from the correctness of his position.

6. 'The distress and obstruction having reached its end, it is overthrown and removed:'—how could it be prolonged?

XII. 'The Great Symbolism' here is sufficiently explained in the first Appendix. The application, however, is here again difficult, though we may try to find in it a particular instance of the interruption of communication,—in great merit not meeting with its reward.

The subject of the first line is one of the cluster of small men who are able to change their mind, and set their hearts to love their ruler.

The subject of the second line is a 'great man,' and occupies the place in the centre.

The subject of the third line is weak, and does not occupy his correct position;—hence the symbolism.

The fourth line is near the fifth, the ruler's place. It is a strong line in an even place; but acting according to the will of Heaven or of the ruler, its subject gets his purpose carried out.

The subject of the fifth line is the great man, the ruler in his right place. Hence he is successful, and in the last line, we see

XIII. (The trigrams for) heaven and fire form Thung Zăn. The superior man, in accordance with this), distinguishes things according to their kinds and classes.

1. '(The representative of) the union of men is just issuing from his gate :'—who will blame him?

2. '(The representative of) the union of men appears in relation with his kindred :'—that is the path to regret.

3. 'He hides his arms in the thick grass :'—because of the strength of his opponent. 'For three years he makes no demonstration :'—how can he do anything?

4. 'He is mounted on his city-wall;' but yielding to the right, 'he does not proceed to make the attack (he contemplated).' (Where it is said), 'There will be good fortune,' (that shows how) he feels the strait he is in, and returns to the rule of law.

5. The first action of (the representative of) the union of men (here described) arises from his central position and straightforward character. 'The meeting secured by his great host' intimates that the opponents of it have been overcome.

6. '(The representative of) the union of men appears in the suburbs :'—his object has not yet been attained.

---

how the distress and obstruction are come to an end. It was in the order of change that they should do so.

XIII. The style of 'heaven and fire form Thung Zăn' is such as to suggest the appearance of fire ascending up, blazing to the sky, and uniting with it. The application of the symbolism is again perplexing.

In line 1, the party just issuing from his gate has all the world

XIV. (The trigram for) heaven and (that of) fire above it form Tâ Yû. The superior man, in accordance with this, represses what is evil and gives distinction to what is good, in sympathy with the excellent Heaven-conferred (nature).

1. This first NINE, (undivided), of Tâ Yû shows no approach to what is injurious.

2. 'A large waggon with its load' refers to the (virtue) accumulated (in the subject of the line), so that he will suffer no loss (in the conduct of affairs).

3. 'A feudal prince presents his offerings to the son of Heaven:'—a small man (in such a position) does (himself) harm.

4. 'He keeps his great resources under restraint:'— his wisdom discriminates clearly (what he ought to do).

5. 'His sincerity is reciprocated by all the others:'— his sincerity serves to stir and call out what is in their minds. 'The good fortune springing from a display of proper majesty' shows how they might (other-wise) feel too easy, and make no preparation (to serve him).

---

before him, with which to unite. Selfish thoughts disposing to union have no place in him.

In line 2, union (only) with kindred implies narrowness of mind.
For line 3, see note on the Text.
In line 4, stress should be laid on 'yielding to the right.'
For line 5, see note on the Text.
The Khang-hsî editors append the following note to the last paragraph:—'Under line 1 it is said that "union in the open country indicates progress and success," while here it is only said that "with union in the suburbs there is no cause for repentance." Beyond the suburbs was the open country, and till the union reached so far, the object of the hexagram was not attained. We may truly say that Confucius was a skilful reader of the duke of Kâu.' Of course the editors did not doubt Confucius' authorship of all the Appendixes.

6. 'The good fortune attached to the topmost line of Tâ Yû' arises from the help of Heaven.

XV. (The trigram for) the earth and (that of) a mountain in the midst of it form *Kh*ien. The superior man, in accordance with this, diminishes what is excessive (in himself), and increases where there is any defect, bringing about an equality, according to the nature of the case, in his treatment (of himself and others).

1. 'The superior man who adds humility to humility' is one who nourishes his (virtue) in lowliness.

2. 'The good fortune consequent on being firm and correct, where the humility has made itself recognised,' is owing to the possessor's having (the virtue) in the core of his heart.

3. 'The superior man of (acknowledged) merit, and yet humble :'—the myriads of the people will submit to him.

4. 'One, whose action would be in every way advantageous, stirs up his humility the more :'— (but in doing so) he does not act contrary to the (proper) rule.

5. 'He may advantageously use the force of arms :'—correcting, that is, those who do not submit.

XIV. 'Fire above the sky' will shine far; and this is supposed to symbolise the vastness of the territory or of the wealth implied in the possession of what is great. The superior man, in governing men, especially in a time of prosperity and wealth, must set himself to develope what is good in them, and repress what is evil. And this will be in accordance with the will of Heaven, which has given to all men a nature fitted for goodness.

All the comment that is necessary on the symbolism of the several lines may be gathered from the comments on the Text.

6. 'His humility has made itself recognised:'—
(but) all his aims have not yet been attained. 'He
may employ the force of arms, (but only) in correcting (his own) towns and state.'

XVI. (The trigrams for) the earth and thunder
issuing from it with its crashing noise form Yü.
The ancient kings, in accordance with this, composed their music and did honour to virtue, presenting it especially and most grandly to God,

---

XV. The earth is low, and in the midst of it is a high mountain;
but I fail to see how this can symbolise humility. Nor does Regis'
representation of it much improve the case:—'Monte' (ait glossa)
'nihil est altius in terra, quae est summe abjecta. At cum is de-
clivis sit, imago esse potest humilis modestiae.' I find the following
note on the paragraph in my copy of the 'Daily Lessons' (see Preface):—'The five yin lines above and below symbolise the earth;
the one yang line in the centre is "the mountain in the midst of
the earth." The many yin lines represent men's desires; the
one yang line, heavenly principle. The superior man, looking at
this symbolism, diminishes the multitude of human desires within
him, and increases the single shoot of heavenly principle; so does he
become grandly just, and can deal with all things evenly according
to the nature of each. In whatever circumstances or place he is, he
will do what is right.' This is certainly very ingenious, but one
shrinks from accepting a view that is not based on the component
trigrams.

Under line 1, 'nourishes his (virtue)' is, literally, 'pastures himself.' He is all humility. That makes him what he is.

Under line 4, 'the (proper) rule' is the rule proper for the subject
of the line in his circumstances so near the place of the ruler.

Under line 5, 'the refusal to submit' makes an appeal to force
necessary. Even the best and humblest ruler bears the sword, and
must not bear it in vain.

Kü Hsî bases all that is said under line 6 on its being a weak
line; so that the humble ruler is unable even at the close of the
action described in the figure to accomplish all his objects, and
must limit his field even in appealing to arms.

when they associated with Him (at the service) their highest ancestor and their father.

1. 'The (subject of the) first six proclaims his pleasure and satisfaction :'—there will be evil; his wishes have been satisfied to overflowing.

2. '(He sees a thing) without waiting till it has come to pass; with his firm correctness there will be good fortune :'—this is shown by the central and correct position (of the line).

3. 'He looks up (for favours), while he indulges the feeling of satisfaction ; there will be occasion for repentance :'—this is intimated by the position not being the appropriate one.

4. 'From him the harmony and satisfaction come ; great is the success which he obtains :'—his aims take effect on a grand scale.

5. '(The subject of) the fifth six has a chronic complaint :'—this is shown by his being mounted on the strong (line). 'He still lives on without dying :'— he is in the central position, (and its memories of the past) have not yet perished.

6. 'With darkened mind devoted to the harmony and satisfaction (of the time),' as shown in the topmost (line) :—how can one in such a condition continue long?

XVI. 'The Great Symbolism' here is more obscure than usual. A thunderstorm clears the air and removes the feeling of oppression, of which one is conscious before its occurrence. Is this all that is meant by making the trigrams of the earth and thunder form Yü, the hexagram of harmony and satisfaction? What is meant, moreover, by making the thunder 'issue,' as the Chinese text says, from the earth? Then as to the application of this symbolism, I can trace the author's idea but imperfectly. To say that the thunder crash suggested the use of music, as some critics do, is

XVII. (The trigram for the waters of) a marsh and (that for) thunder (hidden) in the midst of it form Sui. The superior man in accordance with this, when it is getting towards dark, enters (his house) and rests.

1. 'He is changing the object of his pursuit:'—but if he follow what is correct, there will be good fortune. 'He goes beyond (his own) gate to find associates:'—he will not fail (in the method he pursues).

2. 'He cleaves to the little boy:'—he cannot be with the two at the same time.

3. 'He cleaves to the man of age and experience:'—by the decision of his will, he abandons (the youth) below.

4. 'He is followed and obtains adherents:'—according to the idea (of the hexagram), this is evil. 'He is sincere in his course:'—showing his intelligence, and leading to achievement.

5. 'He is sincere in fostering what is excellent:'—his position is correct and in the centre.

---

absurd. The use of music at sacrifices, however, as assisting the union produced by those services between God and his worshippers, and the present and past generations, agrees with the general idea of the figure. I must suppose that the writer had in mind the sacrifices instituted by the duke of *K*âu, as related in the Hsiâo King, chap. ix.

Pleasure has operated injuriously on the subject of line 1. He calls attention to himself.

Only a part of the symbolism of line 2 is referred to here. Such an omission is not uncommon;—as in lines 3 and 4 also.

With 'the memories of the past not perishing' compare Mencius, II, Section i, chap. 1. 6-13.

In line 6 the action of the hexagram is over. If one puts off changing his evil way any longer, there remains no more hope for him.

6. 'The sincerity is firmly held and clung to, as shown in the topmost line:'—(the idea of the hexagram) has reached its extreme development.

XVIII. (The trigram for) a mountain, and below it that for wind, form Kû. The superior man, in accordance with this, (addresses himself to) help the people and nourish his own virtue.

1. 'He deals with the troubles caused by his father:'—he feels that he has entered into the work of his father.

2. 'He deals with the troubles caused by his mother:'—he holds to the course of the due mean.

3. 'He deals with the troubles caused by his father:'—in the end there will be no error.

4. 'He views indulgently the troubles caused by his father:'—if he go forward, he will not succeed.

5. 'He deals with the troubles caused by his father, and obtains praise:'—he is responded to (by the subject of line two) with all his virtue.

XVII. An explosion of thunder amidst the waters of a marsh would be succeeded by a tremulous agitation of those waters; so far there would be a following of the movement of the lower trigram by the upper. Then in the application of the symbolism we have an illustration of action following the time, that is, according to the time; which is a common use of the Chinese character Sui. Neither the symbolism, however, nor its application adds much to our understanding of the text.

Paragraph 1 consists of two lines that rhyme; and paragraphs 4 (two lines), 5, and 6 do the same. According to Kû Yen-wû, paragraphs 2 and 3 also rhyme; but this appears to me doubtful. The symbolism of these paragraphs is sufficiently explained in the notes on the Text. Some peculiarities in their style (in Chinese) are owing to the bonds of the rhyme.

6. ' He does not serve either king or feudal lord :'—
but his aim may be a model (to others).

XIX. (The trigram for) the waters of a marsh
and that for the earth above it form Lin. The
superior man, in accordance with this, has his purposes of instruction that are inexhaustible, and
nourishes and supports the people without limit.

1. ' The good fortune through the firm correctness of (the subject of the first line) advancing in
company (with the subject of the second)' is due to
his will being set on doing what is right.

2. ' The good fortune and every possible advantage attending the advance (of the subject of the
second line), in company (with the subject of the
first),' arises from the fact that those (to whom the
advance is made) are not yet obedient to the ordinances (of Heaven).

3. ' He (shows himself) well pleased to advance :'—
his position is not that appropriate to him. ' If he
become anxious, however, about his action,' his error
will not be continued.

4. ' The freedom from error consequent on the

XVIII. ' When the wind,' says _Kh_ăng-ẕze, ' encounters the
mountain, it is driven back, and the things about are all scattered
in disorder ; such is the emblem of the state denoted by Kû.'
' The nourishing of virtue' appears especially in line 6 ; all the
other lines belong to the ' helping of the people.'

The subject of line 1 has entered into the work of his father,
and brings it about that his father is looked on as blameless. The
' due mean' of line 2 is according to the caution in the Text.
The Khang-hsî editors interpret the explanation of line 5 as = ' he
takes up (the course of his father) with all his virtue.' I think they
are wrong.

advance in the highest mode' is due to the (various) appropriateness of the position.

5. 'What befits the great ruler' means the pursuing the course of the due mean.

6. ' The good fortune consequent on the advance of honesty and generosity' is due to the will (of the subject of the line) being set on the subjects of (the first two lines of) the inner (trigram).

XX. (The trigram representing) the earth, and that for wind moving above it, form K w a n. The ancient kings, in accordance with this, examined the (different) regions (of the kingdom), to see the (ways of the) people, and set forth their instructions.

1. ' The looking of a lad shown by the first six, (divided), indicates the way of the inferior people.

XIX. 'The earth descending or approaching the marsh' is, according to Kû Hsî, symbolical of the approach of superiors to the inferior people, and then the two predicates about the superior man are descriptive of him in that approach, the instruction being symbolised by Tui, and the supporting by Khwǎn. The Khanghsî editors, wishing to defend the explanation of lin by ' great,' in Appendix VI, which they ascribe to Confucius, say :—' Lin means " great." The earth above the waters of the marsh shows how full those waters are, rising to the level of the earth, and thus expressing the idea of greatness.' This representation is lame and impotent.

Kû Hsî says he does not understand what is said on line 2. The interpretation in my version is the ordinary one, but I am not satisfied with it. The Khang-hsî editors try to solve the difficulty ; but I am not able to follow them.

The same editors compare the conclusion of paragraph 6 in the symbolism of hexagram 11. ' What is external' there, and 'what is internal here,' have, they say, the same reference,—the state, namely, of the whole kingdom, the expressions differing according to the different standpoints from which they are made. The view in the translation is that of Kû Hsî. It is difficult to hold the balance between them. The newer view, perhaps, is the preferable.

2. 'The firm correctness of a woman, in peeping out from a door' is also a thing to be ashamed of (in a superior man).

3. 'He looks at (the course of) his own life, to advance or recede (accordingly):'—he will not err in the path (to be pursued).

4. 'He contemplates the glory of the kingdom:'—(thence) arises the wish to be a guest (at court).

5. 'He contemplates his own life(-course):'—he should (for this purpose) contemplate (the condition of) the people.

6. 'He contemplates his own character:'—he cannot even yet let his mind be at rest.

XXI. (The trigrams representing) thunder and lightning form Shih Ho. The ancient kings, in accordance with this, framed their penalties with intelligence, and promulgated their laws.

1. 'His feet are in the stocks, and he is deprived of his toes:'—there is no walking (to do evil).

2. 'He bites through the soft flesh, and (goes on)

XX. Wind moving above the earth has the widest sweep, and nothing escapes its influence; it penetrates everywhere. This symbolism is more appropriate to the subject in hand than that of many other hexagrams. Personal influence in a ruler effects much; but the ancient kings wished to add to that the power of published instructions, specially adapted to the character and circumstances of the people. Sun, representing the wind, is well adapted to denote this influence;—see the Analects, XII, xix.

The looking in line 1 is superficial, and does not reach far.

Line 3. 'He will not err in the path to be pursued;'—advancing or receding as is best.

Line 4. 'The glory of the kingdom' is the virtue of the sovereign and the character of his administration. With the sentiment compare Mencius, VII, i, chap. 21. 2.

to bite off the nose :'—(the subject of the line) is mounted on the strong (first line).

3. 'He meets with what is disagreeable and hurtful :'—his position is not the proper one for him.

4. 'It will be advantageous to him to realise the difficulty of his task and be firm, in which case there will be good fortune :'—his light has not yet been sufficiently displayed.

5. 'Let him be firm and correct, realising the peril (of his position), and there will be no error :'—he will possess every quality appropriate (to his position and task).

6. 'He wears the cangue and is deprived of his ears :'—he hears, but will not understand.

XXII. (The trigram representing) a mountain and that for fire under it form Pî. The superior man, in accordance with this, throws a brilliancy around his various processes of government, but does not dare (in a similar way) to decide cases of criminal litigation.

XXI. *Kh*äng-ȝze says that thunder and lightning are always found together, and hence their trigrams go together to give the idea of union intended in Shih Ho. The one trigram symbolising majesty and the other brightness or intelligence, the application of the hexagram here is easier and more natural than in many other cases.

1. 'There is no walking :'—that is, the subject of the line will not dare to offend any more.

2. '"Being mounted on the strong first line" means,' says *Kh*äng-ȝze, 'punishing a strong and vehement man, when severity is required, as is denoted by the central position of the line.'

4. 'His light has not been sufficiently displayed ;' that is, there is still something for him to do :—he has to realise the difficulty of his position and be firm.

1. 'He can discard a carriage and walk on foot :'—righteousness requires that he should not ride.

2. 'He adorns his beard :'—he rouses himself to action (only) along with the (subject of the) line above.

3. 'The good fortune consequent on his ever maintaining firm correctness' is due to this,—that to the end no one will insult him.

4. 'The place occupied by the fourth six, (divided),' affords ground for doubt (as to its subject) ; but '(as the subject of the third pursues) not as a robber, but as intent on a matrimonial alliance,' he will in the end have no grudge against him.

5. 'The good fortune falling to the fifth six, (divided),' affords occasion for joy.

6. 'The freedom from error attached to (the subject of) the topmost line, with no ornament but the (simple white),' shows how he has attained his aim.

XXII. 'A mountain,' says *Khǎng-ʒze,* 'is a place where we find grass, trees, and a hundred other things. A fire burning below it throws up its light, and brings them all out in beauty ; and this gives the idea of ornament, or being ornamented. The various processes of government are small matters, and elegance and ornament help their course ; but great matters of judgment demand the simple, unornamented truth.'

The subject of line 1 does not care for and does not need ornament. He will walk in the way of righteousness without it.

Paragraph 3 tells us that it is not ornament, but correct firmness, which secures the respect of others.

In the fourth place, and cut off from line 1 by 2 and 3, we might doubt how far the subject of 4 would continue loyal to the subject of 1. But he does continue loyal, through the character and object of the subject of 3.

The Khang-hsî editors say :—' Line 5 occupies the place of honour, and yet prefers simplicity and exalts economy ; its subject

XXIII. (The trigrams representing) the earth, and (above it) that for a mountain, which adheres to the earth, form Po. Superiors, in accordance with this, seek to strengthen those below them, to secure the peace and stability of their own position.

1. ' He overthrows the couch by injuring its legs :' —thus (he commences) his work of ruin with what is lowest (in the superior man).

2. ' He destroys the couch by injuring its frame :'— (the superior man) has as yet no associates.

3. That ' there will be no error on the part of this one among the overthrowers' arises from the difference between him and the others above and below.

4. ' He has overthrown the couch, and (proceeds to injure) the skin (of him who lies on it):'—calamity is very near at hand.

5. ' He obtains for them the favour that lights on the inmates of the palace :'—in the end there will be no grudge against him.

6. ' The superior man finds himself in a carriage :'—he is carried along by the people. ' The small men (by their course) overthrow their own dwellings :'—they can never again be of use to them.

---

might change and transform manners and customs;'—it is a small matter to say of him that he affords occasion for joy.

The subject of line 6 has more of the spirit of the hexagram than in most hexagrams. His being clothed in simple white crowns the lesson that ornament must be kept in a secondary place.

XXIII. ' A mountain,' says Yü Fan (towards the end of the Han dynasty), ' stands out high above the earth ; here it appears as lying on the earth :—plainly it has been overturned.' On the

XXIV. (The trigram representing) the earth and that for thunder in the midst of it form Fû. The ancient kings, in accordance with this, on the day of the (winter) solstice, shut the gates of the passes (from one state to another), so that the travelling merchants could not (then) pursue their journeys, nor the princes go on with the inspection of their states.

1. 'Returning (from an error) of no great extent' is the prelude to the cultivation of the person.

2. 'The good fortune attendant on the admirable return (of the subject of the second line)' is due to his condescension to the virtuous (subject of the line) below.

3. Notwithstanding 'the perilous position of him

---

other hand, Liû Mû (early in the Sung dynasty) says :—' A mountain has the earth for its foundation. If the earth be thick, the mountain preserves its height. So it is with the sovereign and people.' The application might be deduced from either view.

It is hard to tell whether 'the lowest' in paragraph 1 should be supplemented as I have done. If not, then the explanation is a mere truism.

Khăng-żze is precise and decisive in supplementing the explanation of paragraph 2 as in the translation.

See on the Text of lines 3 and 4.

On paragraph 5, the Khang-hsî editors say admirably :—' The fifth line is weak, and yet occupies the most honourable place in the figure,—emblematic of a queen; and as its subject leads on the subjects of the other lines to obtain the favours given to the inmates of the palace, she, it is plain, has neither jealousy nor any other injurious temper that might incur blame for tending to overthrow the ruler.'

Paragraph 6 shows the ruler restored to the favour of the people, and the restoration of concord in the state. The small men have done their worst, and there is an end of their attempts— for a time.

who has made many returns,' there will be no error through (his aiming after righteousness).

4. 'He moves right in the centre (among those represented by the other divided lines), and yet returns alone :'—his object is to pursue the (proper) path.

5. 'The noble return, giving no ground for repentance,' is due to (the subject of the line) striving to perfect himself in accordance with his central position.

6. 'The evil consequent on being all astray on the subject of returning' is because the course pursued is contrary to the proper course for a ruler.

XXIV. 'Thunder in the midst of the earth' is thunder shut up and silent, just able to make its presence felt. So is it with the first genial stirrings of life after the winter solstice ; so is it with the first returning steps of the wanderer to virtue. As the spring of life has to be nursed in quietness, so also has the purpose of good. The ancient statutes here referred to must have been like the present cessation from public and private business at the time of the new year, when all the Chinese people are for a time dissolved in festivity and joy.

Canon McClatchie translates here :—' The ancient kings on this culminating day (i. e. the seventh) closed their gates,' &c. 'Culminating day' does not give us the meaning so well as 'the day of the solstice ;' but where does the translator find the explanatory 'the seventh,' which he puts in parentheses ? In my own 'salad' days of Chinese knowledge I fancied there might be in paragraph 1 of the Text some allusion to a primitive sabbath ; but there is no ground for introducing 'seven days,' or 'the seventh day,' into this paragraph of the Great Symbolism.

'The virtuous subject of the first line' is in paragraph 2 called ẑăn, 'the benevolent' or 'loving.' It is the only case in all the symbolism of the Yî where we find that term used as an adjective. It is emphatic here for 'humanity,' man in his ideal.

The other paragraphs present nothing for remark beyond what has been said on the Text of the duke of Kâu.

XXV. The thunder rolls all under the sky, and to (every)thing there is given (its nature), free from all insincerity. The ancient kings, in accordance with this, (made their regulations) in complete accordance with the seasons, thereby nourishing all things.

1. When 'he who is free from insincerity makes any movement,' he will get what he desires.

2. 'He reaps without having ploughed:'—(the thought of) riches to be got had not risen (in his mind).

3. 'The passer-by gets the ox:'—this proves a calamity to the people of the neighbourhood.

4. 'If he can remain firm and correct there will be no error:'—he firmly holds fast (his correctness).

5. 'Medicine in the case of one who is free from insincerity!'—it should not be tried (at all).

6. 'The action (in this case) of one who is free from insincerity' will occasion the calamity arising from action (when the time for it is) exhausted.

XXV. The composition of the hexagram is given here in a manner different from what we have met with in the account of any of the preceding figures; and as the text is not called in question, I have made the best I could in the translation of the two commencing clauses. The application of the symbolism to what the ancient kings did is also hard to comprehend.

The paragraph on line 1 is another way of saying that in the course of things real goodness may be expected to be fortunate,— 'by the appointment of Heaven.'

Paragraph 2. 'The thought of getting rich had not risen in his mind:'—he did what he did, because it was right, not because of the gain it would bring him.

On paragraph 3, it is said, 'The superior man seeks simply to be free from insincerity, and leaves the questions of happiness and calamity to Heaven.'

Paragraph 5. 'Sickness ought not to happen to one who

XXVI. (The trigram representing) a mountain, and in the midst of it that (representing) heaven, form Tâ *Khû*. The superior man, in accordance with this, stores largely in his memory the words and deeds of former men, to subserve the accumulation of his virtue.

1. 'He is in a position of peril; it will be advantageous for him to stop his advance :'—he should not rashly expose himself to calamity.

2. '(He is as) a carriage from which the strap under it has been removed :'—being in the central position, he will incur no blame.

3. 'There will be advantage in whatever direction he may advance :'—(the subject of) the topmost line is of the same mind with him.

4. 'The great good fortune indicated by the fourth six, (divided),' shows that there is occasion for joy.

5. 'The good fortune indicated by the fifth six, (divided),' shows that there is occasion for congratulation.

6. 'In command of the firmament of heaven:'—the way is grandly open for movement.

---

is perfectly sincere. If it do happen, he must refer it to some inexplicable will of Heaven. As that has afflicted, so it will cure.'

Paragraph 6. 'When a thing is over and done, submission and acquiescence are what are required, and not renewed attempts at action.'

XXVI. I have quoted, in the Introduction, p. 37, *K*û Hsî's remark on the Great Symbolism here. *Kh*ǎng-ʒze says :—'Heaven is the greatest of all things, and its being in the midst of a mountain gives us the idea of a very large accumulation. And so great

XXVII. (The trigram representing) a mountain and under it that for thunder form ䷚. The superior man, in accordance with this, (enjoins) watchfulness over our words, and the temperate regulation of our eating and drinking.

1. 'You look at me till your (lower) jaw hangs down:'—(the subject of the line) is thus shown unfit to be thought noble.

2. 'The evil of advance by the subject of the second six, (divided),' is owing to his leaving in his movements his proper associates.

3. 'For ten years let him not take any action:'— his course is greatly opposed (to what is right).

4. 'The good fortune attached to looking down- wards for (the power to) nourish,' shows how brilliant will be the diffusion (of that power) from (the subject of the line's) superior position.

5. 'The good fortune from abiding in firmness' is due to the docility (of the subject of the line) in following (the subject of the line) above.

6. 'The good fortune, notwithstanding the peril

---

is the labour of the superior man in learning, acquiring, and remem- bering, to accumulate his virtue.'

Paragraph 1. The 'calamity' is that of opposition from, or re- pression by, the subject of line 4.

Paragraph 3. When the action of the hexagram has reached line 6, its work is done. The subject of 6 will no longer exercise repression, but join with that of 3, assisting him to advance.

Paragraph 4. The subject of line 4 has indeed occasion for joy. Without the use of punishment for crimes committed, by precau- tion anticipating them, without any trouble he has repressed evil. The 'joy' gives place in paragraph 5 to 'congratulation,' the people being all interested in the action of the ruler.

of his position, of him from whom comes the nourishing,' affords great cause for congratulation.

XXVIII. (The trigram representing) trees hidden beneath that for the waters of a marsh forms Tâ Kwo. The superior man, in accordance with this, stands up alone and has no fear, and keeps retired from the world without regret.

1. 'He places mats of the white mâo grass under things set on the ground:'—he feels his weakness and his being in the lowest place, (and uses extraordinary care).

2. 'An old husband and a young wife:'—such association is extraordinary.

3. 'The evil connected with the beam that is weak' arises from this, that no help can be given (to the condition thus represented).

4. 'The good fortune connected with the beam curving upwards' arises from this, that it does not bend towards what is below.

5. 'A decayed willow produces flowers:'—but how can this secure its long continuance? 'An old

---

XXVII. I do not think that the Great Symbolism here is anything but that of a thunderstorm, dispersing the oppression that hangs over nature, and followed by genial airs, and the reviving of all vegetation. But there is nothing analogous to the thunder in the application. 'Words,' it is said, 'nourish virtue; food and drink nourish the body.'

Paragraph 1. As Mencius said, 'He that nourishes the little belonging to him is a little man.'

Paragraph 2. Neither the subject of line 1, nor of line 6, is the proper associate of 2.

The other paragraphs are sufficiently illustrated in the notes on the Text.

wife and a young husband :'—this also is a thing to be ashamed of.

6. 'Evil follows wading with (extraordinary) boldness (through the stream):'—but (the act) affords no ground for blame.

XXIX. (The representation of) water flowing on continuously forms the repeated Khan. The superior man, in accordance with this, maintains constantly the virtue (of his heart) and (the integrity of) his conduct, and practises the business of instruction.

1. 'In the double defile, he enters a cavern within it :'—he has missed his (proper) way, and there will be evil.

2. 'He will get a little (of the deliverance) that he seeks :'—he will not yet escape from his environed position.

3. 'Whether he comes or goes, he is confronted by a defile :'—he will never (in such circumstances) achieve any success.

XXVIII. *Kh*äng-*z*ze says on the Great Symbolism:—'The waters of a marsh moisten and nourish the trees. When here it is said that they destroy and extinguish the trees, their action is very extraordinary.' This explanation is very far-fetched; and so is what the same scholar says on the application of it. I need not give it here, nor have I found, or myself made out, any other more easy and natural.

Paragraph 2. 'Such an association is extraordinary:'—the characters also imply, perhaps, that it is successful.

Paragraph 3. The beam being broken, any attempt to sustain it will have no effect in supporting the roof.

Paragraph 5. The shoots produced in line 2 will grow into a new and vigorous tree. The flowers here will soon decay, and the withered trunk continue the same. For what will a young man marry an old woman? There will be no children;—it can only be from some mercenary object.

4. '(Nothing but) a bottle of spirits and a sub-sidiary basket of rice:'—(these describe) the meeting at this point of (those who are represented by) the strong and weak lines.

5. 'The water in the defile is not full (so as to flow away):'—(the virtue indicated by) the central situation is not yet (sufficiently) great.

6. 'The sixth line, divided, shows its subject missing his (proper) course:'—'there will be evil for three years.'

XXX. (The trigram for) brightness, repeated, forms Lî. The great man, in accordance with this, cultivates more and more his brilliant (virtue), and diffuses its brightness over the four quarters (of the land).

1. 'The reverent attention directed to his con-fused steps' is the way by which error is avoided.

2. 'The great good fortune (from the subject of the second line) occupying his place in yellow' is owing to his holding the course of the due mean.

3. 'A position like that of the declining sun:'—how can it continue long?

4. 'How abrupt is the manner of his coming!'—none can bear with him.

5. 'The good fortune attached to the fifth SIX,

XXIX. The application of the Great Symbolism is here more perplexing even than usual. What is said of the superior man is good, but there is no reference in it to the subject of danger.

The subject of line 3 goes and comes, moves up and down, backwards and forwards; making no advance. This can be of no use in extricating him from the danger.

Those represented in line 4 by the strong and weak lines are the ruler and his minister.

(divided),' is due to its occupying the place of a king or a prince.

6. 'The king employs him in his punitive expeditions :'—the object is to bring the regions to a correct state.

Section II

XXXI. (The trigram representing) a mountain and above it that for (the waters of) a marsh form Hsien. The superior man, in accordance with this, keeps his mind free from pre-occupation, and open to receive (the influences of) others.

1. 'He moves his great toe :'—his mind is set on what is beyond (himself).

2. Though 'there would be evil; yet, if he abide (quiet) in his place, there will be good fortune :'—through compliance (with the circumstances of his condition and place) there will be no injury.

3. 'He moves his thighs :'—he still does not (want to) rest in his place. His will is set on 'following others :'—what he holds in his grasp is low.

4. 'Firm correctness will lead to good fortune,

XXX. In the Great Symbolism Lî is used in the sense of brightness. There was no occasion to refer to its other meaning. 'The great man' rather confirms the interpretation of the 'double brightness' in the treatise on the Thwan as indicating the ruler.

Paragraph 2. As yellow is a 'correct' colour, so is the due mean the correct course.

Paragraph 3. 'The declining sun,' say the Khang-hsî editors, 'is an emblem of the obscuration coming over the virtue of the mind.'

Paragraph 4. 'None can bear with him' refers to the second part of the symbolism of the line, which is not given here.

and prevent all occasion for repentance :'—there has not yet been any harm from (a selfish wish to) influence. 'He is unsettled in his movements :'— (his power to influence) is not yet either brilliant or great.

5. 'He (tries to) move the flesh along the spine above the heart :'—his aim is trivial.

6. 'He moves his jaws and tongue :'—he (only) talks with loquacious mouth.

XXXI. In various ways the waters of a marsh, placed high above the adjacent land, will descend to water and fertilise them. This symbolism agrees sufficiently well with the idea of influence passing between a superior and inferior party in relation with each other. There is nothing in the representation, however, to suggest particularly the relation between husband and wife; and the more I think of it, the more doubtful it becomes to me that king Wan intended by the trigrams of this figure to give the idea of man and wife. The application of the symbolism is sufficiently appropriate. The commentators see in it especially the lesson of humility— emptiness of self, or poverty of spirit—in order that the influences to which we are subjected may have free course.

Paragraph 1. What is beyond one's self is represented by line 4, a proper correlate of 1. There is the desire to influence; but it is ineffectively exhibited.

Paragraph 2. 'Compliance (with the circumstances of his condition and place)' is merely another way of 'being firm and correct.'

Paragraph 3. The language, 'What he holds in his grasp is low,' makes Kû Hsî and the older commentators generally understand low of lines 1 and 2, and their weak subjects. But 'following' leads the mind to the lines above, as the Khang-hsî editors point out. 'Low' is to be understood in the sense of 'mean.'

Paragraph 4. The 'being firm and correct' appears here as equivalent to the want of 'a selfish wish to influence.'

Paragraph 5. The triviality of the aim explains the ineffectiveness of the movement, but not its giving no occasion for repentance. That the mei which are moved are behind and above the region of the heart seems too mechanical and trivial an explanation.

XXXII. (The trigram representing) thunder and that for wind form Hăng. The superior man, in accordance with this, stands firm, and does not change his method (of operation).

1. 'The evil attached to the deep desire for long continuance (in the subject of the first line)' arises from the deep seeking for it at the commencement (of things).

2. 'All occasion for repentance on the part of the subject of the second NINE, (undivided), disappears :'— he can abide long in the due mean.

3. 'He does not continuously maintain his virtue :'—nowhere will he be borne with.

4. (Going) for long to what is not his proper place, how can he get game?

5. 'Such firm correctness in a wife will be fortunate :'—it is hers to the end of life to follow with an unchanged mind. The husband must decide what is right, and lay down the rule accordingly :— for him to follow (like) a wife is evil.

6. 'The subject of the topmost line is exciting himself to long continuance :'—far will he be from achieving merit.

XXXII. How the interaction of wind and thunder symbolises the lesson of the hexagram, and especially the application in this paragraph of that symbolism, is a question I have not been able to solve.

Paragraph 1. The stress of what is said under line 1 is here made to lie on its being the first line of the figure.

Paragraph 2. Line 2 is in the centre of its trigram, and that position, here as often elsewhere, symbolises the course of its subject.

Paragraph 3. The Khang-hsî editors make the application here = 'nowhere can he bear (to remain).'

XXXIII. (The trigram representing) the sky and below it that for a mountain form T h u n. The superior man, in accordance with this, keeps small men at a distance, not by showing that he hates them, but by his own dignified gravity.

1. There is 'the perilousness of the position shown by the retiring tail:'—but if 'no movement' be made, what disaster can there be?

2. 'He holds it as by (a thong from the hide of) a yellow ox:'—his purpose is firm.

3. 'The peril connected with the case of one retiring, though bound,' is due to the (consequent) distress and exhaustion. 'If he were (to deal as in) nourishing a servant or concubine, it would be fortunate for him:'—but a great affair cannot be dealt with in this way.

4. 'A superior man retires notwithstanding his likings; a small man cannot attain to this.'

5. 'He retires in an admirable way, and with firm correctness there will be good fortune:'—this is due to the rectitude of his purpose.

6. 'He retires in a noble way, and his doing so will be advantageous in every respect:'—he who does so has no doubts about his course.

From paragraph 5 it appears that what is right will vary in different cases. The lesson of the hexagram is perseverance in what is right in each particular case.

XXXIII. *K*û Hsî says :—' The sky is illimitable ; a mountain is high, but has its limits ; the union of these is an emblem of retiring.' I do not understand such embleming. *K*h*ă*ng-ʒze says :— ' Below the sky is a mountain. The mountain rises up below the sky, and its height is arrested, while the sky goes up higher and higher, till they come to be apart from each other. In this we have an emblem of retiring and avoiding.' We feel somewhat as

XXXIV. (The trigram representing) heaven and above it that for thunder form Tâ *K*wang. The superior man, in accordance with this, does not take a step which is not according to propriety.

1. 'He manifests his vigour in his toes:'—this will certainly lead to exhaustion.

2. 'The second NINE,(undivided),shows that with firm correctness there will be good fortune:'—this is due to its being in the centre, (and its subject exemplifying the due mean).

3. 'The small man uses all his strength; in the case of the superior man it is his rule not to do so.'

4. 'The fence is opened and the horns are not entangled:'—(the subject of the line) still advances.

5. 'He loses his ram and hardly perceives it:'—he is not in his appropriate place.

6. 'He is unable either to retreat or to advance:'—this is owing to his want of care. 'If he realise the difficulty (of his position), there will be good fortune:'—his error will not be prolonged.

---

if there were a meaning in this; but, as in many other cases, both the symbolism and its application are but dimly apprehended.

The symbolism of the various lines is sufficiently explained on the Text. Paragraph 5 is but a repetition of the Text without additional explanation.

XXXIV. In illustration of the symbolism of the trigrams here, *K*hǎng-ʒze says well:—'Thunder rolling above in the sky and making all things shake is the emblem of great power.' In passing on to its application he starts with a beautiful saying of antiquity, that 'the strong man is he who overcomes himself.' That this thought was in the mind of the writer of the paragraph on the Great Symbolism I can well believe; but the analogy between the natural and the moral and spiritual worlds in passing from the phenomenon of thunder to this truth is a thing to be felt, and that can hardly be described.

XXXV. (The trigram representing) the earth and that for the bright (sun) coming forth above it form 3in. The superior man, according to this, gives himself to make more brilliant his bright virtue.

1. 'He appears wishing to advance, but (at the same time) being kept back :'—all-alone he pursues the correct course. 'Let him maintain a large and generous mind, and there will be no error :'—he has not yet received an official charge.

2. 'He will receive this great blessing :'—for he is in the central place and the correct position for him.

3. 'All (around) trust him :'—their (common) aim is to move upwards and act.

4. '(He advances like) a marmot. However firm and correct he may be, his position is one of peril :'—his place is not that appropriate for him.

5. 'Let him not concern himself whether he fails or succeeds :'—his movement in advance will afford ground for congratulation.

6. 'He uses his horns only to punish (the rebellious people of) his city :'—his course of procedure is not yet brilliant.

Paragraph 1. 'This will lead to exhaustion ;' and from that will follow distress and other evils.

The central position and the due moral mean in paragraph 2 is another instance of the felt analogy referred to above.

In paragraph 3 nothing is added to the Text; and on the symbolism nothing is said.

Paragraph 5. 'He is not in his appropriate place :' this is said simply because an odd place ought to be filled by a strong line.

XXXV. The sun rising above the earth, and then travelling up to his meridian height, readily suggests the idea of advancing. On

XXXVI. (The trigram representing) the earth and that for the bright (sun) entering within it form Ming Î. The superior man, in accordance with this, conducts his management of men ;—he shows his·intelligence by keeping it obscured.

1. 'The superior man (is revolving his) going away:'—(in such a case) he feels it right not to eat.

2. 'The good fortune of (the subject of) the second SIX, divided,' is due to the proper fashion of his acting according to his circumstances.

3. With the aim represented by 'hunting in the south' a great achievement is accomplished.

4. 'He has (just) entered into the left side of the belly (of the dark land):'—he is still able to carry out the idea in his (inner) mind.

5. 'With the firm correctness of the count of Kî,' his brightness could not be (quite) extinguished.

6. 'He had at first ascended to (the top of) the sky:'—he might have enlightened the four quarters

---

the application of this symbolism, Hû Ping-wǎn (Yüan dynasty) says :—' Of strong things there is none so strong as heaven ; and hence the superior man after its pattern makes himself strong ; of bright things there is none so bright as the sun, and after its pattern he makes himself bright.'

If the subject of line 1 had received an official charge, then when unrecognised by his sovereign, and obstructed in his progress, his correct course would have been to cease to advance, and retire from the office in which he was not allowed to carry out his principles.

There is nothing said on line 2 to explain particularly the symbolism of ' the grandmother' in the Text.

' The course of procedure' in paragraph 6 has still an element of force in it, which is more than ' the firm correctness' that was to king Wǎn the ideal character of a feudal lord, and therefore his light is not yet that of the full-orbed sun.

of the kingdom. 'His future shall be to go into the earth :'—he has failed to fulfil the model (of a ruler).

XXXVII. (The trigram representing) fire, and that for wind coming forth from it, form *K*iâ *Z*ăn. The superior man, in accordance with this, orders his words according to (the truth of) things, and his conduct so that it is uniformly consistent.

1. 'He establishes restrictive regulations in his household :'—(he does so), before any change has taken place in their wills.

2. 'The good fortune attached to the second SIX, (divided),' is due to the docility (of its subject), operating with humility.

3. When 'the members of the household are treated with stern severity,' there has been no (great) failure (in the regulation of the family). When 'wife and children are smirking and chattering,' the (proper) economy of the family has been lost.

4. 'The family is enriched, and there is great

XXXVI. The application of the Great Symbolism here is in itself sufficiently natural ; but this meaning of the hexagram hardly appears in the text, till we come to the sixth line.

Paragraph 1. 'He thinks it right not to eat ;'—he does not purposely fast ; but when he has nothing to eat, he does not complain. He thinks it right that it should be so in the case.

Paragraph 2. 'The proper fashion of acting' is suggested by the weak line's being in the central place.

Paragraph 3. 'The great achievement is accomplished ;' but such achievement was not what prompted to action.

Paragraph 4. 'The idea in his inner mind' is the idea of withdrawing from the position and escaping ; but the meaning is obscure. See on the Text.

good fortune:'—this is due to the docility (belonging to the subject of the line), and its being in its correct place.

5. 'The influence of the king' extends to his family:'—the intercourse between them is that of mutual love.

6. 'The good fortune connected with the display of majesty' describes (the result of) the recovery of the true character.

XXXVII. The Symbolism here is certainly far-fetched. 'As wind,' it is said, 'comes first from fire, so does transforming influence emanate from the family.' But the subject of the hexagram is the regulation and not the influence of the family. Then the application is good for the superior man's cultivation of himself; but this again is only connected indirectly with the regulation of the family.

The sooner preventive measures are presented to the youthful mind the better; but does not prohibition imply that a change in the good will has taken place?

In paragraph 2 'docility' is suggested by the weak line. 'The humility' comes out of Sun, the upper trigram, whose attribute is pliant flexibility.

Yü Yen (Yüan dynasty) ingeniously observes on paragraph 4 that the riches of a family are not to be sought in its wealth, but in the affection and harmony of its members. Where these prevail, the family is not likely to be poor, and whatever it has will be well preserved.

The mention 'of mutual love' is unusual in Chinese writings, and must be considered remarkable here. 'The husband,' says Khäng-ȝze, 'loves his helpmate in the house; the wife loves him who is the pattern for the family.' But however admirable the sentiment is, it comes from the mind of the writer, and is not drawn from the Text.

Paragraph 6. It is said on this, that the majesty is not designedly assumed or put on; but the effect of the character remoulded and perfected. The words of Mencius are aptly quoted in illustration of the lesson :—'If a man himself do not walk in the (right) path, it will not be walked in (even) by his wife and children.'

XXXVIII. (The trigram representing) fire above, and that for (the waters of) a marsh below, form Khwei. The superior man, in accordance with this, where there is a general agreement, yet admits diversity.

1. 'He meets with bad men (and communicates with them):'—(he does so), to avoid the evil of their condemnation.

2. 'He happens to meet with his lord in a bye-passage:'—but he has not deviated (for this meeting) from the (proper) course.

3. 'We see his carriage dragged back:'—this is indicated by the inappropriateness of the position (of the line).

'There is no (good) beginning, but there will be a (good) end:'—this arises from his meeting with the strong (subject of the topmost line).

4. 'They blend their sincere desires together, and there will be no error:'—their (common) aim is carried into effect.

5. 'With his hereditary minister (he unites closely and easily) as if he were biting through a piece of skin:'—his going forward will afford ground for congratulation.

6. 'The good fortune symbolised by meeting with (genial) rain' springs from the passing away of all doubts.

XXXVIII. The application here of the Symbolism is correct, but neither of them comes up to the idea of disunion which is in Khwei.

The various paragraphs seem to need no illustration beyond what may be found in the notes on the Text.

XXXIX. (The trigram representing) a mountain, and above it that for water, form *K*ien. The superior man, in accordance with this, turns round (and examines) himself, and cultivates his virtue.

1. 'Advancing will conduct to (greater) difficulties, while remaining stationary will afford ground for praise:'—the proper course is to wait.

2. 'The minister of the king struggles with difficulty on difficulty:'—in the end no blame will be attached to him.

3. 'He advances, (but only) to (greater) difficulty; he remains stationary, and returns to his former associates:'—they, (represented in) the inner (trigram), rejoice in him.

4. 'To advance will (only be to) encounter (greater) difficulties; he remains stationary, and unites (with the subject of the line above):'—that is in its proper place and has the solidity (due to it in that position).

5. 'He struggles with the greatest difficulties, while friends are coming (to help him):'—he is in the central position, and possesses the requisite virtue.

6. 'To advance will (only) increase the difficulties, while his remaining stationary will (be productive of) great (merit):'—his aim is to assist the (subject of the line) inside of him.

'It will be advantageous to meet the great man:'—by his course he follows that noble (lord of the figure).

XXXIX. The Symbolism is described here a little differently from the form of it in Appendix I. *K*ẚng-ʓze brings the same meaning out of it, however, in the following way :—'We have here a steep and difficult mountain, and again on the top of that there

XL. (The trigram representing) thunder and that for rain, with these phenomena in a state of manifestation, form *K*ieh.   The superior man, in accordance with this, forgives errors, and deals gently with crimes.

1. The strong (fourth) line and the weak line here are in correlation:—we judge rightly in saying that 'its subject will commit no error.'

2. 'The good fortune springing from the firm correctness of the second NINE,(undivided),'is due to its subject holding the due mean.

3. For 'a porter with his burden to be riding in a carriage' is a thing to be ashamed of. 'It is he himself that tempts the robbers to come:'—on whom besides can we lay the blame? (See Appendix III, i, 48.)

4. 'Remove your toes:'—the places (of this line

---

is water; each of the two trigrams is an emblem of perilousness. There is peril, both above and below, in the figure; and hence it represents the difficulties of the state.' The application of the symbolism is illustrated by the words of Mencius, 'When we do not, by what we do, realise (what we desire), we must turn inwards and examine ourselves in every point.'

From the lesson in paragraph 2 we saw that the moral value of conduct is independent of failure or success. It is said, 'Though the difficulties be too great for him to overcome, the sage accepts his desire, in order to stimulate others to loyal devotedness.'

On paragraph 3, Khung Ying-tâ says:—'Of the three lines of the lower trigram only the third is yang, above the two others which are of the yin nature. They cling to it, and are represented as if rejoicing in it.

The view given of paragraph 4 is that of the Khang-hsî editors.

'The friends' in paragraph 5 are the subjects of the second line, the correlate of 5, and also of the two other lines of the lower trigram.

Sû Shih (A.D. 1036–1101) remarks on paragraph 6 that by 'the inside,' and 'the noble,' we are to understand the subject of line 5.

and of the third and first) are all inappropriate to them.

5. When 'the superior man executes his function of removing (whatever is injurious to the idea of the hexagram),' small men will of themselves retire.

6. 'A prince with his bow shoots a falcon:'—thus he removes (the promoters of) rebellion.

XLI. (The trigram representing) a mountain and beneath it that for the waters of a marsh form Sun. The superior man, in accordance with this, restrains his wrath and represses his desires.

1. 'He suspends his own affairs and hurries away (to help the subject of the fourth line) :'—the (subject of that) upper (line) mingles his wishes with his.

XL. It is a common saying that thunder and rain clear the atmosphere, and a feeling of oppression is relieved. The last paragraph of Appendix I, however, leads us to understand the Symbolism of the phenomena of spring. The application seems to refer to the gentle policy of a conqueror forward to forgive the opposition of those who offer no more resistance.

The subject of line 2 is a minister or officer; and the Khang-hsî editors say that while straightforwardness, symbolised by the arrow, is the first duty of an officer, if he do not temper that quality by pursuing the due medium, which is symbolised by the yellow colour of the arrow, but proceed by main force, and that only, to remove what is evil, he will provoke indignation and rebellion. The 'three foxes' are not alluded to in this second paragraph.

On paragraph 4 the same editors say :—'The subject of this line is not in the central nor in an odd place; he has for his correlate the subject of line 1 and for his close associate that of line 3, both of which lines are weak in strong places. Hence it is said, that they are all in places inappropriate to them.'

What paragraph 5 says, that 'the small men retire,' means that believing in the sincerity of the ruler's determination to remove all evil men, they retire of themselves, or strive to conform to his wishes.

2. 'It will be advantageous for (the subject of) the second NINE, (undivided), to maintain his firm correctness :'—his central position gives its character to his aim.

3. 'One man, walking,' (finds his friend) :—when three are together, doubts rise among them.

4. 'He diminishes the ailment under which he labours :'—this is matter for joy.

5. 'The great good fortune attached to the fifth SIX, (divided),' is due to the blessing from above.

6. 'He gives increase to others without taking from what is his own :'—he obtains his wish on a grand scale.

XLI. 'The waters of a marsh are continually rising up in vapour to bedew the hill above it, and thus increase its verdure ; what is taken from the marsh gives increase to the hill.' This is very far-fetched. In the application again the superior man acts only on himself, and for himself ;—which has nothing to do with those of low degree giving to those above them. This application, however, agrees with what, as we have seen on the Text, was *Kh*äng-ȝze's view of the meaning of the hexagram.

The explanation appended to paragraph 1 seems to be to account for the subject of line 1 hurrying away to the help of line 4.

'His aim' is to abide where he is, and help the subject of 5 by the exhibition of 'firm correctness.'

The Khang-hsî editors observe that paragraph 3 is true indeed of three men ; and not of three men only, but of many repetitions of thought or action.

The same editors say on paragraph 5 that 'the blessing from above is explained, by many, of the oracles obtained through divining with the tortoise-shell ; but that looking at the text on line 2 of the next hexagram, and that Tî (spoken of there) is the lord of all spirits, the term " above" here is most naturally explained of Heaven's mind, whose acceptance cannot be gainsaid by men or spirits.'

*Kh*äng-ȝze says on paragraph 6, though I do not see the rele-

XLII. (The trigram representing) wind and that for thunder form Yî. The superior man, in accordance with this, when he sees what is good, moves towards it; and when he sees his errors, he turns from them.

1. 'If the movement be greatly fortunate, no blame will be imputed to him:'—though it is not for one in so low a position to have to do with great affairs.

2. 'Parties add to his stores:'—they come from beyond (his immediate circle) to do so.

3. 'Increase is given by means of what is evil and difficult:'—as he has in himself (the qualities called forth).

4. 'His advice to his prince is followed:'—his (only) object in it being the increase (of the general good).

5. '(The ruler) with sincere heart seeks to benefit (all below):'—there need be no question (about the result). '(All below) with sincere heart acknowledge (his goodness):'—he gets what he desires on a great scale.

6. 'To his increase none will contribute:'—this expresses but half the result. 'Many will seek to assail him:'—they will come from beyond (his immediate circle) to do so.

---

vancy of his remarks:—'Dwelling on high, and taking nothing from those below him, but on the contrary giving more to them, the superior man accomplishes his aim on a grand scale. The aim of the superior man is simply to be increasing what others have;—that and nothing else.'

XLII. The Symbolism here is different from what we gather from the former Appendix. Sun no longer symbolises wood, but, as

XLIII. (The trigram representing) heaven and that for the waters of a marsh mounting above it form Kwâi. The superior man, in accordance with this, bestows emolument on those below him, and dislikes allowing his gifts to accumulate (undispensed).

1. 'Without (being able to) succeed, he goes forward:'—this is an error.

2. 'Though hostile measures be taken against him, he need not be anxious:'—he pursues the course of the due mean.

3. 'The superior man looks bent on cutting off the culprit:'—there will in the end be no error.

4. 'He walks slowly and with difficulty:'—he is not in the place appropriate to him.

'He hears these words, but does not believe them:'—he hears, but does not understand.

5. 'If his action be in harmony with his central

---

it more commonly does, wind. Thunder and wind, it is supposed, increase each the other; and their combination gives the idea of increase. Then the application, good in itself, must be treated very nicely, as it is by the Khang-hsî editors, in order to make out any connexion between it and the Symbolism.

Paragraph 1. 'One in a low position should not move in great affairs;'—not a son, it is said, while his father is alive; nor a minister, while his ruler governs; nor a member of an official department, while its head directs its affairs. If such a one do initiate such an affair, only great success will excuse his rashness.

Paragraph 2. Line 5 is the proper correlate of 2; and its subject will be among the contributing parties. But others 'beyond' will be won to take part with him.

Paragraph 3. There is a soul of good even in men who seem only evil; and adversity may quicken it.

Paragraph 6. As in line 2 the attractive power of benevolence is shown, so in line 6 we have the repulsive power of selfishness exhibited. Mark the 'from beyond' in both paragraphs.

position, there will be no error :'—but his standing in the due mean is not yet clearly displayed.

6. 'There is the misery of having none on whom to call :'—the end will be that he cannot continue any longer.

XLIV. (The trigram representing) wind and that for the sky above it form Kâu. The sovereign, in accordance with this, delivers his charges, and promulgates his announcements throughout the four quarters (of the kingdom).

1. 'Tied and fastened to a metal drag :'—(this

XLIII. We can only understand the mounting of the waters of a marsh up into the sky of the phenomenon of evaporation ; and certainly the waters so formed into clouds will be condensed, and come down again as rain. This may be taken as an image of dispersion, but not of displacement in the sense of the Text of the hexagram.

The first clause of the application follows naturally enough from the above interpretation of the Symbolism. Kû Hsî says he does not understand the second clause. Many critics adopt the view of it which appears in the translation.

Paragraph 2 does not mention the precautionary measures taken in the Text by the subject of the line, from which the conclusion would follow quite as naturally as from his central position. The Khang-hsî editors, however, say that the not having recourse lightly to force is itself the due course.

Line 3 responding, and alone of all the strong lines responding to 6, may appear at first irresolute, and not prepared for decided measures; but 'in the end' its subject does what is required of him.

The contiguity of line 5 to the divided 6, is supposed to have some bad effect on its subject, so that while he does what his central position requires, it is not without an effort. 'If a man,' says Khäng-ȝze, 'cherish a single illicit desire in his mind, he has left the right way. The admonition here conveyed is deep.'

describes the arrest of) the weak (line) in its advancing course.

2. 'He has a wallet of fish :'—it is right for him not to allow (the subject of the first line) to get to the guests.

3. 'He walks with difficulty :'—but his steps have not yet been drawn (into the course of the first line).

4. 'The evil' indicated by there being 'no fish in the wallet' is owing to (the subject of the line) keeping himself aloof from the people.

5. 'The subject of the fifth NINE,(undivided),keeps his brilliant qualities concealed :'—as is indicated by his central and correct position.

'(The good issue) descends (as) from Heaven :'—his aim does not neglect the ordinances (of Heaven).

6. 'He receives others on his horns :'—he is exhausted at his greatest height, and there will be cause for regret.

XLIV. Wind, blowing all-under the sky, penetrates everywhere, and produces its natural effect; and it is a good application of this phenomenon that follows; but it has nothing to do with the meaning of Kâu and the interpretation of the hexagram, as taught in the Text. The Khang-hsî editors perceive this, and deal with the Symbolism after a method of their own, on which it is unnecessary to enter.

Paragraph 1. My supplement, 'This describes the arrest of,' is a conclusion from the whole of the Text on the line. All the commentaries have it.

In the 'Daily Lecture' it is said that the lesson of paragraph 2 is that 'the subject of the line should make the repression of 1 his own exclusive work, and not allow it to pass on to the subject of any of the other lines.' That view is rather different from the one indicated in my supplement.

'His steps have not been drawn into the course of the first

XLV. (The trigram representing the) earth and that for the waters of a marsh raised above it form 3hui. The superior man, in accordance with this, has his weapons of war put in good repair, to be prepared against unforeseen contingencies.

1. 'In consequence disorder is brought into the sphere of his union:'—his mind and aim are thrown into confusion.

2. 'He is led forward; there will be good fortune, and freedom from error:'—(the virtue proper to) his central place has not undergone any change.

3. 'If he go forward, he will not err:'—in the subject of the topmost line there is humility and condescension.

4. 'If he be grandly fortunate, he will receive no blame:'—(this condition is necessary, because) his position is not the one proper to him.

5. 'There is the union (of all) under him in the place of dignity:'—(but) his mind and aim have not yet been brilliantly displayed.

---

line:'—we have to supply, 'and therefore there will be no great error.'

Paragraph 4. See what is said on the Text. But that the subject of the line stands alone is owing, it is here implied, to his own impatience. If he could exercise forbearance, he would find a proper opportunity to check the advance of the subject of line 1.

The subject of line 5, while mindful of his task in the hexagram,— to repress the advance symbolised by 1,—yet keeps his wise plans concealed till the period of carrying them into execution, determined by the ordinances of Heaven, has arrived. Then comes the successful stroke of his policy as if it were directly from Heaven.

The subject of line 6 really accomplishes nothing to repress the advance of the unworthy; but he keeps himself from evil communication with them. He is not to be charged with blameable error, though more and better might have been expected of him.

6. 'He sighs and weeps:'—he does not yet rest in his topmost position.

XLVI. (The trigram representing) wood and that for the earth with the wood growing in the midst of it form Shăng. The superior man, in accordance with this, pays careful attention to his virtue, and accumulates the small developments of it till it is high and great.

1. 'He is welcomed in his advance upwards, and there will be great good fortune:'—(the subjects of) the upper (trigram) are of the same mind with him.

2. 'The sincerity of the subject of the second NINE, undivided,' affords occasion for joy.

3. 'He advances upwards (as into) an empty city:'— he has no doubt or hesitation.

4. 'The king employs him to prevent his offerings on mount *Khî* :'—such a service (of spiritual Beings) is according to (their mind).

XLV. What has this Great Symbolism to do with the idea and preservation of union? The question is answered in this way:—A marsh whose waters are high up above the earth must be kept in by banks and dykes, to keep them together, to preserve them from being dispersed. So the union of a people must be preserved by precautions against what would disturb and destroy it. Of such precautions the chief is to be prepared to resist attack from without, and to put down internal sedition.

Paragraph 3. The topmost line is the last in T u i, whose attribute is complacent satisfaction, appearing in flexibility or docility.

Paragraph 5. 'His mind and aim have not yet been brilliantly displayed:'—this is in explanation of the case that some may even still not have confidence in him.

Paragraph 6. The topmost position is that of the trigram; the subject of the line might bid farewell to all the work of the hexagram; but he cannot bear to do so.

5. 'He is firmly correct, and will therefore enjoy good fortune. He ascends the stairs (with all due ceremony) :'—he grandly succeeds in his aim.

6. 'He blindly advances upwards,' and is in the highest place:—but there is decay in store for him, and he will not (preserve) his riches.

XLVII. (The trigram representing) a marsh, and (below it that for a defile, which has drained the other dry so that there is) no water in it, form Khwăn. The superior man, in accordance with this, will sacrifice his life in order to carry out his purpose.

1. 'He enters a dark valley:'—so benighted is he, and without clear vision.

2. 'He is straitened amidst his wine and viands:'—(but) his position is central, and there will be ground for congratulation.

XLVI. See what has been said on the Great Symbolism in Appendix I. The application which is made of it here may be accepted, though it has nothing to do with the teaching of the Text about the gradual rise of a good officer to high social distinction and influence.

Paragraph 1. Instead of finding in this the three lines of Khwăn and their subjects, Khăng-ȝze makes 'the upper' denote only line 2.

Paragraph 2. The subject of line 2 in his loyal devotion to 5 will do much good and benefit many; hence we have the words, 'affords occasion for joy.'

Paragraph 3. 'He has no doubt or hesitation :'—but this is presuming rather on his strength.

Paragraph 4. The Khang-hsî editors say :—'Such an employment of men of worth to do service to spiritual Beings is serving them according to their mind.'

Paragraph 6. When one has reached the greatest height, he should think of retiring. Ambition otherwise may overleap itself.

3. 'He lays hold of thorns :'—(this is suggested by the position of the line) above the strong (line).

'He enters his palace, and does not see his wife :'—this is inauspicious.

4. 'He proceeds very slowly (to help the subject of the first line):'—his aim is directed to (help) that lower (line). Although he is not in his appropriate place, he and that other will (in the end) be together.

5. 'His nose and feet are cut off :'—his aim has not yet been gained.

'He is leisurely, however, in his movements, and is satisfied :'—his position is central and (his virtue) is correct.

'It will be well for him to be (as sincere as) in sacrificing :'—so shall he receive blessing.

6. 'He is straitened as if bound with creepers :'—(his spirit and action) are unsuitable.

'(He says), "If I move, I shall repent of it." And he does repent (of former errors), which leads to good fortune :'—so he (now) goes on.

XLVII. The first sentence of the Great Symbolism is constructed differently from any which has presented itself in the previous 46 hexagrams. Literally translated, it would be 'a marsh with no water is Khwăn;' and this might certainly suggest to us a condition of distress. But how does this come out of the trigrams? The upper one is Tui, representing a marsh; and the lower is Khân, representing water in a defile. The collocation of the two suggests the running of the water from the marsh or lake into the stream, which will soon empty the other. Such is the view which occurred to myself; and it is the same as that given by *K*û Hsî :—' The water descending and leaking away, the marsh above will become dry.' The application is good in itself, but the concatenation between it and the Symbolism is hardly discernible.

XLVIII. (The trigram representing) wood and above it that for water form 3ing. The superior man, in accordance with this, comforts the people, and stimulates them to mutual helpfulness.

1. 'A well so muddy that men will not drink of it:'—this is indicated by the low position (of the line).

'An old well to which the birds do not come:'— it has been forsaken in the course of time.

2. 'A well from which by a hole the water escapes, and flows away to the shrimps:'—(the subject of this second line has) none co-operating with him (above).

3. 'The well has been cleared out, but is not used:'—(even) passers-by would be sorry for this.

A prayer is made 'that the king were intelligent:'—for then blessing would be received.

4. 'A well the lining of which is well laid. There will be no error:'—the well has been put in good repair.

5. 'The waters from the cold spring are (freely) drunk:'—this is indicated by the central and correct position (of the line).

6. 'The great good fortune' at the topmost place

So stupid is the subject of line 1 that by his own act he increases his distress.

The Khang-hsî editors say that the 'ground for congratulation in paragraph 2 is the banqueting and sacrificing.' I rather think it is the measure of help, which it is intimated the subject will give in removing the straitness and distress of the time.

See the extract from the Khang-hsî editors on the symbolism of the third line of the Text.

The difficulties attending the symbolism of the Text of lines 4, 5, and 6 are not lightened by what we find in this Appendix.

indicates the grand accomplishment (of the idea in the hexagram).

XLIX. (The trigram representing the waters of) a marsh and that for fire in the midst of them form Ko. The superior man, in accordance with this, regulates his (astronomical) calculations, and makes clear the seasons and times.

1. 'He is bound with (the skin of) a yellow ox :'—he should in his circumstances be taking action.

2. 'He makes his changes when some time has passed :'—what he does will be matter of admiration.

3. 'The change (contemplated) has been three times fully discussed :'—to what else should attention (now) be directed ?

4. 'The good fortune consequent on changing (existing) ordinances' is due to the faith reposed in his aims.

5. 'The great man produces his changes as the tiger does when he changes his stripes :'—their beauty becomes more brilliant.

XLVIII. The Great Symbolism here may well enough represent a well, it being understood that the water which is above the wood is that raised by it for irrigation and other uses. What is said, moreover, in the application is more akin to the idea of the hexagram than in most of the other cases. It is certainly one way in which the ruler should nourish the people.

It is said on paragraph 1 :—'Those who have a mind to do something in the world, when they look at this line, and its symbolism, will learn how they ought to exert themselves.'

Rather in opposition to what I have said on the Text of line 4, the 'Daily Lecture' observes here :—'The cultivation of one's self, which is represented here, is fundamental to the government of others.'

6. 'The superior man produces his changes as the leopard does when he changes his spots:'—their beauty becomes more elegant.

'Small men change their faces:'—they show themselves prepared to follow their ruler.

L. (The trigram representing) wood and above it that for fire form Ting. The superior man, in accordance with this, keeps his every position correct, and maintains secure the appointment (of Heaven).

1. 'The caldron is overturned, and its feet turned upwards:'—but this is not (all) contrary (to what is right).

'There will be advantage in getting rid of what was bad:'—thereby (the subject of the line) will follow the more noble (subject of the fourth line).

2. 'There is the caldron with the things (to be cooked) in it:'— let (the subject of the line) be careful where he goes.

'My enemy dislikes me:'—but there will in the end be no fault (to which he can point).

3. 'There is the caldron with (the places for) its

XLIX. Wise men, occupying themselves with the determination of the seasons and questions of time, have in all ages based their judgments on the observation of the heavenly bodies. We find this insisted on in the first book of the Shû, by the ancient Yâo. But how this application of the Great Symbolism really flows from it, I must confess myself unable to discover. Once, however, when I was conversing about the Yî with a high Chinese dignitary, who was a well-read scholar also so far as his own literature was concerned, he referred to this paragraph as proving that all our western science had been known to Fû-hsî and Confucius !

What is said on the several lines is sufficiently illustrated in the notes on the Text.

ears changed :'—(its subject) has failed in what was required of him (in his situation).

4. 'The contents designed for the ruler's use are overturned and spilt :'—how can (the subject of the line) be trusted?

5. 'The caldron has yellow ears :'—the central position (of the line) is taken as (a proof of) the solid (virtue of its subject).

6. 'The rings of jade' are at the very top :—the strong and the weak meet in their due proportions.

LI. (The trigram representing) thunder, being repeated, forms *K*ăn. The superior man, in accordance with this, is fearful and apprehensive, cultivates (his virtue), and examines (his faults).

1. 'When the (time of) movement comes, he will be found looking out with apprehension :'— that feeling of dread leads to happiness.

L. The Great Symbolism here has come before us in the treatise on the Thwan. Of the application of that symbolism I can only say that, as has been seen in many other hexagrams, while good enough in itself, it is far-fetched.

The same remark may be made on the explanation of the Text of the first line. I can myself do little more than guess at its meaning. The Khang-hsî editors observe that nothing is said about the case of the 'concubine' in the Text; but that it is covered by the 'following the more noble,' 'so condensed and complete are the words of the sage!'

The same editors find a pregnant sense in the conclusion of paragraph 2 :—'There will be no fault in me to which my enemy can point, and his disposition to find fault will be diminished.'

'What was required of the caldron in the third line was that that line and line 5, instead of 6, should be correlates;' but there is little meaning in such a statement.

The subject of line 4 cannot be trusted again. He has failed in doing what was his proper work.

'He yet smiles and talks cheerfully:'—the issue (of his dread) is that he adopts (proper) laws (for his course).

2. 'When the movement approaches, he is in a position of peril:'—(a weak line) is mounted on a strong (one).

3. 'He is distraught amid the startling movements going on:'—(the third line) is in a position unsuitable to it.

4. 'Amid the startling movements, he sinks supinely in the mud:'—the light in him has not yet been brilliantly developed.

5. 'He goes and comes amid the startling movements, and (always) in peril:'—full of risk are his doings.

'What he has to do has to be done in his central position:'—far will he be from incurring any loss.

6. 'Amid the startling movements he is in breathless dismay:'—he has not found out (the course of) the due mean.

'Though evil (threatens), he will not fall into error:'—he is afraid of being warned by his neighbours.

LII. (Two trigrams representing) a mountain, one over the other, form Kăn. The superior man, in

---

LI. The account of the Great Symbolism here calls for no remark. Nor does the application of it; but may it not be too late to fear, and order anew one's thoughts and actions when the retributions in providence are taking place? Commentators are haunted by the shadow of this question; but they are unable rightly to meet it.

Paragraph 1 is the same as 2 in Appendix I.

Paragraph 4. Compare paragraph 4 of hexagram 21, Appendix II.

accordance with this, does not go in his thoughts beyond the (duties of the) position in which he is.

1. 'He keeps his toes at rest:'—he does not fail in what is correct (according to the idea of the figure).

2. 'He cannot help him whom he follows:'—(he whom he follows) will not retreat to listen to him.

3. 'He keeps the loins at rest:'—the danger (from his doing so) produces a glowing heat in the heart.

4. 'He keeps the trunk of his body at rest:'—he keeps himself free (from agitation).

5. 'He keeps his cheek bones at rest:'—in harmony with his central position he acts correctly.

6. 'There is good fortune through his devotedly maintaining his restfulness:'—to the end he shows himself generous and good.

LII. According to the view of the Khang-hsî editors, the application should be translated:—'The superior man, in accordance with this, thinks anxiously how he shall not go beyond the duties of his position.' It is difficult to decide between this shade of the meaning, and the more common one which I have followed.

The toes play a great part in walking; but they are here kept at rest, and so do not lose the correct idea of Kăn.

There is no correlation between lines 2 and 3, and thence the subject of 3 will hold on its upward way without condescending to 2.

*Kh*ăng-ʒze finds an unsatisfactory auspice in paragraph 4. Line 4 represents a great minister who should be able to guide all to rest where they ought to be; but he can only keep himself from agitation.

Yü Păn (Ming dynasty) says on paragraph 5:—'Words should not be uttered rashly. Then, when uttered, they will be found

LIII. (The trigram representing) a mountain and above it that for a tree form *K*ien. The superior man, in accordance with this, attains to and maintains his extraordinary virtue, and makes the manners of the people good.

1. 'The danger of a small officer (as represented in the first line)' is owing to no fault of his in the matter of what is right.

2. 'They eat and drink joyfully and at ease :'—but not without having earned their food.

3. 'A husband goes and does not return :'—he separates himself from his comrades.

'A wife is pregnant, but will not nourish her child :'—she has failed in her (proper) course.

'It might be advantageous in resisting plunderers :'—by acting as here indicated men would preserve one another.

4. 'They may light on the flat branches :'—there is docility (in the line) going on to flexible penetration.

5. 'In the end the natural issue cannot be prevented. There will be good fortune :'—(the subject of the line) will get what he desires.

6. 'Their feathers can be used as ornaments. There will be good fortune :'—(the object and character of the subject of the line) cannot be disturbed.

---

accordant with principle. But it is only the master of the virtue belonging to the due mean who can attain to this.'

LIII. The Khang-hsî editors, to bring out the suitability of the Great Symbolism and its application, say :—'A tree springing up on the ground is a tree as it begins to grow. A tree on a hill is high and large. Every tree when it begins to grow, shows its

LIV. (The trigram representing the waters of) a marsh and over it that for thunder form K wei M ei. The superior man, in accordance with this, having regard to the far-distant end, knows the mischief (that may be done at the beginning).

1. 'The younger sister is married off in a position ancillary to that of the real wife:'—it is the constant practice (for such a case).

'Lame on one leg, she is able to tramp along :'— she can render helpful service.

2. 'There will be advantage in maintaining the firm correctness of a solitary widow:'—(the subject of

---

branches and twigs gradually becoming long. Every morning and every evening show some difference; and when the tree is high and great, whether it be of an ordinary or extraordinary size, it has taken years to reach its dimensions. This illustrates the difference between the advance in Shăng (46) and that in Kien. Then the maintenance of extraordinary virtue in the application and the improvement of manners is a gradual process. The improvement of the manners, moreover, flows from the maintenance of the extraordinary virtue; which implies also a gradual operation and progress.'

Paragraph 1. The danger is the result of circumstances; the small officer has not brought it on himself.

Paragraph 2. Only the geese appear in this paragraph; but the writer is thinking of the advancing officer. I cannot but think that in the language and sentiment also there is an echo of the Shih King, I, ix, ode 6.

The 'separation from his comrades' has respect to line 3 not finding its correlate in 6. 'The wife's failing in her proper course' has respect to the line being undivided and not in the centre.

Khăng-3ze says, on paragraph 4, that humility and right-doing will find rest and peace in all places and circumstances.

Paragraph 5. 'The natural issue cannot be prevented :'—the wife will have a child; minister and ruler will meet happily.

Paragraph 6. See on the Text. But it is difficult to see the aptness of the symbolism.

the line) has not changed from the constancy (proper to a wife).

3. 'The younger sister who was to be married off is in a mean position:'—this is shown by the improprieties (indicated in the line).

4. (The purpose in) 'protracting the time' is that, after waiting, the thing may be done (all the better).

5. 'The sleeves of the younger sister of (king) Tî-yî, when she was married away, were not equal to those of her (half-) sister, who accompanied her:'—such was her noble character, indicated by the central position of the line.

6. '(What is said in) the sixth six, (divided), about there being nothing in the basket' shows that the subject of it is carrying an empty basket.

LV. (The trigrams representing) thunder and lightning combine to form Făng. The superior man, in accordance with this, decides cases of litigation, and apportions punishments with exactness.

1. 'Though they are both of the same character, there will be no error:'—if the subject of this

---

LIV. Thunder rolling above is supposed to produce movement in the waters of the marsh below. The combination of this symbolism in Kwei Mei is recognised as an evil omen in the case which the name denotes. The application of it is not inappropriate.

Paragraph 1. 'It is the constant practice (for such a case)' seems to mean that an ancillary wife has no right to the disposition of herself, but must do what she is told. Thus it is that the mean position of the younger sister does not interfere with the service she can render.

The addition to the Text of 'the purpose' in paragraph 4 is to show that the putting marriage off is on the part of the lady and not on the other side.

line seek to overpass that similarity, there will be calamity.

2. 'Let him cherish his feeling of sincere devotion, that it shall appear being put forth:'—it is by sincerity that the mind is affected.

3. 'There is an (additional) screen of a large and thick banner:'—great things should not be attempted (in such circumstances).

'He breaks his right arm:'—in the end he will not be fit to be employed.

4. 'He is surrounded by a screen large and thick:'—the position of the line is inappropriate.

'At midday he sees the constellation of the Bushel:'—there is darkness and no light.

'He meets with the subject of the line, undivided like himself. There will be good fortune:'—action may be taken.

5. 'The good fortune indicated by the fifth six, (divided),' is the congratulation (that is sure to arise).

6. 'He has made his house large:'—he soars (in his pride) to the heavens.

'He looks at his door, which is still, with no one about it:'—he (only) keeps himself withdrawn from all others.

LV. Lightning appears here as the natural phenomenon of which Lî is the symbol. The virtues attributed to the two trigrams are certainly required in the application of them which is subjoined; but that application has little or nothing to do with the explanation of the hexagram supplied by the Text.

I hardly understand the conclusion of paragraph 1. My translation of it is according to the view of Kû Hsî, if I rightly understand that.

Paragraph 2. It is by such sincerity that the mind is affected,—that is, the mind of the ruler occupying line 5.

LVI. (The trigram representing) a mountain and above it that for fire form Lü. The superior man, in accordance with this, exerts his wisdom and caution in the use of punishments and not allowing litigations to continue.

1. 'The stranger is mean and meanly occupied:'—his aim is become of the lowest character, and calamity will ensue.

2. 'He is provided with good and trusty servants:'—he will in the end have nothing of which to complain.

3. 'The stranger burns his lodging-house:'—and he himself also suffers hurt thereby. When, as a stranger, he treats those below him (as the line indicates), the right relation between him and them is lost.

4. 'The stranger is in a resting-place:'—but he has not got his proper position.

'He has the means of livelihood, and the axe:'—but his mind is not at ease.

5. 'In the end he will obtain praise and a (high) charge:'—he has reached a high place.

6. 'Considering that the stranger is here at the very height (of distinction),' with the spirit that possesses him, it is right he (should be emblemed by a bird) burning (its nest).

Line 3 has a correlate in 6, which is weak, and as it were out of the game. The light in 3 moreover is hidden. Hence the symbolism; and through the blindness of its subject his hurt, which unfits him to be employed.

The line undivided like 4 is 1; perhaps we might translate— 'He meets with the subject of the parallel line.'

No one but himself has any confidence in the subject of line 6. He holds himself aloof from others, and they leave him to himself.

'He loses his ox(-like docility) too readily and easily:'—to the end he would not listen to (the truth about the course to be pursued).

LVII. (Two trigrams representing) wind, following each other, form Sun. The superior man, in accordance with this, reiterates his orders, and secures the practice of his affairs.

1. '(Now) he advances, (now) he recedes:'—his mind is perplexed.

'It would be advantageous for him to have the

LVI. Different attempts are made to bring the idea of a travelling stranger out of the trigrams Kăn and Lî; but none of them is satisfactory. Let Khung Ying-tâ's view serve as a specimen of them :—'A fire on a mountain lays hold of the grass, and runs with it over the whole space, not stopping anywhere long, and soon disappearing ;—such is the emblem of the traveller.' The application may be derived well enough from the attributes of the trigrams ; but does not fit in with the lessons of the Thwan and Hsiang.

The meanness of the subject of line 1 does not arise from the nature of his occupation ; but from his mind and aim being emptied of all that is good and ennobling.

Strong and trusty servants are the most important condition for the comfort and progress of the traveller ; and therefore it alone is resumed and expanded.

The subject of line 3 treats those below him with violence and arrogance, which of course alienates them from him.

'He has not got into his proper position' seems to say no more than that 4 is a strong line in an even place.

It is difficult to say what 'he has reached a high place' means. The fifth line is not in this hexagram the ruler's seat ; but by his qualities and gifts the subject of it attracts the attention and regard of his friends and of his ruler.

The spirit that possesses the subject of line 6 is one of haughty arrogance, with which the humility that ought to characterise him cannot co-exist. His careless self-sufficiency has shut his mind against all lessons of wisdom.

firmness of a brave soldier :'—his mind would in that case be well governed.

2. 'The good fortune springing from what borders on confusion' is due to the position (of the line) in the centre.

3. 'The regret arising from the violent and repeated efforts to penetrate' shows the exhaustion of the will.

4. 'He takes game in his hunting, enough for the threefold use of it :'—he achieves merit.

5. 'The good fortune of (the subject of) the fifth NINE, undivided,' is owing to its correct position and its being in the centre.

6. 'The representative of penetration is beneath a couch :'—though occupying the topmost place, his powers are exhausted.

'He has lost the axe with which he executed his decisions :'—though he try to be correct, there will be evil.

LVII. I have said on the Thwan that some commentators make the upper trigram symbolical of the ordinances of the ruler and the lower symbolical of the obedience of the people. E. g., Khäng-ȝze says :—'Superiors, in harmony with the duty of inferiors, issue their commands; inferiors, in harmony with the wishes of their superiors, follow them. Above and below there are that harmony and deference; and this is the significance of the redoubled Sun. When governmental commands and business are in accordance with what is right, they agree with the tendencies of the minds of the people who follow them.'

Paragraph 2 seems to say that the sincerity of purpose indicated by the central position of the second line conducts its subject to the right course, despite the many considerations that might distract him.

'The will is exhausted' in paragraph 3 intimates that 'the repeated efforts' made by its subject have exhausted him. He can now only regret his failures.

LVIII. (Two symbols representing) the waters of a marsh, one over the other, form Tui. The superior man, in accordance with this, (encourages) the conversation of friends and (the stimulus of) their (common) practice.

1. 'The good fortune attached to the pleasure of (inward) harmony' arises from there being nothing in the conduct (of the subject ôf the line) to awaken doubt.

2. 'The good fortune attached to the pleasure arising from (inward sincerity)' is due to the confidence felt in the object (of the subject of the line).

3. 'The evil predicated of one's bringing around himself whatever can give pleasure' is shown by the inappropriateness of the place (of the line).

4. 'The joy in connexion with (the subject of) the fourth NINE, (undivided),' is due to the happiness (which he will produce).

5. 'He trusts in one who would injure him :'— his place is that which is correct and appropriate.

6. 'The topmost six, (divided), shows the pleasure (of its subject) in leading and attracting others :'— his (virtue) is not yet brilliant.

What is said in paragraph 6 proceeds on a different view of the Text from that which I have followed.

LVIII. The application of the Great Symbolism here will recall to many readers the Hebrew maxims in Proverbs xxvii. 17, 19. The sentiment of it, however, does not readily fit in to the teaching of the hexagram as set forth in the Text.

There is nothing in the conduct of the subject of line 1 to awaken suspicion. He has as yet taken no action; but it was not necessary to say anything like this about the subject of line 2, his central position being an assurance that he would never do anything of a doubtful character.

LIX. (The trigram representing) water and that for wind moving above the water form Hwân. The ancient kings, in accordance with this, presented offerings to God and established the ancestral temple.

1. 'The good fortune attached to the first SIX, (divided),'is due to the natural course (pursued by its subject).

2. 'Amidst the prevailing dispersion, he hurries to his contrivance (for security):'—he gets what he desires.

3. 'He has no regard to his own person:'—his aim is directed to what is external to himself.

4. 'He scatters the (different) parties (in the state), and there is great good fortune:'—brilliant and great (are his virtue and service).

5. 'The accumulations of the royal (granaries) are dispersed, and there is no error:'—this is due to the correctness of the position.

6. 'His bloody wounds are gone:'—he is far removed from the danger of injury.

Line 3 should be strong, and the desire of pleasure which is the idea of the hexagram leads its weak subject to the course which is so emphatically condemned.

Paragraph 5 is incomplete. Does the correctness and appropriateness of the position of the subject of the line afford any explanation of his trusting the subject of the weak line above, who would only injure him? It ought to keep him on the contrary from doing so. The commentators have seen this, and say that the paragraph is intended by way of caution.

The action of the hexagram should culminate and end in line 5. But the subject of it has not made brilliant attainment in the firmness and correctness by which the love of pleasure should be controlled.

LIX. The 'in accordance with this' must be equivalent to—'to remedy the state of things thus symbolised.' What follows certainly

LX. (The trigram representing) a lake, and above it that for water, form *K*ieh. The superior man, in accordance with this, constructs his (methods of) numbering and measurement, and discusses (points of) virtue and conduct.

1. 'He does not quit the courtyard outside his door :'—he knows when he has free course and when he is obstructed.

2. 'He does not quit the courtyard inside his gate. There will be evil :'—he loses the time (for action) to an extreme degree.

3. In 'the lamentation for not observing the (proper) regulations,' who should there be to blame?

4. 'The progress and success of the quiet and natural (attention) to all regulations' is due to the deference which accepts the ways of (the ruler) above.

5. 'The good fortune arising from the regulations enacted sweetly and acceptably' is due to (the line)

---

amounts to this, that the ancient kings considered the services of religion, sincerely and earnestly attended to, as calculated to counteract the tendency to mutual alienation and selfishness in the minds of men. How they operated to have this beneficial effect we are not told. Nor is it easy to account for the extension of what is said in the Text about the establishment of the ancestral temple to the presentation also of offerings to God. Probably the writer had the same idea in his mind as in the Great Symbolism of hexagram 16, q. v.

'The natural course' pursued by the subject of line 1 is, probably, that required by the time.

'What the subject of line 2 desired' would be his success in counteracting the prevailing tendency to disunion.

The view given of paragraph 5 is that propounded by *K*û Hsî.

For paragraph 6 see the note on line 6 under the Text.

occupying the place (of authority) and being in the centre.

6. 'The regulations are severe and difficult. Even with firm correctness there will be evil :'—the course (indicated by the hexagram) is come to an end.

LXI. (The trigram representing the waters of) a marsh and that for wind above it form *K*ung Fû. The superior man, in accordance with this, deliberates about cases of litigation and delays (the infliction of) death.

1. 'The first NINE, (undivided), shows its subject resting (in himself). There will be good fortune :'— no change has yet come over his purpose.

2. 'Her young ones respond to her :'—from the (common) wish of the inmost heart.

3. 'Now he beats his drum, and now he leaves off :'—the position (of the line) is the appropriate one for it.

LX. Various explanations of the Great Symbolism have been attempted. E. g., *Kh*ăng-ʒze says :—'The water which a lake or marsh will contain is limited to a certain quantity. If the water flowing in exceed that, it overflows. This gives us the idea of *K*ieh.' What is found on the application of it is to my mind equally unsatisfactory.

The subject of line 1 knows when he might have free course and when he is obstructed, and acts accordingly. He is regulated by a consideration of the time.

The subject of line 1 ought not to act, and he is still. The subject of line 2 ought to act, and he also is still. The error and the effect of it are great.

The subject of line 3 shows by his lamentation how he blames himself.

The other three paragraphs are sufficiently explained in what is said on the Text.

4. 'A horse the fellow of which disappears:'—he breaks from his (former) companions, and mounts upwards.

5. 'He is perfectly sincere, and links others to him in closest union:'—the place (of the line) is the correct and appropriate one.

6. 'Chanticleer (tries to) mount to heaven:'—but how can (such an effort) continue long?

LXII. (The trigram representing) a hill and that for thunder above it form Hsiâo Kwo. The superior man, in accordance with this, in his conduct exceeds in humility, in mourning exceeds in sorrow, and in his expenditure exceeds in economy.

1. 'There is a bird flying (and ascending) till the result is evil:'—nothing can be done to avoid this issue.

2. 'He does not attempt to reach his ruler:'—

LXI. Dissatisfied with previous attempts to explain the Great Symbolism, the Khang-hsî editors say:—'The wind penetrates things. The grass and trees of the level ground are shaken and tossed by it; the rocky valleys and caverns in their sides have it blowing round about them; and it acts also on the depths of the collected waters, the cold of which disappears and the ice is melted before it. This is what makes it the emblem of that perfect sincerity which penetrates everywhere. The litigations of the people are like the deep and dark places of the earth. The kings examine with discrimination into all secret matters connected with them, even those which are here mentioned, till there is nothing that is not penetrated by their perfect sincerity.' But all this is greatly strained. The symbolism of the eight trigrams gets pretty well played out in the course of the 64 hexagrams.

1. 'No change has come over the purpose:'—the sincerity, that is, perfect in itself and of itself, continues.

2. One bond of loving regard unites the mother bird and her young; so answers the heart of man to man.

a minister should not overpass the distance (between his ruler and himself).

3. 'Some in consequence find opportunity to assail and injure him. There will be evil:'—how great will it be!

4. 'He meets the exigency (of his situation), without exceeding (the proper course):'—(he does so), the position being inappropriate (for a strong line).

'If he go forward, there will be peril, and he must be cautious:'—the result would be that his course would not be long pursued.

5. 'There are dense clouds, but no rain:'—(the line) is in too high a place.

6. 'He does not meet the exigency (of his situation), and exceeds (his proper course):'—(the position indicates) the habit of domineering.

LXIII. (The trigram representing) fire and that for water above it form Kî 3î. The superior

---

LXII. The Khang-hsî editors endeavour to show the appropriateness of the Great Symbolism in this way:—'When thunder issues from the earth, the sound of it comes with a rush and is loud; but when it reaches the top of a hill it has begun to die away and is small.' There is nothing in the Chinese about the hills being high; and readers will only smile at the attempted explanation. The application of the symbolism, or rather of the idea of the hexagram, is good, and in entire accordance with what I have stated that idea to be.

Nothing can be done to avoid the issue mentioned in paragraph 1, for the subject of the line brings it on himself.

Paragraph 2 deals only with the symbolism in the conclusion of what is stated under line 2. The writer takes the view which I have given on the Text.

For paragraphs 3 and 4 see the notes on the Text.

In line 5 the yin line is too high. If the line were yang, the auspice would be different.

man, in accordance with this, thinks of evil (that may come), and beforehand guards against it.

1. 'He drags back his wheel:'—as we may rightly judge, there will be no mistake.

2. 'In seven days she will find it:'—for the course pursued is that indicated by the central position (of the line).

3. 'He was three years in subduing it:'—enough to make him weary.

4. 'He is on his guard all the day:'—he is in doubt about something.

5. 'The slaughtering of an ox by the neighbour in the east is not equal to (the small sacrifice of) the neighbour in the west:'—because the time (in the latter case is more important and fit).

'His sincerity receives the blessing:'—good fortune comes on a great scale.

6. 'His head is immersed; the position is perilous:'—how could such a state continue long?

LXIV. (The trigram representing) water and that for fire above it form Wei 3i. The superior man, in accordance with this, carefully discriminates among (the qualities of) things, and the (different) positions they (naturally) occupy.

1. 'His tail gets immersed:'—this is the very height of ignorance.

LXIII. Water and fire coming together as here, fire under the water, each element occupies its proper place, and their interaction will be beneficial. Such is the common explanation of the Great Symbolism; but the connexion between it and the application of it, which also is good in itself, is by no means clear.

The notes on the different lines present nothing that has not been dealt with in the notes on the Text.

2. 'The second NINE,(undivided),shows good fortune arising from being firm and correct:'—it is in the central place, and the action of its subject thereby becomes correct.

3. '(The state of things is) not yet remedied. Advancing will lead to evil:'—the place (of the line) is not that appropriate for it.

4. 'By firm correctness there is good fortune, and cause for repentance disappears:'—the aim (of the subject of the line) is carried into effect.

5. '(We see) the brightness of a superior man:'— the diffusion of that brightness tends to good fortune.

6. 'He drinks and gets his head immersed:'— he does not know how to submit to the (proper) regulations.

LXIV. In this last hexagram we have water below and fire above, so that the two cannot act on each other, and the Symbolism may represent the unregulated condition of general affairs, the different classes of society not harmonising nor acting together. The application follows naturally.

*K*û Hsî and others suspect an error in the text of paragraph 1; yet a tolerable meaning comes from it as it stands.

The Khang-hsî editors observe on paragraph 2 that an undivided line in the second place, and a divided line in the fifth place, are both incorrect, and yet it is often said of them that with firm correctness in their subjects there will be good fortune ;—such is the virtue of the central position. This principle is at last clearly enunciated in this paragraph.

*Kh*ǎng-ɀze says :—' The subject of line 4 has the ability which the time requires, and possesses also a firm solidity. He can carry out therefore his purpose. There will be good fortune, and all cause for repentance will disappear. The smiting of the demon region was the highest example of firm correctness.'

Both the symbols in paragraph 6 indicate a want of caution, and an unwillingness to submit one's impulses to the regulation of reason and prudence.

APPENDIX III

The Great Appendix   Section I

Chapter I. 1. Heaven is lofty and honourable; earth is low. (Their symbols), *Kh*ien and Khwǎn, (with their respective meanings), were determined (in accordance with this).

Things low and high appear displayed in a similar relation. The (upper and lower trigrams, and the relative position of individual lines, as) noble and mean, had their places assigned accordingly.

Movement and rest are the regular qualities (of their respective subjects). Hence comes the definite distinction (of the several lines) as the strong and the weak.

(Affairs) are arranged together according to their tendencies, and things are divided according to their classes. Hence were produced (the interpretations in the Yî, concerning) what is good [or lucky] and evil [or unlucky].

In the heavens there are the (different) figures there completed, and on the earth there are the (different) bodies there formed. (Corresponding to them) were the changes and transformations exhibited (in the Yî).

2. After this fashion a strong and a weak line were manipulated together (till there were the eight trigrams), and those eight trigrams were added, each to itself and to all the others, (till the sixty-four hexagrams were formed).

3. We have the exciting forces of thunder and lightning; the fertilising influences of wind and rain; and the revolutions of the sun and moon, which give rise to cold and warmth.

4. The attributes expressed by *Kh*ien constitute the male; those expressed by Khwăn constitute the female.

5. *Kh*ien (symbolises Heaven, which) directs the great beginnings of things; Khwăn (symbolises Earth, which) gives to them their completion.

6. It is by the ease with which it proceeds that *Kh*ien directs (as it does), and by its unhesitating response that Khwăn exhibits such ability.

7. (He who attains to this) ease (of Heaven) will be easily understood, and (he who attains to this) freedom from laborious effort (of the Earth) will be easily followed. He who is easily understood will have adherents, and he who is easily followed will achieve success. He who has adherents can continue long, and he who achieves success can become great. To be able to continue long shows the virtue of the wise and able man; to be able to become great is the heritage he will acquire.

8. With the attainment of such ease and such freedom from laborious effort, the mastery is got of all principles under the sky. With the attainment of that mastery, (the sage) makes good his position in the middle (between heaven and earth).

Chapter I is an attempt to show the correspondency between the phenomena of external nature ever changing, and the figures of the Yî King ever varying. The first four paragraphs, it is said, show, from the phenomena of production and transformation in external

Chapter II. 9. The sages set forth the diagrams, inspected the emblems contained in them, and appended their explanations;—in this way the good fortune and bad (indicated by them) were made clear.

10. The strong and the weak (lines) displace each other, and produce the çhanges and transformations (in the figures).

11. Therefore the good fortune and evil (mentioned in the explanations) are the indications of the right and wrong (in men's conduct of affairs), and the repentance and regret (similarly mentioned) are the indications of their sorrow and anxiety.

---

nature, the principles on which the figures of the Yî were made. The fifth and sixth paragraphs show, particularly, how the attributes represented by the figures *Kh*ien and Khwăn are to be found in (the operations of) heaven and earth. The last two paragraphs show both those attributes embodied or realised in man. The realisation takes place, indeed, fully only in the sage or the ideal man, who thus becomes the pattern for all men.

In paragraph 3 we have five of the six derivative trigrams;—the six 'children,' according to the nomenclature of the Wăn arrangement. 'Thunder' stands for *k*ăn (☳), 'lightning' for lî (☲), 'wind' for sun (☴), and 'rain' for khan (☵). 'The sun,' however, is also an emblem of lî, and 'the moon' one of kăn (☶), generally said to represent 'mountains,' while tui (☱), representing 'collections of water,' has no place in the enumeration. *K*û Hsî says that in paragraph 3 we have the natural changes seen in the phenomena of the sky, while in 4 we have such changes as find body and figure on the earth.

Paragraphs 5 and 6 have both been misunderstood from neglect of the peculiar meaning of the character *k*ih (知), and from taking it in its common acceptation of 'knowing.' Both commentaries and dictionaries point out that it is here used in the sense of 'directing,' 'presiding over.' In paragraph 7, however, it resumes its ordinary significancy.

12. The changes and transformations (of the lines) are the emblems of the advance and retrogression (of the vital force in nature). Thus what we call the strong and the weak (lines) become the emblems of day and night. The movements which take place in the six places (of the hexagram) show the course of the three extremes (i. e. of the three Powers in their perfect operation).

13. Therefore what the superior man rests in, in whatever position he is placed, is the order shown in the Yî; and the study which gives him the greatest pleasure is that of the explanations of the several lines.

14. Therefore the superior man, when living quietly, contemplates the emblems and studies the explanations of them; when initiating any movement, he contemplates the changes (that are made in divining), and studies the prognostications from them. Thus ' is help extended to him from Heaven; there will be good fortune, and advantage in every movement.'

Chapter II, paragraphs 9–14, is divided into two parts. The former contains paragraphs 9–12, and tells us how the sages, king Wăn and the duke of *K*âu, proceeded in making the Yî, so that the good fortune and bad of men's courses should be indicated by it in harmony with right and wrong, and the processes of nature. Paragraphs 13, 14 form the second part, and speak of the study of the Yî by the superior man, desirous of doing what is right and increasing his knowledge, and the advantages flowing from it.

I can follow to some extent the first two statements of paragraph 12, so far as the ideas of the writer are concerned, though asserting any correspondence between the changes of the lines of the diagrams, and the operations of external nature, as in the succession of day and night, is merely an amusement of the fancy. I all but fail, however, to grasp the idea in the last statement. In the trigram, the first line represents earth; the second, man; and the

Chapter III. 15. The Thwan speak of the emblematic figures (of the complete diagrams). The Yâo speak of the changes (taking place in the several lines).

16. The expressions about good fortune or bad are used with reference to (the figures and lines, as) being right or wrong (according to the conditions of time and place); those about repentance or regret refer to small faults (in the satisfying those conditions); when it is said 'there will be no error,' or 'no blame,' there is reference to (the subject) repairing an error by what is good.

17. Therefore the distinction of (the upper and lower trigrams and of the individual lines) as noble or mean is decided by the (relative) position (of the lines); the regulations of small and great are found in the diagrams, and the discriminations of good and bad fortune appear in the (subjoined) explanations.

18. Anxiety against (having occasion for) repentance or regret should be felt at the boundary line (between good and evil). The stirring up the thought of (securing that there shall be) no blame arises from (the feeling of) repentance.

---

third, heaven; in the hexagram, the first and second lines are assigned to earth; the third and fourth, to man; and the fifth and sixth, to heaven. These are the three Powers, and each Power has 'a Grand Extreme,' where its nature and operation are seen in their highest ideal. This is to some extent conceivable; but when I try to follow our author, and find an analogy between the course of these extremes and the movements in the places of the diagrams, I have no clue by which to trace my way. For the concluding sentence of paragraph 14 see the duke of *K*âu on the last line of hexagram 14.

19. Thus of the diagrams some are small, and some are great; and of the explanations some are startling, and some are unexciting. Every one of those explanations has reference to the tendencies (indicated by the symbols).

Chapter IV. 20. The Yî was made on a principle of accordance with heaven and earth, and shows us therefore, without rent or confusion, the course (of things) in heaven and earth.

21. (The sage), in accordance with (the Yî), looking up, contemplates the brilliant phenomena of the heavens, and, looking down, examines the definite arrangements of the earth ;—thus he knows the causes of darkness (or, what is obscure) and light (or, what is bright). He traces things to their beginning, and follows them to their end ;—thus he knows what can be said about death and life. (He

---

Chapter III, paragraphs 15–19, gives additional information about the constituent parts of the Yî, that is, the Text of the classic as we have it from king Wăn and his son. The imperial editors say that it expands the meaning of the fourth paragraph, the third of chapter 2. It does do so, but this account hardly covers all its contents.

To understand the names 'small and great,' as used of the diagrams in paragraphs 17 and 19, it should be noted that hexagrams to which the divided or yin line gives their character are termed 'small,' and those where the undivided or yang line rules are called 'great.' Kâu (44, ▤), Thun (33, ▤), and Phei (12, ▤) are instances of the former class; Fû (24, ▤), Lin (19, ▤), and Thâi (11, ▤) of the other.

It is observed by Zhâi Khing (early in the Ming dynasty) that the terms 'diagrams' and 'explanations' must be understood not only of the whole figures but also as embracing the several lines.

perceives how the union of) essence and breath form things, and the (disappearance or) wandering away of the soul produces the change (of their constitution);—thus he knows the characteristics of the anima and animus.

22. There is a similarity between him and heaven and earth, and hence there is no contrariety in him to them. His knowledge embraces all things, and his course is (intended to be) helpful to all under the sky;—and hence he falls into no error. He acts according to the exigency of circumstances without being carried away by their current; he rejoices in Heaven and knows its ordinations;—and hence he has no anxieties. He rests in his own (present) position, and cherishes (the spirit of) generous benevolence;—and hence he can love (without reserve).

23. (Through the Yî), he comprehends as in a mould or enclosure the transformations of heaven and earth without any error; by an ever-varying adaptation he completes (the nature of) all things without exception; he penetrates to a knowledge of the course of day and night (and all other connected phenomena);—it is thus that his operation is spirit-like, unconditioned by place, while the changes which he produces are not restricted to any form.

Chapter IV, paragraphs 20-23, is intended still more to exalt the Yî, and seems to say that the sage by means of it can make an exhaustive study of all principles and of human nature, till he attains to the knowledge of the ordinances of Heaven. Such is the account of the chapter given by Kû Hsî; but the second character in paragraph 21 must be understood in the signification which it has in all the sixty-four sentences which explain the emblematic structure of the hexagrams, as='in accordance with' and not 'by means of.' The

Chapter V. 24. The successive movement of the inactive and active operations constitutes what is called the course (of things).

---

imperial editors append to their statement of *K*û's account, that it must be borne in mind that the sages had not to wait till the Yî was made to conduct their exhaustive study. They had done that before, and the Yî may be considered as a talk on the results, drawn out in its own peculiar style. It holds the mirror up to nature; but its authors knew nature before they made it.

In paragraph 21, 'the brilliant phenomena of the heavens' are the various shining bodies of the sky, with their rising and setting; 'the definite arrangements of the earth' are the different situations of its parts according to the points of the compass, and its surface as diversified by mountain and valley; and by the study of these the causes of day and night are known as being the expansion and contraction of the elementary ether. The same thing produces the facts of birth or life and death.

ᴣing, which I have translated 'essence,' denotes the more subtle and pure part of matter, and belongs to the grosser form of the elementary ether; *kh*î, or 'spirit,' is the breath, still material, but purer than the ᴣing, and belongs to the finer, and more active form of the ether. Here *kh*î is 'the breath of life.' In the hwun or 'soul (animus),' the *kh*î predominates, and the ᴣing in the pho or animal soul. At death the hwun wanders away, ascending, and the pho descends and is changed into a ghostly shade. So did the ancient Chinese grope their way from material things to the concept and representation of what was immaterial.

For my 'characteristics of the anima and animus,' Dr. Medhurst rendered 'the circumstances and conditions of the Kwei Shăns' (Theology of the Chinese, pp. 10–12); but he observes that 'the Kwei Shăns in the passage are evidently the expanding and contracting principles of human life.' The kwei shăns are brought about by the dissolution of the human frame, and consist of the expanding and ascending shăn, which rambles about in space, and of the contracted and shrivelled kwei, which reverts to earth and nonentity. It is difficult to express one's self clearly on a subject treated so briefly and enigmatically in the text.

We must understand that the subject of the predicates in this and the next two paragraphs is 'the sage,' who has endeavoured to give a transcript of his views and doings in the Yî. The character,

25. That which ensues as the result (of their movement) is goodness; that which shows it in its completeness is the natures (of men and things).

26. The benevolent see it and call it benevolence. The wise see it and call it wisdom. The common people, acting daily according to it, yet have no knowledge of it. Thus it is that the course (of things), as seen by the superior man, is seen by few.

27. It is manifested in the benevolence (of its operations), and (then again) it conceals and stores up its resources. It gives their stimulus to all things, without having the same anxieties that possess the sage. Complete is its abundant virtue and the greatness of its stores!

28. Its rich possessions is what is intended by 'the greatness of its stores;' the daily renovation which it produces is what is meant by 'the abundance of its virtue.'

29. Production and reproduction is what is called (the process of) change.

30. The formation of the semblances (shadowy forms of things) is what we attribute to *Kh*ien; the giving to them their specific forms is what we attribute to Khwăn.

31. The exhaustive use of the numbers (that turn

---

which I have translated by 'spirit-like' in paragraph 23, is different from *kh*î in paragraph 21. It is shăn, a character of the phonetic class, while its primary material signification has not been satisfactorily ascertained. 'The Chinese,' says P. Regis (vol. ii. p. 445), 'use it in naming the soul, true angels, and the genii of idolaters; and the Christian Chinese use it when they speak of God, of the Holy Spirit, of angels, and of the soul of man. For what else could they do?'

up in manipulating the stalks), and (thereby) knowing (the character of) coming events, is what we call prognosticating; the comprehension of the changes (indicated leads us to) what we call the business (to be done).

32. That which is unfathomable in (the movement of) the inactive and active operations is (the presence of a) spiritual (power).

Chapter V, paragraphs 24–32, still shows us the Yî fashioned so as to give a picture of the phenomena of the external universe; but the writer dwells more on the latter, and the different paragraphs give an interesting view of his ideas on the subject. He supposes a constant change from rest to movement and from movement to rest, through which all things are formed, now still, now in motion, now expanding, now contracting. It is customary to speak of two forms of an original ether as the two elementary principles, but they are really one and the same ether, in a twofold condition, with a twofold action. By their successive movement the phenomena of existence are produced,—what I have called 'the course (of things)' in paragraph 24. It is attempted, however, by many native scholars and by some sinologists, to give to tâo, the last character in that paragraph, the meaning of 'reason,' that which intelligently guides and directs the movements of the two elements. But this view is not in harmony with the scope of the chapter, nor can the characters be fairly construed so as to justify such an interpretation.

The imperial editors say that the germ of the Mencian doctrine about the goodness of human nature is in paragraph 25; but it says more widely, that 'every creature is good,' according to its ideal as from the plastic yin and yang. But few, the next paragraph tells us, can understand the measure of this goodness.

'The benevolent operations' in the course of things in paragraph 27 are illustrated from the phenomena of growth and beauty in spring and summer; and the cessation of these in autumn and winter may be called 'a concealing and storing them up.'

Paragraph 29 seems to state the origin of the name Yî as applied to the book, the Yî King.

In paragraph 30 the names Khien and Khwăn take the place of yin and yang, as used in paragraphs 24 and 32. In Khien,

Chapter VI. 33. Yes, wide is the Yî and great!
If we speak of it in its farthest reaching, no limit
can be set to it; if we speak of it with reference to
what is near at hand, (its lessons are) still and
correct; if we speak of it in connexion with all
between heaven and earth, it embraces all.

34. There is *Kh*ien. In its (individual) stillness
it is self-absorbed; when exerting its motive power
it goes straight forward; and thus it is that its productive action is on a grand scale. There is Khwăn.
In its (individual) stillness, it is self-collected and
capacious; when exerting its motive power, it de-
velopes its resources, and thus its productive action
is on a wide scale.

35. In its breadth and greatness, (the Yî) corre-

---

the symbol of heaven, every one of its three lines is undivided; it
is the concentration of the yang faculty; so Khwăn, the symbol
of the earth, is the concentration of the yin. The critics themselves call attention to the equivalence of the symbolic names here
given to yin and yang. The connexion of the two is necessary
to the production of any one substantial thing. The yang originates a shadowy outline which the yin fills up with a definite substance. So actually in nature Heaven (*Kh*ien) and Earth (Khwăn)
operate together in the production of all material things and
beings.

The 'numbers,' mentioned in paragraph 31, are not all or any
numbers generally, but 7, 8, 9, 6, those assigned to the four 'emblematic figures,' that grow out of the undivided and divided lines,
and by means of which the hexagrams are made up in divination.
The 'future or coming events' which are prognosticated are not
particular events, which the diviner has not already forecast, but the
character of events or courses of actions already contemplated, as
good or evil, lucky or unlucky, in their issue.

The best commentary on paragraph 32 is supplied by paragraphs
8–10 of Appendix VI. The 'Spirit' is that of 'God;' and this
settles the meaning of tâo in paragraph 24, as being the course of
nature, in which, according to the author, 'God worketh all in all.'

sponds to heaven and earth; in its ever-recurring changes, it corresponds to the four seasons; in its mention of the bright or active, and the dark or inactive operation, it corresponds to the sun and moon; and the excellence seen in the ease and ready response (of its various operations) corresponds to the perfect operations (presented to us in the phenomena of nature).

Chapter VII. 36. The Master said:—' Is not the Yî a perfect book?' It was by the Yî that the sages exalted their virtue, and enlarged their sphere of occupation. Their wisdom was high, and their rules of conduct were solid. That loftiness was after the pattern of heaven; that solidity, after the pattern of earth.

Chapter VI, paragraphs 33–35, goes on further to celebrate the Yî as holding up the mirror to nature in all its operations and in its widest extent. The grandiloquent language, however, amounts only to this, that, when we have made ourselves acquainted with the phenomena of nature, we can, with a heated fancy, see some analogy to them in the changes of the diagrams and lines of the Yî book.

*Kh*ien and Khwăn must be taken as the same names are understood in paragraph 30 above.

' The Yî,' with which paragraph 33 begins, must be understood also at the commencement of paragraph 35. The character which I have translated by ' corresponds' throughout this last chapter, should not, it is observed, have stress laid upon it. *K*û Hsî says that it is simply equal to the ' there is a similarity' of paragraph 22. 'The bright or active element' and 'the dark or inactive' are in the original, ' the yang and the yin.' The correspondence predicated between them and the sun and moon, the brightness and warmth of the one, and the paleness and coldness of the other, shows us how those names arose, and that it is foreign to the original concept of them to call them ' the male and female principles:'—with the last clause compare paragraphs 6–8.

37. Heaven and earth having their positions as assigned to them, the changes (of nature) take place between them. The nature (of man) having been completed, and being continually preserved, it is the gate of all good courses and righteousness.

Chapter VIII. 38. The sage was able to survey all the complex phenomena under the sky. He then considered in his mind how they could be figured, and (by means of the diagrams) represented their material forms and their character. Hence these (diagrams) are denominated Semblances (or emblematic figures, the Hsiang).

39. A (later) sage was able to survey the motive influences working all under the sky. He contemplated them in their common action and special nature, in order to bring out the standard and proper tendency of each. He then appended his

---

Chapter VII, paragraphs 36, 37, is understood to set forth how the sages embodied the teachings of the Yî in their character and conduct. But when it is said that ' it was by the Yî that they exalted their virtue and enlarged their sphere of occupation,' the meaning can only be that what they did in these directions was in harmony with the principles which they endeavoured to set forth in the symbols of the Yî.

' Their rules of conduct were solid,' in paragraph 36, is, literally, ' their rules were low.' To the height of heaven reached by the wisdom of the sages, the author opposes the low-lying earth, between which and their substantial practices and virtues he discovered some analogy.

It will be seen that the chapter commences with ' The Master said.' Kû Hsî observes that ' as the Ten Appendixes were all made by the Master, these words are out of place, and that he conjectures that wherever they occur here and elsewhere, they were added after the sage's time.' Their occurrence very seriously affects the question of the authorship of the Appendixes, which I have discussed in the Introduction, pages 28-31.

explanation (to each line of the diagrams), to determine the good or evil indicated by it. Hence those
(lines with their explanations) are denominated Imitations (the Yâo).

40. (The diagrams) speak of the most complex
phenomena under the sky, and yet there is nothing
in them that need awaken dislike; the explanations
of the lines speak of the subtlest movements under
the sky, and yet there is nothing in them to produce
confusion.

41. (A learner) will consider what is said (under
the diagrams), and then speak; he will deliberate
on what is said (in the explanations of the lines), and
then move. By such consideration and deliberations
he will be able to make all the changes which he
undertakes successful.

42. 'Here hid, retired, cries out the crane;
    Her young's responsive cry sounds there.
    Of spirits good I drain this cup;
    With thee a cup I'll freely share.'

The Master said:—'The superior man occupies
his apartment and sends forth his words. If they
be good, they will be responded to at a distance of
more than a thousand lî;—how much more will they
be so in the nearer circle! He occupies his apartment and sends forth his words. If they be evil,
they will awaken opposition at a distance of more
than a thousand lî;—how much more will they do
so in the nearer circle! Words issue from one's
person, and proceed to affect the people. Actions
proceed from what is near, and their effects are seen
at a distance. Words and actions are the hinge and
spring of the superior man. The movement of that

hinge and spring determines glory or disgrace. His
words and actions move heaven and earth ;—may he
be careless in regard to them ?'

43. '(The representative of) the union of men first
cries out and weeps, and afterwards laughs.'   The
Master said, on this :—

  ' The ways of good men (different seem).
  This in a public office toils;
  That in his home the time beguiles.
  One man his lips with silence seals;
  Another all his mind reveals.
  But when two men are one in heart,
  Not iron bolts keep them apart;
  The words they in their union use,
  Fragrance like orchid plants diffuse.'

44. ' The first six, (divided), shows its subject
placing mats of the white grass beneath what he
sets on the ground.'   The Master said :—' To place
the things on the ground might be considered sufficient; but when he places beneath them mats
of the white grass, what occasion for blame can
there be ? Such a course shows the height of carefulness. The white grass is a trivial thing, but,
through the use made of it, it may become important. He who goes forward using such careful art
will not fall into any error.'

45. ' A superior man toiling laboriously and yet
humble ! He will bring things to an end, and with
good fortune.'   The Master said on this :—' He
toils with success, but does not boast of it; he
achieves merit, but takes no virtue to himself from
it ;—this is the height of generous goodness, and
speaks of the man who with (great) merit yet places

himself below others. He wishes his virtue to be more and more complete, and in his intercourse with others to be more and more respectful;—he who is so humble, carrying his respectfulness to the utmost, will be able to preserve himself in his position.'

46. 'The dragon (is seen) beyond his proper haunts; there will be occasion for repentance.' The Master said on this:—'He is noble, but is not in his correct place; he is on high, but there are no people to acknowledge him; there is a man of virtue and ability below, but he will not assist him. Hence whatever movement he may make will give occasion for repentance.'

47. 'He does not quit the courtyard before his door;—there will be no occasion for blame.' The Master said on this:—'When disorder arises, it will be found that (ill-advised) speech was the stepping-stone to it. If a ruler do not keep secret (his deliberations with his minister), he will lose that minister. If a minister do not keep secret (his deliberations with his ruler), he will lose his life. If (important) matters in the germ be not kept secret, that will be injurious to their accomplishment. Therefore the superior man is careful to maintain secrecy, and does not allow himself to speak.'

48. The Master said:—'The makers of the Yî may be said to have known (the philosophy of) robbery. The Yî says, "He is a burden-bearer, and yet rides in a carriage, thereby exciting robbers to attack him." Burden-bearing is the business of a small man. A carriage is the vehicle of a gentleman. When a small man rides in the vehicle of a gentle-

man, robbers will think of taking it from him.
(When one is) insolent to those above him, and
oppressive to those below, robbers will wish to
attack him. Careless laying up of things excites
to robbery, (as a woman's) adorning of herself
excites to lust. What the Yî says about the burden-
bearer's riding in a carriage, and exciting robbers
to attack him, (shows how) robbery is called out.'

Chapter VIII, paragraphs 38–48. In the first two paragraphs
here we have an account of the formation of the diagrams, and of
the explanation of the whole hexagrams and of the individual
lines. 'The sage' in paragraph 38 is intended presumably of
Fû-hsî; but we cannot say, from it, whether the writer thought of
him as having formed only the eight trigrams, or all the sixty-four
hexagrams. In the diagrams, however, we have semblances, or
representations, of the phenomena of nature, even the most complex, and hard to be disentangled. Paragraph 39 goes on to
speak of the explanation more especially of the individual lines, by
the duke of Kâu, as symbolical of good luck or evil, as they turned
up in the processes of divination.

Paragraph 40 declares the usableness (so to speak) of the diagrams and the explanations of them; and 41 shows us how a
learner or consulter of the Yî would actually proceed in using it.

In paragraphs 42–48 we have the words of Confucius on seven
lines in so many hexagrams, or rather his amplification of the
words of the duke of Kâu's explanations of their symbolism. The
lines are 2 of hexagram 61; 5 of 13; 1 of 28; 3 of 15; 6 of 1;
1 of 60; and 3 of 40. What Confucius says is not without interest, but does not make the principles on which the Yî was
made any clearer to us. It shows how his object was to turn the
symbolism that he found to a moral or ethical account; and no
doubt he could have varied the symbolism, if he had been inclined
to do so.

I have spoken in the preceding chapter of the difficulty which
the phrase 'The Master said' presents to our accepting the Appendix as from the hand of Confucius himself. But his words in
paragraph 43 are in rhyme. He did not speak so. If he rhymed
his explanation of the symbolism of the line that is the groundwork of that paragraph, why did he not rhyme his explanations of

Chapter IX. 49. To heaven belongs (the number) 1 ; to earth, 2 ; to heaven, 3 ; to earth, 4 ; to heaven, 5 ; to earth, 6 ; to heaven, 7 ; to earth, 8 ; to heaven, 9 ; to earth, 10.

50. The numbers belonging to heaven are five, and those belonging to earth are (also) five. The numbers of these two series correspond to each other (in their fixed positions), and each one has another that may be considered its mate. The heavenly numbers amount to 25, and the earthly to 30. The numbers of heaven and earth together amount to 55. It is by these that the changes and transformations are effected, and the spirit-like agencies kept in movement.

51. The numbers of the Great Expansion, (multiplied together), make 50, of which (only) 49 are used (in divination). (The stalks representing these) are divided into two heaps to represent the two (emblematic lines, or heaven and earth). One is then taken (from the heap on the right), and placed (between the little finger of the left hand and the next), that there may thus be symbolised the three (powers of heaven, earth, and man). (The heaps on both sides) are manipulated by fours to represent the four seasons; and then the remainders are returned, and placed (between) the two middle fingers of the left hand, to represent the intercalary month. In five years there are two intercalations, and therefore there are two operations; and afterwards the whole process is repeated.

52. The numbers (required) for *Kh*ien (or the

---

the other lines ?   To answer these questions categorically is beyond our power.   The facts that suggest them increase the difficulty in ascribing this and the other additions to the Yî to the later sage.

undivided line) amount to 216; those for K h wăn (or the divided line), to 144. Together they are 360, corresponding to the days of the year.

53. The number produced by the lines in the two parts (of the Yî) amount to 11,520, corresponding to the number of all things.

54. Therefore by means of the four operations is the Yî completed. It takes 18 changes to form a hexagram.

55. (The formation of) the eight trigrams constitutes the small completion (of the Yî).

56. If we led on the diagrams and expanded them, if we prolonged each by the addition of the proper lines, then all events possible under the sky might have their representation.

57. (The diagrams) make manifest (by their appended explanations), the ways (of good and ill fortune), and show virtuous actions in their spiritual relations. In this way, by consulting them, we may receive an answer (to our doubts), and we may also by means of them assist the spiritual (power in its agency in nature and providence).

58. The Master said:—' He who knows the method of change and transformation may be said to know what is done by that spiritual (power).'

Chapter IX, paragraphs 49-58, is of a different character from any of the preceding, and treats, unsatisfactorily, of the use of numbers in connexion with the figure of the Yî and the practice of divination.

In the Thang edition of the Yî, published in the seventh century, paragraph 49 is the first of the eleventh chapter according to the arrangement now followed. Khăng-ȝze restored it to its present place, which it occupied, as has been proved, during the Han

Chapter X. 59. In the Yî there are four things characteristic of the way of the sages. We should set the highest value on its explanations to guide

---

dynasty, and to which it properly belongs. It and the next paragraph should be taken together, and are distinct from what follows, though the Thang edition is further confused in placing 51 before 50.

In 49 and 50 'heaven' and 'earth' are used as we have seen *Kh*ien and Khwăn are in paragraphs 30 and 34. Odd numbers belong to the strong or undivided line, which is symbolical of the active operation in nature, and the even numbers to the weak or divided line, symbolical of its inaction. The phraseology of the paragraphs, however, can only be understood by a reference to 'the river map,' which has been given in the Introduction, pages 15, 16.

The map, as it appeared on the back of 'the dragon-horse,' consisted of so many circles, and so many dark circular markings, the former, it was assumed, being of the yang character, and the latter of the yin. Fû-hsî for the circle substituted the strong or undivided line (————), and for the dark markings the weak or divided (—— ——). It will be seen that the yang symbols are the 1, 3, 5, 7 and 9 circles, and the yin are the 2, 4, 6, 8 and 10 circular markings, which is the pictorial delineation of paragraph 49. The only thing to be said upon it is that the arrangement of the five circles and ten circular markings is peculiar, and evidently devised 'for a purpose.' So far, however, as we know, no figure of the map was attempted till after the beginning of our twelfth century.

The same figure is supposed to illustrate what is said in paragraph 50: 'The numbers of the two series correspond to each other in their fixed positions.' 1 and 2, and 3 and 4 certainly front each other, and perhaps 5 and 6; but 7 and 8, and 9 and 10 do not do so in the same way. It is said also that 'each has another that may be considered its mate.' So it is with 1 and 6, 2 and 7, 3 and 8, 4 and 9, but hardly with 5 and 10. Further, $1+3+5+7+9=25$; $2+4+6+8+10=30$; and $25+30=55$; all of which points are stated.

The last statement in the paragraph, however, derives no illustration, so far as I can see, from the figure. How can the numbers effect the things that are predicated of them? There is a

us in speaking; on its changes for (the initiation of)
our movements; on its emblematic figures for (definite action as in) the construction of implements;

---

jargon indeed about the formation of the five elements, but in
order to make it appear not reasonable, but capable of being
related, writers call in 'the Lo writing' to the aid of 'the Ho map;'
and 'the five elements' is a division of the constituents of material
things, which is foreign to the Yî.

Paragraph 51 is intended to describe the process of divination
in manipulating the stalks, but the description is confused by introducing into it the four seasons and the subject of intercalation, so
as to be very difficult to understand.

In the middle of the Ho map are the five circles symbolical of
heaven and the ten dark terrestrial markings (five above and five
below the others). These multiplied together give fifty, which form
'the great expansion.' But 50 divining stalks or slips, when
divided, give either two odd numbers or two even; and therefore
one was put on one side. The remaining 49, however divided,
were sure to give two parcels of stalks, one containing an even
number of stalks, and the other an odd, and so might be said fan-
cifully to represent the undivided or strong, and the divided or
weak line. It is needless to go minutely into the other steps of
the process. Then comes in the counting the stalks by four,
because there are four seasons in the year, and those that remain
represent the intercalary days. But how could such a process
be of any value to determine the days necessary to be intercalated
in any particular year? The paragraph shows, however, that,
when it was written, the rule was to intercalate two months in five
years. But it does not say how many days would remain to be
carried on to the sixth year after the second intercalation.

Paragraph 52. The actual number of the undivided and divided
lines in the hexagrams is the same, 192 of each. But the representative number of an undivided line is 9, and of a divided line 6.
Now 9×4 (the number of the emblematic figures) $\times 6$ (the lines of
each hexagram) $= 216$; and $6 \times 4 \times 6 = 144$. The sum of these
products is 360, which was assumed, for the purpose of working
the intercalation, as the standard length of the year. But this was
derived from observation, and other considerations;—it did not
come out of the Yî.

Paragraphs 53–56. The number in 53 arises thus:—192 (the

and on its prognostications for our practice of divination.

60. Therefore, when a superior man is about to take action of a more private or of a public character, he asks (the Yî), making his inquiry in words. It receives his order, and the answer comes as the echo's response. Be the subject remote or near, mysterious or deep, he forthwith knows of what kind will be the coming result. (If the Yî) were not the most exquisite thing under heaven, would it be concerned in such an operation as this?

61. (The stalks) are manipulated by threes and fives to determine (one) change; they are laid on opposite sides, and placed one up, one down, to make sure of their numbers; and the (three necessary)

---

number of each series of lines in the sixty-four hexagrams) × 36 (obtained as above) = 6912, and 192 × 24 = 4608, the sum of which = 11,520. This is said to be 'the number of all things,' the meaning of which I do not know. The 'four operations' are those described in paragraph 31. They were thrice repeated in divination to determine each new line, and of course it took eighteen of them to form a hexagram. The diagrams might be extended ad infinitum, both in the number of lines and of figures, by the natural process of their formation as shown in the Introduction, page 14, without the aid of the divining stalks; and no sufficient reason can be given why the makers of the figures stopped at sixty-four.

It is difficult to believe the first statement in paragraph 57 and to understand the second. What is it 'to Shăn or spiritualise virtuous actions?' The concluding statement approximates to impiety.

We may grant what is affirmed in paragraph 58, but does the Yî really give us any knowledge of the processes of change and transformation in nature? What wiser are we after all the affirmations about numbers? 'Change' = changings, understood actively:—the work of Heaven; 'transformations'=evolution:—the finish given by earth to the changing caused by Heaven.

changes are gone through with in this way, till they form the figures pertaining to heaven or to earth. Their numbers are exactly determined, and the emblems of (all things) under the sky are fixed. (If the Yî) were not the thing most capable of change of all things under heaven, how could it effect such a result as this?

62. In (all these operations forming) the Yî, there is no thought and no action. It is still and without movement; but, when acted on, it penetrates forthwith to all phenomena and events under the sky. If it were not the most spirit-like thing under the sky, how could it be found doing this?

63. The (operations forming the) Yî are the method by which the sages searched out exhaustively what was deep, and investigated the minutest springs (of things).

64. 'Those operations searched out what was deep:'—therefore they could penetrate to the views of all under the sky. 'They made apparent the minutest springs of (things):'—therefore they could bring to a completion all undertakings under the sky. 'Their action was spirit-like:'—therefore they could make speed without hurry, and reached their destination without travelling.

65. This is the import of what the Master said, that 'In the Yî there are four things indicating the way of the sages.'

Chapter X, paragraphs 59–65, enlarges on the service rendered to men by the Yî, owing to the way in which it was made by the sages to express their views and carry into effect their wishes.

Paragraph 59 mentions the four things in which its usefulness appears. 'The emblematic figures' are the four hsiang, which are produced by the manipulation of the undivided and divided

Chapter XI. 66. The Master said :—'What is it that the Yî does? The Yî opens up (the knowledge of the issues of) things, accomplishes the undertakings (of men), and embraces under it (the way of) all things under the sky. This and nothing more is what the Yî does. Thereby the sages, through (divination by) it, would give their proper course to the aims of all under the sky, would give stability to their undertakings, and determine their doubts.'

67. Therefore the virtue of the stalks is versatile

---

lines, and whose representative numbers are 9, 8, 7, 6. 'Divination' appears in the paragraph as pû-shih, which means 'divination by the tortoise-shell and by the stalks.' But the tortoise-shell had nothing to do with the use of the Yî. Before the composition of these Appendixes the two terms must have been combined to express the practice of divination, without reference to its mode.

Paragraph 60 speaks of the explanations and prognostications of the Yî. The 'exquisiteness' ascribed to it would be due to the sages who had devised it, and appended their explanations to it; but the whole thing has no existence save in cloud-land.

Paragraph 61 speaks of the operations with the stalks till the various changes in the results issued in the determination of the emblematic figures, and then in the fixing of the individual lines and entire hexagrams. Even Kû Hsî admits that the references to the different processes are now hardly intelligible.

Paragraph 62. How could the writer speak of the Yî without thought or action as being most 'spirit-like?' If it did what he asserts, those who contrived it might be so described? They would have been beings whose operation was indeed like that of spirits, inscrutable, 'unfathomable' (paragraph 32), even like that of the Spirit of God (VI, 10).

Paragraphs 63 and 64 ought not to be taken as saying that the sages did the things described for themselves by the Yî. They knew them of themselves, and made the Yî that others might come by it to do the same. So the writer imagined. No words could indicate more clearly than those of paragraph 65 that the paragraphs between it and 59 did not come from Confucius, but from the compiler of the Great Appendix, whoever he was.

and spirit-like; that of the diagrams is exact and
wise; and the meaning given by the six lines is
changeful to give (the proper information to men).
The sages having, by their possession of these
(three virtues), cleansed their minds, retired and
laid them up in the secrecy (of their own consciousness). But their sympathies were with the people
in regard both to their good fortune and evil. By
their spirit-like ability they knew (the character of)
coming events, and their wisdom had stored up (all
experiences of) the past. Who could be able to
accomplish all this? (Only our) ancient sages,
quick in apprehension and clear in discernment, of
far-reaching intelligence, and all-embracing knowledge, and with a majesty, going spirit-like to its
objects;—it was only they who could do so.

68. Therefore (those sages), fully understanding
the way of Heaven, and having clearly ascertained
the experience of the people, instituted (the employment of) these spirit-like things, as a provision for
the use of the people. The sages went about
the employment of them (moreover) by purifying
their hearts and with reverent caution, thereby
giving (more) spirituality and intelligence to their
virtue.

69. Thus, a door shut may be pronounced (analogous to) Khwăn (or the inactive condition), and the
opening of the door (analogous to) *Kh*ien (or the
active condition). The opening succeeding the being
shut may be pronounced (analogous to what we
call) a change; and the passing from one of these
states to the other may be called the constant course
(of things).

The (first) appearance of anything (as a bud) is

what we call a semblance; when it has received its complete form, we call it a definite thing.

(The divining-plant having been produced, the sages) set it apart and laid down the method of its employment,—what we call the laws (of divination). The advantage arising from it in external and internal matters, so that the people all use it, stamps it with a character which we call spirit-like.

70. Therefore in (the system of) the Yî there is the Grand Terminus, which produced the two elementary Forms. Those two Forms produced the Four emblematic Symbols, which again produced the eight Trigrams.

71. The eight trigrams served to determine the good and evil (issues of events), and from this determination was produced the (successful prosecution of the) great business (of life).

72. Therefore of all things that furnish models and visible figures there are none greater than heaven and earth; of things that change and extend an influence (on others) there are none greater than the four seasons; of things suspended (in the sky) with their figures displayed clear and bright, there are none greater than the sun and moon; of the honoured and exalted there are none greater than he who is the rich and noble (one); in preparing things for practical use, and inventing and making instruments for the benefit of all under the sky, there are none greater than the sages; to explore what is complex, search out what is hidden, to hook up what lies deep, and reach to what is distant, thereby determining (the issues) for good or ill of all events under the sky, and making all men under heaven full of strenuous endeavours, there

are no (agencies) greater than those of the stalks and the tortoise-shell.

73. Therefore Heaven produced the spirit-like things, and the sages took advantage of them. (The operations of) heaven and earth are marked by (so many) changes and transformations; and the sages imitated them (by means of the Yî). Heaven hangs out its (brilliant) figures from which are seen good fortune and bad, and the sages made their emblematic interpretations accordingly. The Ho gave forth the map, and the Lo the writing, of (both of) which the sages took advantage.

74. In the (scheme of the) Yî there are the four symbolic figures by which they inform men (in divining of the lines making up the diagrams); the explanations appended to them convey the significance (of the diagrams and lines); and the determination (of the divination) as fortunate or the reverse, to settle the doubts (of men).

Chapter XI, paragraphs 66–74, treats of divination, and the scheme of it supplied in the Yî. That scheme must be referred first to Heaven, which produced the spirit-like things,—the divining-plant and the tortoise; and next to the sages, who knew the mind of Heaven, and made the plant and shell subservient to the purpose for which they were intended.

Paragraph 66 answers the question of what the Yî does; and if there were truth or reason in it, the book and its use would be most important. I have closed the quotation of "the Master's" words at the end of the paragraph; but really we do not know if they extend so far, or farther.

Paragraphs 67 and 68 glorify the sages and their work. The virtues of the divining-plant all belonged to them, and it was thus that they were able to organise the scheme of divination. The production of 'the spirit-like things' is, in paragraph 73, ascribed to 'Heaven;' the characters about them in these paragraphs mean no more than is expressed in the translation.

Chapter XII. 75. It is said in the Yî, 'Help is given to him from Heaven. There will be good fortune ; advantage in every respect.' The Master

---

Paragraph 69 shows how the antinomy of the yin and yang pervades all nature, and how the sages turned it, as existing pre-eminently in the divining-plant, to account.

Paragraph 70. Evidently the author had in view here the genesis of the diagrams of the Yî, the number of figures increasing in a geometrical progression with the ratio of 2, while the lines of the figures form an arithmetical progression with the common differ-ence of 1. This is quite plain after 'the two elementary forms (——— and — —)' have been made. They give birth to 'the four emblematic symbols,' each of two lines (═══, ══ ═, ═ ═, ═ ═, known, in this order, as the Grand or old Yang, the young Yin, the young Yang, and the Grand or old Yin). By the addition to each of these symbols first of the yang line, and then of the yin, there arise the eight trigrams, each of three lines ; and the process of formation might be continued indefinitely.

But how was the first step taken in the formation of the two ele-mentary lines? Here, it is said, they were produced by the Thâi Kî, or the Grand Terminus. This is represented in Kû Hsî's ' Youth's Introduction to the Study of the Yî,' by a circle ; but he tells us that that representation of it was first made by Kâu-ʒze (A.D. 1017–1073, called also Kâu Tun-î, Kâu Mâu-shû, and, most of all, Kâu Lien-khî), and that his readers must be careful not to suppose that Fû-hsî had such a figure in his mind's eye. I fail myself to understand how there can be generated from a circle the undivided and the broken line. Given those two lines, and the formation of the sixty-four hexagrams proceeds regularly according to the method above described. We must start from them, whether we can account or not for the rise of the idea of them in the mind of Fû-hsî.

Leaving the subject of the figure of the Thâi Kî, the name gives us hardly any clue to its meaning. Kî is used for the extreme term of anything, as the ridge-pole of a house, or the pinnacle of a pagoda. The comment on the first sentence in the paragraph by Wang Pî (A.D. 226–249) is :—'Existence must begin in non-existence, and therefore the Grand Terminus produced the two elementary Forms. Thâi Kî is the denomination of what has no denomination. As it cannot be named, the text takes the extreme

said:—'Yû (祐) is the symbol of assisting. He whom Heaven assists is observant (of what is right); he whom men assist is sincere. The individual here indicated treads the path of sincerity and desires to be observant (of what is right), and studies to exalt the worthy. Hence "Help is given to him from Heaven. There will be good fortune, advantage in every respect."'

76. The Master said:—' The written characters are

---

point of anything that exists as an analogous term for the Thâi *K*î.' Expanding Wang's comment, Khung Ying-tâ says :—'Thâi *K*î means the original subtle matter, that formed the one chaotic mass before heaven and earth were divided;' and then he refers to certain passages in Lâo-ʒze's Tâo Teh King, and identifies the Thâi *K*î with his Tâo. This would seem to give to Thâi *K*î a material meaning. The later philosophers of the Sung school, however, insist on its being immaterial, now calling it lî, the principle of order in nature, now tâo, the defined course of things, now Tî, the Supreme Power or God, now shän, the spiritual working of God. According to *K*häng-ʒze, all these names are to be referred to that of 'Heaven,' of which they express so many different concepts.

Paragraph 71 speaks of divination in practice, and paragraph 72 celebrates the service done by that through the plant and shell, as equal to, and indeed the complement of, all the other services rendered by heaven and earth, the seasons, the sun and moon, the sages, and the greatest potentates. Surely, it is all very extravagant.

The last two paragraphs resume the theme of the making of the Yî by the sages, and their teaching the practice of divination. Of the Ho map and the Lo writing, I have spoken in the Introduction, pages 14-18. But if we accept the statement that the Lo writing had anything to do with the making of the Yî, we must except Fû-hsî from the sages to whom we are indebted for it. It was to the Great Yü, more than a thousand years later than Fû-hsî, that the Lo disclosed its writing; and Yü is never said to have had anything to do with the Yî. Nor is either of these things mentioned in Section ii, paragraph 11, where the work of Fû-hsî is described more in detail.

not the full exponent of speech, and speech is not
the full expression of ideas ;—is it impossible then
to discover the ideas of the sages ?' The Master
said :—' The sages made their emblematic symbols
to set forth fully their ideas; appointed (all) the
diagrams to show fully the truth and falsehood (of
things); appended their explanations to give the
full expression of their words ; and changed (the
various lines) and made general the method of
doing so, to exhibit fully what was advantageous.
They (thus) stimulated (the people) as by drums
and dances, thereby completely developing the
spirit-like (character of the Yî).'

77. May we not say that *Kh*ien and Khwăn
[= the yang and yin, or the undivided and
divided lines] are the secret and substance of the
Yî? *Kh*ien and Khwăn being established in
their several places, the system of changes was
thereby constituted. If *Kh*ien and Khwăn were
taken away, there would be no means of seeing that
system; and if that system were not seen, *Kh*ien
and Khwăn would almost cease to act.

78. Hence that which is antecedent to the material form exists, we say, as an ideal method, and
that which is subsequent to the material form exists,
we say, as a definite thing.

Transformation and shaping is what we call
change; carrying this out and operating with it is
what we call generalising the method; taking the
result and setting it forth for all the people under
heaven is, we say, (securing the success of) the
business of life.

79. Hence, to speak of the emblematic figures :—
(The sage) was able to survey all the complex phe-

nomena under the sky. He then considered in his mind how they could be figured, and (by means of the diagrams) represented their material forms and their character. Hence those (diagrams) are denominated Semblances. A (later) sage was able to survey the motive influences working all under the sky. He contemplated them in their common action and special nature, in order to bring out the standard and proper tendency of each. He then appended his explanation (to each line), to determine the good or evil indicated by it. Hence those (lines with their explanations) are denominated Imitations (the Yâo).

80. The most thorough mastery of all the complex phenomena under the sky is obtained from the diagrams. The greatest stimulus to movement in adaptation to all affairs under the sky is obtained from the explanations.

81. The transformations and shaping that take place are obtained from the changes (of the lines); the carrying this out and operating with it is obtained from the general method (that has been established). The seeing their spirit-like intimations and understanding them depended on their being the proper men; and the completing (the study of) them by silent meditation, and securing the faith of others without the use of words, depended on their virtuous conduct.

Chapter XII, paragraphs 75–81, endeavours to show how we have in the Yî a representation of the changing phenomena of nature, and such a representation as words or speech could not convey.

Paragraph 75 has a good meaning, taken by itself; but it has no apparent connexion with the rest of the chapter. Kû Hsî thought

SECTION II

Chapter I. 1. The eight trigrams having been completed in their proper order, there were in each the (three) emblematic lines. They were then

---

it was misplaced in its present position, and should be at the end of chapter 8. Compare paragraph 14.

The first two statements of paragraph 76 are general, but made here specially to exalt the Yî, as teaching more clearly and fully than written characters could have done. The Khang-hsî editors decide that 'the emblematic figures' here are the eight trigrams of Fû-hsî,—against the view of Kû Hsî, which restricts them to signify the undivided and divided lines. The repetition of the words, 'The Master said,' is probably the error of an early transcriber.

Paragraphs 77 and 78 refer to the phenomena of nature and the course of human affairs, as suggesting and controlling the formation of the system of the Yî. The formation of that becomes the subject in paragraph 79. Khien and Khwăn are used, as we have already seen them more than once, for the active and inactive conditions in nature, indicated by the divided and undivided lines. It is difficult to translate what is said in paragraph 78, about Tâo and Khî;—what I have called, 'an ideal method' and 'a definite' thing. P. Regis translates the text by—'Quod non est inter figurata aut corporea sed supereminet est rationale, est ratio, Tâo; quod (est) inter figurata subjacetque certae figurae est sensibile, est instrumentum.' But tâo cannot here signify ratio or reason; for tâo and khî are names for the same thing under different conditions; first as a possibility, and next as an actuality. Such is the natural interpretation of the text, and so all the great scholars of the Sung dynasty construed it, as may be seen in the 'Collected Comments' of the imperial edition. So far they were correct, however many of them might stumble and fall in confounding this 'ideal method' with God.

What follows in the paragraph has no connexion with these two statements. P. Regis, who divides his translation into two paragraphs, says:—'Satis patet utramque textus hujus partem non cohaerere.

multiplied by a process of addition till the (six) component lines appeared.

2. The strong line and the weak push themselves each into the place of the other, and hence the changes (of the diagrams) take place. The appended explanations attach to every form of them its character (of good or ill), and hence the movements (suggested by divination) are determined accordingly.

3. Good fortune and ill, occasion for repentance or regret, all arise from these movements.

4. The strong and the weak (lines) have their fixed and proper places (in the diagrams); their changes, however varied, are according to the requirements of the time (when they take place).

5. Good fortune and ill are continually prevailing each against the other by an exact rule.

6. By the same rule, heaven and earth, in their course, continually give forth (their lessons); the sun and moon continually emit their light; all the movements under the sky are constantly subject to this one and the same rule.

Quod ergo illas divisimus, id fecimus majoris perspicuitatis causa, non ratione ordinis qui certe nullus est, ut in re potius assuta quam connexa.'

Paragraph 79 is a repetition of paragraphs 38, 39, 'to introduce,' says Kû Hsî, 'the two paragraphs' that follow.

The editors of the imperial edition find in 80, 81, an amplification mainly of 76, showing how what is said there of the natural phenomena is exhibited in the Yî. The concluding sentence is a declaration (hardly necessary) about the sage makers, to the effect that they were as distinguished for virtuous conduct as for wisdom,—'the proper men' to stand between Heaven and the mass of men as they did.

7. *Kh*ien, (the symbol of heaven, and) conveying the idea of strength, shows to men its easy (and natural) action. *Kh*wăn, (the symbol of earth, and) conveying the idea of docility, shows to men its compendious (receptivity and operation).

8. The Yâo (or lines) are imitative representations of this. The Hsiang, or emblematic figures, are pictorial representations of the same.

9. The movements of the lines and figures take place (at the hand of the operator), and are unseen; the good fortune or ill is seen openly and is beyond. The work to be done appears by the changes; the sympathies of the sages are seen in their explanations.

10. The great attribute of heaven and earth is the giving and maintaining life. What is most precious for the sage is to get the (highest) place— (in which he can be the human representative of heaven and earth). What will guard this position for him? Men. How shall he collect a large population round him? By the power of his wealth. The right administration of that wealth, correct instructions to the people, and prohibitions against wrong-doing;—these constitute his righteousness.

Chapter I, paragraphs 1-10, is an amplification, according to Khung Ying-tâ and the editors of the imperial edition of the present dynasty, of the second chapter of Section i. The latter say that as all the chapters of Section i from the third onwards serve to elucidate chapter 2, so it is with this chapter and all that follow in this Section. The formation of the diagrams, and of their several lines, their indication of good fortune and bad, and the analogy between the processes of nature and the operations of divination, and other kindred subjects, are all touched on.

The order of the eight trigrams in paragraph 1, is *kh*ien, tui,

Chapter II. 11.   Anciently, when Pâo-hsî had
come to the rule of all under heaven, looking up,
he contemplated the brilliant forms exhibited in the
sky, and looking down he surveyed the patterns
shown on the earth.   He contemplated the ornamental appearances of birds and beasts and the
(different) suitabilities of the soil.   Near at hand, in
his own person, he found things for consideration,
and the same at a distance, in things in general.   On
this he devised the eight trigrams, to show fully the

---

lî, *k*ăn, sun, khan, kăn, khwăn.   The three lines of each are
emblematic,—the first of heaven, the second of man, the third of
earth.   This is the most likely explanation of hsiang, 'the emblems' or 'similitudes' here.   Why the maker—'sages'—stopt at
sixty-four figures, of six lines each, is a question that cannot be
answered.

Paragraph 2.   Of course it was a great delusion to suppose that
the changes of lines consequent on divination could be so connected with the movements of life as to justify the characterising
them as good or evil, or afford any guidance in the ordering of
conduct.

Paragraph 4.   Who can tell 'the requirements of the time' amid
the complexity of the phenomena of nature or the ever-varying
events of human experience and history?   The wiser men are, the
more correct will be their judgments in such matters; but is there
any reason for trusting to divination about them?

Paragraphs 5, 6.   It is difficult to say what is 'the exact rule'
intended here; unless it be that the factors in every movement
shall act according to their proper nature.   The Khang-hsî editors
say:—'We see the good sometimes meeting with misfortune, and
the bad with good fortune; but such is not the general rule.'   'The
lessons that heaven and earth give forth' are those concerning the
method of their operation as stated in paragraph 7, and more fully
in 6, 7, 8 of Section i.

What is said in paragraph 10 is striking and important, and in
harmony with the general strain of Confucian teaching;—as in
the Great Learning, chapter 10, and many other places; but I fail
to see its appropriateness in its present place in the Yî.

attributes of the spirit-like and intelligent (operations working secretly), and to classify the qualities of the myriads of things.

12. He invented the making of nets of various kinds by knitting strings, both for hunting and fishing. The idea of this was taken, probably, from Lî (the third trigram, and thirtieth hexagram).

13. On the death of Pâo-hsî, there arose Shǎn-năng (in his place). He fashioned wood to form the share, and bent wood to make the plough-handle. The advantages of ploughing and weeding were then taught to all under heaven. The idea of this was taken, probably, from Yî (the forty-second hexagram).

14. He caused markets to be held at midday, thus bringing together all the people, and assembling in one place all their wares. They made their exchanges and retired, every one having got what he wanted. The idea of this was taken, probably, from Shih Ho (the twenty-first hexagram).

15. After the death of Shǎn-năng, there arose Hwang Tî, Yâo, and Shun. They carried through the (necessarily occurring) changes, so that the people did (what was required of them) without being wearied; yea, they exerted such a spirit-like transformation, that the people felt constrained to approve their (ordinances) as right. When a series of changes has run all its course, another change ensues. When it obtains free course, it will continue long. Hence it was that 'these (sovereigns) were helped by Heaven; they had good fortune, and their every movement was advantageous.' Hwang Tî, Yâo, and Shun (simply) wore their upper and

lower garments (as patterns to the people), and good order was secured all under heaven. The idea of all this was taken, probably, from *Kh*ien and Khwăn (the first and eighth trigrams, or the first and second hexagrams).

16. They hollowed out trees to form canoes; they cut others long and thin to make oars. Thus arose the benefit of canoes and oars for the help of those who had no means of intercourse with others. They could now reach the most distant parts, and all under heaven were benefited. The idea of this was taken, probably, from Hwân (the fifty-ninth hexagram).

17. They used oxen (in carts) and yoked horses (to chariots), thus providing for the carriage of what was heavy, and for distant journeys,—thereby benefiting all under the sky. The idea of this was taken, probably, from Sui (the seventeenth hexagram).

18. They made the (defence of the) double gates, and (the warning of) the clapper, as a preparation against the approach of marauding visitors. The idea of this was taken, probably, from Yü (the sixteenth hexagram).

19. They cut wood and fashioned it into pestles; they dug in the ground and formed mortars. Thus the myriads of the people received the benefit arising from the use of the pestle and mortar. The idea of this was taken, probably, from Hsiâo Kwo (the sixty-second hexagram).

20. They bent wood by means of string so as to form bows, and sharpened wood so as to make arrows. This gave the benefit of bows and arrows, and served to produce everywhere a feeling of awe.

The idea of this was taken, probably, from Khwei (the thirty-eighth hexagram).

21. In the highest antiquity they made their homes (in winter) in caves, and (in summer) dwelt in the open country. In subsequent ages, for these the sages substituted houses, with the ridge-beam above and the projecting roof below, as a provision against wind and rain. The idea of this was taken, probably, from Tâ *K*wang (the thirty-fourth hexagram).

22. When the ancients buried their dead, they covered the body thickly with pieces of wood, having laid it in the open country. They raised no mound over it, nor planted trees around; nor had they any fixed period for mourning. In subsequent ages the sages substituted for these practices the inner and outer coffins. The idea of this was taken, probably, from Tâ Kwo (the twenty-eighth hexagram).

23. In the highest antiquity, government was carried on successfully by the use of knotted cords (to preserve the memory of things). In subsequent ages the sages substituted for these written characters and bonds. By means of these (the doings of) all the officers could be regulated, and (the affairs of) all the people accurately examined. The idea of this was taken, probably, from Kwâi (the forty-third hexagram).

Chapter II, paragraphs 11–23, treats of the progress of civilisation in China, and how the great men of antiquity who led the way in the various steps of that progress were guided by the Yî. Only five of these are mentioned;—the first, Fû-hsî, the beginning of whose reign, according to the least unlikely of the chronological accounts, must be placed in the 34th century B.C., while Shun's

Chapter III. 24. Therefore what we call the Yî is (a collection of) emblematic lines. They are styled emblematic as being resemblances.

---

reign ended in B.C. 2203. The time embraced in this chapter therefore is about twelve centuries and a half. But the writer gives his own opinion that the various discoveries and inventions mentioned were suggested to their authors by certain hexagrams of the Yî. The most commonly received view, however, is that Fû-hsî had only the eight trigrams, and that the multiplication of them to the 64 hexagrams was the work of king Wăn, fully a thousand years later than Shun. This is the view of the editors of the imperial Yî. If it be contended that Fû-hsî himself multiplied his trigrams, and gave their names to the resulting hexagrams, how could he have wrapped up in them the intimations of discoveries which were not made till many centuries after his death? The statements in the chapter cannot be received as historical. It came from another hand, and not from Confucius himself. The writer or compiler gives the legends current about the various inventions of his time. The making of the trigrams is placed first of all to do honour to the Yî. The account of it is different from that given in paragraph 73 of the former Section, and we hear nothing of the Ho map or Lo writing.

Paragraph 11. Pâo-hsî here and in 13 is the same as Fû-hsî. As Pâo is written here, there is no meaning in it; but another character Phâo (庖) is more common, and Phâo-hsî would mean the inventor of the kitchen and cookery. This was the first step towards civilisation, and was appropriately followed by the hunting and fishing—both by means of nets—in paragraph 12.

Paragraphs 13, 14 celebrate the work of Shăn-năng, 'the marvellous or spirit-like husbandman.' There was no metal about the primitive plough. The market for the exchange of commodities, without the use of coin, was an important advance.

The invention of the robes, or of dress, mentioned in paragraph 15, would seem to show that previously men had been in a very rude state. The passage indicates, however, the courtesies and proprieties of social life, in which dress plays an important part, and which now began to be organised.

The infant navigation in paragraph 16 was as little indebted to the use of metal as the agriculture of 13.

Paragraphs 17 and 18 show that in those primitive times there

25. What we call the Thwan (or king Wăn's explanations) are based on the significance (of each hexagram as a whole).

26. We call the lines (of the figures) Yâo from their being according to the movements taking place all under the sky.

27. In this way (we see) the rise of good fortune and evil, and the manifestation of repentance and regret.

---

were already the practices of rapine and war. 'The double gates' were those of the city wall, and of the enclosed suburb. The clapper may still be heard all over China. Bows and arrows, however, came rather later, as in 20.

I suppose 'the sages' in paragraphs 21, 22, 23 refer generally to the great names mentioned in the previous chapters; nor can we define the distinction in the writer or compiler's mind between 'antiquity' and 'the highest antiquity.' Compare what is said on the rise of the coffin in 22 with Mencius' remarks on the same subject in Book III, ii, 5. 4. He would hardly have expressed himself as he did, if he had been familiar with this text. The invention of written characters is generally ascribed to Fû-hsî. Paragraph 23 does not say so, but the inventor is said to have been a sage of a subsequent age to the time of 'high antiquity.' That 'high antiquity' must stretch back very far.

Chapter III, paragraphs 24–27, treats of the Yî as made up of figurative diagrams, which again are composed of lines ever changing, in accordance with the phenomena of nature and human experience, while to the resulting figures their moral character and providential issues are appended by the sages. It may be regarded as an epitome of chapter 2 in Section i.

Paragraph 24. It is observed by the editors of the imperial edition that a chapter should not begin with a 'therefore;' and they are inclined to agree with many critics who would enter this as the last paragraph of the preceding chapter. In that case it would be a summing-up of the concluding sentences of the different paragraphs, the truth and genuineness of which are deservedly suspected. The characters for 'therefore,' however, are very loosely used in these Appendixes.—The lines, as they were intended by

Chapter IV. 28. In the Yang trigrams (or those of the undivided line) there are more of the Yin lines, and in the Yin trigrams (or those of the divided line) there are more of the Yang lines.

29. What is the cause of this? It is because the Yang lines are odd (or made by one stroke), and the Yin lines are even (or made by two strokes).

30. What (method of) virtuous conduct is thus intimated? In the Yang trigrams we have one ruler, and two subjects,—suggesting the way of the superior man. In the Yin trigrams we have two rulers, and one subject,—suggesting the way of the small man.

Fû-hsî, were emblematic; and they are still more so, as interpreted by the duke of Kâu. Meanings are drawn from the figures that resemble or illustrate principles in the subjects to which they are applied.

Paragraph 25. The character rendered 'the significance' means materials, and is illustrated by reference to all the different materials out of which a house is composed. So there are half-a-dozen things about the diagrams, their lineal structure, emblematic intention, their attributes, &c., out of which their interpretation is fashioned.

Paragraph 26. E.g. an undivided line may appear in an odd place, which is right, or in an even place, which is wrong; and the case is the opposite with the divided lines. But what has this to do with the right or wrong of the events divined about?

Chapter IV, paragraphs 28–30. Of the distinction of the trigrams into Yang and Yin.

The trigrams that contain only one undivided line—kăn (≡≡), khan (≡≡), and kăn (≡≡)—are called Yang. The undivided line is called 'the lord' in them. It is just the opposite with the Yin trigrams, in which there are two undivided lines, and one divided,—sun (≡≡), lî (≡≡), and tui (≡≡). These together constitute the 'six children,' or 'three

Chapter V. 31. It is said in the Yî, 'Full of anxious thoughts you go and come; (only) friends will follow you and think with you.' The Master said:—'In all (the processes taking place) under heaven, what is there of thinking? what is there of anxious scheming? They all come to the same (successful) issue, though by different paths; there is one result, though there might be a hundred anxious schemes. What is there of thinking? what is there of anxious scheming?'

32. The sun goes and the moon comes; the moon goes and the sun comes;—the sun and moon thus take the place each of the other, and their shining is the result. The cold goes and the heat comes; the heat goes and the cold comes;—it is by this mutual succession of the cold and heat that the year is completed. That which goes becomes less and less, and that which comes waxes more and more;—it is by the influence on each other of this contraction and expansion that the advantages (of the different conditions) are produced.

33. When the looper coils itself up, it thereby straightens itself again; when worms and snakes

---

sons' and 'three daughters' in the later arrangement of the trigrams, ascribed to king Wǎn.

Paragraph 29. Each part of the divided line counts as one; hence a yang trigram counts as $1 + 2 + 2 = 5$ strokes, four of which are yin, while a yin trigram counts as $2 + 1 + 1 = 4$, only two of which are yang. But this is mere trifling.

In explanation of paragraph 30 it is said that 'we have in the yang trigrams two (or more) subjects serving one ruler, and in the yin one subject serving two rulers, and two rulers striving together for the allegiance of one subject.' This is ingenious, but fanciful; as indeed this distinction of the trigrams into a yang class and a yin is a mere play of fancy.

go into the state of hybernation, they thereby keep
themselves alive. (So), when we minutely investigate the nature and reasons (of things), till we
have entered into the inscrutable and spirit-like in
them, we attain to the largest practical application
of them; when that application becomes the quickest
and readiest, and all personal restfulness is secured,
our virtue is thereby exalted.

34. Going on beyond this, we reach a point which
it is hardly possible to know. We have thoroughly
comprehended the inscrutable and spirit-like, and
know the processes of transformation ;—this is the
fulness of virtue.

35. It is said in the Yî, '(The third line shows its
subject) distressed before a rock, and trying to lay
hold of thorns; entering into his palace and not
seeing his wife :—there will be evil.' The Master
said :—' If one be distressed by what need not distress
him, his name is sure to be disgraced; if he lay hold
on what he should not touch, his life is sure to be
imperilled. In disgrace and danger, his death will
(soon) come ;—is it possible for him in such circumstances to see his wife ?'

36. It is said in the Yî, ' The duke with (his bow)
shoots at the falcon on the top of the high wall; he
hits it :—his every movement will be advantageous.'
The Master said:—' The falcon is a bird (of prey);
the bow and arrow is a weapon (of war); the shooter
is a man. The superior man keeps his weapon concealed about his person, and waits for the proper
time to move ;—doing this, how should his movement be other than successful ? There is nothing
to fetter or embarrass his movement; and hence,
when he comes forth, he succeeds in his object.

The language speaks of movement when the instrument necessary to it is ready and perfect.'

37. The Master said:—'The small man is not ashamed of what is not benevolent, nor does he fear to do what is not righteous. Without the prospect of gain he does not stimulate himself to what is good, nor does he correct himself without being moved. Self-correction, however, in what is small will make him careful in what would be of greater consequence;—and this is the happiness of the small man. It is said in the Yî, "His feet are in the stocks, and he is disabled in his toes:—there will be no (further) occasion for blame."'

38. If acts of goodness be not accumulated, they are not sufficient to give its finish to one's name; if acts of evil be not accumulated, they are not sufficient to destroy one's life. The small man thinks that small acts of goodness are of no benefit, and does not do them; and that small deeds of evil do no harm, and does not abstain from them. Hence his wickedness becomes great till it cannot be covered, and his guilt becomes great till it cannot be pardoned. This is what the Yî says, 'He wears the cangue and his ears are destroyed:—there will be evil.'

39. The Master said:—'He who keeps danger in mind is he who will rest safe in his seat; he who keeps ruin in mind is he who will preserve his interests secure; he who sets the danger of disorder before him is he who will maintain the state of order. Therefore the superior man, when resting in safety, does not forget that danger may come; when in a state of security, he does not forget the possibility of ruin; and when all is in a state of order, he does not

forget that disorder may come. Thus his person is kept safe, and his states and all their clans can be preserved. This is according to what the Yî says, "(Let him say), 'Shall I perish? shall I perish?' (so shall this state be firm, as if) bound to a clump of bushy mulberry trees."'

40. The Master said:—'Virtue small and office high; wisdom small and plans great; strength small and burden heavy:—where such conditions exist, it is seldom that they do not end (in evil). As is said in the Yî, "The tripod's feet are overthrown, and the ruler's food is overturned. The body of him (who is thus indicated) is wet (with shame):— there will be evil."'

41. The Master said:—'Does not he who knows the springs of things possess spirit-like wisdom? The superior man, in his intercourse with the high, uses no flattery, and, in his intercourse with the low, no coarse freedom:— does not this show that he knows the springs of things? Those springs are the slight beginnings of movement, and the earliest indications of good fortune (or ill). The superior man sees them, and acts accordingly without waiting for (the delay of) a single day. As is said in the Yî, "He is firm as a rock, (and acts) without the delay of a single day. With firm goodness there will be good fortune." Firm as a rock, how should he have to wait a single day to ensure his knowing (those springs and his course)? The superior man knows the minute and the manifested; he knows what is weak, and what is strong:—he is a model to ten thousand.'

42. The Master said:—'I may venture to say that the son of the Yen family had nearly attained (the

standard of perfection). If anything that he did was not good, he was sure to become conscious of that; and when he knew it, he did not do the thing again. As is said in the Yî, "(The first line shows its subject) returning from an error that has not led him far away. There is no occasion for repentance. There will be great good."'

43. There is an intermingling of the genial influences of heaven and earth, and transformation in its various forms abundantly proceeds. There is an intercommunication of seed between male and female, and transformation in its living types proceeds. What is said in the Yî, 'Three individuals are walking together and one is made to disappear; there is (but) one man walking, and he gets his mate,' tells us of the effort (in nature) at oneness (of operation).

44. The Master said :—' The superior man (in a high place) composes himself before he (tries to) move others; makes his mind restful and easy before he speaks; settles (the principles of) his intercourse with others before he seeks anything from them. The superior man cultivates these three things, and so is complete. If he try to move others while he is himself in unrest, the people will not (act) with him; if he speak while he is himself in a state of apprehension, the people will not respond to him; if without (certain principles of) intercommunication, he issue his requests, the people will not grant them. When there are none to accord with him, those who (work to) injure him will make their appearance. As is said in the Yî, "(We see one) to whose advantage none will contribute, while some will seek to assail him. He observes no

regular rule in the ordering of his heart:—there will be evil."'

Chapter V, paragraphs 31–44, gives the words of the duke of *K*âu on eleven different lines in the Text of the Yî, along with remarks of Confucius in farther illustration of them. But they seem also to be intended to bring forth more‧ fully the meaning of certain previous utterances about the structure and scope of the Yî.

Paragraphs 31–34 start from the fourth line of the 31st hexagram, which would seem merely to require a steady and unvarying purpose in any one, in order to the full development of his influence. The editors of the imperial edition, however, make the whole a sequel of paragraph 5. But granted that there is no 'anxious scheming' in the processes of the natural world or in the phenomena of insect life, there is really no analogy to their proceedings in the course of the man who makes himself master of 'the nature and reasons of things,' as described in 33 and 34. Nor are 'the nature and reasons of things' to be found in the Yî, as the writer believed they were. Such as it is, it requires immense thought to understand it, and when we have laid hold of it, there is nothing substantial in our grasp. The 'virtue' predicated of such attainment is not so much moral exčellence, as apprehension and the power and ability to invent, and to affect others.

Paragraph 35. See on the third line of Khwăn, the 47th hexagram. If we were to translate the explanations of the line after Confucius, we should put the first two statements hypothetically; but the four that compose it seem to run on in the same way. They are all, I apprehend, hypothetical.

Paragraph 36. See on the last line of *K*ieh, the 40th hexagram.

Paragraph 37. See on the first line of Shih Ho, the 21st hexagram. The 'self-correction in what is small' implies of course that the small man has been 'awed.' What is said about him here is true; but we hardly expect it in this place.

Paragraph 38 should probably begin, like those before and after it, with 'The Master said.' The characters quoted fröm the Yî are again from the text of Shih Ho, on the last line.

Paragraph 39. See on the fifth line of Phî, the 12th hexagram.

Paragraph 40 gives Confucius' views on the fourth line of Ting, the 50th hexagram.

In paragraph 41 we are conducted to the 16th hexagram,—the

Chapter VI. 45. The Master said :—'(The tri-grams) *Kh*ien and Khwăn may be regarded as the gate of the Yî.' *Kh*ien represents what is of the yang nature (bright and active); Khwăn what is of the yin nature (shaded and inactive). These two unite according to their qualities, and there comes the embodiment of the result by the strong and weak (lines). In this way we have the phenomena of heaven and earth visibly exhibited, and can com-prehend the operation of the spiritual intelligence.

46. The appellations and names (of the diagrams and lines) are various, but do not go beyond (what is to be ascribed to the operation of these two con-ditions). When we examine the nature and style

---

second line of it. The being 'firm as a rock' is understood to symbolise the state of 'rest,' the quiet self-possession out of which successful movement and action is understood to spring.

In paragraph 42, 'the son of the Yen family' is Yen Hui, the favourite disciple of Confucius. The passage quoted from the Yî is that on the first line of Fû, the 24th hexagram.

To paragraph 43, as to paragraph 38, I would prefix the cha-racters for 'The Master said.' 'Male and female' is to be taken generally, and not confined to the individuals of the human pair. One Chinese writer says that in the transformations ascribed to heaven and earth, birds, fishes, animals, and plants are included, but from the 'transformation in its living types' plants are excluded, because in their generation there is nothing analogous to the emis-sion and reception of seed. Other Chinese writers, however, are well enough acquainted with the sexual system of plants. It would seem to me that Confucius, if the paragraph were really his, intended only plants or the vegetable world in his reference to the operation of heaven and earth, and had all living tribes in view in his mention of male and female. The passage of the Yî referred to is on the third line of Sun, the 41st hexagram. The application of it is far-fetched.

Paragraph 44. See on the fifth line of Yî, the 42nd hexa-gram.

(of the appended explanations), they seem to express the ideas of a decaying age.

47. The Yî exhibits the past, and (teaches us to) discriminate (the issues of) the future; it makes manifest what is minute, and brings to light what is obscure. (Then king Wăn) opened (its symbols), and distinguished things in accordance with its names, so that all his words were correct and his explanations decisive;—(the book) was now complete.

48. The appellations and names (of the diagrams and lines) are but small matters, but the classes of things comprehended under them are large. Their scope reaches far, and the explanations attached to them are elegant. The words are indirect, but to the point; the matters seem plainly set forth, but there is a secret principle in them. Their object is, in cases that are doubtful, to help the people in their conduct, and to make plain the recompenses of good and evil.

The principal object, it is said, of chapter VI, paragraphs 45–48, is to set forth the views of king Wăn and his son in the explanations which they appended to the diagrams and lines; and in doing this the writer begins in 45, with Fû-hsî's starting, in the formation of his eight trigrams, from the devising of the whole and divided lines, to represent the two primitive forms in nature. The two 'pure' trigrams formed of these lines, unmixed, give rise to all the others, or rather the lines of which they are formed do so; and are thus compared to a gate by which the various diagrams enter to complete the system that is intended to represent the changing phenomena of nature and experience. The next sentence in the above version of paragraph 45 appears in Canon McClatchie's translation of the Yî, as follows:—'*Kh*ien is the membrum virile, and Khwăn is the pudendum muliebre (the sakti of *Kh*ien).' It is hardly possible, on reading such a version, to suppress the exclamation proh pudor! Can a single passage be adduced in support of it from among all the Chinese critics in the

Chapter VII. 49. Was it not in the middle period of antiquity that the Yî began to flourish? Was not he who made it familiar with anxiety and calamity?

50. Therefore (the 10th diagram), Lî, shows us the foundation of virtue; (the 15th), Hsien, its handle; (the 24th), Fû, its root; (the 32nd), Hăng, its solidity; (the 41st), Sun, its cultivation; (the 42nd), Yî, its abundance; (the 47th), Khwăn, its exercise of discrimination; (the 48th), 3ing, its field; and (the 57th), Sun, its regulation.

51. In Lî we have the perfection of harmony; in Hsien, we have the giving honour to others,

---

line of centuries? I believe not. The ideas which it expresses are gratuitously and wantonly thrust into this text of the Yî. 'Khien' and 'Khwăn' are not spoken of thus. If the latter half of the paragraph be unintelligible, this interpretation of the former would make the whole disgusting.

In paragraph 46 the writer passes from the work of Fû-hsî to that of king Wăn and his son, and the composition of the written Yî is referred to 'a decaying age,'—the age, namely, of the tyrant Kâu. Then king Wăn and the duke of Kâu, it is said, deploring the degeneracy of their times and the enormities of the government, indicated, by their treatment of the ancient symbols, their sense of right and wrong, and the methods by which the prevailing evils might be rectified.

Paragraphs 47 and 48 follow and expand the meaning of 45. The editors of the imperial edition say that the former sentence of 47 is the sequel of 45, and the latter of 46, bringing us finally to the explanations and decisions of king Wăn, as the most important portion of the Yî. Kû Hsî, moreover, observes that throughout the chapter, as well as in the chapters that follow, there must be many characters wanting in the text, while there are many also that are doubtful. This is specially the case with 48. Where the order of the characters has been disarranged merely, correction is easy; but where characters are evidently missing, attempts to fill the lacunae are merely guess-work.

and the distinction thence arising; in Fû we have
what is small (at first), but there is in it a (nice)
discrimination of (the qualities of) things; in Hăng
we have a mixed experience, but without any weari-
ness; in Sun we have difficulty in the beginning
and ease in the end; in Yî we have abundance of
growth without any contrivance; in Khwăn we
have the pressure of extreme difficulty, ending in a
free course; in 3ing we have abiding in one's place
and at the same time removal (to meet the movement of others); and in Sun we have the weighing
of things (and action accordingly), but secretly and
unobserved.

52. (The use of) Lî appears in the harmony of
the conduct; of Hsien, in the regulation of ceremonies; of Fû, in self-knowledge; of Hăng, in uni-
formity of virtue; of Sun, in keeping what is harmful
at a distance; of Yî, in the promotion of what is
advantageous; of Khwăn, in the diminution of re-
sentments; of 3ing, in the discrimination of what
is righteous; and of Sun, in the doing of what is
appropriate to time and to circumstances.

Chapter VII, paragraphs 49–52, is occupied with nine hexagrams, as specially indicating how the superior man, or the ruler,
should deal with a time of trouble and solicitude, specially by the
cultivation of his own virtue. Not, we are told, that the same
thing might not be learned from other diagrams, but these nine
specially occurred to the writer, or, as many think, to Confucius.

Paragraph 49 is important as agreeing in its testimony with 46.
The Yî was made in middle-antiquity; that is, in the end of the
Shang dynasty, and the rise of the Kâu; and the maker or makers
had personal and public reasons for anxiety about the signs of
the times.

Paragraph 50 shows the particular phase of virtue in each of the
nine hexagrams that are mentioned; 51, the marvellous character-

Chapter VIII. 53. The Yî is a book which should not be let slip from the mind. Its method (of teaching) is marked by the frequent changing (of its lines). They change and move without staying (in one place), flowing about into any one of the six places of the hexagram. They ascend and descend, ever inconstant. The strong and the weak lines change places, so that an invariable and compendious rule cannot be derived from them ;—it must vary as their changes indicate.

54. The goings forth and comings in (of the lines) are according to rule and measure. (People) learn from them in external and internal affairs to stand in awe.

55. (The book), moreover, makes plain the nature of anxieties and calamities, and the causes of them. Though (its students) have neither master nor guardian, it is as if their parents drew near to them.

56. Beginning with taking note of its explanations, we reason out the principles to which they point. We thus find out that it does supply a constant and standard rule. But if there be not the proper men (to carry this out), the course cannot be pursued without them.

---

istics of each phase; and 52, its use. The 'therefore' with which paragraph 50 commences shows the process of thought by which the writer passed from the anxiety that possessed the mind of the author of the Yî to the use to be derived, in such circumstances, from the study of Lî and the other hexagrams.

Chapter VIII, paragraphs 53–56, describes the method of studying the Yî as consisting very much in watching the changes that take place in the lines, and reflecting on the appended explanations; while, after all, much must depend on there being 'the proper men,' to carry its lessons into practice.

Chapter IX. 57. The Yî is a book in which the form (of each diagram) is determined by the lines from the first to the last, which must be carefully observed. The six lines are mixed together, according to the time (when they enter the figure) and their substance (as whole and divided).

58. There is difficulty in knowing (the significance of) the first line, while to know that of the topmost line is easy;—they form the beginning and the end (of the diagram). The explanation of the first line tasks the calculating (of the makers), but in the end they had (but) to complete this.

59. As to the variously-disposed intermediate lines with their diverse formations, for determining their qualities, and discriminating the right and wrong in them, we should be unprovided but for the explanations of them.

60. Yea, moreover, if we wish to know what is likely to be preserved and what to perish, what will be lucky and what will be unlucky, this may easily be known (from the explanations of the different lines). But if the wise will look at the explanations of the entire diagrams, their thoughts will embrace more than half of this knowledge.

61. The second and fourth lines are of the same

There seems to be a contradiction between the statements in paragraphs 53 and 56 about the book supplying, and not supplying, a standard rule; but the meaning, probably, is that while it does not give a rule generally applicable, it gives rules for particular cases.

Kû Hsî says he does not understand 54, and thinks some characters must have been lost. 'The six places of the hexagram' in 53 are, literally, 'the six empties.' The places are so called, because it is only a temporary possession of them, which is held by the fugitive lines, whether whole or divided.

quality (as being in even places), but their positions (with respect to the fifth line) are different, and their value is not the same; but the second is the object of much commendation, and the fourth the subject of many apprehensions,—from its nearness (to that line). But for a line in a place of weakness it is not good to be far (from the occupant of the place of strength), and what its subject should desire in such a case is (merely) to be without blame. The advantage (here) is in (the second line) being in the central place.

62. The third and fifth lines are of the same quality, (as being in odd places), but their positions are different; and the (occupant of) the third meets with many misfortunes, while the occupant of the fifth achieves much merit:—this arises from one being in the noble position and the other in the mean. Are they occupied by the symbol of weakness? There will be peril. By that of strength? There will be victory.

Chapter IX, paragraphs 56–62, speaks of the hexagrams as made up of the different lines, and various things to be attended to in those lines to determine their meaning.

Paragraph 57. The time or order in which the lines enter determines of course the place and number of each in the figure. Their 'substance' is their form, as whole or divided, being yang or yin.

Paragraph 58 belongs to the first and sixth lines. We are hardly prepared for the statement that 'the maker or makers' had so much difficulty in determining the meaning of the first line. Of course when they had fixed that and completed the figure, explaining all the lines, it was easy for the student to follow their exposition, as paragraph 59 says.

Paragraph 60 seems to say that the work of the duke of *K*âu on each line was but an indicating in detail of the processes of his father's mind in explaining the whole figure.

Chapter X. 63. The Yî is a book of wide comprehension and great scope, embracing everything. There are in it the way of heaven, the way of man, and the way of earth. It then takes (the lines representing) those three Powers, and doubles them till they amount to six. What these six lines show is simply this,—the way of the three Powers.

64. This way is marked by changes and movements, and hence we have the imitative lines. Those lines are of different grades (in the trigrams), and hence we designate them from their component elements. These are mixed together, and elegant forms arise. When such forms are not in their appropriate places, the ideas of good fortune and bad are thus produced.

The last two paragraphs mention several points important to be attended to in studying, more especially, the duke of *K*âu on the several lines. Three different views of the concluding statement,— ' are they occupied,' &c.,—are given in the imperial edition. 'It belongs,' says Wû *K*äng, 'to the fifth line;' ' to the third line,' says Hû Ping-wän (also of the Yüan dynasty); while Hân Hsing-kwo (of the Thang dynasty) held that it belonged to both. The Khang-hsî editors say that ' by discriminating and combining these views, we get to the meaning of the text.' I am unable to do so.

Chapter X, paragraphs 63, 64, speaks of the great comprehensiveness of the Yî, its figures and explanations being applicable to the three Powers—heaven, earth, and man.

With paragraph 63, compare paragraph 4, Appendix VI. In the trigram the upper line represents heaven, the middle line man, and the lowest earth. This paragraph and that other are the nearest approach I know to an attempt to account for the doubling of the number of lines, and stopping with the hexagram; but the doing so was entirely arbitrary. *K*û Hsî says:—' The upper two characters belong to heaven, the middle two to man, and the lower two to earth.' No words could be more express; and yet Canon McClatchie says (p. 354):—' The two upper strokes represent Heaven, or Thâi-yî, the husband; the two middle strokes, Earth, his wife; and the

Chapter XI. 65. Was it not in the last age of Yin, when the virtue of *K*âu had reached its highest point, and during the troubles between king Wăn and (the tyrant) *K*âu, that the (study of the Yî) began to flourish? On this account the explanations (in the book) express (a feeling of) anxious apprehension, (and teach) how peril may be turned into security, and easy carelessness is sure to meet with overthrow. The method in which these things come about is very comprehensive, and must be acknowledged in every sphere of things. If at the beginning there be a cautious apprehension as to the end, there will probably be no error or cause for blame. This is what is called the way of the Yî.

---

two lower strokes, Man, their son; all being animated by the same Divine Reason (tâo) or Supreme God (Chih Shăn).' This note shows how one error, or misunderstanding of the Chinese original, draws other errors with it. The character tâo in the paragraph has not at all the sense of reason, human or divine, but its primary and ordinary signification of the path or course. As Lû Ʒî (Han dynasty) says:—' In the way of heaven there are the changes of day and night, sun and moon; in that of earth, those of hardness and softness, dryness and moisture; in that of man, those of action and rest, of movement and stillness, of good fortune and bad, of good and evil.'

' The imitative lines' in the translation of 64, is simply ' the Yâo' in the Chinese text, which I have rendered according to the account of them in paragraph 8, et al. Their different grades are their position as high or low in the figures (paragraph 1, Section i), and their ' component elements,' literally ' their substance, or thing-nature,' is their structure as being yang or yin, according to the use of wuh in paragraphs 57, 59, et al. A yang line in an even place, or a yin line in an odd, is not in its appropriate place, and gives an indication of what is bad.

Chapter XI, paragraph 65. P. Regis observes on this chapter:—
' I do not hesitate to say that there is found nowhere in the whole

Chapter. XII. 66. (The hexagram) *Kh*ien represents the strongest of all under the sky. Through
this quality its operations are always manifested
with ease, for it knows where there would be peril
and embarrassment. (The hexagram) Khwǎn
represents the most docile of all under the sky.
Through this quality its operations are always manifested with the promptest decision, for it knows
where there would be obstruction.

67. (The sages, who are thus represented, and
who made the Yî,) were able to rejoice in heart
(in the absolute truth of things), and were able (also)
to weigh carefully all matters that could occasion
anxiety; (thus) they fixed the good and bad fortune
(of all things) under the sky, and could accomplish
the things requiring strenuous efforts.

68. Therefore amid the changes and transformations (taking place in heaven and earth), and the
words and deeds of men, events that are to be
fortunate have their happy omens. (The sages)
knew the definite principles underlying the prognostications of the former class, and the future of

---

Yî a passage which affords more light for the explanation of the
book.' Paragraph 49 told us that 'the study of the Yî flourished in
the middle period of antiquity, and that the author of it was familiar
with anxiety and troubles.' That information becomes here more
particular. The Yî, existing when this Appendix was written, was
made in the closing period of the Yin dynasty, and the making of
it was somehow connected with the attempts of the tyrant *K*âu
against king Wǎn. We are not told expressly that the book was
written, in part at least, by king Wǎn; but the tradition to that
effect derives a certain amount of support from what is said here.
The general object of the author is also stated clearly enough,—
to inculcate a cautious and reverent administration of affairs, never
forgetful of the uncertainties of life and fortune.

those of the latter, (now to be) ascertained by divination.

69. The places of heaven and earth (in the diagrams) having been determined, the sages were able (by means of the Yî) to carry out and complete their ability. (In this way even) the common people were able to share with them in (deciding about) the counsels of men and the counsels of spiritual beings.

70. The eight trigrams communicate their information by their emblematic figures. The explanations appended to the lines and the completed figures tell how the contemplation of them affected (the makers). The strong and the weak lines appear mixed in them, and (thus) the good and the evil (which they indicate) can be seen.

71. The changes and movements (which take place in the manipulation of the stalks and the formation of the diagrams) speak as from the standpoint of what is advantageous. The (intimations of) good and evil vary according to the place and nature (of the lines). Thus they may indicate a mutual influence (in any two of them) of love or hatred, and good or evil is the result; or that mutual influence may be affected by the nearness of the lines to, or their distance from, each other, and then repentance or regret is the result; or the influence may be that of truth or of hypocrisy, and then the result is what is advantageous, or what is injurious. In all these relations of the (lines in the) Yî, if two are near and do not blend harmoniously, there may be (all these results),—evil, or what is injurious, or occasion for repentance and regret.

72. The language of him who is meditating a

revolt (from the right) betrays his inward shame; that of him whose inward heart doubts about it diverges to other topics. The words of a good man are few; those of a coarse man are many. The words of one who slanders what is good are un-

---

Chapter XII, paragraphs 66–72, is generally divided into three sections;—the first, embracing 66–68, and treating of the sages, the makers of the Yî, as themselves independent of it, knowing all that it enables us to know, and able to accomplish all that it enables us to accomplish; the second, embracing 69–71, and telling how the sages formed the Yî, and made all men, by means of it, partakers of their now unlimited knowledge and power; the third, comprised in paragraph 72, and saying, if it be genuine and in its proper place, that the ordinary speech of men is as mysterious and indicative of what is in them, as the explanations of the Yî are, when we consider who were its authors.

'The sages,' who are the subject of 65–68, are not mentioned in the text; but 67 makes it plain that the subject must be some personal being or beings. Neither *Kh*ien nor Khwăn can 'rejoice in heart, and weigh carefully matters occasioning anxiety.' The commentators generally interpolate 'the sages;' even Ying-tâ of the Thang dynasty, who does not introduce the sages in his exposition, yet makes the subject to be 'the disposer and nourisher of all things.' He gets to his view by an unnatural interpretation of two characters in 67, which are now thrown out of the text by all critics as not genuine. That 'the sages' is really the subject in the mind of the writer appears from the express mention of them in 69, when also 'heaven and earth' take the place of *Kh*ien and Khwăn. It is absurd, not to say blasphemous, to assume that the sages who made the Yî had the knowledge and ability here ascribed to them; but the theory of the Yî as containing a scheme for the discovery of the future necessitated the ascribing such attributes to them. Compare with the whole Section, and especially with paragraph 68, what is said in 'the Doctrine of the Mean,' chapter 24.

The first Section shows how the sages were themselves independent of the Yî, and had no need of it; the second goes on to tell how they devised and constructed it, to make all men equal to themselves in a knowledge of phenomena and human events, and of their indications of, and issues in, the future. Summing up its

substantial; those of him who is losing what he ought to keep are crooked.

---

lessons, the editors of the imperial edition say, 'There is no passage in the Appendix more full and clear than this on the five points in regard to the lines which the student of the Yî has to attend to. Those points are:—their time, position, quality, mutual nearness, and responsive relation. It is by a consideration of the two latter points, moreover, that he must form his judgment on their appropriateness or inappropriateness in the three others.'

Paragraph 72 has really no connexion with the rest of the chapter. I have stated above how the critics attempt to make out such a connexion; but I agree myself with P. Regis, who appends to his version of the paragraph this note:—' Quae sententiae quidem sapiunt doctrinam Confucianam, at non ordinem, utpote cum praecedentibus minime cohaerentes, sed omnino ab iis abscissae avulsaeque.'

APPENDIX IV

Supplementary to the Thwan and Yâo on the first and second
Hexagrams, and showing how they may be interpreted of man's
nature and doings

SECTION I *KHIEN*

Chapter I. 1. What is called (under *Kh*ien) 'the
great and originating' is (in man) the first and chief
quality of goodness; what is called 'the penetrating'
is the assemblage of excellences; what is called 'the
advantageous' is the harmony of all that is right;
and what is called 'the correct and firm' is the
faculty of action.

2. The superior man, embodying benevolence, is
fit to preside over men; presenting the assemblage
of excellences, he is fit to show in himself the union
of all propriety; benefiting (all) creatures, he is fit to
exhibit the harmony of all that is right; correct and
firm, he is fit to manage (all) affairs.

3. The fact that the superior man practises these
four virtues justifies the application to him of the
words—'*Kh*ien represents what is great and originating, penetrating, advantageous, correct and firm.'

The title of this Appendix is in Chinese the Wăn Yen *K*wan,
'The Record of Wăn Yen;' and according to the analogy of
the titles of the three Appendixes that follow, Wăn should perform the part of a verb and Yen that of a substantive. So the
characters are usually taken, and to Wăn is given the meaning of
'Explaining (Shih);' and to Yen that of 'Words or Sentences,'
meaning the Thwan of king Wăn, and the Yâo of the duke of
*K*âu on the first two hexagrams. The document treats of these,

Chapter II. 4. What is the meaning of the words under the first NINE, (undivided), 'The dragon lies hid (in the deep);—it is not the time for active doing?.' The Master said :—'There he is, with the powers of the dragon, and yet lying hid. The influence of the world would make no change in him; he would do nothing (merely) to secure his fame. He can live, withdrawn from the world, without regret; he can experience disapproval without trouble of mind. Rejoicing (in opportunity), he carries his principles

and of no others. 'It shows the amount and depth of meaning in them,' says *K*û Hsî, 'and the other hexagrams may be treated after the analogy supplied here.' Confucius, it is said by others, died before he was able to carry out the plan which he had formed. But, as I have shown in the Introduction (pp. 28–30), it is more than doubtful whether we have in this Appendix anything at all directly from the sage.

Chapter I, paragraphs 1–3, shows how the attributes of *Kh*ien, as explained by king Wăn, are to be understood of the constituent principles of human nature. What is remarkable is, that we find paragraphs 1, 2, with very little variation, in one of the narratives of the *3*o *K*wan, as having been spoken by a marchioness-dowager of Lû in B.C. 564, several years before Confucius was born. One so familiar as *K*û Hsî was with all the classical literature of his country could not be ignorant of this. His solution of the questions arising from it is, that anciently there was this explanation of the characters of king Wăn; that it was employed by Shû *K*iang (of Lû), and that Confucius also availed himself of it; while the chronicler used, as he does below, the phraseology of 'The Master said,' to distinguish the real words of Confucius from such ancient sayings. But who was this chronicler? No one can tell. The legitimate conclusion from *K*û's criticism is this, that so much of this Appendix as is preceded by 'The Master said' is from Confucius ;—so much and no more.

The ascription in paragraph 3 of 'the four virtues' to the superior or normal man, man in his best estate, and yet inferior to 'the sagely man,' is Confucian,—after the style of the teaching of the Master in the Analects.

into action; sorrowing (for want of opportunity), he keeps with them in retirement. Yes, he is not to be torn from his root (in himself).' This is 'the dragon lying hid.'

5. What is the meaning of the words under the second NINE, ' The dragon shows himself and is in the field;—it will be advantageous to see the great man?' The Master said:—' There he is, with the dragon's powers, and occupying exactly the central place. He is sincere (even) in his ordinary words, and earnest in his ordinary conduct. Guarding against depravity, he preserves his sincerity. His goodness is recognised in the world, but he does not boast of it. His virtue is extensively displayed, and transformation ensues. The language of the Yî, " The dragon shows himself and is in the field;—it will be advantageous to see the great man," refers to a ruler's virtue.'

6. What is the meaning of the words under the third NINE, ' The superior man is active and vigilant all the day, and in the evening (still) careful and apprehensive;—the position is dangerous, but there will be no mistake?' The Master said:—' The superior man advances in virtue, and cultivates all the sphere of his duty. His leal-heartedness and good faith are the way by which he advances in virtue. His attention to his words and establishing his sincerity are the way by which he occupies in his sphere. He knows the utmost point to be reached, and reaches it, thus showing himself in accord with the first springs (of things); he knows the end to be rested in, and rests in it, thus preserving his righteousness in accordance with that end. Therefore he occupies a high position without pride, and a low

position without anxiety. Thus it is that, being active and vigilant, and careful (also) and apprehensive as the time requires, though his position be perilous, he will make no mistake.'

7. What is the meaning of the words under the fourth NINE, ' He is as if he were leaping up, (but still) is in the deep;—there will be no mistake?' The Master said :—' He finds no permanent place either above or below, but he does not commit the error (of advancing). He may advance or recede ;— there is no permanent place for him : but he does not leave his fellows. The superior man, advancing in virtue and cultivating the sphere of his duty, yet wishes (to advance only) at the (proper) time, and therefore there is no mistake.'

8. What is the meaning of the words under the fifth NINE, ' The dragon is on the wing in the sky;— it will be advantageous to see the great man?' The Master said :—' Notes of the same key respond to one another; creatures of the same nature seek one another; water flows towards the place that is (low and) damp; fire rises up towards what is dry; clouds follow the dragon, and winds follow the tiger :— (so) the sage makes his appearance, and all men look to him. Things that draw their origin from heaven move towards what is above; things that draw their origin from the earth cleave to what is below :—so does everything follow its kind.'

9. What is the meaning of the words under the topmost NINE, ' The dragon exceeds the proper limits ;—there will be occasion for repentance ?' The Master said :—' The position is noble, but it is not that of office; (its occupant) dwells on high, but he has no people (to rule); and the men of talent

and virtue in the positions below will give him no
aid;—should he move in such a case, there will be
occasion for repentance.'

In chapter II, paragraphs 4–9, Confucius is introduced, explaining, with considerable amplification, what is said by the duke
of *K*âu under the several lines of the hexagram. 'The dragon'
becomes the symbol of 'the superior man;' and of 'the great man,'
or the sage upon the throne. The language approaches at times to
the magniloquence of Mencius, while in paragraph 8 the voice hardly
seems to be that of the sage at all.

With paragraph 5, compare chapters 8 and 14 of 'the Doctrine of the Mean,' agreeing much in language and sentiment
with what we have here. The line, a strong or undivided line, and
therefore yang, is said to be 'exactly in the central place;' but
the line is in the second, an even place, that proper to a yin line;
and in other passages this might be explained in an unfavourable
way. The Chinese character *k*äng has the meaning given to it,
now of 'exact,' and now of 'correct,' the latter being always
favourably interpreted.

Paragraph 8. The fifth is almost always the place of honour and
authority in the hexagram, and therefore 'the great man' here continues to be the great man, 'the sage.' The argument is that as
things of the same kind respond to and seek one another, so is it
with the sage and ordinary man. They are of the same kind,
though far apart; and when a sage appears, all other men look to
him with admiration and hope. The continuity of the illustrations,
however, is broken by the introduction of the dragon and clouds,
and the tiger and wind. Are these of the same kind? *K*û Hsî
says he does not think that the real dragon and real tiger are
intended; but he does not tell us how he understood the terms.
Ȝâi *K*ʰing (early in the Ming dynasty) says:—'The dragon feels
the influence of the clouds surcharged with rain, and rises from the
deep, and when the tiger feels the approach of the cold winds he
roars. Thus when the dragon rises, the clouds are sure to collect;
and when the tiger screams, the winds follow;' but all this does not
help us to appreciate any better the words of the text. And the
concluding illustration is nearly as foreign to our way of conceiving
things. By 'things that draw their origin from heaven' all animals
—moving creatures—are intended; and by those that draw their
origin from the earth are intended all plants,—things that stand and

Chapter III. 10. 'The dragon lies hid;—it is not the time for active doing:'—the position is (too) low.

11. 'The dragon shows himself and is in the field:'—the time (requires him still) to be unemployed.

12. 'All the day active and vigilant:'—(he now) does his (proper) business.

13. 'He is as if he were leaping up, (but still) is in the deep:'—he is making trial of himself.

14. 'The dragon is on the wing in the sky:'—(the subject of the line) is on high and ruling.

15. 'The dragon exceeds the proper limit, and there will be occasion for repentance:'—when things have been carried to extremity, calamity ensues.

16. Undivided lines appear in all these representations of the great and originating power denoted by *K h*ien:—(what follows in the Yâo tells us how) all under the sky there will be good order.

---

do not move. The former turn their heads to the sky, and the latter their roots to the earth. So we read in *K*û Hsî; but I continue to wonder that Confucius selected such illustrations and spoke in such a style.

Paragraph 9. As I have said above, the place of honour and authority in the hexagram belongs to the fifth line, and no other plays so unimportant a part as the sixth; and hence it is represented here as having 'no place' at all. Before he whom it represents is called to act, the battle has been won or lost. Movement from him will only accelerate and intensify the result.

Chapter III, paragraphs 10–16, goes over again the Yâo of the duke of *K*âu with very brief explanations, grounded chiefly on the consideration of the place or position occupied by the several lines, and the time of their introduction into the action of the hexagram.

Paragraph 16. See the note on the Text of *K h*ien, corresponding to this line, page 58, and also that on paragraph 7 of the symbolism of the figures and lines, Section i, page 165. There is the same

Chapter IV. 17. 'The dragon lies hid in the deep;—it is not the time for active doing:'—the energy denoted by the undivided line is laid up and hid away as in the deep.

18. 'The dragon appears in the field:'—all under heaven (begins to be) adorned and brightened.

19. 'All the day active and vigilant:'—continually, as the time passes and requires, does he act.

20. 'He is as if he were leaping up, (but still) is in the deep:'—a change is taking place in the method indicated by (this) *Kh*ien diagram.

21. 'The dragon is on the wing in the sky:'—this shows that his place is based on his heavenly virtue.

22. 'The dragon exceeds the (proper) limit;—there will be occasion for repentance:'—the time is come to an end, and so also is his opportunity.

23. Undivided NINES appear in all these representations of the great and originating power denoted by *Kh*ien:—and (from what follows in the Yâo) we see the model (of action) afforded by Ḥeaven.

---

difficulty in understanding the first part of the short paragraph; the conclusion of it must be a consequence of the language of the Yâo, though it is not repeated here.

Chapter IV, paragraphs 17-23, goes over the same ground for a third time, treating the various paragraphs chiefly from the standpoint of time.

Paragraph 17 tells us that time and circumstances are essential, as well as inward power, to successful development and demonstration. In paragraph 18, the words of the Yâo about meeting with the great man are not quoted, but they prompted the latter half of it.

Paragraph 19. Compare the language on paragraph 6, towards the end.

Paragraph 20. The subject passes here from the lower trigram and enters into the upper. We are told not to lay stress on 'the method of *Kh*ien.' In paragraph 21 we have the sage upon the

Chapter V. 24. The 'greatness' and 'originating' represented by *Kh*ien refer to it as (the symbol of) what gives their beginning (to all things), and (also) secures their growth and development.

25. 'The advantageousness and the correctness and firmness' refer to its nature and feelings (as seen in all the resulting things).

26. *Kh*ien, (thus) originating, is able with its admirable benefits to benefit all under the sky. We are not told how its benefits are conferred; but how great is (its operation)!

27. How great is (what is emblemed by) *Kh*ien!— strong, vigorous, undeflected, correct, and (in all these qualities) pure, unmixed, exquisite!

28. The six lines, as explained (by the duke of *K*âu), bring forth and display (its meaning), and everything about it is (thus) indirectly exhibited.

29. (The great man) at the proper time drives with these six dragons through the sky. The clouds move, and the rain is distributed; all under heaven enjoys repose.

---

throne. Time and opportunity are both in progress in 19; here in 22, they are both passed, have reached their extremity or end.

Paragraph 23:—see on paragraph 16. 'The model of heaven,' says Wû *Kh*ăng, 'is the due blending of the strong and active with the weak and passive, the regulation of movement in accordance with the highest reason, so that there shall be neither excess nor deficiency.'

Chapter V, paragraphs 24–29. The author here, leaving the treatise on the symbolism of the Yâo, turns to that on the Thwan, or expositions of king Wăn, and amplifies it, not quoting from it, however, so fully and exactly, as he has done in the previous chapters from the Yâo.

Paragraphs 24 and 25 are based on the statement of the significance of the Thwan under *Kh*ien, and not on the treatise on the symbolism. The originating power cannot be separated from that of penetration and development. The latter issues from the former

Chapter VI. 30. In the superior man his conduct
is (the fruit of) his perfected virtue, which might be
seen therefore in his daily course; but the force of
that phrase, 'lying hid,' requires him to keep retired, and not yet show himself, nor proceed to the
full development of his course. While this is the
case, the superior man (knows that) it is not the
time for active doing.

31. The superior man learns and accumulates the
results of his learning; puts questions, and discriminates among those results; dwells magnanimously
and unambitiously in what he has attained to; and
carries it into practice with benevolence. What the
Yî says, 'The dragon appears in the field:—it will
be advantageous to meet with the great man,' has
reference to the virtuous qualities of a ruler (as
thus described).

32. In the third NINE, there is a twofold (symbol
of) strength, but (the position) is not central. (Its

---

as the summer follows on the spring, according to an illustration
of Kû Hsî. 'The advantageousness' and 'firm correctness,' he
compares also to the autumn and winter, saying that the Khien
power in its essence, as it is in itself, is best described by these two
latter characteristics, while the two former describe it in its operation. It is thus that he tries to give his readers an idea of what he
understood by 'nature and feelings' in 25. But this chapter treats
of the Khien power in nature rather than in humanity. Confining
our view to the power so operating, we cannot say that the description of it in 26 and 27 is magniloquent or hyperbolical.

Paragraph 28 returns to the explanations of the lines of the
hexagram by the duke of Kâu, which exhibit the power in different
positions and relations, bringing out all its significance; and then
29 confines us to the fifth line, in which we have its ideal. The
spheres of nature and of men seem to be in the view of the
author, and therefore I introduce 'the great man,' as the subject,
after the example of the best critics. Like the clouds and the rain to
the thirsty earth, so is the rule of the sage to expectant humanity.

occupant) is not in heaven above, nor is he in the field beneath. Therefore there must be active vigilance and cautious apprehension as the time requires; and though (the position be) perilous, there will be no mistake.

33. In the fourth NINE, there is (the symbol of) strength, but (the position) is not central. (Its occupant) is not in heaven above, nor is he in the field beneath, nor is he in the place of man intermediate. Hence he is in perplexity; and being so, he has doubts about what should be his movements, and so will give no occasion for blame.

34. The great man is he who is in harmony, in his attributes, with heaven and earth; in his brightness, with the sun and moon; in his orderly procedure, with the four seasons; and in his relation to what is fortunate and what is calamitous, in harmony with the spirit-like operations (of Providence). He may precede Heaven, and Heaven will not act in opposition to him; he may follow Heaven, but will act (only) as Heaven at the time would do. If Heaven will not act in opposition to him, how much less will men! how much less will the spirit-like operation (of Providence)!

35. The force of that phrase—'exceeding the proper limits'—indicates the knowing to advance but not to retire; to maintain but not to let perish; to get but not to lose.

36. He only is the sage who knows to advance and to retire, to maintain and to let perish; and that without ever acting incorrectly. Yes, he only is the sage!

___

Chapter VI, paragraphs 30–36. The author leaving the Thwan, turns again to the treatise on the symbolism of the Yâo, his main

Section II Khwăn

Chapter I. 1. (What is indicated by) Khwăn is most gentle and weak, but, when put in motion, is

---

object being to show how reasonable are the decisions and lessons of the duke of *K*âu.

The subject of paragraph 30 has the virtue ; but his position in the lowest place shows that his time is not yet come.

In paragraph 31 we have the superior man developing, by means of the processes described, into 'the great man,' with the attributes of a ruler, the appearance of whom is a blessing to men.

The twofold symbol of strength in paragraph 32 is the yang or undivided line in the third place (odd) proper to it. There will be no mistake, because the subject of the line, in the exercise of his caution, will abstain from any forward movement.

According to paragraph 63 of last Appendix, Section ii, both the third and fourth lines in the hexagram belong to man, and are intermediate between those of heaven and those of earth. Khung Ying-tâ, to get over the difficulty in what is said on the fourth line, says that, as a matter of fact and locally, man is nearer earth than heaven, and is aptly represented therefore by the third line and not by the fourth ;—I prefer to point out the inconsistency, and leave it. The subject of this fourth line will move very cautiously, and so escape blame.

The eulogium of 'the great man' in paragraph 34 cannot fail to recall to the classical scholar the thirty-first and other chapters of 'the Doctrine of the Mean,' where the sage is described as 'The Equal of Heaven.' In one sentence here he is spoken of as sometimes taking precedence of Heaven, which then does not act in opposition to him ! I do not know of any statement about the sage, coming without doubt from Confucius, that is so extravagant as this. It is difficult—in fact impossible—to say from the Yî itself, what we are to understand by the kwei shăn, which I have translated here by 'the spirit-like operations (of Providence).' The compound denomination does not often occur in the book. In Appendix III, Section i, 21, kwei is the anima and shăn the animus ; and in paragraph 50, I have translated the terms by 'the contracting and expanding operations.' In Appendix I, page 226 and page 259, the name is used as in the present text. That second instance and this

hard and strong; it is most still, but is able to give every definite form.

2. 'By following, it obtains its (proper) lord,' and pursues its regular (course).

3. It contains all things in itself, and its transforming (power) is glorious.

4. Yes, what docility marks the way of Khwăn! It receives the influences of heaven, and acts at the proper time.

Chapter II. 5. The family that accumulates goodness is sure to have superabundant happiness, and the family that accumulates evil is sure to have superabundant misery. The murder of a ruler by

---

paragraph were evidently constructed, the one on the model of the other. I think it likely that the breath or air, *khî*, became the name with the earliest Chinese for their first concept of spirit; then the breath inspired or inhaled was called kwei, and became the name for the grosser part of the spirit, returning to the earth; and shăn, the breath exhaled or expired, the name for the subtler and intellectual spirit, ascending to a state of activity and enjoyment. The explanations of the terms in the *R* Yâ and other dictionaries seem to justify this view. The combination kwei shăn is sometimes best translated by 'spiritual beings.' The school of the Sung philosophy understand by it—the contracting and expanding of the primary matter, or that matter conceived of in two forms or with two opposite qualities. *Kh*ăng-ჳze says here that 'Heaven and earth are another name for tâo, and kwei shăn another name for "the vestiges of making and transformation;" and that the sage being in harmony with the tâo or practical reason of the universe, how can men or the kwei shăn be contrary to him?' Whatever be thought of the Sung speculations and theories, I think that a translator ought to give an indication of the primary meaning of the name kwei shăn.

Paragraphs 35 and 36 suggest the description of Confucius by Mencius, V, ii, 1, 5, as the one among the sages who was most governed by the consideration of time, doing continually what the circumstances of the time required.

his minister, or of his father by a son, is not the result of the events of one morning or one evening. The causes of it have gradually accumulated,—through the absence of early discrimination. The words of the Yî, ' He treads on the hoar-frost ; the strong ice will come (by and by),' show the natural (issue and growth of things).

6. 'Straight' indicates the correctness (of the internal principle), and 'square,' the righteousness (of the external act). The superior man, (thus represented), by his self-reverence maintains the inward (correctness), and in righteousness adjusts his external acts. His reverence and righteousness being (thus) established, his virtues are not solitary instances or of a single class. 'Straight, square, and great, working his operations, without repeated efforts, in every respect advantageous :'—this shows how (such a one) has no doubts as to what he does.

7. Although (the subject of) this divided line has excellent qualities, he (does not display them, but) keeps them under restraint. ' If he engage with them in the service of the king, and be successful, he will not claim that success for himself:'—this is the way of the earth, of a wife, of a minister. The way of the earth is—'not to claim the merit of achievement,' but on behalf (of heaven) to bring things to their proper issue.

8. Through the changes and transformations produced by heaven and earth, plants and trees grow luxuriantly. If (the reciprocal influence of) heaven and earth were shut up and restrained, we should have (a state that might suggest to us) the case of men of virtue and ability lying in obscurity. The words of the Yî, ' A sack tied up :—there will be

no ground for blame or for praise,' are in reality a lesson of caution.

9. The superior man (emblemed here) by the 'yellow' and correct (colour), is possessed of comprehension and discrimination. He occupies the correct position (of supremacy), but (that emblem) is on (the lower part of) his person. His excellence is in the centre (of his being), but it diffuses a complacency over his four limbs, and is manifested in his (conduct of) affairs:—this is the perfection of excellence.

10. (The subject of) the yin (or divided line) thinking himself equal to the (subject of the) yang, or undivided line, there is sure to be 'a contest.' As if indignant at there being no acknowledgment of the (superiority of the subject of the) yang line, (the text) uses the term 'dragons.' But still the (subject of neither line) can leave his class, and hence we have 'the blood' mentioned. The mention of that as being (both) 'azure and yellow' indicates the mixture of heaven and earth. Heaven's (colour) is azure and earth's is yellow.

The hexagram Khwăn is dealt with in Section ii, and much more briefly than *Kh*ien in Section i. Much less distinct, moreover, is the attempt in it to show how the attributes of the hexagram are to be understood of the principles of human nature. The most important portion of the Section, perhaps, is paragraph 5, the first of chapter II, and I have spoken of it in the Introduction, pages 47 and 48.

APPENDIX V

Treatise of Remarks on the Trigrams

Chapter I. 1. Anciently, when the sages made the Yî, in order to give mysterious assistance to the spiritual Intelligences, they produced (the rules for the use of) the divining plant.

2. The number 3 was assigned to heaven, 2 to earth, and from these came the (other) numbers.

3. They contemplated the changes in the divided and undivided lines (by the process of manipulating the stalks), and formed the trigrams; from the movements that took place in the strong and weak lines, they produced (their teaching about) the separate lines. There ensued a harmonious conformity to the course (of duty) and to virtue, with a discrimination of what was right (in each particular case). They (thus) made an exhaustive discrimination of what was right, and effected the complete development of (every) nature, till they arrived (in the Yî) at what was appointed for it (by Heaven).

Chapter I, paragraphs 1-3, treats of the rise of the scheme of the Yî from the wonderful qualities of the divining plant, the use of certain numbers, and the formation of the lineal figures.

P. Regis translates paragraph 1 by—'The ancient (sages), the most excellent men, were the authors of the Yî-king, in making which they were assisted by an intelligent spirit, who for their help produced the plant called Shih.'

But the text will not admit of this version, nor have I found the view given in it in any Chinese writer. It is difficult to make up one's mind whether to translate—'the sage,' or 'the sages.' Khung Ying-tâ contends that the writer had Fû-hsî and him alone in his

Chapter II. 4. Anciently, when the sages made the Yî, it was with the design that (its figures) should be in conformity with the principles underlying the natures (of men and things), and the ordinances (for them) appointed (by Heaven). With this view they exhibited (in them) the way of heaven, calling (the lines) yin and yang; the way of earth, calling (them) the weak (or soft) and the strong (or hard); and the way of men, under the names of benevolence

---

mind. To me it seems otherwise. Fû-hsî, if we accept the testimony of universal Chinese consent, made the eight trigrams; but he did not make the Yî, which, by the same consent, was the production of king Wăn and his son.

The text would seem to say that the sages 'produced' the plant, but this is so extravagant that the view indicated in my supplementary clause appears in all the best commentators. So understood, the Yî may be said to 'give mysterious assistance to the spiritual Intelligences,' or, if we take that name as singular (according to the analogy of chapter 6), to the Divine Being in affording a revelation of His will, as in paragraph 3. We may well say that it is a pity the revelation should be so enigmatical; but the author, it must be remembered, is writing from his own standpoint. Wăn and his son, as I have endeavoured to show in the Introduction, merely wished to convey, under the style and veil of divination, their moral and political lessons.

On paragraph 2 it is said that heaven is round; and as the circumference of a circle is three times its diameter, hence 3 is the number of heaven. Again, earth is square, and as the circumference of a square is four times its length or breadth, or it consists of two pairs of equal sides, hence 2 is the number of earth.

The concluding statement about 'the other numbers' is understood of the manipulation of the divining stalks, as in Appendix III, i, 51. That manipulation, thrice repeated, might leave three stalks each time, and $3 \times 3 = 9$; or 2, being in the same way in all $= 6$; or twice 3 and once $2 = 8$; or twice 2 and once $3 = 7$. These are the numbers of the 4 binary symbols, employed in forming the new figures; ▬▬▬, the old yang, $= 9$; ▬▬ ▬▬, the young yin, $= 8$; ▬▬ ▬▬, the young yang, $= 7$; and ▬▬ ▬▬, the old yin, $= 6$.

and righteousness. Each (trigram) embraced (those) three Powers; and, being repeated, its full form consisted of six lines. A distinction was made of (the places assigned) to the yin and yang lines, which were variously occupied, now by the strong and now by the weak forms, and thus the figure (of each hexagram) was completed.

Chapter III. 5. (The symbols of) heaven and earth received their determinate positions; (those for) mountains and collections of water interchanged their influences; (those for) thunder and wind excited each other the more; and (those for) water and fire did each other no harm. (Then) among these eight symbols there was a mutual communication.

6. The numbering of the past is a natural process; the knowledge of the coming is anticipation. Therefore in the Yî we have (both) anticipation (and the natural process).

Chapter II. The top line in each trigram thus belongs to the category of heaven; the bottom line to that of earth; and the middle line to that of man. The odd places should be occupied, 'correctly,' by the undivided lines; and the even by the divided. The trigram being increased to the hexagram, lines 5 and 6 were assigned to heaven; 1 and 2 to earth; and 3 and 4 to man. 5 is the yang characteristic of heaven, and 6 the yin; so 1 and 2 in regard to earth; while 3 represents the benevolence of man, and 4 his righteousness. But all this is merely the play of fancy, and confuses the mind of the student.

Chapter III, paragraphs 5 and 6, is understood, though not very clearly, by referring to the circular arrangement of the trigrams according to Fû-hsî, as shown in Figure 2, of Plate III. Paragraph 5 refers to the correlation of Khien and Khwăn, Kăn and Tui, Kăn and Sun, Khân and Lî. Paragraph 6 is less easy of apprehension. Starting in the same figure from Khien and numbering on the left we come to Kăn by a natural process. Then

Chapter IV. 7. Thunder serves to put things in motion; wind to scatter (the genial seeds of) them; rain to moisten them; the sun to warm them; (what is symbolised by) Kăn, to arrest (and keep them in their places); (by) Tui, to give them joyful course; (by) *Kh*ien, to rule them; and by Khwăn, to store them up. Ɣ

Chapter V. 8. God comes forth in *K*ăn (to His producing work); He brings (His processes) into full and equal action in Sun; they are manifested to one another in Lî; the greatest service is done for Him in Khwăn; He rejoices in Tui; He struggles in *Kh*ien; He is comforted and enters into rest in Khân; and He completes (the work of the year) in Kăn.

9. All things are made to issue forth in *K*ăn, which is placed at the east. (The processes of production) are brought into full and equal action in Sun, which is placed at the south-east. The being brought into full and equal action refers to the purity and equal arrangement of all things. Lî gives the idea of brightness. All things are now made mani-

---

we turn back, and numbering on the right, from Sun, we come by a backward process to Khwăn. The same process is illustrated on a large scale by the circular arrangement of the 64 hexagrams in Plate I. But what the scope of the paragraph is I cannot tell, and am tempted to say of it, as P. Regis does, 'Haec observatio prorsus inanis est.'

In chapter IV we have the same circular arrangement of the trigrams, though they are named in a different order; the last first and the first last. The first four are mentioned by their elemental names; the last four by the names of their lineal figures. No special significance is attached to this. If it ever had any, it has been lost.

fest to one another. It is the trigram of the south. The sages turn their faces to the south when they give audience to all under the sky, administering government towards the region of brightness :—the idea in this procedure was taken from this. Khwăn denotes the earth, (and is placed at the south-west). All things receive from it their fullest nourishment, and hence it is said, 'The greatest service is done for Him in Khwăn.' Tui corresponds (to the west) and to the autumn,—the season in which all things rejoice. Hence it is said, 'He rejoices in Tui.' He struggles in *Kh*ien, which is the trigram of the north-west. The idea is that there the inactive and active conditions beat against each other. Khan denotes water. It is the trigram of the exact north,—the trigram of comfort and rest, what all things are tending to. Hence it is said, 'He is comforted and enters into rest in Khan. Kăn is the trigram of the north-east. In it all things bring to a full end the issues of the past (year), and prepare the commencement of the next. Hence it is said, 'He completes (the work of the year) in Kăn.'

Chapter V, paragraphs 8 and 9, sets forth the operations of nature in the various seasons, as being really the operations of God, who is named Tî, 'the Lord and Ruler of Heaven.' Those operations are represented in the progress by the seasons of the year, as denoted by the trigrams, according to the arrangement of them by king Wăn, as shown also in Plate III, Figure 2.

'The greatest service is done for Tî in Khwăn;' Yang Wan-lî (of our twelfth century, but earlier than *K*û Hsî) says :—'Khwăn is a minister or servant. Tî is his ruler. All that a ruler has to do with his minister is to require his service.' 'On the struggles in *Kh*ien' he says :—'*Kh*ien is the trigram of the north-west, when the yin influence is growing strong and the yang diminishing.'

The 'purity' predicated in paragraph 9 of things in Sun, was

Chapter VI. 10. When we speak of Spirit we mean the subtle (presence and operation of God) with all things. For putting all things in motion there is nothing more vehement than thunder; for scattering them there is nothing more effective than wind; for drying them up there is nothing more parching than fire; for giving them pleasure and satisfaction there is nothing more grateful than a lake or marsh; for moistening them there is nothing more enriching than water; for bringing them to an end and making them begin again there is nothing more fully adapted than Kăn. Thus water and fire contribute together to the one object; thunder and wind do not act contrary to each other; mountains and collections of water interchange their influences. It is in this way, that they are able to change and transform, and to give completion to all things.

---

explained by *K*ăng Khang-*kh*ăng (our second century) as equivalent to 'newness,' referring to the brightness of all things in the light of spring and summer. On 'all things receive from the earth their fullest nourishment' the same Yang, quoted above, says:— 'The earth performs the part of a mother. All things are its children. What a mother has to do for her children is simply to nourish them.'

Chapter VI is the sequel of the preceding. There ought to have been some mention of Shân or 'Spirit' in chapter 5. It is the first character in this chapter, and the two characters that follow show that it is here resumed for the purpose of being explained. As it does not occur in chapter 5, we must suppose that the author of it here brings forward and explains the idea of it that was in his mind. Many of the commentators recognise this,—e. g. Liang Yin, as quoted in the Introduction, p. 33.

Two other peculiarities in the style of the chapter are pointed out and explained (after a fashion) by 3hui *K*ing (earlier, probably, than the Sung dynasty):—'The action of six of the trigrams is described, but no mention is made of *Kh*ien or Khwăn. But

Chapter VII. 11. *Kh*ien is (the symbol of) strength; Khwăn, of docility; *K*ăn, of stimulus to movement; Sun, of penetration; Khan, of what is precipitous and perilous; Lî, of what is bright and what is catching; Kăn, of stoppage or arrest; and Tui, of pleasure and satisfaction.

---

heaven and earth do nothing, and yet do everything; hence they are able to perfect the spirit-like subtilty of the action of thunder, wind, and the other things. (Moreover), we have the trigram Kân mentioned, the only one mentioned by its name, instead of our reading "mountains." The reason is, that the putting in motion, the scattering, the parching, and the moistening, are all the palpable effects of thunder, wind, fire, and water. But what is ascribed to Kăn, the ending and the recommencing all things, is not so evident of mountains. On this account the name of the trigram is given, while the things in nature represented by the trigrams are given in those other cases. The style suitable in each case is employed.'

Chapter VII mentions the attributes, called also the 'virtues,' of the different trigrams. It is not easy to account for the qualities— 'their nature and feelings'—ascribed to them. Khung Ying-tâ says:—'*Kh*ien is represented by heaven, which revolves without ceasing, and so it is the symbol of strength; Khwăn by the earth, which receives docilely the action of heaven, and so it is the symbol of docility; *K*ân by thunder, which excites and moves all things, and so it is the symbol of what produces movement; Sun by wind, which enters everywhere, and so it is the symbol of penetration; Khân by water, found in a place perilous and precipitous, and the name is explained accordingly; Lî by fire, and fire is sure to lay hold of things, and so it is the symbol of being attached to; Kân by a mountain, the mass of which is still and arrests progress, and so it is the symbol of stoppage or arrest; and Tui by a lake or marsh, which moistens all things, and so it is the symbol of satisfaction.'

The Khang-hsî editors consider this explanation of the qualities of the trigrams to be unsatisfactory, and certainly it has all the appearance of an ex post facto account. They prefer the views of the philosopher Shâo (of our eleventh century), which is based on the arrangement of the undivided and divided lines in the figures. This to me is more unsatisfactory than the other. The editors say,

Chapter VIII. 12. *Kh*ien (suggests the idea of) a horse; Khwăn, that of an ox; *K*ăn, that of the dragon; Sun, that of a fowl; Khan, that of a pig; Lî, that of a pheasant; Kăn, that of a dog; and Tui, that of a sheep.

Chapter IX. 13. *Kh*ien suggests the idea of the head; Khwăn, that of the belly; *K*ăn, that of the feet; Sun, that of the thighs; Khan, that of the ears; Lî, that of the eyes; Kăn, that of the hands; and Tui, that of the mouth.

Chapter X. 14. *Kh*ien is (the symbol of) heaven, and hence has the appellation of father. Khwăn is (the symbol of) earth, and hence has the appellation of mother. *K*ăn shows a first application (of Khwăn to *Kh*ien), resulting in getting (the first of) its male (or undivided lines), and hence is called 'the oldest son.' Sun shows a first application (of *Kh*ien to Khwăn), resulting in getting (the first of) its female (or divided lines), and hence is called 'the oldest daughter.' Khan shows a second application

---

moreover, that Shâo's account of the three yang trigrams, *K*ăn, Khan, and Kăn is correct, and that of the three yin, Sun, Lî, and Tui incorrect; but this would be based on king Wăn's arrangement, which does not appear to have place here.

Chapter VIII. In the Great Appendix, p. 383, it is said that Fû-hsî, in making his trigrams, was guided by 'the consideration of things apart from his own person.' Of such things we have a specimen here. The creatures are assigned, in their classes, to the different trigrams, symbolising the ideas in the last chapter. We must not make any difference of sex in translating their names.

Chapter IX. Fû-hsî found also 'things near at hand, in his own person,' while making the trigrams. We have here a specimen of such things.

(of Khwăn to *Kh*ien), resulting in getting (the second of) its male (or undivided lines), and hence is called 'the second son.' Lî shows a second application (of *Kh*ien to Khwăn), resulting in getting the second of its female (or divided lines), and hence is called 'the second daughter.' Kăn shows a third application (of Khwăn to *Kh*ien), resulting in getting (the third of) its male (or undivided lines), and hence is called 'the youngest son.' Tui shows a third application (of *Kh*ien to Khwăn), resulting in getting (the third of) its female (or divided lines), and hence is called 'the youngest daughter.'

Chapter XI. 15. *Kh*ien suggests the idea of heaven; of a circle; of a ruler; of a father; of jade; of metal; of cold; of ice; of deep red; of a good horse; of an old horse; of a thin horse; of a piebald horse; and of the fruit of trees.

16. Khwăn suggests the idea of the earth; of a mother; of cloth; of a caldron; of parsimony; of a turning lathe; of a young heifer; of a large waggon; of what is variegated; of a multitude; and of a handle and support. Among soils it denotes what is black.

17. *K*ăn suggests the idea of thunder; of the dragon; of (the union of) the azure and the yellow; of development; of a great highway; of the eldest son; of decision and vehemence; of bright young bamboos; of sedges and rushes; among horses, of

---

Chapter X has been discussed in the Introduction, pp. 49 and 50. Let it simply be added here, that the account which it does give of the formation of the six subsidiary trigrams is inconsistent with their gradual rise from the mutual imposition of the undivided and divided lines.

the good neigher; of one whose white hind-leg appears, of the prancer, and of one with a white star in his forehead. Among the productions of husbandry it suggests the idea of what returns to life from its disappearance (beneath the surface), of what in the end becomes the strongest, and of what is the most luxuriant.

18. Sun suggests the idea of wood; of wind; of the oldest daughter; of a plumb-line; of a carpenter's square; of being white; of being long; of being lofty; of advancing and receding; of want of decision; and of strong scents. It suggests in the human body, the idea of deficiency of hair; of a wide forehead; of a large development of the white of the eye. (Among tendencies), it suggests the close pursuit of gain, even to making three hundred per cent in the market. In the end it may become the trigram of decision.

19. Khan suggests the idea of water; of channels and ditches (for draining and irrigation); of being hidden and lying concealed; of being now straight, and now crooked; of a bow, and of a wheel. As referred to man, it suggests the idea of an increase of anxiety; of distress of mind; of pain in the ears;—it is the trigram of the blood; it suggests the idea of what is red. As referred to horses, it suggests the idea of the horse with an elegant spine; of one with a high spirit; of one with a drooping head; of one with a thin hoof; and of one with a shambling step. As referred to carriages, it suggests one that encounters many risks. It suggests what goes right through; the moon; a thief. Referred to trees, it suggests that which is strong, and firm-hearted.

20. Lî suggests the emblem of fire; of the sun; of lightning; of the second daughter; of buff-coat and helmet; of spear and sword. Referred to men, it suggests the large belly. It is the trigram of dryness. It suggests the emblem of a turtle; of a crab; of a spiral univalve; of the mussel; and of the tortoise. Referred to trees, it suggests one which is hollow and rotten above.

21. Kăn suggests the emblem of a mountain; of a by-path; of a small rock; of a gateway; of the fruits of trees and creeping plants; of a porter or a eunuch; of the (ring) finger; of the dog; of the rat; of birds with powerful bills; among trees, of those which are strong, with many joints.

22. Tui suggests the emblem of a low-lying collection of water; of the youngest daughter; of a sorceress; of the mouth and tongue; of the decay and putting down (of things in harvest); of the removal (of fruits) hanging (from the stems or branches); among soils, of what is strong and salt; of a concubine; and of a sheep.

Chapter XI may be made to comprehend all the paragraphs from the 15th to the end, and shows how universally the ideas underlying the Yî are diffused through the world of nature. The quality of the several trigrams will be found with more or less of truth, and with less or more of fancy, in the objects mentioned in connexion with them. More needs not to be said on the chapter than has been done in the Introduction, pp. 53 and 54.

APPENDIX VI

The Orderly Sequence of the Hexagrams

SECTION I

1–3. When there were heaven and earth, then afterwards all things were produced. What fills up (the space) between heaven and earth are (those) all things. Hence (*Kh*ien and Khwăn) are followed by *K*un[1]. *K*un denotes filling up.

3–6. *K*un is descriptive of things on their first production. When so produced, they are sure to be in an undeveloped condition. Hence *K*un is followed by Măng. Măng is descriptive of what is undeveloped,—the young of creatures and things. These in that state require to be nourished. Hence Măng is followed by Hsü. Hsü is descriptive of the way in which meat and drink (come to be supplied)[2]. Over meat and drink there are sure to be contentions[2]. Hence Hsü is followed by Sung.

6–8. Sung is sure to cause the rising up of the multitudes[3]; and hence it is followed by Sze. Sze has the signification of multitudes[3], and between multitudes there must be some bond of union. Hence it is followed by Pî, which denotes being attached to.

8–11. (Multitudes in) union must be subjected to some restraint. Hence Pî is followed by Hsiâo

*Kh*û.   When things are subjected to restraint, there
come to be rites of ceremony, and hence Hsiâo
*Kh*û is followed by Lî [4].   The treading (on what
is proper) leads to Thâi, which issues in a state of
freedom and repose, and hence Lî is followed by
Thâi.

11–16.   Thâi denotes things having free course.
They cannot have that for ever, and hence it is
followed by Phî (denoting being shut up and restricted).   Things cannot for ever be shut up, and
hence Phî is followed by Thung Zän.   To him
who cultivates union with men, things must come
to belong, and hence Thung Zän is followed by
Tâ Yû.   Those who have what is great should
not allow in themselves the feeling of being full, and
hence Tâ Yû is followed by *Kh*ien.   When great
possessions are associated with humility, there is
sure to be pleasure and satisfaction; and hence
*Kh*ien is followed by Yü.

16–19.   Where such complacency is awakened, (he
who causes it) is sure to have followers [5].   They
who follow another are sure to have services (to
perform), and hence Sui is followed by Kû [6].   Kû
means (the performance of) services.   He who performs such services may afterwards become great,
and hence Kû is followed by Lin.   Lin means
great [6].

19–23.   What is great draws forth contemplation,
and hence Lin is followed by Kwân.   He who
attracts contemplation will then bring about the
union of others with himself, and hence Kwân is
followed by Shih Ho.   Shih Ho means union.
But things should not be united in a reckless or
irregular way, and hence Shih Ho is followed by

Pî.   Pî denotes adorning.   When ornamentation
has been carried to the utmost, its progress comes
to an end; and hence Pî is followed by Po.   Po
denotes decay and overthrow.

23–26. Things cannot be done away for ever.
When decadence and overthrow have completed
their work at one end, redintegration commences at
the other; and hence Po is followed by Fû.   When
the return (thus indicated) has taken place, we have
not any rash disorder, and Fû is followed by Wû
Wang.   Given the freedom from disorder and insincerity (which this name denotes), there may be the
accumulation (of virtue), and Wû Wang is followed
by Tâ *Kh*û.

26–30. Such accumulation having taken place,
there will follow the nourishment of it; and hence
Tâ *Kh*û is followed by Î.   Î denotes nourishing.
Without nourishment there could be no movement,
and hence Î is followed by Tâ Kwo.   Things cannot for ever be in a state of extraordinary (progress);
and hence Tâ Kwo is followed by Khân.   Khân
denotes falling into peril.   When one falls into peril,
he is sure to attach himself to some person or thing;
and hence Khân is followed by Lî.   Lî denotes
being attached, or adhering, to.

Section II

31, 32.   Heaven and earth existing, all (material)
things then got their existence.   All (material) things
having existence, afterwards there came male and
female.   From the existence of male and female
there came afterwards husband and wife.   From

husband and wife there came father and son. From father and son there came ruler and minister. From ruler and minister there came high and low. When (the distinction of) high and low had existence, afterwards came the arrangements of propriety and righteousness.

The rule for the relation of husband and wife is that it should be long-enduring. Hence Hsien is followed by Hăng. Hăng denotes long enduring[7].

32–37. Things cannot long abide in the same place; and hence Hăng is followed by Thun. Thun denotes withdrawing. Things cannot be for ever withdrawn; and hence Thun is succeeded by Tâ Kwang. Things cannot remain for ever (simply) in the state of vigour; and hence Tâ Kwang is succeeded by Зin. Зin denotes advancing. (But) advancing is sure to lead to being wounded; and hence Зin is succeeded by Ming Î. Î denotes being wounded. He who is wounded abroad will return to his home; and hence Ming Î is followed by Kiâ Zăn.

37–40. When the right administration of the family is at an end, misunderstanding and division will ensue; and hence Kiâ Zăn is followed by Khwei. Khwei denotes misunderstanding and division; and such a state is sure to give rise to difficulties and complications. Khwei therefore is followed by Kien. Kien denotes difficulties; but things cannot remain for ever in such a state. Kien therefore is followed by Kieh, which denotes relaxation and ease.

40–44. In a state of relaxation and ease there are sure to be losses; and hence Kieh is followed by Sun. But when Sun (or diminution) is going on without end, increase is sure to come. Sun therefore is followed by Yî. When increase goes on without end, there is sure to come a dispersing of it, and hence Yî is followed by Kwâi. Kwâi denotes dispersion. But dispersion must be succeeded by a meeting (again). Hence Kwâi is followed by Kâu, which denotes such meeting.

44-48. When things meet together, a collection is then formed. Hence Kâu is followed by Зhui, which name denotes being collected. When (good men) are collected and mount to the highest places, there results what we call an upward advance; and hence Зhui is followed by Shăng. When such advance continues without stopping, there is sure to come distress; and hence Shăng is followed by Khwăn. When distress is felt in the height (that has been gained), there is sure to be a return to the ground beneath; and hence Khwăn is followed by Зing.

48, 49. What happens under Зing requires to be changed, and hence it is followed by Ko (denoting change).

49-55. For changing the substance of things there is nothing equal to the caldron; and hence Kŏ is followed by Ting. For presiding over (that and all other) vessels, no one is equal to the eldest son, and hence Ting is followed by Kăn. Kăn conveys the idea of putting in motion. But things cannot be kept in motion for ever. The motion is stopped; and hence Kăn is followed by Kăn, which gives the idea of arresting or stopping. Things cannot be kept for ever in a state of repression, and hence Kăn is followed by Kien, which gives the idea of

(gradually) advancing. With advance there must
be a certain point that is arrived at, and hence
*K*ien is succeeded by Kwei Mei. When things
thus find the proper point to which to come, they
are sure to become great. Hence Kwei Mei is
succeeded by Făng, which conveys the idea of
being great.

55–57. He whose greatness reaches the utmost
possibility, is sure to lose his dwelling; and hence
Făng is succeeded by Lü (denoting travellers or
strangers). We have in it the idea of strangers who
have no place to receive them, and hence Lü is
followed by Sûn, which gives the idea of (penetrating
and) entering.

57–59. One enters (on the pursuit of his object),
and afterwards has pleasure in it; hence Sûn is followed by Tui. Tui denotes pleasure and satisfaction. This pleasure and satisfaction (begins)
afterwards to be dissipated, and hence Tui is followed by Hwan, which denotes separation and
division.

59–62. A state of division cannot continue for
ever, and therefore Hwan is followed by 3ieh.
3ieh (or the system of regulations) having been
established, men believe in it, and hence it is followed by *K*ung Fû. When men have the belief
which *K*ung Fû implies, they are sure to carry
it into practice; and hence it is succeeded by
Hsiâo Kwo.

62–64. He that surpasses others is sure to remedy
(evils that exist), and therefore Hsiâo Kwo is
succeeded by *K*î 3î. But the succession of events
cannot come to an end, and therefore *K*î 3î is

succeeded by Wei 3í, with which (the hexagrams)
come to a close.

The few sentences on this Appendix in the Introduction, pp. 54,
55, are sufficient. It shows the importance of the meaning of the
name in the attempt to explain the lineal figures, and prepares us
to expect on each one a brief enigmatical essay, which, it has
been seen, is the nature of the Text. But the writer, whoever
he was, is by no means careful always to follow that Text in the
significance of the characters, as will appear in the few instances to
which attention is called in the following notices. The treatise
is too slight to require, or to justify, an exhibition of all its
inaccuracies.

[1] But *K*un does not denote filling up. It is the symbol of
being in a state of distress and difficulty. The writer is thinking
of the result of the interaction of heaven and earth as being to fill
all between them with the various forms of living beings; and to
represent that he gives the result of *K*un, and not its meaning.
He makes a blunder which might have been easily avoided, for he
adds immediately that the character is descriptive of things on their
first production.

[2] It is difficult to follow the writer here. Hsü in the Text is
the symbol of the idea of waiting. Does he mean that a provision
of food and drink can only be made gradually? There is nothing
in the character Hsü to awaken in the mind the idea of nourishment. Then the genesis of contention which is given is strange.
The writer probably had in his mind the lines of the Shih, II, i,
ode 5. 3 :—

> ' The loss of kindly feeling oft
>   From slightest things shall grow.
>   Where all the fare is dry and spare,
>   Resentments fierce may glow.'

But what is allowable, good even, in poetry, is out of place in this
treatise.

[3] Contention on a great scale will put all the population of a
state in excitement and motion, and military measures of repression
will be necessary. But the idea of the multitudes in Sze would
seem to be simply that of number, and not that of a numerous
host. In a feudal kingdom, however, all the able-bodied people
might be required to join the army.

⁴ Lî, the name of the 10th hexagram, is the symbol for a shoe, and the act of treading or walking. It seems here to be derived from the homophonous lî, the symbol of acts of ceremony. The identity of sound or name must be considered as accidental. A measured step would be one of the first ways in which the inward sense of propriety would manifest itself.

⁵ By the subject of Tâ Yû and Khien we must understand the possessor of the kingdom,—the great man who in his greatness is yet distinguished by humility. He attracts followers.

⁶ For the true meaning of Kû and Lin, the names of hexagrams 18, 19, see what is said in the notes on the Text of them.

⁷ The same reference should be made to the notes on the Text of Hsien and many of the other hexagrams that follow.

APPENDIX VII

Treatise on the Hexagrams taken promiscuously, according to the opposition or diversity of their meaning.

This last of the Appendixes is touched on very briefly in the concluding paragraph of the Introduction, p. 55. It is stated there to be in rhyme, and I have endeavoured to give a similar form to the following version of it. The rhymes and length of the lines in the original, however, are very irregular, and I found it impossible to reproduce that irregularity in English.

1, 2.   Strength in *Kh*ien, weakness in Khwăn we find.

8, 7.   Pî shows us joy, and Sze the anxious mind.

19, 20.   Lîn gives, Kwân seeks;—such are the several themes

Their different figures were to teach designed.

3.   *K*un manifests itself, yet keeps its place;

4.   'Mid darkness still, to light Măng sets its face.

51, 52.   *K*ăn starts; Kăn stops. In Sun and Yî are seen

41, 42.   How fulness and decay their course begin.

26.   Tâ *Kh*û keeps still, and waits the proper time.

25.   Wû Wang sets forth how evil springs from crime.

45, 46. Good men in Ʒhui collect; in Shăng
they rise:

15, 16. *Kh*ien itself, Yü others doth despise.

21, 22. Shih Ho takes eating for its theme; and
Pî
Takes what is plain, from ornament quite
free.

58, 57. Tui shows its scope, but Sun's we do
not see.

17, 18. Sui quits the old; Kû makes a new
decree.

23. We see in Po its subject worn away;
24. And Fû shows its recovering from decay.

35. Above in Ʒin the sun shines clear and
bright;
36. But in Ming Î 'tis hidden from the
sight.

48, 47. Progress in Ʒing in Khwăn encounters
blight.

31. Effect quick answering cause in Hsien
appears;
32. While Hăng denotes continuance for
years.

59, 60. Hwân scatters; but Ʒieh its code of
rules uprears.

40. Relief and ease with *K*ieh are sure to
come;
41. Hard toil and danger have in *K*ien their
home.

38. Khwei looks on others as beyond its care;
37. *K*iâ *Z*ăn all includes within its sphere.

12, 11. While Phî and Thâi their different scopes prefer,

34, 33. Tâ Kwang stops here as right; withdraws Thun there.

14. Tâ Yû adhering multitudes can show;

13. Thung Zăn reflects their warm affection's glow.

50, 51. Ting takes what's new; the old is left by Ko.

61, 62. Sincere is Kung Fû; but exceeds, Hsiâo Kwo.

55, 56. Făng tells of trouble; Lü can boast few friends.

30, 29. Fire mounts in Lî; water in Khân descends.

9. Hsiâo Khû with few 'gainst many foes contends.

10. Movement in Lî, unresting, never ends.

5. Hsü shows its subject making no advance:

6. In Sung we seek in vain a friendly glance;

28. And Tâ Kwo's overthrown with sad mischance.

44. Kâu shows a meeting, where the many strong
   Are met by one that's weak, yet struggles long.

53. In Kien we see a bride who will delay
   To move until the bridegroom takes his way.

27. Body and mind are nourished right in Î;

63. All things are well established in Kî Ȝî.

54. Kwei Mei reveals how ends the virgin life;
64. Wei 3î how fails the youth (to get a wife).

43. The strong disperse the weak; Kwâi teaches so.
    Prospers the good man's way; to grief all small
    men go.

TRANSLITERATION OF ORIENTAL ALPHABETS ADOPTED FOR THE TRANSLATIONS OF THE SACRED BOOKS OF THE EAST

| CONSONANTS. | MISSIONARY ALPHABET. | | | Sanskrit. | Zend. | Pehlevi. | Persian. | Arabic. | Hebrew. | Chinese. |
	I Class.	II Class.	III Class.							
Gutturales.										
1 Tenuis	k	.	.	क	.	५	४	५	.	k
2 ,, aspirata	kh	.	.	ख	.	.	.	.	.	kh
3 Media	g	.	.	ग	.	५	.	.	.	.
4 ,, aspirata	gh	.	.	घ	.	.	.	.	.	.
5 Gutturo-labialis	q	.	.	.	.	५	.	.	.	.
6 Nasalis	ṅ (ng)	.	.	ङ	{ʒ (ng)} {ɯʃ(n)}	.	.	.	.	h, hs
7 Spiritus asper	h	.	.	ह	ʮ(ʮ hὲ)	५	- ~	- ~	ה ח	h, hs
8 ,, lenis	,	.	.	.	.	.	-	-	.	.
9 ,, asper faucalis	ʿh	.	ʾh	.	.	.	०५५०	०५५०	ה ए ד ה	.
10 ,, lenis faucalis	ʿh	.	.	.	.	.	.	.	.	.
11 ,, asper fricatus	.	ʿh	.	.	.	.	.	.	.	.
12 ,, lenis fricatus	.	ʿh	.	.	.	.	.	.	.	.
Gutturales modificatae (palatales, &c.)										
13 Tenuis	k	.	.	च	.	५	८	.	.	k
14 ,, aspirata	kh	.	.	छ	.	५	.	४	७०	kh
15 Media	g	.	.	ज	.	.	.	.	.	.
16 ,, aspirata	gh	.	ʾh	झ	.	.	०५	०५	.	.
17 ,, Nasalis	ṅ	.	ʾh	ञ	.	.	.	.	.	.

CONSONANTS (continued)	MISSIONARY ALPHABET			Sanskrit.	Zend.	Pehlevi.	Persian.	Arabic.	Hebrew.	Chinese.
	I Class.	II Class.	III Class.							
18 Semivocalis	y			य	३	ﻦ	ى	ى	·	y
19 Spiritus asper		(j)								
20 ,, lenis		(j)								
21 ,, asper assibilatus		s		श						z
22 ,, lenis assibilatus		z								
Dentales.										
23 Tenuis	t			त						t
24 ,, aspirata	th		TH	थ						th
25 ,, assibilata	d									
26 Media	d			द						n
27 ,, aspirata	dh		DH	ध						l
28 ,, assibilata				ध						
29 Nasalis	n			न						
30 Semivocalis	l	l	L							s
31 ,, mollis 1				ल						
32 ,, mollis 2				ळ						
33 Spiritus asper 1	s		s (S)	स						z
34 ,, asper 2										ž, ǰh
35 ,, lenis	z		z (ž)							
36 ,, asperrimus 1			z (ž)							
37 ,, asperrimus 2			z (ž)							

								Translit.	Translit. 2
Dentales modificatae (linguales, &c.)									
38 Tenuis								t	
39 „ aspirata								th	
40 Media								d	
41 „ aspirata								dh	
42 Nasalis								n	
43 Semivocalis									
44 „ fricata						R		r	
45 „ diacritica									
46 Spiritus asper								sh	sh
47 „ lenis								zh	
Labiales.									
48 Tenuis								p	p
49 „ aspirata								ph	ph
50 Media								b	
51 „ aspirata								bh	
52 Tenuissima									
53 Nasalis								m	m w
54 Semivocalis								w	
55 „ aspirata								hw	
56 Spiritus asper								f	f
57 „ lenis								v	
58 Anusvâra								m	
59 Visarga								h	

VOWELS.	MISSIONARY ALPHABET. I Class	II Class	III Class	Sanskrit.	Zend.	Pehlevi.	Persian.	Arabic.	Hebrew.	Chinese.
1 Neutralis	0									ă
2 Laryngo-palatalis	ə									
3 „ labialis	ð									a
4 Gutturalis brevis	a	(a)					ا	ا	ا	ă
5 „ longa	ā			आ		á fin. ৪ init.	ا	ا	ا	ā
6 Palatalis brevis	i	(ĕ)		इ						ĭ
7 „ longa	ī			ई						
8 Dentalis brevis	ǐ									
9 „ longa	ǐ̄									
10 Lingualis brevis	ri									
11 „ longa	r̃ī									
12 Labialis brevis	u	(u)		उ			و	و	و	ŭ
13 „ longa	ū			ऊ			و	و	و	ū
14 Gutturo-palatalis brevis	e	(e)			ᔆ(e)	—				ĕ
15 „ longa	ê (ai)	(ai)				ᔆ				ē
16 Diphthongus gutturo-palatalis	äi			ऐ						äi, ĕi
17 „	ei (ĕi)									ei, ĕi
18 „	oi (ŏu)									
19 Gutturo-labialis brevis	o	(o)				—				ŏ
20 „ longa	ô (au)	(au)		औ		—				
21 Diphthongus gutturo-labialis	äu			औ		(au)				åu
22 „	eu (ĕu)									
23 „	ou (ŏu)									
24 Gutturalis fracta	ä									
25 Palatalis fracta	ï									ü
26 Labialis fracta	ö									

BANTAM NEW AGE BOOKS

Bantam New Age Books are for all those interested in reflecting on life today and life as it may be in the future. This important new imprint features stimulating works in fields from biology and psychology to philosophy and the new physics.

☐	25388	**DON'T SHOOT THE DOG** Karen Pryor	**$3.95**
☐	25344	**SUPERMIND: THE ULTIMATE ENERGY** Barbara B. Brown	**$4.95**
☐	24147	**CREATIVE VISUALIZATION** Shatki Gawain	**$3.95**
☐	24903	**NEW RULES: SEARCHING FOR SELF-FULFILLMENT IN A WORLD TURNED UPSIDE DOWN** Daniel Yankelovich	**$4.50**
☐	25223	**STRESS AND THE ART OF BIOFEEDBACK** Barbara Brown	**$4.95**
☐	24682	**THE FIRST THREE MINUTES** Steven Weinberg	**$3.95**
☐	26076	**MAGICAL CHILD** Joseph Chilton Pearce	**$4.50**
☐	25748	**ZEN/MOTORCYCLE MAINTENANCE** Robert Pirsig	**$4.95**
☐	25982	**THE WAY OF THE SHAMAN** Michael Harner	**$4.50**
☐	25437	**TO HAVE OR TO BE** Fromm	**$4.50**
☐	24562	**LIVES OF A CELL** Lewis Thomas	**$3.95**
☐	14912	**KISS SLEEPING BEAUTY GOODBYE** K. Kolbenschlag	**$3.95**

Prices and availability subject to change without notice.

Bantam Books, Inc., Dept. NA, 414 East Golf Road, Des Plaines, Ill. 60016

Please send me the books I have checked above. I am enclosing $_____
(please add $1.50 to cover postage and handling). Send check or money order
—no cash or C.O.D.'s please.

Mr/Mrs/Miss _____

Address _____

City _____ State/Zip _____

NA—5/86
Please allow four to six weeks for delivery. This offer expires 11/86.

BANTAM
SHOP·AT·HOME
C·A·T·A·L·O·G

Special Offer
Buy a Bantam Book
for only 50¢.

Now you can have an up-to-date listing of Bantam's hundreds of titles plus take advantage of our unique and exciting bonus book offer. A special offer which gives you the opportunity to purchase a Bantam book for only 50¢. Here's how!

By ordering any five books at the regular price per order, you can also choose any other single book listed (up to a $4.95 value) for just 50¢. Some restrictions do apply, but for further details why not send for Bantam's listing of titles today!

Just send us your name and address and we will send you a catalog!

BANTAM BOOKS, INC.
P.O. Box 1006, South Holland, Ill. 60473

Mr./Mrs./Miss/Ms. _____
(please print)

Address _____

City _____ State _____ Zip _____
FC(A)—11/85
Please allow four to six weeks for delivery. This offer expires 5/86.

Shirley MacLaine Times Three!!!

☐ **Dancing In the Light**   05094-X **$17.95**

By the bestselling author of OUT ON A LIMB.

From her fabulous fiftieth birthday party attended by hundreds of celebrities through a crisis that nearly takes her mother's life to sun-drenched Santa Fe for the life-altering experience that provides a stunning new vision of herself, her future and the fate of our world, she looks for answers to spiritual questions.

☐ **Don't Fall Off the Mountain**   25234-8 **$4.50**

"Honest, candid, outspoken . . . a brave and charming book."
—The New York Times

From her Virginia roots, to stardom, marriage, motherhood and her enlightening travels to mysterious corners of the world, her story is exciting and poetic, moving and humorous—the varied and life-changing experiences of a talented, intelligent and extraordinary woman.

☐ **Out On a Limb**   25045-0 **$4.50**

"A stunningly honest, engrossing account of an intimate journey inward."

—Literary Guild Magazine

"From Stockholm to Hawaii to the mountain vastness of Peru, from disbelief to radiant affirmation, she at last discovers the roots of her very existence . . . and the infinite possibilities of life.

Bantam Books, Inc., Dept. SM, 414 East Golf Road, Des Plaines, Ill. 60016

Please send me the books I have checked above. I am enclosing $_____ (Please add $1.50 to cover postage and handling. Send check or money order—no cash or C.O.D.'s please.)

Mr/Ms _____

Address _____

City/State _____ Zip _____

SM—5/86

Please allow four to six weeks for delivery. This offer expires 11/86. Prices and availability subject to change without notice.

IF YOU'VE ENJOYED OTHER BOOKS FROM OUR NEW AGE LIST, WE'RE SURE YOU'LL WANT TO ADD MORE OF THEM TO YOUR COLLECTION

☐	25000	**MUSIC IN EVERY ROOM: AROUND THE WORLD IN A BAD MOOD** John Krich	$3.95
☐	24798	**BETWEEN HEALTH & ILLNESS . . .** B. Brown	$3.95
☐	24171	**REENCHANTMENT OF THE WORLD** M. Berman	$4.95
☐	23391	**ON HUMAN NATURE** T. Wilson	$4.95
☐	23636	**THE HEART OF PHILOSOPHY** Jacob Needleman	$3.95
☐	23471	**ECOTOPIA** E. Callenbach	$3.95
☐	25617	**END TO INNOCENCE** S. Kopp	$4.50
☐	20215	**ENTROPY: NEW WORLD VIEW** J. Rifkin	$3.95
☐	23398	**MEDUSA AND THE SNAIL** L. Thomas	$3.50
☐	24024	**MYSTICISM & THE NEW PHYSICS** M. Talbot	$3.95
☐	01475	**SEVEN TOMORROWS** J. Ogilvy & Hawken & P. Schwartz (A Large Format Book)	$7.95

Prices and availability subject to change without notice.

Bantam Books, Inc., Dept. NA5, 414 East Golf Road, Des Plaines, Ill. 60016

Please send me the books I have checked above. I am enclosing $_____
(please add $1.50 to cover postage and handling). Send check or money order
—no cash or C.O.D.'s please.

Mr/Mrs/Miss_____

Address_____

City_____ State/Zip_____

NA5—5/86

Please allow four to six weeks for delivery. This offer expires 11/86.

DON'T MISS
THESE CURRENT
Bantam Bestsellers

☐	25570	**JEALOUSIES** Justine Harlowe	$3.95
☐	25571	**MAXWELL'S TRAIN** Christopher Hyde	$3.50
☐	25944	**PRETTY IN PINK** H. B. Gilmore	
☐	25621	**HOLD THE DREAM**	$4.50
		Barbara Taylor Bradford	
☐	25547	**SWEET REASON** Robert Littel	$3.50
☐	25540	**MOONDUST AND MADNESS**	$3.95
		Janelle Taylor	
☐	25890	**PLEASURES** Diana Sydney	$3.95
☐	05097	**THE SISTERS** Robert Littel	$16.95
		(A Bantam Hardcover Book)	
☐	25416	**THE DEFECTION OF A. J. LEWINTER**	$3.95
		Robert Littel	
☐	25432	**THE OCTOBER CIRCLE** Robert Littel	$3.95
☐	23667	**NURSES STORY** Carol Gino	$3.95
☐	24978	**GUILTY PARTIES** Dana Clarins	$3.50
☐	24257	**WOMAN IN THE WINDOW** Dana Clarins	$3.50
☐	24184	**THE WARLORD** Malcolm Bosse	$3.95
☐	23920	**VOICE OF THE HEART**	$4.50
		Barbara Taylor Bradford	
☐	25053	**THE VALLEY OF HORSES** Jean M. Auel	$4.95
☐	25042	**CLAN OF THE CAVE BEAR** Jean M. Auel	$4.95

Prices and availability subject to change without notice.

Buy them at your local bookstore or use this convenient coupon for ordering.

Bantam Books, Inc., Dept. FB, 414 East Golf Road, Des Plaines, Ill. 60016

Please send me the books I have checked above. I am enclosing $_____
(please add $1.50 to cover postage and handling). Send check or money order
—no cash or C.O.D.'s please.

Mr/Mrs/Miss_____

Address_____

City_____ State/Zip_____

FB—5/86

Please allow four to six weeks for delivery. This offer expires 11/86.